authorship

and

film

Previously published in the AFI Film Readers series
edited by Charles Wolfe and Edward Branigan

Westerns
Janet Walker

Masculinity
Peter Lehman

Violence and American Cinema
J. David Slocum

The Persistence of History
Vivian Sobchack

Home, Exile, Homeland
Hamid Naficy

Black Women Film and Video Artists
Jacqueline Bobo

The Revolution Wasn't Televised
Lynn Spigel and Michael Curtin

Classical Hollywood Comedy
Henry Jenkins and Kristine Brunovska Karnick

Disney Discourse
Eric Smoodin

Black American Cinema
Manthia Diawara

Film Theory Goes to the Movies
Jim Collins, Ava Preacher Collins, and Hilary Radner

Theorizing Documentary
Michael Renov

Sound Theory/Sound Practice
Rick Altman

Fabrications
Jane M. Gaines and Charlotte Herzog

Psychoanalysis and Cinema
E. Ann Kaplan

authorship

and

film

edited by

david a. gerstner

and

janet staiger

routledge
new york and london

Published in 2003 by
Routledge
29 West 35th Street
New York, NY 10001
www.routledge-ny.com

Published in Great Britain by
Routledge
11 New Fetter Lane
London EC4P 4EE
www.routledge.co.uk

Routledge is an imprint of the Taylor & Francis Group.
Printed in the United States of America on acid-free paper.

10 9 8 7 6 5 4 3 2 1

Library of Congress Cataloging-in-Publication Data

Authorship and film : trafficking with Hollywood / edited by David A.
Gerstner and Janet Staiger.
    p. cm. — (AFI film readers)
  Includes bibliographical references and index.
  ISBN 0-415-93993-3 (alk. paper) — ISBN 0-415-93994-1 (pbk. : alk.
paper)
    1. Motion picture authorship. 2. Motion pictures and literature.
  3. Auteur theory (Motion pictures) I. Gerstner, David A., 1966- II.
Staiger, Janet. III. Series.

PN1996 .A94 2002
808.2'3—dc21   2002151656

Dedicated

by David to Dave and Jean Gerstner

and by Janet to Mercedes de Uriarte,

Michelangelo Signorile, and

Allucquére Rosanne Stone

contents

acknowledgments ix

introduction xi

part one. authorship studies in review

1. the practices of authorship 3
   david a. gerstner

2. authorship approaches 27
   janet staiger

part two. authorship and identity in hollywood

3. the auteur theory: 61
   michael curtiz, and *casablanca*
   peter wollen

4. i hear music and . . . 77
   darryl and irving write history with *alexander's ragtime band*
   george f. custen

5. stepping out from behind the grand silhouette: 97
   joan harrison's films of the 1940s
   christina lane

part three. authorship and identity near and far from hollywood

6. intentions and mass culture: 119
   oscar micheaux, identity, and authorship
   hugh bartling

7. cundieff's revision of masculinity in film,   137
    or, a "hard" man is not necessarily good to find
    jacqueline fulmer

8. john waters goes to hollywood: 157
    a poststructural authorship study
    walter metz

9. len lye: 175
    reading with the body
    roger horrocks

10. *a lost man*:
    willie varela and the american avant-garde   193
    chon a. noriega

11. grassroots authors:
    collectivity and construction in community video   213
    cindy hing-yuk wong

part four.   the author-function

12. reframing a biographical legend: 235
    style, european filmmakers, and the sideshow
    cinema of tod browing
    matthew solomon

13. robert stigwood: producer, author, text   247
    michael deAngelis

14. making films asian american: 263
    shopping for fangs and the discursive auteur
    sarah projansky and kent a. ono

bibliography   281

biographies   297

indexes   301

acknowledgments

We would like to thank Mark DeOca, Janet Manfredonia, Edward Miller, Charles Silver, Michelangelo Signorile, Catherine Burke, and the William Evans Fellowship at the University of Otago for help along the way. Additionally, our thanks go to Bill Germano and Gilad Foss from Routledge for their good counsel and support. David dedicates this to his parents Dave and Jean Gerstner. Janet dedicates it to Mercedes de Uriarte, Michelangelo Signorile, and Allucquére Rosanne Stone for fighting the good fight, which is, after all, another form of authoring.

introduction

The question is: Why bother looking at authorship yet again? Several reasons exist. First, the purely pragmatic one that authorship is an enabling tool. Every scholar (even those who subscribe to the "death of authorship") speaks of going to a Robert Altman film. Coming to terms with our own ambivalence about the name of the author and the author-function is worthwhile. Second, and perhaps the truth behind the first, is that we don't think the author is dead. In the *Imaginary Signifier*, Christian Metz discusses our disavowal of childhood ideas, but points out that underneath it all we still retain our narcissism and our desire for the other. In fact, Roland Barthes did not really declare the author dead except rhetorically in that [his essay] was an attempt to make a place for the reader. Indeed, Barthes references Proust, Sade, and other authors as significant agents. Third, although authorship may be subject to the wiles of humanism and capitalism, it also has functions for social action. Contemporary poststructuralist theory may be working to articulate a dynamics of agency not yet fully evident. As our essays indicate, the drive to produce such understandings in the production of media texts matters to academics and those producing the texts.

As the two chapters by the co-editors suggest, the past five years have seen a resurgence in the analysis of authorship. This anthology contributes to these discussions by not containing the study of authorship. Rather, this collection offers multiple strategies for analyzing authorship at this time. Additionally, because our concern is the enabling of agency for minority production, the significance of identity has been a major line of investigation.

Each person will come to these questions differently. An ironic example of this occurred during the shaping of the anthology. Planning to write a single review of the literature, we were confounded by both the similarities and differences of our reading of the scholarship. Rather than try to force a single chapter that cramped our individual voices, we have elected to submit two chapters. The repetition of sources does not by any means yield the same meaning to two different individuals just as multiple directors who come to the same script will not produce the same film (e.g., Alfred Hitchcock and Gus Van Sant). There is no truth, just production. Yet this production has effects.

The chapters in this anthology provide methodological exemplars for poststructuralist authorship study. One exemplar is in how identities raise the import of authorship studies and intersect with significant cultural concerns. The chapters surveyed include identities involving nation (Peter Wollen, George Custen, Hugh Bartling, Roger Horrocks, Matthew Solomon), ethnicity and race (Custen, Bartling, Chon Noriega, Cindy Hing-Yuk Wong, Sarah Projansky, Kent A. Ono), class (Bartling, Walter Metz, Wong), sex and gender (Jacqueline Fulmer, Horrocks, Projansky, Ono), and sexual orientation (Metz, Michael DeAngelis). For all of those authors studied, identity matters, but the solutions may differ.

The solutions differ in whether the individual works within the system or chooses alternatives, such as a trash aesthetics (John Waters), an aesthetics of sensuality (Len Lye and Willie Varela), a collaborative, authorless production mode (grassroots filmmakers), a system of parody and satire (Rusty Cundieff), or revisions of genre formulas (Joan Harrison and Oscar Micheaux). Thus, these chapters also raise authorship study exemplars in terms of cinematic mode, narrative form, genre, and industrial practice. From classical Hollywood to avant-garde, the individuals considered here function within the constraints and possibilities of the cultural fields and systems that inform the filmmaking conventions in which they operate. What is at stake, of course, is negotiating these systems through the [marking] of their identities in relationship to these conventions and methods of filmmaking.

The chapters also consider how the term "author" itself serves marketplace interests, identity politics, and social movements for cultural change. What becomes significant, perhaps, is the way the political and identity lines blur in relationship to this "author-function." Are there differences, say, between the way Robert Stigwood marketed his name and the way independent filmmakers such as Quentin Lee and Justin Lin market but also resist the cache of their names? Even with collective authorship, the individual videomakers may seem to privilege themselves by including themselves in their own films and thereby creating a recognition factor within the community in which the films are shown. But the stakes are very different in the case of youth in Philadelphia versus Alfred Hitchcock in Hollywood. In naming an author, a function is served. The effect of the naming, however, is worth exploring to understand better the seemingly endless countenance toward the privileged place of the author but also the potential for expression, social change, and identification.

authorship

studies

in review

the practices

of authorship

d a v i d   a .   g e r s t n e r

Finally, in constructing alternatives to Hollywood, we must recognize
that the historical centrality of that mode creates a constant and complex interchange with other modes. No absolute, pure alternative to
Hollywood exists. . . . You can trace a Hollywood technical process
such as back projection from its classical use to its cubistic
possibilities in films like *The Chronicle of Anna Magdalena Bach*
(1968). Likewise, Hollywood's mode of production continues to
exert a power that can be opposed only by a knowledge of its past
and its functions. The historical and aesthetic importance of the classical Hollywood cinema lies in the fact that to go beyond it we must
go through it.

—David Bordwell, *The Classical Hollywood Cinema*

David Bordwell's provocative suggestion that the production of cinema—from Hollywood itself to national and avant-garde cinemas—has
no ideological recourse other than to respond to the terms established

by the classical Hollywood mode of production frames the discussion of cultural production as one that is contained by ideological repetition operating through dominant institutional practices.[1] Bordwell's claims recall, yet not so pessimistically, Theodor Adorno's axiom (a writer who is, however, never far behind Bordwell's thoughts[2]) that "Whenever Orson Welles offends against the tricks of the trade, he is forgiven because his departures from the norm are regarded as calculated mutations which serve all the more strongly to confirm the validity of the system."[3] The move toward radical difference (and certainly a radical cinema) in twentieth-century culture-industry practices is, in other words, always already hegemonically inscribed from within.

But if the terms of the dominant mode of film production preclude cultural production from without, what possibilities exist for the cultural producer, or as Walter Benjamin terms it, "author as producer,"[4] to intervene and resist the larger institutional framework? Is it critically true to say that when Welles "offends against the tricks of the trade," he is simply affirming the "validity of the system"? In what ways might the filmmaker-as-film author challenge rather than submit to the ideological saturation of Hollywood production? Is the film author merely an ideological tool of a corporatized, homogeneous culture? What critical purpose might the function of the author serve in critical theory against, on the one hand, theories that support a culture of containment or, on the other hand, the bourgeois enterprise that reifies the author position?

This anthology does not claim to rescue, resuscitate, or reclaim "the author" as the *raison d'être* of film studies. Rather, these chapters explore the above questions and *put into practice* methodologies of film authorship that intervene in the landscape of theoretical and historical possibilities associated with critical cinema studies (and, perhaps, in other fields of media as well). At the outset, this collection of writings initially seeks to address the pivotal placement of the film author or auteur in film and other media studies.[5] From what theoretical models does film scholarship draw to develop this area of study? Why and how does auteur studies take on such a significant role in film scholarship? How has this concept been worked and reworked in different historical periods for different ideological reasons? Within the strong current toward interdisciplinary study in the academy, film studies finds itself hard pressed to identify itself as an isolationist discipline. In what relationship, then, does film studies sit with other disciplines concerned with issues of authorship?

Identifying the singular and great author of the text is indeed not reserved for film studies. The long-standing tradition of the sole artist as creative force has evolved for centuries and can be traced from the arts' relationship to the sacral through our contemporary period of late capitalism.[6] The privileged station of the author/artist solidified the abstract qualities of both meaning and exchange value for particular historical economies. During the era of mass-produced art (late nineteenth and early twentieth centuries) where the purity of art was perceived as threatened by loss of original value, the art-critical and market-emphasized focus of one great man and his masterwork of art neatly packaged the illusion of artist and masterpiece.

The history of film criticism and scholarship that emerged during the early years of the twentieth century fits into this historical discourse that stitches together artist-and-masterpiece theories in order to signal film's stake in the realm of the so-called high arts. Like literature before it, film went through the hoops and hurdles of art criticism so as to overcome its vulgar associations with and reputation as mere popular entertainment.[7] Once consecrated by the likes of art historians and critics Sadakichi Hartmann, Vachel Lyndsay, Erwin Panofsky, and Rudolf Arnheim, the role of the filmmaker served as a conduit that raised film into the paean of the sanctified Arts.

A second area this book considers is the ongoing fascination with and interest in the auteur specifically in film studies (or what Dana Polan has recently called "Auteur Desire").[8] Although film, for the most part, is produced as a collaborative medium, the urge and desire to discuss theoretically and market film in relation to the auteur are striking. Years of film criticism have drawn upon issues of authorship and theoretical models of the auteur to explore an array of cinematic topics; the interest has simply not waned. Yet, if such inquiries still find momentum in film scholarship, the critical tools for analyzing the author's body of work (if not the body of the author) have undergone important and significant rethinking throughout these periods.

Against the backdrop of poststructuralist strategies that unraveled the traditionally established place of the author, a new critical position surfaced in which the reader of the text became its writer (note: the author position was not necessarily removed here; its position was reconsidered albeit with varying theoretical implications). Thus, the third interest in my reevaluation of film authorship is the way in which a text is consumed, appropriated, and reproduced given the complicated relationships of production, reception, and spectatorship. Seen this way, the reader/consumer of texts is also the writer/producer of texts. How might authorship be understood in light of this critical shift that initially positioned the author's vision as unique and the mark of Truth to one that privileged authorship as an act of interpretive and, to be sure, culturally productive possibilities? Reception studies as well as deconstruction with its emphasis on *écriture* have challenged old-guard theories of both the intentional fallacy and the affective fallacy. In doing so, these critical theories have opened new territory upon which to rethink the terms of authorship and cultural production.

The final area explored in this book is the state of contemporary political and ideological relevance accorded the film author. With the emergence of cultural studies in academia the interface of race, class, and gender with the production of art took on a particular urgency. As these fields of political and ideological import open around theories of intersectionality, the position of the author takes on new force. This is not to say that the question of the author has not historically carried political concerns and relevance (see my discussion below). But the sometimes overdetermined backlash against author studies in film scholarship has sharpened the focus around just why such a backlash occurs. In feminist-, queer-, and race-film studies, for example, the rethinking of the work by filmmakers such as Rainer Werner Fassbinder, Lois Weber, Dorothy Arzner, Maya Deren, Derek Jarman, Isaac Julien, Marlon Riggs, Oscar Micheaux, Julie Dash, Kenneth Anger, and Andy Warhol indicates what Pam Cook describes as the continuing "pleasures" and "transformations" made available through film-author studies particularly in the struggles over ideological, cultural, and political relations (Cook, 114).[9] The abrasive and hasty dismissal of the auteur or author studies begs the question that perhaps the lady doth protest too much.

the politics of authorship

The auteur theory in cinema is rooted in the theatrics of a political gesture. The theory and its critical champions emerged in postwar France when a group of young cinéastes encountered a deluge of Hollywood cinema (embargoed under the Occupation) and expressed dissatisfaction with the production of what they and other left intellectuals saw as a banal "tradition of quality" in French cinema. Alexandre Astruc's article, "The Birth of a New Avant-garde: *La Caméra-stylo*," in 1948 acted as an *agent provocateur* that challenged a "tendency" or what was sardonically perceived by François Truffaut and his cinéaste compatriots at *Cahiers du Cinéma* as "a *certain* tendency" of the French Cinema.[10]

Astruc's emphasis on *la caméra-stylo* functioned as a critical intervention to break the then current model of cinema's reliance on literature as its primary source of storytelling. *La caméra-stylo* should not merely be understood in direct correlation to the literary author's pen but as a metaphor for grasping the cinema as a "means of expression, just as all the other arts have been before it" (17). It was more than the equivalent between pen and camera as a strict translation might suggest. *La caméra-stylo* indicated the director's creative ability to "translate his obsessions" (18) and "write ideas" (19) so as to reach the profound achievements that exist in great literature and painting. As Astruc would have it, cinema, like the other arts, is its own creative medium with discrete creative properties that when fully realized through the authorial hand of the film's maker the critic may distinguish "between the man who conceives the work and the man who writes it" (22).

Astruc's notion of the cinematic auteur resonated soundly with the upstart Truffaut who argued for a new French cinema that was grounded in radical and political impulses that only a true auteur could provide. In his 1953 manifesto for a new French cinema, "A Certain Tendency of the French Cinema," Truffaut railed against "psychological realism" and the "Tradition of Quality" (nothing more than a filmed novel) in the national cinema that, as he saw it, denigrated the spirit toward a pure cinema (232). French filmmakers' reliance on literary adaptation for their cinematic narrative "destroyed the audience's ability to comprehend a cinema of difference" because to rely on literary form lacked the essence of cinema.

Written in polemic form, Truffaut called for filmmakers to strip away their literary sensibilities. True filmmakers are those who produce cinema from scenario to mise-en-scène. In this way, Truffaut reiterated Astruc's stylistic concern and assertion: The cinematic is expressed by the visual (mise-en-scène), not the literary word. The emphasis on mise-en-scène has since had a long-standing and substantial impact on auteur studies. John Caughie argues that "the attention to mise-en-scène, even to the extent of a certain historically necessary formalism, is probably the most important positive contribution of auteurism to the development of a precise and detailed film criticism, engaging with the specific mechanisms of visual discourse, freeing it from literary models, and from the liberal commitments which were prepared to validate films on the basis of their themes alone."[11] Who were the great French cinematic auteurs according to Truffaut that successfully broke from the bondage of the literary word? Jean Renoir, Robert Bresson, Jean Cocteau, Abel Gance, Max Ophuls, and Jacques Tati were *les auteurs du cinéma* who ultimately created a cinematic transformation couched in the spirit of the other arts yet pure in its own specific properties.

The effect of Truffaut's *la politiques des auteurs* was profound particularly on fellow cinéastes Eric Rohmer, Claude Chabrol, and Jean Domarchi who favored an auteur approach for film criticism. These auteurists would later write for the influential *Cahiers du Cinéma* while several of them fancied themselves auteurs and made films under the aegis of the *nouvelle vague*.[12] Yet for all the bravado attending Truffaut's political edge of the auteur, the theory, as Jim Hillier explains, was underlined by "an essentially romantic conception of art and the artist" in which "art transcended history" (6).[13] André Bazin, arguably Truffaut's surrogate father figure, challenged his colleagues at *Cahiers* "who are most firmly convinced that the *politique des auteurs* is well founded."[14] For Bazin, the genius-artist is no simple matter and should not and must not be hastily determined. Indeed, Bazin does not relinquish the genius-artist in the other arts. The "danger" in which his cinéaste comrades partook was their polemic discharge on the auteur that slid suspiciously into "an aesthetic personality cult" (257).

What about Hollywood? If the auteur in European cinema was readily identifiable as an artist of integrity and therefore produced a complete work of art, it was because (especially in the cases of those filmmakers held in high regard by the *Cahiers*) these directors were afforded the opportunity to work *outside* a strict studio environment. Is it possible for the auteur to be identified in the great factory-produced art of America? As far as American film critic Andrew Sarris was concerned, the answer was yes! If the French recognized the importance of Hollywood directors why were American critics unable to see their contribution to the cinema? Yet, to make the case that popular culture and mass-produced art was worthy of critical discussion was no easy matter. Aside from a handful of writers such as artists and critics James Agee and Parker Tyler or anthropologist Hortense Powdermaker, Hollywood film was not even a gleam in the eye of most American art critics and historians. In 1968, Sarris published his own manifesto, *The American Cinema: Directors and Directions 1929–1968*, in which he critiqued the "snobberies" of art criticism in order to explore the "twilight periods of [Hollywood's] greatest artists."[15]

Sarris sought to bring critical analysis to Hollywood cinema against the backdrop of critical condescension. To do this he identified the film's director (following the *Cahiers*'s agenda of auteurist criticism) as the criterion of value.[16] Sarris opposed the more contemporary practice of film criticism that relied on a review of the star, screenwriter, and/or producer. To counter this, he established a set of evaluative criteria upon which he determined the worth of the American director as auteur. His evaluation process included technical competence, presence of a distinct visual style, and the emergence of "interior meaning" that, as he saw it, arose from the tension between the director (auteur) and the conditions of production with which he or she worked (i.e., Hollywood studio system). Clearly, Sarris's methodology slipped dangerously into overly subjective analysis. What Sarris provided, however (and weighed heavily on a posteriori film criticism), was an analysis of Hollywood cinema that prescribed (rather than proscribed) the possibility of creative agency in the industrial arts.

Now well rehearsed in the canon of film scholarship, Sarris hierarchically categorized America's auteurs. From top to bottom, his list began with the "Pantheon Directors" (D.W. Griffith, Hawks, John Ford, Welles), was followed, in part, by what he called "The Far Side of Paradise Directors" (Nicholas Ray, Vincente Minnelli), "Expressive Esoterica Directors" (Donald Siegel), and, toward the lower rungs of the barrel, "Oddities, One-Shots, and Newcomers" where "classification" is defied (Francis Ford Coppola, Roger Corman). He further clarified the difference between auteur and *metteurs-en-scène*. Caughie succinctly describes the distinction where "the one consistently [expresses] his own unique obsessions, the other a competent, even highly competent filmmaker" (9).

Sarris's goal in "Toward a Theory of Film History" was to shake film criticism out of its cultural blindness to the critical engagement of

Hollywood cinema. Once critics moved beyond the Hollywood clichés, the "personal signature styles" of the directors were discerned, the mise-en-scène was carefully scrutinized, and every single Hollywood film by a particular director was viewed, Sarris was convinced that Hollywood could hold its own with the rest of the world. Foreign films, documentary films, and avant-garde films, according to Sarris, were not morally superior. The Hollywood auteur existed once discovered by the rigorous critic.

The race for the great American auteurs was on! In America, England, and France a cottage industry developed around auteurship and was successfully marketed in both the academy and Hollywood. There were dissenters (who, of course, fueled the marketability of the debate itself). V.F. Perkins in *Film as Film* appeared to wobble in his final determination of the auteur theory. On the one hand, the "ultimate unity" of a film as a coherent vision is a "dubious proposition" since the "distance between conception and delivery is so great."[17] On the other hand, Perkins concludes that the director "is in control throughout the period in which virtually all significant relationships [of production] are defined. He [*sic*] has possession of the means through which all other contributions acquire meaning *within* the film" (184).

The writer who most insistently challenged Sarris and his theory of the Hollywood auteur was Pauline Kael. In her essay, "Circles and Squares," Kael suggests that the "auteur theory is an attempt by adult males to justify staying inside the small range of experience of their boyhood and adolescence."[18] But what truly astonished Kael was that the auteur critic refused to exercise taste and judgment within their area of study. There are "bad" critics such as Sarris who, according to Kael, lack rigor and are "undisciplined" (21). She challenged what she saw as Sarris's "three circles of the Auteur Theory" as well as the formulaic rigidity, yet "conflicting implications" (21), she perceived in the theory. For Kael: "Criticism is an art, not a science" (14).

Kael takes to task Sarris's three determining factors for auteur status: technical competence (or the "outer circle"), distinguishable personality of the directory (or the "middle circle"), and, mise-en-scène (or the "inner circle") (14–20). For Kael, Sarris's auteur-theory model is a rote practice that ludicrously reduces *all* films to a privileged status of art. Indeed, the auteur theory, "silly as it is, can nevertheless be a dangerous theory . . . because it offers nothing but commercial goals to the young artists who may be trying to do something in film" (25).

Cook writes that Britain's critical assessment of authorship in film was shaped somewhat differently than the polemic-aesthetic positions taken in America and France. Film criticism during the 1950s in Britain functioned through the contradictory economies of the personal-taste determinations of critics and emerging Marxist social criticism (Cook, 147). Journals such as *Movie*, *Sequence*, and *Sight and Sound* became the hotbed for these often-contentious debates. Key critical and theoretical models were foreground and appealed to intellectual's new critical discourses quickly emerging in film studies. To be sure, structuralism and a political rethinking of ideology through the work of Louis Althusser introduced a different set of stakes into the auteur debate.

Peter Wollen, a contributor to this collection, intervened with a model of the auteur that suggested "*auteur* theory does not limit itself to acclaiming the director as the main author of a film. It implies an operation of decipherment; it reveals authors where none had been seen before."[19] Wollen stressed that the study of the auteur is not strictly formalist. Rather it is one of decipherment *and* analysis facilitated by structuralist theory. In this way, Wollen turned to Hawks and Ford where he argued that the "great directors must be defined in terms of shifting relations, in their singularity as well as their uniformity" (104).

The auteur theory investigates the "stylistic expressions" of the filmmaker similar to the way one considers a musician's interpretation of a score or a commission charged to a painter. The material may originate from several hands (the composer, the patron, the publisher) but the artist's interpretation is a transformation of the "original" score or, in the case of film, screenplay (105–8).

Following Wollen's work, Ed Buscombe, in his important overview of the auteur debate up to this point, suggests that there are possible areas in which the question of the auteur may be fruitfully explored so as to "squeeze out the auteur from his position of prominence, and transform the notion of him which remain."[20] He recommends three alternatives to the romantic auteur regimen: (1) examine the effects of cinema on society; (2) consider the effect of society on cinema or "the operation of ideology, economics, technology, etc."; and (3) study "the effects of films on other films" (84). Buscombe's shift from the romantic sensibilities of the *Cahiers* group and Sarris to a more culturally political critique and use of the auteur finds a point of departure in Wollen's early work. Buscombe, however, opens the theory into wider fields of investigation especially toward a more rigorous and ideological analysis.

Indeed, as the notion of the auteur traversed the 1960s and into the early 1970s when the political environment altered considerably in academic thinking in Europe and America, the questions of ideology, spectatorship, and modes of cultural production were placed center stage in the new debates around the auteur. The *Cahiers'* collectively authored article, "Cinema/Ideology/Criticism," filtered the auteur status of Ford through a Marxist analysis that highlighted what the writers saw as Ford's ideological critique of class and social structure in "John Ford's *Young Mr. Lincoln*" (1939).[21] Writers such as Daniel Dayan and Nick Browne lay bare the absent structure of ideology in the formal construction of the Hollywood film.[22] Stephen Heath pushed and opened the auteur envelope further when he asked, "what can it mean . . . to speak of the author as a source of discourse?"[23]

Heath clarifies and expands upon Buscombe's three approaches to auteur studies. "[W]hat is in question," writes Heath, "is the production through the development of [Buscombe's] proposals, of new objects the formalisation of which will provide not so much an insight as a theoretical grasp of film as signifying practice, a new problematic in which traditional notions are radically displaced" (88). Intersecting at the structuralist/poststructuralist convergence, Heath's and Buscombe's notes may be seen as a critical move from the emphasis on authorship per se to a textual, ideological, and theoretical analysis of the subject/spectator in relationship to the text. Indeed, as I will chart below, the concept of authorship has cut across a wide and diverse spectrum of political and cultural ideology.

authorship as (sentient) discourse

The anxiety over (auto)biography and authorial intention is remarkable for both its dogged insistence and overwhelmingly accepted dicta within critical-theory circles. It is tempting to argue that the critical discourse around the loss of subjectivity and conscious-individual intention occurred following the apocalyptic images and cultural effects of World War II.[24] The modernist idea of unique authorship and, in another modernist register, collective political practice and intervention seemingly evaporated, or was made abstract, with the Atomic Age. In the now classic and seminal work of New Criticism, "The Intentional Fallacy" (1946), W. K. Wimsatt and Monroe Beardsley make clear that "the design of the author or intention of the author is neither available nor desirable as a standard for judging the success of work of literary art."[25] Delving into "author psychology . . . takes the form of inspirational promotion" that runs the risk of "confusing personal and poetic studies; and there is the fault of writing the personal as if it were poetic" (477). For the New Critics, the work of poetry is understood only on its own (poetic and linguistic) terms.

Similarly, in "The Affective Fallacy" (1949), Wimsatt and Beardsey rejected the "confusion" that "emotive" and "psychological effects" of the reader may have with their encounter with the text.[26] Most discomfiting for Wimsatt and Beardsley was, at least since the Romantic era, the blurred line between criticism and art where the text was evaluated through discrete subjectivity. Art criticism thus "approximated the tone of the Buchmanite confession" (41). To confess one's experience, in other words, neglected the work itself and its ability to stand on its own poetic terms and historical "patterns" of language and form. Thus, although art/poetry is a "discourse about emotions and objects," the reasoned and objective critic must be clear that the "emotions correlative to the objects of poetry become a part of the matter dealt with—not communicated to the reader like an infection or disease" (52). Critical distance allowed pure critical objectivity and a shield from contamination of "emotions."

11

But have theories that trouble authorship, intention, and reader affect truly jettisoned the author? Or is it that the subsequent use of these critiques of agency and intention by scholars and others—critiques enmeshed within their own historical and ideological logic—reduces the complexities of these theories to an oversimplified erasure of the author? Through a closer reading of some of the apposite theoretical works on which film studies have drawn, I would like to suggest that claims for the "death of the author" and intentionality in the twentieth century might identify not so much an end point of a discourse of authorship. Instead, authorship is situated in these critical works as a transformative point of departure for theoretical and political intervention.

When Michel Foucault wrote his essay, "What Is an Author?," he emphasized the genealogical production of meaning surrounding the bourgeois construct of authorship.[27] In other words, Foucault's theory of the master author was a discourse secured through a particular ideology. It was not that the author did not exist. The author, or "author-function" (107), as Foucault called it, existed to the extent that the concept upheld bourgeois sensibilities of art and circulated as an important operative of that ideology. Two key theorists, however, wrote in advance of Foucault (as well as other structuralist and poststructuralist thinkers) and were instrumental in carving out the complexities of authorship in bourgeois culture. These authors are Mikhail Bakhtin and Walter Benjamin. Although their writings found academic popularity in the 1960s and 1970s, Bakhtin's and Benjamin's critical models of authorship were conceived during the 1930s.

Bakhtin was concerned with "naïve biographism" when he wrote his work on Rabelais, "Forms of Time and Chronotope in the Novel."[28] At the same time, Bakhtin was quick to point out ("first and foremost") that the materials attending the "chronotopes of the author and the listener or reader" are seated in intimate relationship with the work of art and are "not dead, [they are] speaking, signifying" (252). So concerned was Bakhtin about cursory understanding of the author that he posited a new term—"author-creator"—distinct from what might be perceived as "the author as human being" (253).[29] Because the chronotope was embodied in the work of art, Bakhtin insisted that the author-creator has a "dialogical character" (256) and "presence" that exist tangentially and in "mutual interaction between the world represented in the work and the world outside the work" (255).

Through this *rondelet-Bakhtin*, a "single but complex event that we might call the work in the totality of all its events" includes the "givenness of the work, and its text, and the world represented in the text, and the author-creator, and the listener or reader" (255). The reader is an active participant and producer of meaning in Bakhtin's dialogic characterization of the work. To write of Rabelais without privileging the concept of the author (naive biographism), Bakhtin necessarily reconceived the author position to include the multilayered dimensions associated with the phenomenological experience of the work of art in space and time [what he refers to as the "here and now" (169)]. Bakhtin's work on authorial intention, as Gary Saul Morson and Caryl Emerson argue, "is far more complex than either intentionalists or their opponents have imagined" (430).

During the same period (late 1930s) when Bakhtin developed his dissertation on Rabelais under the Stalinist regime, Benjamin was working through the authorship question against the personality-driven fascist regime of the Nazis. It is clear from Benjamin's body of work that he struggled with his own productive role as a bourgeois intellectual in the interests of the proletariat movement. What was most difficult for Benjamin was how to consider the cultural *effect* of the author and his or her relationship to bourgeois interests in the service of proletariat revolution. The position of the (bourgeois) artist/author was never far from Benjamin's ruminations on Marxism. Was it possible, in other words, to speak of authorship without falling into the trap of bourgeois and (by extension) fascist ideology?

Similar to Bakhtin's phenomenological theory of experience with the work of art, Benjamin often considered the moment of the "here and now" as central to grasping the interconnectedness between author, work, and reader. Benjamin, however, saw the "here and now" as a space–time relationship that straddled a nebulous line between revolutionary activity and false consciousness that defined bourgeois ideology.[30] What is important about Benjamin's writing is that the critical *questioning* of the ideological emplacement of the work of art overrode the impetus to assert reactionary and ineffectual dogma about politics and culture.

To be reactionary, Benjamin wrote in "The Author as Producer," meant "[the work's] effect could never be revolutionary" (1934, 227). As he saw it, the distinction between the reactionary and the revolutionary characterized the "author as producer" *as* one who either sided with the proletariat in attitude (reactionary) or as a producer of what his friend Bertolt Brecht termed *Umfunktionierung* (functional transformation) (228). What this suggested for Benjamin was that although "the bourgeois apparatus of production and publication can assimilate astonishing quantities of revolutionary themes" (224), those modes of production can undergo *Umfunktionierung* "which is able first to induce other producers to produce" (233). This "apparatus is better the more consumers it is able to turn into producers—that is, readers or spectators into collaborators" (233). Importantly, Brecht's conscious intervention in bourgeois theatrical narrative "constantly counteracts an illusion in the audience" (235).[31]

It is precisely through the productive activity of the author and his or her "demand *to think*, to reflect on his position in the process of production" (236; emphasis in original) and its effect on the reader that broke the illusion of ideology. For Benjamin, there are "writers who *matter*" (236, emphasis in original). The "writers who matter" are not simply privileged names assigned to the culturally void strata of bourgeois culture. Rather, the writers who matter are agents who engage with revolutionary, creative, and collective practices and function as prescient agents for the commingled and direct relationship between reader and work.

> It is not enough, however, to repeat the empty affirmation that the author has disappeared. For the same reason, it is not enough to keep repeating (after Nietzsche) that God and man have died a common death. Instead, we must locate the space left empty by the author's disappearance, follow the distribution of gaps and breaches, and watch for the openings that this disappearance uncovers.
>
> —Michel Foucault, "What Is an Author?"

Foucault's remarks emphasize his refusal to simply negate or privilege "empty affirmations" about the position of the author (105). His strategy, rather, investigates how the discourse of authorship is produced and produces meaning. Indeed, the claims that the author has disappeared reaffirm authorship precisely through the discursive "gaps and breaches" that its "disappearance uncovers." As I have discussed, postwar French critics rethought the place of the author (especially in the cinema). Opposing bourgeois sensibilities associated with the "tradition of quality cinema," Truffaut and the other theorists and filmmakers saw themselves as *agents provocateurs*. This sort of "reactionary" response that posed the radical cultural producer against the traditional author, however, lent itself to a critical inquiry by scholars such as Roland Barthes, Foucault, and subsequently Jacques Derrida. Recalling (although indirectly) Benjamin's distinction between "reactionary" and "revolutionary" bourgeois production and authorial intervention, this group of French thinkers, against the backdrop of the politically charged 1960s, challenged the modernist/bourgeois privileging of the author (radical or otherwise).

The break from author(ity) was a hallmark of radical 1960s politics in both France and America. Barthes's shift from structuralist formulations to a theoretical approach more in line with poststructuralist thinking ushered in a complex (and certainly political) consideration of the author. To grasp his idea of the author it is necessary to understand the distinction that Barthes makes between "work" and "text." Although published after "The Death of the Author" (1968), Barthes's essay, "From Work to Text," emphasizes that the "work is a fragment of substance, occupying a portion of the space of books (in a library, for example); the Text on the other hand is a methodological tool."[32] Relevant to my discussion here is that the Text "is not a coexistence of meanings but a passage, a traversal; thus it answers not to an interpretation, even a liberal one, but to an explosion, a dissemination" (171). Such a key distinction was made earlier by Barthes in "The Death of the Author" when he suggested that "To give a text an Author is to impose a limit on that text, to furnish it with a final signified, to close the writing."[33]

In this essay, Barthes intersects, in many ways, with Bakhtin's and Benjamin's theories of the author. His positing the reader of the text as "the space on which all the quotations that make up a writing are inscribed without any of them being lost; a text's unity lies not in its origin but in its destination" (Barthes, 1968, 148) echoes Bakhtin's and Benjamin's insistence on the readerly act of consumption *as* production. Strikingly, Barthes's suggests that the reader's active role with the Text, one that displaces the bourgeois privilege of the author, occurs because "every text is eternally written *here and now*"(Barthes, 1968 145; emphasis in original). The sense of the "here and now" that reverberates in these theories addresses the phenomenological and active relationship between producer, work, and consumer where the presence of the text yields "multiple writings" that resist a foreclosed interpretation. Thus, the reader-as-producer makes meaning not to secure it for the past or for the future ("ultimate meaning"), but for the "here and now."

This is why perhaps Foucault was reticent to subscribe to "empty affirmation" and reactionary polemics that purportedly erased the "author-function." If the author matters, it is because the author serves an ideological function. "The author-function," Foucault writes, "is therefore characteristic of the mode of existence, circulation, and functioning of certain discourses within a society" (108). To dismiss the author *in toto* is to misunderstand how authorship functions within cultural ideology. Marx and Freud, for example, are what Foucault calls "founders of discursivity." They are not "just the author" of major works such as *Communist Manifesto* or *The Interpretation of Dreams*; "they both have established an endless possibility of discourse" (114).

Barthes's and Foucault's theories of authorship resonated with varying degrees on the work of subsequent French thinkers Pierre Bourdieu and Michel de Certeau. In his essay, "The Production of Belief," Bourdieu (turning predominantly to Foucault) argues that "the ideology of creation, which makes the author the first and last source of value of his work, conceals the fact that the cultural businessman (art dealer, publisher, etc.) is at one and the same time the person who exploits the labour of the 'creator' . . . by putting it on the market, by exhibiting, publishing or staging it, consecrates a product which he has discovered and which would otherwise remain a mere natural resource."[34] As Bourdieu sees it, the question of degree of "conscious strategy" in the field of cultural production has "no simple answer."[35]

De Certeau turns toward both Barthes and Foucault to identify the author through the strategies and tactics of cultural place. De Certeau, in one instance, suggests that "A different world (the reader's) slips into the author's place," and, in another, he defines the "author position" as "the nominal center where the fictional unity of the work is produced."[36] Again, a symbiotic relationship between work and text creates the vital dynamic between producer and consumer. When Gilles Deleuze wrote his treatise on the cinema he claimed that there is "no room for metaphor" in Astruc's "camera-pen."[37] The machine of the cinematic apparatus intermingles with spectatorial corporeality. "But what is important," writes Deleuze, "is the possibility of a cinema of the brain which brings together all the powers, as much as the cinema of the body equally brought them together as well" (205). Hitchcock, Carl Dreyer, Tony Conrad, Godard, and other authors, according to Deleuze, are granted "very great position in cinema" (63).[38]

"New Criticism," writes Gaytatri Chakravorty Spivak, "although it vigorously argued the self-enclosure and 'organic unity' of the text," was similar to Derrida's "insight" that "the text belongs to language."[39] Deconstructionist emphasis on the text's polysemic interpretive possibilities introduced yet another fold into questions of authorship or, more precisely, intention and the reader as writer of meaning. Since Derrida argued that *écriture* was an act of "inscription" facilitated not only by the stroke of a pen but through "cinematography, choreography . . . [writing is] pictorial, musical, sculptural" (9). The mark left through the gesture of writing found meaning because of its iterability or repetition. In other words, the mark of writing "makes sense" in relationship to the context in which the mark emerged. But "context" is not determinable as such. Does this suggest that authorial intention is determinable as such? Although this is not the place to address Derrida's notions of "trace" and "*differance*," it is important to stress that to understand the intentionality of the mark, of what remains, it is necessary to understand that, as Jonathan Culler argues, "Intention . . . is not something prior to the text that determines its meaning but is an important organizing structure identified in readings that distinguish an explicit line of argumentation from its subversive other."[40] The mark is always in excess of some transparent meaning intended through the conscious act of its author. In this way, intention is not decided and determined by the simple reorganizing of an author's context by the historian. Indeed, as Culler tells us, although "meaning is context bound [and] context is boundless" (128), the truth of intention is unknowable.[41]

Indeed, "[t]he category of intention," writes Derrida in "Signature Event Context," "will not disappear; it will have its place, but from this place it will no longer be able to govern the entire scene and the entire system of utterances."[42] For Derrida, writing is communication, ideological (in the sense that signs represent ideal content), and "an effective *intervention*" that, through deconstruction, resists the traces of the dominant forces "which organized the—to say it quickly—logocentric

16

hierarchy" (Derrida 1971, 329–30). It is here, then, that I turn to the ways in which issues of authorship and intention have recently operated as political intervention, especially in film studies.

the body of work and the work of the body

Oscar Wilde scandalously once wrote, "One should either be a work of art, or wear a work of art."[43] Later, and reflecting on his screen-test actors, Andy Warhol said, "Their lives became part of my movies, and of course the movies became part of their lives; they'd get so into them that pretty soon you couldn't really separate the two, you couldn't tell the difference—and sometimes neither could they."[44] These remarks that commingle artist with work of art point to an important theoretical concept of *techné* that has interested writers such as Socrates, Heidegger, Derrida, and Foucault. Such a theory, I suggest, offers a profitable way to engage with questions of authorship particularly in film studies.

In his third volume of the *History of Sexuality*, Foucault charts the subtle yet significant shifts from Socratic claims for the "art of existence" to the Roman's more functional philosophy of "the cultivation of the self."[45] What *techné* stresses is the symbiotic relationship between the body (cultural producer) and technology. Technology (and the similarities between *techné* and technology should not be underestimated here) of the twentieth century further raised the ante on the relationship between body and object. But if philosophers such as Heidegger saw body and technology unified in such a way that solidified the presence of meaning, deconstruction and poststructuralist arguments sought to destabilize the totalizing effects presumed with that presence. "As something that *goes on*," Samuel Weber tells us, "technics moves *away* from itself in being what it is."[46] Here, *technics* is about Doing. For those cultural producers at the margins the issue of authorship as a productive force rests not so much in reifying the privileged status or Being of the author. Rather, the intervention of authorship challenges the authorities that have decidedly announced, *once and for all*, the parameters and limitations of the body's involvement in the processes of cultural production.

In America, poststructuralism was received with both warm embrace and firm resistance. Foucault's reception was particularly complicated because his work was engaged by feminist and gay and lesbian theorists who, on the one hand, reveled in Foucault's toppling of methodological hierarchies yet, on the other hand, had concern that Foucault's purported loss of the subject gave little succor to what was so urgently at stake for these theorists: *bodies*. As I have shown, however, Foucault was not wont to eliminate the subject/body as much as he sought to understand how the subject/body was ideologically produced. I will return to feminist and queer theorists' writings on authorship and subjectivity below. What is important here, however, is to consider Foucault's theory of discourse and authorship as it found a significant place in the methodological approaches of authorship in the traditional disciplines of the humanities.[47]

Writers such as Edward Said who later followed Foucault's analytical model of authorial discourse insisted that (*unlike* Foucault according to Said) there is a "determining imprint of individual writers upon the otherwise anonymous collective body of texts constituting a discursive formation like Orientalism."[48] For Said, the political stakes are high in his elegiac work, *Orientalism*. His Foucauldian analysis that draws together a complex set of discursive practices to reveal the formation of the "Orient" through "Occidental" texts relies on an investigation of author(ity) that is neither "mysterious [nor] natural": "it is formed, irradiated, disseminated; it is instrumental, it is persuasive; it has status, it establishes canons of taste and value; it is virtually indistinguishable from certain ideas it dignifies as true from traditions, perceptions, and judgments it forms, transmits, reproduces" (19–20).

Abdul R. JanMohamed challenges those that suggest Said's argument outlines a top-bottom hierarchical structure where the colonized culture is erased by the imperialist's crush of moral and juridical imperative.[49] Homi Bhabha, for example, counters that hegemony is made risible by ironic inflection enacted by the colonized upon the regulatory terms established by the imperialists. Yet, as JanMohamed argues, "Bhabha's unexamined conflation allows him to circumvent entirely the dense history of the material conflict between European and natives and to focus on colonial discourse as if it existed in a vacuum" (79). For JanMohamed, the colonized author (here he refers to V.S. Naipaul) is inextricably enmeshed in the matrix of imperialist commodification and "can also be inducted, under the right circumstances, to fulfill the author-function of the colonialist writer" (82). A "profound symbiotic relationship" between the work of the colonized author and imperialist practices is so entrenched that it is "impossible to determine which form of commodification takes precedence, so entirely are the two forms intertwined" (83).

In America, African–Americans confront a similar conundrum regarding the move to elevate the stature of the author and its canonization. Does such a gesture merely mimic white culture's claims of good taste and authority? Is it possible to mark the presence of black authorship—to assert privilege where none had existed before—as an intervention on the white canon? The risks are high. But as J. Ronald Green makes clear, "auteur studies are still valid."[50] In his work on Oscar Micheaux, Green insists that auteur studies "[remain] vital to the politics of representation" (xvi). To simply refuse the existence of these lives (such as Micheaux's) smacks of doctrinaire principles that seek to shape the contours and parameters of scholarship. Micheaux's case significantly raises the strategy of authorship as Micheaux consistently overlaps the biographical with the body of work. Pearl Bowser and Louise Spence demonstrate that Micheaux's films and novels "were acts of recollection and imagination, creations and re-creations shaped by his personal experience *and* the desire to construct an image of himself for his audience."[51] The recording of the author's experience as valid, as worthwhile, not only grants privilege to the writer but provides a site where author and spectator/reader might convene in a cultural sphere in which such pleasures of identification are in short supply.

Inserting authorial presence as a dynamic enterprise among author, work, and spectator resists a liberal posture of "nonrace" (or indeed *non*homosexual) where the celebratory announcement, "we're all the same," effectively elides cultural difference. Such a relationship offers, Jane Gaines suggests, "a chance to redefine the motion picture producer [Micheaux here] as an instigator and an actualizer, someone who not only designs the work but who orchestrates its reception."[52] Across media, the lives and works of black authors resonate and share in the cultural and political lives of those who engage with the text.[53]

Like African-American and postcolonialist writers, feminists, gays and lesbians, Chicano/Chicana, and Asian scholars have cautioned against hasty dismissal of the authority of the author precisely because such a status provides for both a critique of the power relations attending the position of the author and locates a site of pleasure and political identification. Constance Penley, for example, asks, "What happens . . . when a woman director attempts to locate and convey the 'discourse of a woman' in a representational form which is entirely male?"[54] This was the project of Cook's and Claire Johnston's work on Dorothy Arzner in the early 1970s. Such feminist intervention quickly and vitally put the breaks on the other androcentric project of declaring auteur and authorship studies dead—fait accompli.[55]

Following Nancy K. Miller's essay, "The Text's Heroine: A Feminist Critic and Her Fictions," Lauren Rabinowitz argues that Foucault's "author-function" as engaged by feminists "is important as such for feminist theory because it marks critical sites for understanding the cultural underpinnings and enunciation of any specifically female discourse."[56] Rabinowitz's intervention in the canon of avant-garde cinema with the work of Maya Deren, Shirley Clarke, and others situated women practitioners of film alongside their male counterparts. The important distinction here is that Rabinowitz sought the "enunciation of any specifically female discourse" (23). The specificity of the discourse raised more questions than perhaps were answered. What is a "specifically female discourse"? Does this imply only white women? African-American women? Lesbians? In addition, does the work of Cook, Johnston, and Rabinowitz merely serve canon formation in film studies by carving spaces for gender difference?

In 1990, Judith Butler (*Gender Trouble*) and Eve Kosofsky Sedgwick (*Epistemology of the Closet*) critiqued essentialist presumptions about gender and paved the way for queer theorists to deconstruct issues of canon, authority, and corporeality.[57] Authorship again reemerged with a new set of political objectives and agendas. Butler's work, for example, was instrumental for Judith Mayne's queer study of Arzner where "stylization" of "gender performatives" is revealed and *de*naturalized for the pose they ideologically assume.[58] In the tradition of auteur studies, Mayne draws upon textual analysis (mise-en-scène) in order to reconfigure the workings of the author within its reshaping by feminists and gay and lesbian scholars.

Douglas Crimp's provocative reading of Fassbinder through Barthes's theories of autobiography, "Fassbinder, Franz, Fox, Elvira, Armin and All the Others," may be situated in what I have sketched elsewhere as a queer-modernist tradition in authorship and the work of art.[59] Crimp's commingling of Fassbinder and Barthes (not to mention Crimp himself) decadently privileges the "I" of the text as both reader and writer—two indissoluble figures who are not so much distinct and separate as much as sensual inventions of one another.[60] For Crimp, Fassbinder's and Barthes's "biographeme" does not simply "humanize" the author's oeuvre. This intermingling, or to use Barthes's terms, "conversation with friends" (Barthes quoted in Crimp, 265), abolishes individuality while animating the pleasures Fassbinder discovered through his reading of *Berlin Alexanderplatz*: "A second-hand life, dictated by literature: an 'I' invented by someone else" (270). Crimp's phenomenological model recalls Bakhtin's "author-creator" and, of course, Barthes's experiential text.

In queer theory, such sensualness is the sine qua non of the author/reader/writer dynamic. Michael Moon, in his work on Walt Whitman, tells us, "I believe these 'fluid' or boundary-dissolving powers which, according to Whitman, are potential in both texts and persons stand in more than merely analogical relation to one another in his texts. They do so because fundamental to Whitman's project are the transformative equations between 'body' and 'text' on which he insists; his own body *can* be successfully projected through, and partially transformed into, his printed text, and his readers in turn *can* engage in contact with the actual physical presence of the author, at least in liminal terms, as they read his book."[61] Often perverse, the entanglement of subject and text, the irreducible management of self and other, rendered queer subjectivity with the work as a political act of pleasure and agency.

In her essay, "The Author as Receiver," Kaja Silverman considers Godard's form of cinematic production as both an "auto-portrait" and "biographical erasure."[62] Silverman points to Godard's film *JLG/JLG: Self-Portrait in December* (1995) in which the filmmaker cinematically conjures his death and indeed "the death of himself as the author" (20). Godard's conscious gesture toward "authorial suicide" ["Godard signals again his determination to try again to engineer his suicide," (21)] is perceived by Silverman as a performative of the text in which the filmmaker "erases himself as a bodily presence" (23). This is a troubling effect for "those of us who have labored within the field of post-structuralist theory" especially as such theory has inalterably (or so it seems) broken down the privileged presence of authority control of the text. To speak of Godard's "determination" to commit suicide within his own work, however, still grants the author a franchise on the claims for textual authority.

The issue of authorship is certainly perplexing, particularly for those "who have labored" with poststructuralist theory and issues of agency. The pleasures and politics associated with authorship studies must to a certain ideological degree remain suspect. If not, authorship runs the risk of becoming drivel for trivia masters and film-industry public relations. To engage critically with authorship necessarily demands a rethinking along an intellectual continuum in which the pleasures and politics of authorship studies resist any one authoritative theoretical position. To claim the author dead is in itself an act of authorial privilege and hubris. "The death of the author," writes Silverman, "is thus better understood as an ongoing process than as a realizable event" (34). It is my hope that this collection of essays interrogates the status of the film author and indeed the "ongoing process" of his or her purported death. If the author's death is fixed on the distant horizon, its transformative possibilities remain to be seen.

the practices of authorship

notes

1. Some (Sergei Eisenstein, for example) have argued that the idea of the cinematic narrative structure predates the actual invention of the cinematic apparatus. Sergei Eisenstein, "Dickens, Griffith, and the Film Today" [1944], reprinted in *Film Form: Essays in Film Theory* [1949], trans. and ed. Jay Leyda (New York: Harcourt, Brace & Co., 1977), 195–255; see further, Alan Spiegel, *Fiction and the Camera Eye: Visual Consciousness in Film and the Modern Novel* (Charlottesville: University Press of Virginia, 1976); Wylie Sypher, *Rococo to Cubism in Art and Literature: Transformations in Style, in Art and Literature from the Eighteenth to the Twentieth Century* (New York: Vintage Books, 1960), esp. 257–293.
2. David Bordwell, Janet Staiger, and Kristin Thompson, *The Classical Hollywood Cinema: Film Style and Modes of Production to 1960* (London: Routledge & Kegan Paul, 1985), 60, 83.
3. Theodor Adorno and Max Horkheimer, *Dialectic of Enlightenment* [1947] (New York: Continuum, 1993), 129.
4. Walter Benjamin, "The Author as Producer" [1934], in *Reflections: Essays, Aphorisms, Autobiographical Writings*, ed. Peter Demetz, trans. Edmund Jephcott (New York: Schocken Books, 1986).
5. To be clear, we use the term "auteur" in its historical usage. We will use "auteur" when the writer of a particular work specifically posits its use (as in the case of the French New Wave critics) or when engaged in debate by subsequent writers such as Andrew Sarris, Pauline Kael, and Peter Wollen.
6. See Pam Cook, *The Cinema Book* (London: British Film Institute, 1994), 114; and Peter Bürger's economy of art that shifts from the sacral, the courtly, and, finally, the bourgeois in *Theory of the Avant-Garde* [1974, 1979], trans. Michael Shaw (Minneapolis: University of Minnesota Press, 1984), 47–49.
7. Literature in the nineteenth century was once moralized upon in the same

way that some contemporary reviewers look upon television. See Ann Douglas, *The Feminization of American Culture* (New York: Anchor Books, 1988), 9; Michael Davitt Bell *Culture, Genre, and Literary Vocation: Selected Essays on American Literature* (Chicago: University of Chicago Press, 2001), 39; and, of course, Marshall McLuhan, *Understanding Media: The Extensions of Man* [1964], (Cambridge, MA: MIT Press, 1994).

8. Dana Polan, "Auteur Desire," *Screening the Past*, no. 12 (March 2001), http://www.latrobe.edu.au/screeningthepast/firstrelease/fr0301/dpfr12a.htm (accessed March 1, 2001).

9. Cook, 114. James Naremore advises that although "[c]ritical discourse on individual personalities can easily serve the interests of the culture industry. . . it can also serve quite different ends. It's well to remember that auteurism itself was never really a theory; it took on different political meanings at different conjunctures, and its original French practitioners were a diverse group." "Authorship and the Cultural Politics of Film Criticism," *Film Quarterly* 44, no. 1 (Fall 1990): 14–21.

10. Alexandre Astruc, "The Birth of a New Avant-garde: La Caméra Stylo," in *The New Wave: Critical Landmarks*, ed. Peter Graham (London: British Film Institute, 1968), 17–23; François Truffaut, "A Certain Tendency of the French Cinema," *Movies and Methods*, Vol. I, ed. Bill Nichols (Berkeley: University of California Press, 1976), 224–37.

11. John Caughie, "Introduction," in *Theories of Authorship: A Reader*, ed. John Caughie (London: Routledge & Kegan Paul, 1981), 13. As Geoffrey Nowell-Smith points out, "It was in establishing what the *film said*, rather than reasons for liking or disliking it, that authorship criticism validated itself as an approach" [quoted in *Cahiers du Cinéma: The 1950s, Neo-Realism, Hollywood, New Wave*, ed. Jim Hillier (Cambridge, MA: Harvard University Press, 1985), 11 (emphasis added)]. See further on mise-en-scène, Nowell-Smith's *Luchino Visconti*, (1967; reprint Garden City, NY: Doubleday, 1968), 10; Nowell-Smith, "Minnelli and Melodrama" [1977], reprinted in *Home is Where the Heart Is: Studies in Melodrama and the Woman's Film*, ed. Christine Gledhill (1987; reprinted, London: British Film Institute, 1992), 70–74; Thomas Elsaesser, "Tales of Sound and Fury: Observations on the Family Melodrama" [1972], reprinted in *Home is Where the Heart Is*, ed. Gledhill, 43–69; Thomas Elsaesser, "Vincente Minnelli" [1969], reprinted in *Genre: The Musical*, ed. Rick Altman (London: Routledge & Kegan Paul, 1981), 8–27.

12. Jim Hillier places the *Cahiers du Cinéma* (first published in 1951) in historical relationship to the journal's predecessor, *Revue du Cinéma* (1929–31 and 1946–49). The latter was "strikingly similar" to *Cahiers* in that it published articles on filmmakers such as Pabst, Eisenstein, Chaplin, Hawks, and Borzage (2). The *Cahiers* "inherited a great deal both generally from French culture and very specifically from a tradition of film cultural concerns and interests well established since the 1920s"; Jim Hillier, "Introduction" in *Cahiers du Cinéma*, 3.

13. See further, Caughie, 10.

14. André Bazin, "On the *Politique des auteurs*" [1957], trans. Peter Graham, reprinted in *Cahiers du Cinéma*, 248.

15. Andrew Sarris, *The American Cinema: Directors and Directions, 1929–1968* (New York: E. P. Dutton & Co., 1968), 22. His polemic was earlier published in *Film Culture* no. 28 (Spring 1963): 1–51.

16. Sarris insists on the term "auteur" and not the English translation "author" because "it is neither adequate nor accurate as a translation" (27).

17. V. F. Perkins, *Film as Film: Understanding and Judging Movies* (Middlesex, UK: Penguin Books, 1972), 160.

18. Pauline Kael. "Circles and Squares," *Film Quarterly* 16, no. 3 (Spring 1963): 26.

19. Peter Wollen, *Signs and Meanings in the Cinema*, 3rd ed., rev. and enl. (Bloomington: Indiana University Press, 1972), 77.

20. Ed Buscombe, "Ideas of Authorship," *Screen* 14, no. 3 (Autumn 1973): 84.

21. Editors of *Cahiers du Cinéma*, "John Ford's *Young Mr. Lincoln*" [1970], reprinted in *Movies and Methods*, Vol. 1, 493–529.

22. Daniel Dayan, "The Tutor-Code of Cinema"[1974], reprinted in *Movies and Methods*, Vol. 1, 438–51; Nick Browne, "The Spectator-in-the-Text: The Rhetoric of *Stagecoach* [1975], in *Movies and Methods*, Vol. 2, ed. Bill Nichols (Berkeley: University of California Press, 1985), 458–75.

23. Stephen Heath, "Comment on "The Idea of Authorship [*sic*]," *Screen* 14, no. 3 (Autumn 1973): 87.

24. Michael Leja describes the existential angst of this period as the "Modern Man" discourse where "the erasure of [subjective] difference in Modern Man discourse was a considerable convenience," *Reframing Abstract Expressionism: Subjectivity and Painting in the 1940s* (New Haven: Yale University Press, 1993), 237.

25. W. K. Wimsatt, Jr. and M. C. Beardsely, "The Intentional Fallacy," in *Sewanee Review* 54, no. 3 (1946): 468.

26. W. K. Wimsatt, Jr. and M. C. Beardsely, "The Affective Fallacy," in *Sewanee Review* 57, no. 1 (1949): 33.

27. Michel Foucault, "What Is an Author?" [1975], *Foucault Reader*, ed. Paul Rabinow, trans. Josué V. Havari (New York: Pantheon Books, 1984), 101–120.

28. "We will give the name *chronotope* [literally 'time space,']" writes Bakhtin, "to the intrinsic connectedness of temporal and spatial relationships that are artistically expressed in literature." "Forms of Time and of the Chronotope in the Novel," in *The Dialogic Imagination: Four Essays by M.M. Bakhtin*, ed. Michael Holquist, trans. Caryl Emerson and Michael Holquist (Austin: University of Texas Press, 1981), 84.

29. Bakhtin began his query into authorship during the 1920s in his essay, "Author and Hero." For a critical-biographical sketch of Bakhtin's work see Gary Saul Morson and Caryl Emerson, *Mikhail Bakhtin: Creation of a Prosaics* (Stanford: Stanford University Press, 1990), 63–100.

30. See, for example, Walter Benjamin, "Theses on the Philosophy of History" [1939–40], in *Illuminations*, ed. Hannah Arendt, trans. Harry Zohn (New York: Schocken Books, 1969), 253–64.

31. For a discussion of Brechtian technique in the Hollywood melodrama see Jon Halliday, *Sirk on Sirk: Interviews with Jon Halliday* (New York: Viking Press, 1972), 23.

32. Roland Barthes, "From Work to Text" [1971], reprinted in *Art After Modernism: Rethinking Representation*, ed. Brian Willis (New York: The New Museum of Contemporary Art, 1984), 169–74.

33. Roland Barthes, "The Death of the Author" [1968], in *Image Music Text*, trans. and ed. Stephen Heath (New York: Hill and Wang, 1977), 142–48.

34. Pierre Bourdieu, "The Production of Belief: Contribution to an Economy of Symbolic Goods" [1986], trans. Richard Nice, *The Field of Cultural Production: Essays on Art and Literature*, ed. Randal Johnson (New York: Columbia University Press, 1993), 76–7.

35. Bourdieu, "The Field of Cultural Production" [1983], trans. Richard Nice, ed. Randal Johnson, in *The Field of Cultural Production*, 72.

36. Michel de Certeau, *The Practice of Everyday Life*, trans. Steven Rendall (Berkeley: University of California Press, 1984), xxi; de Certeau, *Heterologies: Discourse on the Other* [1986], trans. Brian Massumi (Minneapolis: University of Minnesota Press, 1995), 152.

37. Gilles Deleuze, *Cinema 2: The Time-Image* [1985], trans. Hugh Tomlinson and Robert Galeta (Minneapolis: University of Minnesota Press, 1989), 173–74.

38. Kathleen Burnett, "Toward a Theory of Hypertextual Design," *Postmodern Culture* no. 2 (January 1993), http://jefferson.village.virginia.edu/pmc/issue.193/burnett.193. Burnett shows how Deleuze and Félix Guattari posit

hypermedia as "rhizomorphic" where "perception of connectivity is entirely left to the user. . . . Distinctions between author and reader. . .disintegrate as the reader participates in authorship, constituent in polis, and end-user in the search itself."

39. Gayatri Chakrovorty Spivak, "Translator's Preface," in Jacques Derrida, *Of Grammatology* [1974], trans. Gayatri Chakrovorty Spivak (Baltimore: Johns Hopkins University Press, 1974), lxxiv.

40. Jonathan Culler, *On Deconstruction: Theory and Criticism after Structuralism* (Ithaca, NY: Cornell University Press, 1982), 218.

41. Art historian Michael Baxandall argues otherwise. As he sees it, intention and context are realized through practice: "intentionality . . . assumes purposeful-ness—or intent or, as it were, 'intentiveness'—in the historical actor but even more in the historical object themselves." Intention here is certainly informed by "cultural circumstances" where authorial intention is a purposeful gesture *acted on a work*. Michael Baxandall, *Patterns of Intention: On the Historical Explanation of Pictures* (New Haven: Yale University Press, 1985), 41–42.

42. Jacques Derrida, "Signature Event Context" [1971], in *Margins of Philosophy*, trans. Alan Bass (Chicago: University of Chicago Press, 1982), 326. Derrida critiques J. L. Austin's insistence that the intention of the utterance is know-able through context or what Derrida refers to as the "teleological jurisdiction of a total field whose *intention* remains the organizing center" (323).

43. Oscar Wilde, "Phrases and Philosophies for the Use of the Young," in *The Complete Works of Oscar Wilde: Stories, Plays, Poems, and Essays*, ed. J. B. Foreman (New York: Harper & Row, 1989), 1206.

44. Andy Warhol and Pat Hackett, *Popism: The Warhol Sixties* (San Diego: Harcourt & Brace, 1980), 180.

45. Michel Foucault, *The History of Sexuality: Volume Three, The Care of the Self* (New York: Vintage, 1986), 44.

46. Samuel Weber, *Mass Mediauras: Form Technics Media* (Stanford: Stanford University Press, 1996), 63.

47. Leja calls Foucault the "preeminent analyst" of discourses (271).

48. Edward Said, *Orientalism* (New York: Vintage Books, 1979), 23.

49. Abdul R. JanMohamed, "The Economy of Manichean Allegory: The Function of Racial Difference in Colonialist Literature," in *"Race," Writing, and Difference*, ed. Henry Louis Gates, Jr. (Chicago: University of Chicago Press, 1985), 79.

50. J. Ronald Green, *The Cinema of Oscar Micheaux* (Bloomington: Indiana University Press, 2001), xvi.

51. Pearl Bowser and Louise Spence, *Writing Himself into History: Oscar Micheaux, His Silent Films, and His Audiences* (New Brunswick, NJ: Rutgers University Press, 2000), 37.

52. Jane Gaines, *Fire and Desire: Mixed-Race Movies in the Silent Era* (Chicago: University of Chicago Press, 2001), 123.

53. See further, Angela Davis, *Blues Legacies and Black Feminism: Gertrude "Ma" Rainey, Bessie Smith, and Billie Holiday* (New York: Pantheon Books, 1998); Amiri Baraka, "Spike Lee at the Movies," in *Black American Cinema*, ed. Manthia Diawara (Routledge: New York, 1993), 145–53.

54. Constance Penley, "Introduction: The Lady Doesn't Vanish: Feminism and Film Theory," in *Feminism and Film Theory*, ed. Constance Penley (New York: Routledge, 1988), 5.

55. See, for example, Pam Cook and Claire Johnston, "The Place of Woman in the Cinema of Raoul Walsh" [1974], reprinted in *Feminism and Film Theory*, ed. Penley, 25–35.

56. Lauren Rabinowitz, *Points of Resistance: Women, Power and Politics in the New York Avant-garde Cinema, 1943–71* (Urbana: University of Illinois Press, 1991), 23.

57. Judith Butler, *Gender Trouble: Feminism and the Subversion of Identity* (New

York: Routledge, 1990); Eve Kosofsky Sedgwick, *Epistemology of the Closet* (Berkeley: University of California Press, 1990).

58. Judith Mayne, *Directed by Dorothy Arzner* (Bloomington: Indiana University Press, 1994), 5.

59. Douglas Crimp, "Fassbinder, Franz, Fox, Elvira, Armin and All the Others," in *Queer Looks: Perspectives on Lesbian and Gay Film and Video*, ed. Martha Gever, John Greyson, and Pratibha Parmar (New York: Routledge, 1993), 257–74; David A. Gerstner, "Queer Modernism: The Cinematic Aesthetic of Vincente Minnelli," in *Modernity* 2, no. 1 (2000): http://www.eiu.edu/~modernity/modernity.html; David A. Gerstner, "Queer Angels of History Take It and Leave It from Behind," in *Stanford Humanities Review: Inside the Film Archive, Practice, Theory, Canon* 7, no. 2 (Autumn 1999): 150–65.

60. Crimp labels his endnotes "The Voices in the Text" because "in order to speak one must seek support from other texts" (273).

61. Michael Moon, *Disseminating Whitman: Revision and Corporeality in* Leaves of Grass, (Cambridge, MA: Harvard University Press, 1991), 69. Moon: "the text is designed to impel readers to discover and reclaim their own 'real bodies,' first in the text and then in themselves, and thereby to undo to some degree the culture's devaluations of bodiliness" (131).

62. Kaja Silverman, "The Author as Receiver," *October* 96 (Spring 2001): 19, 24.

authorship

approaches

two

janet staiger

In the second half of the twentieth century, two major problems with authorship studies developed. One problem was the final victory of poststructuralist thinking in which changing notions of the individual as agent cast grave doubts on self-representation or external analysis as sources of explaining intent or rationales for actions. This is the death of the author problem. A second problem was the victory of mass-mediated media in the marketplace of ideas. Mass media is a problem not only because of its multiple-authored collaborative systems of production but because it thrives on intertextuality. Genres and formulas provide the foundations for its emplotments of fictional and nonfictional representations, although intertextuality through stars, stylistic flourishes, and other textual traces also produces a lineage of voices difficult to trace.

Yet authorship does matter. It matters especially to those in non-dominant positions in which asserting even a partial agency may seem to be important for day-to-day survival or where locating moments of alternative practice takes away the naturalized privileges of normativity.

It matters for those who purchase or consume mass media: choosing to see a film directed by Lizzie Borden or Steven Spielberg involves cultivated taste cultures, and it involves political preferences.

Authorship is always a way of looking at films, and obviously other ways exist as do other questions. For my purposes here, "authorship" will be the term used to cover the research question of causality for the film. As I shall point out, several dodges to this question have occurred over the span of authorship study. These include (1) producing a version of formalism in which authorship questions are avoided by claiming that textual analysis suffices to discuss authorship and (2) converting the question to one of reception. As I discuss authorship approaches, these two dodges will be pointed out. Still, I do not want to argue that other research questions—ones that rightfully do utilize formalist critical methods or reception analysis—are irrelevant or invalid. The issue is merely determining the theoretical approaches that best tackle certain questions: here, the question of causality for a mass-media text.

This causal research question, however, is not limited to answers supplied by authorship studies. As has become dogma over the past thirty years, the author is a historical notion. That we require human agents or individual authors to explain the existence of discourses is a historical ideology associated with the appearance of humanism and capitalism.[1] Instead, theories of causality for texts can have broader causal sources such as economic, social, cultural, political, and psychological developments. These sorts of production determinants are often behind authors when scholars focus on specific human agents and individuals. But analyzing individuals, or even groups of individuals working collaboratively, is not a necessary move to explain the causes for the production of a text.

Authorship is, however, useful for humanism and capitalism. As Michel Foucault points out in "What Is an Author?" the concept has functions. He describes four: (1) pointing by name to a person creates a designation; (2) the designation permits categorizing (a method by which to group texts and hence useful to criticism or to capitalist profit making); (3) the categorizing may (and likely will) produce status in our culture; and (4) the categorizing infers meaning on the texts: "revealing, or at least characterizing, its mode of being" (107). This is what Foucault labels "the author-function." Authored texts, he continues, differ from texts "without" authors such as anonymous posters or contracts (which have creators but not authors). Authored texts also, however, create the opportunity for discipline—for punishing or rewarding individuals on the basis of what they write, for searching for authors when they are not named, and for creating a "rational being that we call 'author'" (110). Such a construction of rationality rewards a culture invested in individuals as having so-called coherence or powers of creating since it suggests a discourse of full agency that it is handy for capitalism to promote. Thus, any textual criticism that operates within this ideology of authorship "has required authors and has categorized and hierarchised artifacts accordingly. What [this] criticism provides are criteria by which acts of authorship are identified and in doing that criticism actually creates the possibility for either the position of authors *or* for the category of creativity" (Alvarado, 19).[2]

Authorship studies that are pursued for such reasons fit within humanist and capitalist ideologies. Other reasons for authorship studies can exist, however; indeed, scholars devoted to poststructuralism and Marxism admit to the trouble they feel with the death of the author. In fact, taking studies of the author off the table can eliminate the politically crucial question of causality for texts—something highly undesirable from the point of view of critical theory. Thus, rather than accept the death of the author, the response needs to be a reconceptualization of authoring from the vantage of poststructuralist theories of the subject and agency. Even as Foucault points out the author-function as it has operated in humanism and capitalism, he rejects killing off authors. Disagreeing with Roland Barthes's analysis of the author's death,[3] Foucault claims that writing is not the author's death as Barthes would have it but the evidence of the author's absence; what needs to be rejected is constructing the "empirical character of the author into a transcendental anonymity" (605–6).

As I shall discuss below, the attempted death of the author comes at a time particularly nonadvantageous for some individuals—feminists, gay and lesbian activists, and antiracists. Depriving us of our voices just as we are speaking more loudly seems a plot. In fact, Barthes expresses a melancholy in his *The Pleasure of the Text*: "As institution, the author is dead . . . but in the text, in a way, I *desire* the author."[4] Is it a surprise that Barthes would seek this figure? Others, too, recognize a regret almost as soon as the author is declared an inert corpus. Thomas Elsaesser writes in 1979, "The auteur is the fiction, the necessary fiction one might add, become flesh and historical in the director, for the name of a pleasure that seems to have no substitute in the sobered-up deconstruction of the authorless voice of ideology."[5] In a recent special issue devoted to authorship, Adrian Martin surveys reasons for still wanting to write about authors, suggesting the following: (1) to create "'the richness of experience that may result'" (quoting Tag Gallagher), (2) to explain how films are made, (3) to expand from an earlier shorter list the catalogue of directors whose "world visions" or "signatures" are discussed, and (4) to examine, as Elsaesser writes, "the 'name of a pleasure.'"[6]

These reasons need to be respected but also analyzed. Several of them repeat humanist and capitalist discourses or at least can lapse into such ideologies. Other reasons may, however, have politically productive outcomes. As David Eng and Shinhee Han argue about the political implications of forgetting homelands for immigrants, assuming melancholia is a pathology produces a very particular kind of subject—one without historical pasts and cultural differences.[7] Their point is that describing melancholia as an illness may well be a strategy of assimilationist discourse. Similarly, forgetting authorship and individuals takes away a history necessary for social activism and utopic imaginings. Authorship discourse may have positive political effectivity. The question isn't whether to pursue authorship studies—at least at this historical moment—but how to do so without reproducing humanist and capitalist author-functions. It is this objective that this anthology pursues.

However, to reach the point at which such an objective might be pursued requires distinguishing the sorts of authorship studies anthologized here from authorship studies pursued elsewhere. The history of authorship studies has involved various strategies that I shall organize into seven approaches.[8] In all cases, I would like to see these approaches as twentieth-century strategies for turning gossip about production into science. Moreover, all of these approaches assume some form of the communications model whereby the author produces a message for a reader. How each of these terms—"author," "produces," "message," and "reader"—is further defined produces the variations among these approaches. In particular, however, I will distinguish the various approaches on the bases of how they construct the author as a "subject," an "agent," and "coherent." This sequence does not imply *necessarily* a hierarchy, progress, or improvement but rather historical change.

authorship as *origin*

Tracing the handwork of production is a Western, Judeo-Christian obligation. What (godly) source produced this writing? The implications in such an approach, deriving as it does from a religious hermeneutic tradition, include the evaluation of writings on the basis of the biography of the author. If the author's life was devote, wholesome, upright, then the writings—a flow of the author's morality onto the page—must display and reveal the morality of the life, and, of course, vice (pun intended) versa.[9]

Thus, in authorship as origin, the author is conceptualized as a free agent, the message is a direct expression of the author's agency, and production is untroubled philosophically or linguistically—although rational individuals might debate interpretation. The reader stands in mirror status to the author—also a free agent, although in cases in which vice is, indeed, the message then U.S. law argued for some time that the message proved the intent of the author and the author's morality, and it proceeded to protect those with weak minds. David Bordwell discusses such criticism as having two tacit models: (1) a "transmission" theory in which meanings are "put there" deliberately (or "only partially") and (2) an "object-centered theory of meaning" whereby the object determines in itself its meanings. Critics using this approach may "use the artist's writings, interviews, and recollections to support ascribed meanings" on the basis of the "psychological unity which binds the artist's thought and behavior to the finished work."[10]

American New Criticism operates within this approach to authorship with several additional restrictions. A basic premise is that evidence for interpretation of a work is internal to the text and public information.[11] No amount of contextual (including biographical) evidence could validate a specific interpretation. This might seem contrary to the description of the approach of authorship as origin, but it is not. This is because the New Criticism claim is that the results of the author's handwork are obvious within the work. Thus, uncomplicated origin from the author's mind through the hand is assumed, and, like the courts do, New Criticism appeals to a public discussion of the textual outcome to determine the meanings 'and values of the text. Moreover, second and third premises of New Criticism are that form and content cannot be split, and evaluative criteria are universal and public as well. For example, Cleanth Brooks writes in *The Well Wrought Urn* that form holds content from which the critic can see "the underlying attitudes, the world view, the quality of mind, the informing spirit" of the work's maker (225). New Critics use the evaluative criteria to privilege transcendental and universal statements over historical and political commentary.

These three premises lead to rejecting other criteria for ranking works. One optional criterion would be comparing the outcome of the poem to the author's intent—the so-called intentional fallacy (Wimsatt and Beardsley, 468).[12] What W. K. Wimsatt and M. C. Beardsley argue is that "the design or intention of the author is neither available or desirable as a standard for judging either the meaning or the value of a work of art."[13] Here, the fallacy is not that authors have no self-accessible intent or that intelligent people cannot determine that intent but that intent is not the basis on which to judge the work's meaning or value. Reasons for this are that (1) no logical reason exists to use the cause of the work for evaluation—that would produce the genetic fallacy; (2) the intent may be malevolent, but the outcome what was hoped for, making the work "successful"; and (3) the evidence for successful intent is in the poem—it worked!

Authorship as origin still continues as an approach in mass-mediated, multiple-worker culture, but it has been revised as primary and subsidiary origins. Who is the prime mover in producing the message? What portions of the work can be traced to whose fingertips? Thus, a work such as Pauline Kael's *The Citizen Kane Book* does not attempt to claim all authorship is traceable to Herman Mankiewitz—only those specific portions of the script that flowed from his antagonistic relationship to various members of the film community. As she writes, "[Orson] Welles and Mankiewicz wanted to do something startling, something that would cap the invasion of the Martians . . . . This time

[Welles] and Mankiewicz meant to raise cain."[14] Kael explains why Mankiewicz's authorship has been obscured in favor of Welles's contributions: "As a result of [Mankiewicz's] wicked sense of humor in drawing upon Welles' character for Kane's, his own authorship was obscured" (73).

Another film scholar working early in this approach is Bordwell. In his 1971 essay on *Citizen Kane*, Bordwell produces a New Criticism analysis of the film, attributing authorship to Welles. Bordwell's essay nearly duplicates Brooks' approach to John Donne's "Canonization."[15] Brooks studies the formal structure of the poem first, going through the poem and reexpressing what it literally says (11–17; 218). He notes that metaphors and contrasts exist but that a paradox resolves the tensions. This Brooks calls the theme. He then revisits the poem considering its rhetorical organization: the levels of meaning, symbolizations, clashes of connotation, paradoxes, and ironies. Likewise, in his analysis, Bordwell reads *Citizen Kane* once for a formal opposition of objectivity versus subjectivity and how this tension is duplicated in the closing, point-of-view structures, and other devices. He then reviews the movie for symbolic motifs and stylistic "pyrotechnics," emphasizing tensions and ambiguities. At all times, origin is a simple attribution to Welles, with evidence of meaning from the textual analysis.

In 1976, Bordwell added a cautionary note to his essay about the New Criticism method he used, but he continues to produce origin studies of directors. His three director-centered books are *The Films of Carl-Theodor Dreyer* (1981), *Ozu and the Poetics of Cinema* (1988), and *The Cinema of Eisenstein* (1993).[16] In *Dreyer*, he revises his method into the "biographical legend" approach proposed by Boris Tomashevsky (1981, 4). In the biographical-legend approach, a critic does not claim to find an author's intent but considers how the public reputation of the individual influences the public's interpretation of a work: "The biographical legend may justify production decisions and even create a spontaneous theory of the artist's practice. More important, the biographical legend is a way in which authorship significantly shapes our perception of the work" (9).[17] Such an approach, however, deals with *reading strategies* of a text (see below) and not with its production. When actually discussing Dreyer, Bordwell still assumes an intentional origin—Dreyer—animates the justification for his grouping of texts into a unit for study. He writes, "the interest of Carl-Theodor Dreyer's films lies neither in their thematic unity nor in their testimony to a unique personal vision. Dreyer's work claims our attention today because it poses important problems for the study of cinema as art, industry, and historical process" (1).

Disassociating himself with New Criticism's evaluative criteria of transcendental resolution of paradoxes and auteurism's assumption of personality and personal vision, Bordwell specifies these critical problems to be the aesthetic functions for the ambiguity and transgressions in films directed by Dreyer. In his work on Yasujiro Ozu, Bordwell asserts that "the filmmaker is a rational, intentional agent" (Bordwell, 1988, 2). Finally, for Sergei Eisenstein, he specifically places Eisenstein in his historical context as a maker of films to describe what happens formally and stylistically in that cinema. Thus, Bordwell's approach to authorship may not include some features of New Criticism (such as a presumption of unified, coherent texts), but initially grouping on the basis of the historical body of the individual places Bordwell's studies in this approach. Moreover, though, he explicitly indicates that he considers directors as intentional agents, knowable perhaps not through their statements about their work but through the public consequences of the set of texts attributed to them as directors. Thus, he produces an origin approach to authorship, although his approach with revision might have potential use in new authorship theory (see the last approach).

authorship as *personality*

Prime mover easily flows into the conception of authorship as personality. One characteristic that distinguishes this approach from the former is that causal force (control over parts of the parts of production) is overlaid with personal idiosyncrasies. Some applications of this approach retain the religious foundations of origin studies in disguised form although other applications locate authors in mundane historical circumstances. Thus, this approach may use variant theories of the individual that do not necessarily imply that the author has total self-awareness and free agency. Here is an opening into the morass of philosophical and linguistic troubling of agency in which context or family or trauma may produce distortions and repressions or even cover-ups in an author's external flowing of self into the medium. In authorship as personality, intention is not assumed, and consciousness is not all that may inflect the individual's expression. Thus, the author is no longer a fully conscious agent but often ideally has a coherent personality that appears in the production of the text.

Catherine Belsey describes the ideological source of this sort of approach as it first appears in literary criticism and labels it "expressive realism."[18] Coming from Romanticism and the theorizing of John Ruskin, expressive realism is not just the conveyance of a faithful representation of nature; the artistic individual is "noble" or unusual by virtue of the special insight into the world that is transmitted into and through the artwork. This is also the view of M. H. Abrams.[19] In his *The Mirror and the Lamp*, Abrams distinguishes expressive criticism as theorizing "poetry [to be] the overflow, utterance, or projection of the thought and the feelings of the poet" (21–22). This leads to an evaluative hierarchy that privileges poetry that expresses feelings (rather than ideas), is mimetic to an internal state of mind rather than the external world, and is its own end. An example of such a position would be the beliefs of Walt Whitman intended "to disseminate affectionate physical presence from [the author] to [the audience] fervently and directly," desiring to express a "radical-body politics."[20] Not only were concepts to be transmitted but a bodily presence.

In film studies, the auteurism of French critics and the British and U.S. adaptations provide significant examples.[21] Most scholars suggest that, beyond the general influence of Romanticism and expressive realism (and occasionally surrealism[22]), one major reason for such an authorship approach to cinema is because it allows films to be treated as art. If individuals impart aesthetically sophisticated insights through movies, then art exists. Conversely, if scholars find such insights in movies, sentient beings are assumed to have put them there.[23] The circular logic is obvious in statements such as an example from Andrew Sarris: "the time has come to recognize that directors, like painters, sculptors, writers, et al., must reveal themselves through their work if their work is to have any meaning."[24]

Additionally, however, authorship as personality has specific historical conditions. Developed during and after World War II most obviously in France but in nascent forms elsewhere, authorship-as-personality analysis permitted a means of marking out French films as different from Hollywood product and, thus, potentially increasing their market value. Authorship-as-personality analysis also allowed French critics to align themselves with a younger generation of Hollywood directors who were represented as breaking through the constraints of Hollywood formulas and mass-media production practices. Thus, French authorship-as-personality analysis has been important not only in elevating cinema to the category of art but also in confusing that category since the critics include commercial Hollywood product within its boundaries and find mainstream directors to be artists and even rebels against the system.

Essays in journals from the 1930s and more significantly the writings of André Bazin during the 1940s are early statements of authorship-as-personality. Bazin promoted attention to the revelation of phenomenal reality and, thus, paid significant attention to technical aspects of the cinematic medium.[25] Emphasizing how a director chose aesthetically to organize materials, Bazin wrote about directors but also about genres and sociocultural aspects of cinema. Other writers also concerned themselves with describing the potential power of cinema as expressive as is obvious in Alexandre Astruc's "The Birth of a New Avant-Garde: *La Caméra-Stylo*."[26] Astruc writes that cinema is "becoming a language," which allows it to "break free from the tyranny of what is visual, from the image for its own sake . . . to become a means of writing just as flexible and subtle as written language." For Astruc, cinema might be able to "express ideas" equivalent to the "novels of Faulkner and Malraux, to the essays of Sartre and Camus" (18–20).

Obviously, Astruc's attitude about cinematic specificity differs from that of Bazin who privileges the ability of the cinematic *image* to record and display a profilmic spatial relation among humans and their material world. Still, Astruc's optimism about recent cinema and his expressive model of authorship are part of the contemporaneous French discourse. It continues to be part of French critical heritage and is obvious in the combination of Sarris, Bazin, and Astruc expressed by Gilles Deleuze in the beginning of his authorship study: "The great directors of the cinema may be compared, in our view, not merely with painters, architects and musicians, but also with thinkers. They think with movement-images and time-images instead of concepts."[27] He continues, "the history of the cinema is a long martyrology," making manifest both the religious and rebel discourses latent in much authorship-as-personality studies.

Indeed, Bazin's preference for revealing phenomenological relations through specific constructions of mise-en-scène would color the location where many critics would seek evidence of expressive authorship. The logic is that directors may be handed a script, but they are the individuals charged with controlling the acting, lighting, staging, and use of set design. So one naturally would look to those features of the film for directors' authorial statements. Moreover, the critical strategy is to assume the "director as the creative source of meaning" and the "output as an oeuvre, a repetition and enrichment of characteristic themes and stylistic choices" (Bordwell, 1989, 44). Indeed, as the authorship-as-personality approach would develop, the standard assumption is that the *body* of the director ensures a unified perspective on the world, and *repetition* is where the critic finds the director's perspective. Debates about what perspectives should be valued did occur as the *Cahiers du Cinéma* critics praised Howard Hawks, George Cukor, Nicholas Ray, and Otto Preminger whereas *Positif* writers who aligned with surrealism, anticlericalism, and pro-Soviet Marxism preferred directors such as John Huston, Federico Fellini, and Jerry Lewis and genres such as film noir, musicals, and horror and fantasy films. *Positif* also read the Hollywood cinema as subversive "pop" culture and an indication of resistance within American society (Bordwell, 1989, 48; Elsaesser, 1975, 206–13).

However despite those differences, both groups implicitly sought rebels. As Bill Nichols remarks, "a frequent tenet of *auteur* criticism is that a tension exists between the artist's vision and the means at his disposal for realizing it: studio pressure, genre conventions, star demands, story requirements. These constraints are also seen as a source of strength, imposing discipline and prompting cunning subversions."[28] For example, Lotte Eisner's discussion of F. W. Murnau illustrates this: "whereas [Fritz] Lang attempts to give a faithful reproduction of the famous paintings he sometimes uses, Murnau elaborates the memory he has kept of them and transforms them into personal visions."[29]

What is the cause for this? Besides Murnau's ability as an artist, Eisner attributes this in part to his need to hide his sexual preference: "Murnau had homosexual tendencies. In his attempt to escape from himself, he did not express himself with the artistic continuity that makes it so easy to analyze the style of, say, Lang. But all his films bear the impress of his inner complexity, of the struggle he waged within himself against a world in which he remained despairingly alien" (98). Eisner assumes that an individual's personal identity will be conveyed into the text, that the experiences of an oppressed minority will produce more inhibitions to direct expression of that identity, but that it is still available for study through close stylistic analysis of recurring patterns within the director's films.

Thus, attention to successive stylistic features, especially in mise-en-scène, distinguishes the early approach of French authorship-as-personality from other approaches to authorship. However, auteurism is a more specific approach to authorship-as-personality analysis within this larger trend. To count as auteurism, two additional features are necessary. One is the distinction that a *unified* personal vision *should* be expressed; the other is that an *evaluation* of the entire oeuvre is justified on the basis of the quality of coherence to the expression of that vision. It is this move promoted by François Truffaut in 1954 that creates auteurism as a polemic and sets it apart from a more routine authorship-as-personality approach.[30] Moreover, at least for Truffaut and his allies, a very specific personal vision was required: "an optimistic image of human potentialities within an utterly corrupt society" (Hillier, 6) is one version; another is "a justification, couched in aesthetic terms, of a culturally conservative, politically reactionary attempt to remove film from the realm of social and political concern" (Hess, 1974a, 19). As John Hess describes the appropriate narrative's features, they include a character in "extreme physical, psychological, and spiritual isolation" (expressed visually in the film) who is tested but changes from a former baseness to a elevated moral realm. This for Hess, however, is not so much a proof of an expression of a personality as much as a privileging of a particular world view. In fact, it is a method to denigrate the political views of Truffaut's despised directors from the Popular Front whom Truffaut considers "anti-clerical and anti-militarist." What Hess points to is the ideological parasites attached to the evaluative scheme. Indeed, Truffaut lingers on Jean Aurenche and Pierre Bost's "profanation and blasphemy": vomiting, a "refusal to be sprinkled with holy water," and the "homosexual relationships of characters" (Truffaut, 228).

Truffaut's values need to be distinguished from Bazin's.[31] Indeed, Bazin provides one of the strongest criticisms of the excesses of auteurism in his 1957 essay "On the *Politique des Auteurs*." At least three major points constitute Bazin's reproof. First, he rejects their excesses, especially claims such as that the worst work of an auteur was more worthy of attention than the best works of a mere *metteur-en-scène* or that a director who makes a great film must invariably continue to make meritorious films. Second, Bazin accuses the auteurists of the fallacy of assuming that difference from conventions constitutes improvement. Thus, auteurists implicitly denigrate contributions from the social and historical context in seeking personal signatures. Bazin has a great respect for the material conditions in which directors work and does not think those conditions always hindered filmmaking. Third, he notes their Romanticism: "The *politique des auteurs* consists, in short, of choosing the personal factor in artistic creation as a standard of reference, and then assuming that it continues and even progresses from one film to the next" (255). Thus, auteurists do not fully consider the circumstances of collaboration, of genres and formulas, and schools of filmmaking. In fact, the reason for *repetition* may not be any personal vision and triumph of a constrained auteur but the influence of one of these other determinants. Looking for authors is only a recent critical trend, beginning in the eighteenth century; appreciating a work of art does not require locating an individual source for it. Here Bazin's remarks predate Foucault's work on the historical discourse of authorship that would influence other approaches to authorship. Bazin reasons: an "individual transcends society, but society is also and above all *within* him" and concludes "*Auteur*, yes, but what *of*?" (Bazin, 251, 258). Thus, Bazin's essay criticizes all the features of French auteurism: its emphases on a unified personal vision and its systems of evaluation.

British and U.S. auteurism continued many features of French auteurism: the presumption of expressive authorship via the guarantee of the body of the director, a critical attention to mise-en-scène (particularly spatial relations) when considering style, analysis of repetitions from film to film in order to find the unified personal vision, and a demarcation of difference from conventions so as to argue for subversion of and elevation over the normative and mundane.[32] In England, Oxford graduates formed the core for the journal *Movie*, which was a major site for British auteurism. In response, *Sight and Sound* and Penelope Houston accused the *Movie* writers of a "spatial relation criticism" that ignored humanistic themes (Durgnat, 70).

In the United States, Sarris was practicing a version of authorship-as-personality analysis as early as 1956 (Bordwell, 1989, 48–50). Sarris proselytized for "wrenching" directors from "their historical environments" in order to do aesthetic analysis and elevating some directors into pantheons based on coherent "personal signatures."[33] Thus, Sarris out-auteured some of the French. In his 1962 defense of auteurism, he stated three premises that he correlated with "circles": the outer circle is "technique" with the premise that "the technical competence of a director is a criterion of value"; the middle circle is "personal style" with the premise that "the distinguishable personality of the director is a criterion of value"; and the inner circle is "interior meaning" with the premise that interior meaning is "the ultimate glory of the cinema as an art" and is "extrapolated from the tension between a director's personality and his material" (Sarris, 1962, 132–33). Such a thesis is somewhat different from the *Cahiers'* auteurism in that Sarris opens the door to less intent and more conflict on the part of the director. Indeed, as Bordwell points out, "Sarris edited the first collection of interviews with film directors" (1989, 50) in 1967, providing material grounds for claims about their actions.

However, those contributions weren't relevant to Kael who saw in Sarris's criticism multiple problems including sexism.[34] In her scathing "Circles and Squares," Kael began by noticing that Sarris concluded his 1962 essay noting his joy as an auteur critic when he observed that "one of the screen's most virile directors [Raoul Walsh] employed an essentially feminine narrative device to dramatize the emotional vulnerability of his heroes" (Sarris, 1962, 135). Kael writes,

> We might also ask why this narrative device is "essentially feminine"; is it more feminine than masculine to be asleep, or to talk in one's sleep, or to reveal feelings? Or, possibly, does Sarris regard the device as feminine because the listening woman becomes a sympathetic figure and emotional understanding is, in this "virile" context, assumed to be essentially feminine? Perhaps only if one accepts the narrow notions of virility so common in our action films can this sequence be seen as "essentially feminine," and it is amusing that a critic can both support these clichés of the male world and be so happy when they are violated. (1963, 13)

Whether Sarris's stereotyping set off her reproaches, Kael continued to lambaste him for numerous reasons including assuming that looking for repetitions in an artist's work is something unusual rather than the normal strategy of art critics, describing what he is doing as theory, privileging technique over entertainment, assuming distinguishing personality will result in an artistically praiseworthy text, commending artists for their bad work along with their good, encouraging directors to take up any script offered because it might produce that tension that will illuminate their personality, and becoming a "connoisseur of trash" (1963, 12–17). Kael concludes her essay by noticing that Sarris was able to publish his essay in Jonas Mekas's *Film Culture*, a journal devoted to independent and experimental cinema. In fact, she associates Sarris's essay with Andy Warhol's "Campbell Soup Can" on the grounds that both Sarris's "theory" and Warhol's art object were instances of attempts to transcend mass production. She believes that Sarris and independent filmmakers share many attitudes: no desire for a "balanced view" of a film, an attempt "to ignore cultural determinants," and a preference for "virility." Auteurists "are so enthralled with their narcissistic male fantasies" staged within "the small range of experience of their boyhood and adolescence" (1963, 26). Sarris responded to Kael, reasserting his position that auteurism was a valuable method for studying film history (1968), and versions of auteurism continue today.

Kael's observation of the side-by-side publication of Sarris's 1962 essay with writings by independents does deserve extension. Although Mekas afforded Sarris a place for his essay, other writers in *Film Culture* were by no means obsequious to Sarris. Two additional responses to his essay are at least amusing as well as insightful. One response was published two issues after Sarris's 1962 essay: Charles Boultenhouse's "The Camera as a God."[35] In his response, Boultenhouse argues that there are two "absurd" claims, including: "One is [to claim] that commercial film is a natural kind of Pop Art; the other is that commercial film conceals a director of such creative intensity that he can be regarded as an author (in the higher sense)" (137). Although Boultenhouse enjoyed Parker Tyler's reading of Hollywood as "divine," at least Tyler did his interpretations "playfully and consciously." Only directors who write their own scripts, such as experimental filmmakers, deserved to have "artistic intentions" attributed to them. Boultenhouse's essay is a direct commentary on contemporaneous debates stirred up about art *versus* or *in* Hollywood.[36]

But a more indirect response is parody. Also published in *Film Culture* at the same time were Jack Smith's campy accolades to Maria Montez as a "great" actress and David Ehrenstein's interview with Warhol in which Ehrenstein asks Warhol all the clichéd questions aimed toward directors, including who was Warhol's favorite director. He replied: "Jack Smith."[37] Sarris did reply to these writers. In *The American Cinema*, he wrote: "The forest critic cannot admit even to himself that he is beguiled by the same vulgarity his mother enjoys in the Bronx. He conceals his shame with such cultural defense mechanisms as pop, camp, and trivia, but he sneaks into movie houses like a man of substance visiting a painted woman" (24).

Indeed, Sarris's point is significant. The pleasures both of Hollywood and of authorship entrance scholars! Additionally, auteurism has been important in breaking down high/low culture distinctions. Moreover, authorship-as-personality analysis, and its variant auteurism, continue unabated today, with scholars usually attempting to avoid some of the fallacies—such as doing a much better job placing the director within historical circumstances,[38] not elevating directors to romantic geniuses, and judging films on grounds other than who the director is. Two examples of this show the circumscription of claims. First is Jon Halliday's remarks about Douglas Sirk: "Precisely because a film is a composite product, the conditions of work need to be specified before any assessment of the role of a participant can be undertaken. This is particularly important in Sirk's case, since the ups and downs in his career are attributable to the conditions of production and not to oscillations in his own artistic vision."[39] Here Halliday reproduces the individual in conflict with a system, perhaps unable to secure adequate control over the whole project, but Halliday still represents Sirk as "unified." A second example is Elsaesser on Vincente Minnelli. Elsaesser expressly indicates his goal is to determine "the fundamental *unity* of Minnelli's vision."[40] However, he distinguishes his aim from that of Sarris's and *Movie*'s by looking for the unity in Minnelli's *themes* rather than style: "My contention is that all Minnelli's films aspire to the condition of the musical. . . . It furnishes his great theme: the artist's struggle to appropriate external reality as the elements of his own world, in a bid for absolute creative freedom" (12–13). By the end of the 1960s, authorship-as-personality criticism might focus on either or both themes and style. Thus, these writers, and others following them, reproduce the authorship-as-personality approach, assuming (1) the body of the director proves a coherent—if conflicted—personality, and (2) repetition within an oeuvre and deviation from the norm are where to find the personally expressive gestures of that person.

authorship as a *sociology of production*

Contemporaneous with the rise of U.S. auteurism was the development of liberal and radical theories of authorship within a sociology of production. Indeed, Bazin called for such production research (142), and by the early 1970s, such contextualization was common. One of the earliest strong examples of authorship-within-a-sociology-of-production approach that takes up some of the authorship-as-personality assumptions is Edward Buscombe's 1974 consideration of Raoul Walsh during his tenure at Warner Bros. Buscombe discusses the constraints that the firm placed on all of its directors, including ideological allegiances of the studio heads and preferred genres. However, as pointed out by Colin MacCabe, Buscombe continues to describe Walsh in auteur terms: as "whole and autonomous," liable only to "circumscribed areas laid down by society."[41] Also part of this trend were Perkins (1972), John Ellis, and Charles Barr (Cook, 276–82). Graham Petrie went so far as to reconstruct the auteur hierarchy into a worker hierarchy. Dividing directors into groups based on their opportunities for controlling their work situation, Petrie has three categories: (1) "creators"; (2) "misfits, rebels, unfortunates, and professionals"—those with enough control to justify discussion of "*some at least* of their films as displaying artistic coherence and continuity"; and (3) "scene-stealers and harmonizers"—any one with "some discernible impact on the film" (e.g., Greta Garbo, Val Lewton, Gregg Toland, Michael Curtiz) (32–4).

Because scholars acknowledged that the creation of mass-mediated art required creativity and ingenuity as well as efficiency and routine work patterns, conceptualizing the working arrangements of individuals within structures of relations internal and external to a company as well as hierarchies provided a socially theorized response to these matters rather than the personality explanation as offered within the authorship-as-personality approach. Such an approach has both *structural-functional* (liberal) and *critical* (Marxist) versions.[42] In the former, individuals take up roles that serve institutional needs. The individual should be socialized to the norms and values of the industry although role strain may result, producing deviance or even anomie. Thus, Buscombe and the other auteurists are well within this sociological theory derived from Emile Durkheim, Max Weber, and other sociologists of labor organization. In the latter version, workers contribute their labor to a mode of production that has various features such as division of skills, routinized work sequences, and heirarchies of power by which the mode extracts surplus value from the employees. Resistance and alienation may occur. This approach is indebted to Marxism, but in the 1960s theorizing by Louis Althusser, Pierre Macherey, and Terry Eagleton spurred on applications to mass media (Alvarado, 12).

In the sociology-of-production approach to authorship, depending on the social theory, authors are considered as taking up roles or functioning as workers. Authors produce messages as a consequence of the production experience, usually reflecting to a larger (rather than lesser) degree the fact that the firm producing the work operates within dynamics supporting capitalism (although sociologies of social states are also possible as well as theorizations of alternative work modes within capitalism). In this approach to authorship, production organization and the place of the individual as taking up a role or exchanging labor for wages are described in much greater detail because it is the producing portion of the equation in which a sociology of production has greatest theoretical felicity.

More recent examples in media studies of this sort of approach to authorship include the work of Paul DiMaggio, Paul M. Hirsch, Joseph Turow, and Robert L. Carringer, who are good instances of the structural–functionalist approach; I have pursued a critical-theory approach.[43] Carringer in particular has explored what he describes as the "collaborative" process; everyone who makes "a distinguishable contribution to the film" is a collaborator (1985, ix). In *The Making of "Citizen Kane,"* Carringer details the production process and the workers who were involved in various aspects of the final film. Using interviews and recently accessible archives with production records, correspondence, and script drafts, Carringer is able to describe very specifically the actions of individuals on the work team. A more explicit statement of his position is in his recent essay (2001) in which he disagrees with an interpretation of Alfred Hitchcock's *Strangers on a Train*. Again, drawing on precise historical information about the making of the film, Carringer suggests that Hitchcock is the "primary" author with a set of strategies for working with others, here intentionally cross-casting Robert Walker and Farley Granger into roles with sexual orientations opposite those of the actors in real life.

Carringer remains within a theory of the worker as a subject with agency and coherency. This is a common (but not inevitable) outcome in this liberal sociology. People are free to take up a role or not. Moreover, as Alvarado points out, "it is interesting that this view of creativity invariably locates the concept with the notion of authorship in its individuality, i.e., the possibility of 'group creativity' is rarely if ever, evoked (or even perhaps 'corporate creativity')" (20). Additionally, another outcome in liberal sociology is to shift authorship to another worker in the system, often the producer or the scriptwriter.[44] Such a maneuver duplicates the Romantic version of authorship, with "its continual desire to identify the true author out of the complex of creative personnel" (Caughie, 2). Indeed, a sociology of production that still views workers as subjects with coherency and agency, even while recognizing that they work within a labor force, has not escaped some of the troubles of the authorship-as-origin or -personality approaches. In fact, neoliberal economic theory supports using individuated authorship as a brand name within its marketing and promotion (see Foucault on the author-function), although authorship rights are now being given to corporations because of the profit advantages of claiming those intellectual-property rights.

Contemporary critical theory as an alternative sociology of production does reconceptualize the individual worker into a poststructural subject within a work mode. As Alvarado discusses, Macherey's replacement of terms in his *Theory of Literary Production* provided a strong theoretical option. By describing artistic outcomes as "products" rather than "texts," Macherey forced thinking of the communication process as labor rather than "creation" (Alvarado, 12–13). In 1981, Alvarado calls for a study of the industry that would "understand production as an ensemble of activities involving diverse and discrete skills brought together and organized/articulated in relation to specific objectives . . . these activities are brought into play by the discursive structures of the production but are also more or less determined by other discursive structures" (13). Simultaneously, I (1985) produced such a study of the Hollywood mode of production. Influenced by Marxist labor theory, Althusser, Raymond Williams, and Jean-Louis Comolli, I considered how Hollywood's management system developed historically to produce a detailed division of labor and created hierarchies of control and power. Avoiding an economic determinism, I stressed that discursive preferences of narrative construction, realism, causal coherence and continuity, spectacle, stars, and genres had a relative autonomy in producing and subsequently influencing the standard work procedures. Moreover, I pointed out that the necessity for innovation with a range of options for product differentiation is embedded in the capitalism system. Thus, firms encourage creativity rather than constrain it, rather than as auteurism often pictures the situation.[45] Such a theory of the subject is well within poststructuralism. Despite this, my system remains merely a template to describe routine work behavior. It does not attempt to explain why individuals might pursue enacting those routines in particular ways that reinforce (or not) dominant discourses. Thus, it lacks any theory of agency—a problem common with other poststructural approaches to authorship.

authorship as *signature*

With the arrival of structuralism and poststructuralism, reconceptualizations of agency and "self" produced further backing away from agency for an individual within a mode of production. Although auteurism had not always claimed full conscious intent, auteurism tended to seek a somewhat organic, controlling personality as it postulated authorship out of a possibly troubled, biographical person. Because structuralism and poststructuralism recast the biographical person as structured within discourses that are by no means coherent or knowable, the authorship-as-signature strategy could postulate recurrence of authorship traits only through various pieces of artwork as determined by the places that the biographical author inhabited within historical contexts. Repetition was unconscious because of the place of the individual within historical structures. As Stephen Heath phrases it: "The interrogation of a group of films within this history is not the revelation of the author but the tracing in the series of texts of the insistence of the unconscious" (1973, 90). Here Heath is making a direct psychoanalytical application, but other writers within this approach to authorship have considered the causal sources not as a culturally produced expression of the unconscious but (also) as a culturally produced expression of insistent cultural, social, and political contexts.

In the signature approach to authorship, the author is known by repetition among the various texts "signed" by a historical person. The message is an expression of the variable features produced unintentionally but traceable across a set of films because of the continuing and coherent presence of the person writing those texts. The French engagement with Ferdinand de Saussure's linguistic theory and the applications in anthropology by Claude Lévi-Strauss directly influenced this approach whose early users include Geoffrey Nowell-Smith, Jim Kitses, Alan Lovell, and Peter Wollen.[46]

Scholars such as Stephen Crofts (2000, 89) often cite Nowell-Smith's 1967 study, *[Luchino] Visconti*, as the first employment because of the description of method: Nowell-Smith writes that he seeks "a structural hard core of basic and often recondite motifs."[47] However, a careful reading of the book indicates that Nowell-Smith still operates in an auteurist mode. He argues that his goal is "liberating Visconti from the heritage of past polemics" (9) that linked Visconti to Italian neo-Realism and saw his later work as declining. Instead, Visconti's entire set of films should be viewed "as the product of a single intelligence" whose work "is far more complex and interesting, as well as more *coherent* than is generally imagined" (9, emphasis mine). As he develops his proposition, Nowell-Smith speaks of Visconti as a person acting: "Visconti has in fact purified the story line" (19); as perhaps not intending some outcomes (22, 53, 177); as having or lacking control over the production (177); as a conflicted individual, which explains a central tension in the work: "[The ambiguity] strikes deeper and reflects a constant tension in Visconti's work between an intellectual belief in the cause of progress and an emotional nostalgia for the past world that is being destroyed" (177); and as a person whose perceptions are revealed through the art: "above all the films are works of art. They *reveal* the world [as]. . . it can be perceived and experienced by a particular individual at a particular time" (177, emphasis mine). What has been taken for structuralism is a variant of American New Criticism and auteurism. "Structure" in *Visconti* does not refer to an underlying mythic opposition to be resolved, a preliterate way of thinking, but to patterns and repetitions.

A more precise example of this approach is Wollen's comparison of the films of Ford and Hawks in *Signs and Meaning in the Cinema*.[48] Explicitly drawing on semiotic and structuralist theory, Wollen creates an analogy of the director being like a culture in making the same narrative over and over, with variations (78, 93–4, 104–7, 113). A director has "preoccupations" and a script affects those authorial preoccupations, working as a "catalyst" (113). The director is like a conductor of a musical composition or the stager of a theatrical play who marks the performance with his or her own accent (106–7). Thus, Wollen does produce a structural theory of the director as a subject, one who may have little or no conscious agency and whose coherence is only a matter of continuing preoccupations. Still, Wollen writes to create an evaluative hierarchy of directors: "Hawks could be a lesser director [but] . . . [h]is real claim as an author lies in the presence, together with the dramas, of their inverse, the crazy comedies" (90–91). This desire for coherence of the whole and corollary evaluative stance is not required in authorship-as-signature, and Wollen reevaluates it in his 1972 appended commentary. There he changes the terms for evaluation from "coherence" to "productivity," especially any productivity that "overthrows established ways of reading or looking" (171–72). Moreover, he stresses that the structure created by the critical act should be distinguished from the biographical individual: "But Fuller or Hawks or Hitchcock, the directors, are quite separate from 'Fuller' or 'Hawks' or 'Hitchcock', the structures named after them, and should not be methodologically confused" (168). This disjunctive move escapes problems of seeing the structure as consequences of personality but also is a minor dodge as Wollen does not then provide an alternative theory of the subject that would account for the existence of the signature across all texts worked on by the director. He leaves the revised theory in a formalism wherein the critic does textual analysis to discover the signature but cannot attribute it to any specific causal thesis.

As Alvarado remarks about this approach to authorship, it still assumes a unity to the subject (25). Moreover, users of the approach have yet to account for problems of application from structural anthopology. Charles Eckert and Brian Henderson raise several of these. Is a film equal to a myth? Is a director's oeuvre equal to a myth? Why do some directors have their personal myths in their films and others don't? How would the critic account for other structures (signatures) that should also be in a film? Although structuralism had the value of "scientificness" (Caughie, 125), as a theory of individual authorship, problems existed. Thus, critics tried other solutions.

authorship as *reading strategy*

Perhaps not an approach to authorship as much as an end run or a recognition of actual practices by readers and thus "dodge number one," the approach to authorship in which the reader produces a representation of the author and uses that representation as a reading strategy does merit inclusion within this review, if only to point out what it does and does not explain. Increasingly as authors become more difficult to discuss and as the variables of readers' interpretations are foregrounded, approaching authorship from the perspective of the reader has had some fruitful outcomes. Here authorship is not a puzzle of locating agency within a biographical individual. Instead, authorship is a fantasy construction of a reader that may have value to the reader in producing interpretations of the text that have personal value. Authors, then, are defined as readers' fictional representations that participate in the readers' interpretation of messages supposedly produced by those fictional representations.

This approach derives from the development of reception studies. Deeply influential is Barthes's "The Death of the Author" in which he asserts, "the birth of the reader must be at the cost of the death of the Author" (148). By this he means that as soon as material has been expressed in a text, its integral meaning disappears as the reader possesses the signifiers, interpreting them from the reader's subjective position. This death is apparent in the discourse of the author who is a "modern figure" (142–43) but also in the "I" of the text that is no longer the "I" of an author (or narrator) but is "empty outside of the very enunciation which defines it" (145).

In film studies, Heath took up Barthes's points in his discussions of Buscombe and Wollen: if the structure "Fuller" is separate from the director Fuller, then the "author . . . may return as a *fiction* . . . of a certain pleasure which begins to turn the film . . . into a plurality, a play of assemblage and dispersion" (1973, 91, emphasis in original).

Nowell-Smith also observes that if critics consider the author to be a "sub-code" (see below), this could lead to seeing the author as a construction of the reader.[49] Considering the author as a reading strategy is a viable approach if the research question is about readers' practices (Staiger, 1992, 2000). However, it avoids the problem of causality for the *production* of the film and is, thus, "a dodge."

authorship as *site of discourses*

A further extension of the poststructuralist turn in late twentieth-century theorizing of the individual is approaching the author as a site of discourses, which will be "dodge number two." In this revision of the author-as-signature approach, agency is further removed because repetition is not assumed to be due to an insistent unconscious writing by a present entity with a particular historical body but due to the insistent unconscious writing by material discourses. An individual author's relation to the text is within history, but a history of a special poststructuralist cast. As MacCabe writes, the text is an order of discourses, an aesthetic manifestation of fantasies and ideologies that are "based and find its support in the dominant symbolic orders—which can be identified through an attention to other artistic and social practices" (130).

The author here is still a body but a body devoid of agency *and continuity* and, potentially, of significance. A major source for this approach is Foucault, who expresses the resituation of these matters:

> One can well imagine a culture where discourse can exist without authorship. One would no longer entertain the questions that have been rehashed for so long: Who is really speaking? Is it really he and not someone else? With what authenticity, or with what originality? And what has he expressed? But, other questions like these would arise: What are the modes of existence of this discourse? Where did it come from? How does it circulate? Who can appropriate it? What sites are prepared for possible future subjects? Who can take over the diverse functions of agency? And behind all these questions one would hardly notice the stirring of an indifference: "What difference does it make who is speaking?" (1975, 614)

Part of the answer to Foucault's series of questions is from Barthes and others who significantly redefine the author as contradictory, a tablet upon and through which culture writes its historical discourses. This is finally the poststructural subject, devoid of knowing intention and without coherence or continuity. Barthes's description is memorable:

> the text is a tissue of quotations drawn from the innumerable centers of culture. . . . The writer can only imitate a gesture that is always anterior, never original. His only power is to mix writings, to counter the ones with the others,

in such a way as never to rest on any of them. Does he wish to *express himself*, he ought at least to know that the inner "thing" he thinks to "translate" is itself only a ready-formed dictionary, its words only explainable through other words, and so on indefinitely. (1968, 146; emphasis in original)

In film studies, the very direct source for the authorship-as-site-of-discourse are the editors of the *Cahiers du Cinéma*'s analysis of *Young Mr. Lincoln* (1939) who take up declarations by Macherey and Barthes in their 1971 study of the film. In this application, the author becomes one of several textual "subcodes" to be decoded. Articulations of this causal claim include Nowell-Smith:

> The author (external to the text) records his presence through the signs of this sub-code, to which the reader (also external to the text) can then attribute codic pertinence, or not, as the case may be. Auteur films, on this interpretation, can then be distinguished from non-auteur films by the degree to which the authorial sub-code imposes itself as a necessary component of reading on any spectator of average or above average cinematic literacy. (1976, 29).

In Nowell-Smith's discussion, he suggests that genres have subcodes but no source, whereas the industry's sociology of production does not produce a subcode (28). This description produces the appearance or disappearance of the author depending on whether the authorial subcode "imposes" itself on the reader and is, thus, either another example of authorship as reading strategy or a formalism in which the critical analysis of the text determines the existence of the author.

A slightly better articulation of the approach is Caughie's: "The activity of the critical spectator is then directed, not towards discovering the thread of personality in the work of a director, or placing him on an evaluative scale, but rather investigating the way in which the directorial subcode operates in the film, how it interacts with, modifies, and is modified by the other codes and sub-codes which also operate."[50] This phrasing, however, still produces a formalism as it assumes either the critical reader already knows the directorial subcode (and thus would have no trouble distinguishing it from the other codes and subcodes) or the reader can determine the subcode from textual evidence.

I do not think any way out of the quandary of formalism exists, which is why this approach has been labeled a dodge. However, the approach does set the stage for the next one that I think does eliminate the potential formalism of the authorship-as-site-of-discourse approach. What this approach does accomplish beyond its strong expression of a poststructuralist subject is to offer an important reevaluation of a text as contradictory, fragmented, and citational of other texts. This reduces the desire to seek resolution of contradictions or to find coherent authorial statements. It produces a critical practice that does not look to the structure of the whole but is often a linear reading of the text in the mode of Barthes's discussion in *S/Z* or the *Cahiers's* study of *Young Mr. Lincoln*. This linearity, when combined with an emphasis on how the text affects a reader, can produce a critical discussion of what subject positions are available in the text.[51] The subject positions, however, are hypothesized places for an ideal reader and, once again, can produce a formalist criticism.

Canonical examples of this approach are Paul Willeman's interpretation of *Pursued* and Heath's analysis of *Touch of Evil*.[52] Willemann describes Walsh as "the organizer of the discourse," which is a castration scene. Employing Lacanian psychoanalytical tools, Willemann does not suggest that the narrative is a display of an interiority of the director's personality; instead, Walsh is the individual through which a dominant cultural discourse is arranged into celluloid. Similarly, Heath approaches *Touch of Evil* as having five determinations: narrative order, author style, star weighting, ideological message, and technical accomplishment (1975, 11). Of the ten segments for commenting, one is "author": "the sole interest here is in the author as an effect of the text and only in so far as the effect is significant in the production of the filmic system, is a textual effect" (1975, 37–38). In other words, the author is only an author if perceived—and we are back to formalism.

Approaching authorship-as-site-of-discourses is still attempted with variable degrees of success. The study of Fritz Lang's films by Tom Gunning is a good case to display the difficulties of trying to pay attention to all of these problems.[53] Ultimately, Gunning slips among four approaches: site of discourses, reading strategy, signature, and personality. As an example of the first two approaches: "This figure of Lang seems to be . . . connecting [his films] to an enunciating labor, to a source from which they derive. But it is a source whose existence is indicated by the films themselves; a source we find only by reading backwards from them, as through the films, or our careful viewing of them, create the figure of Lang as much as vice versa" (3); "the author . . . is, I would maintain, a creature of the reader's or viewer's desire" (4). Gunning considers this critical tactic as "somewhat novel" (3) within authorial study, but, as I have indicated, thinking of the author as a construct of the reader has a prominent history in authorship criticism. Gunning then shifts to representing Lang as a real person who is present by his absence through his "imprint": "absent except in the imprint left behind" (5).[54] Echoing Wollen's discussion in *Signs and Meaning in the Cinema*, Gunning emphasizes Lang's hand—literally and figuratively—in his films. Scripts are a "libretto for which Lang supplied a full orchestration into images" (6). They are catalysts: "Lang's contribution is alchemical, a chain reaction of reinterpretation and visualization, opening up the film (and the viewer) to non-verbal meanings" (6). Finally, within the actual discussion of Lang's career, Gunning shifts to the author-as-personality and auteurist vocabulary.

"I feel that Lang's strongest work was made in Germany before 1934. However, I also feel there is no question that the same film-maker, with the same essential stylistics and preoccupations not only continued to work out the design of his authorship in his Hollywood films, but also developed further some of the most profound insights of the last German sound films. . . . [N]one of his films are totally bereft of interest" (204). Why? Because Lang has finally to deal with Hollywood as a system.

The formalism of this approach occurs in part because agency is eliminated in the causal model. As I stated, the approach of authorship as site of discourses represents the biographical individual as a tablet for culture, without agency although potentially with individuality. The author may be a historically constituted subject that is the locus of social, psychological, and cultural discourses and practices; the author may no longer be a great person. But the author no longer seems to matter. Such a proposition dodges the material reality of human actions. Agency needs to be reconceived.

authorship as *technique of the self*

The point is that for many people in a nondominant situation, who is speaking does matter. A consequence of feminism, identity politics, and queer theory has been the demand for a retheorization of agency within the advances of poststructuralist philosophy. As early as 1977, Pam Cook decries the "problems and contradiction for women, and for feminist film-makers" between the seemingly "politically correct" position of "suppression of the 'personal'" and the significance "self-expression" has for political action.[55] As Nancy Hartstock protests, "Why is it that just at the moment when so many of us who have been silenced begin to demand the right to name ourselves, to act as subjects rather than objects of history, that just then the concept of subjecthood becomes problematic."[56] Or subjecthood is represented as "textual energies" or "preoccupations."[57] Others expressing this complaint include Nancy K. Miller who writes: "What matters who's speaking? I would answer it matters, for example, to women who have lost and still routinely lose their proper name in marriage, and whose signature— not merely their voice—has not been worth the paper it was written on. . . . Only those who have [power] can play with not having it."[58]

New theory justifying a revised conception of agency comes from speech-act propositions or from poststructuralism, but the point is to rescue the expression of the self as a viable, if contingent, act—a potent one with real effects. Thus, the author is reconceptualized as a subject having an ability to act as a conscious analyzer of the functionality of citations in historical moments. What do I mean here? One source for this is the later writing of Foucault.[59] In his famous statement about power, Foucault writes, "Where there is power, there is resistance, and yet, or rather consequently, this resistance is never in a position of exteriority in relation to power" (1976, 95). Describing a classic deconstruction proposition that oppositions are not relational or reactional but imbedded within their attempted expulsion, Foucault is saying that an act of resistance does not reply to power but is power turned inside out. This discussion of agency rebukes intention but it does not deny outcome. Actions have consequences.

But it is in the next two books that Foucault provides the basis for a new analysis of agency. In *The Use of Pleasure*, Foucault indicates that by considering the problem of power and agency in terms of historical practices of sexuality, his work has shifted from "a history of systems of morality based . . . on interdictions" to a history of "ethical problematizations based on practices of the self" (1984a, 13). Morality is how an individual obeys or resists a standard of conduct; ethics is "the manner in which one ought to form oneself as an ethical subject acting in reference to the prescriptive elements that make up the code" (26). Morality can be code driven (lots of laws) or ethic oriented (self-regulation) (30). In Western culture, sexual discourses refer to the need to care for one's self as an "art of existence" (1984b, 43). To pursue this fashioning of the self requires "self-knowledge," gained through "recipes, specific forms of examination, and codified exercises" (58). The reason isn't to shame one's self but to habituate one's behavior to achieve one's goals.

When I apply this discussion to the act of authoring rather than sexual ethics, authoring as an "art of existence" becomes a repetitive assertion of "self-as-expresser" through culturally and socially laden discourses of authoring. Individuals author by duplicating recipes and exercises of authorship. Authorship is also a technique of the self, creating and recreating the individual as an acting subject within history. The message produced should not be considered a direct expression of a wholly constituted origin with presence or personality or preoccupations. Yet the message is produced from circumstances in which the individual conceives a self as able to act. The individual believes in the author-function, and this works because the discursive structure (our culture) in which the individual acts also believes in it.

How this happens may also be explained through Judith Butler's extension of J. L. Austin's speech-act theory. As she writes, an individual can express a performative statement that is a "discursive practice that enacts or produces that which it names."[60] An example is "I pronounce you man and wife" stated by someone with the authority (power) to make this statement in a serious manner. However, the power to make this act happen "is not the function of an originating will, but is always derivative" (13) from the fact that the performative statement *repeats* statements in the discursive system that previously have produced the effect of marrying two people. Moreover, it is said in circumstances that abide by other discursive rules—in the United States, it works only if it is said to a male and a female. As Butler notes, "to the extent that [a performative] acquires an act-like status in the present, it conceals or dissimulates the conventions of which it is a repetition" (12).

Thus, in application to the issue of agency in authorship, an approach of authorship as technique of the self would note that a directorial (or other) choice is a performative only as it is given that directors may make a choice. A performative statement works because it is a citation of authoring by an individual having the authority to make an authoring statement. In film, firms hire directors to make these choices, and the division of labor places them into a work structure with specific authority to make authoring statements. As Butler points out, citations work only if they fit within boundaries of the norms they cite, although norms do not exist prior to and separate from the citation. The citation affirms and produces the norm. "In this sense, the agency denoted by the performativity of 'sex' [or 'authorship'] will be directly counter to any notion of a voluntarist subject who exists quite apart from the regulatory norms which she or he opposes. The paradox of subjectivation (*assujetissement*) is precisely that the subject who would resist such norms is itself enabled, if not produced, by such norms. Although this constitutive constraint does not foreclose the possibility of agency, it does locate agency as a reiterative or rearticulatory practice, immanent to power, and not a relation of external opposition to power" (15; interpolation mine). Thus, rebellious or resistant authorship would be understood as a particular kind of citation with the performative outcome of asserting agency against the normative. Moreover, a *repetitive* citation of a performative statement of "authoring choice" produces the "author" (who is different from the subject making the statements). If the subject repeatedly cites the same sorts of performatives, then repetition occurs (which critics perceive in a subject's oeuvre), providing the critical observation that such-and-such distinguishes this subject's authoring practices. However, all authoring statements by a subject are part of the subject's authorship and constitute the technique of that self. What an author *is*, is the repetition of statements.

In film studies some examples exist of individuals taking this approach to authorship. In an excellent review of feminist film theory on authorship, Catherine Grant describes the conflict discussed above between the recognition of the socially constructed subject of poststructuralism and a desire to understand expressions by members of groups of specific selves such as women, feminists, gays, and people of color. Grant notes that Susan Martin-Márquez uses Butler's notion of agency as model for women writers in which a woman "may opt to take up a number of different subject positions through her writing 'depending upon how her choice is constrained and the ways in which the forms are already culturally and institutionally defined and internalized by her.'"[61]

As part of these discussions, scholars have observed some authoring practices that they have claimed are methods for self-expression by authors with features of the self in minority categories. In other approaches to authorship, such expressive methods would be described as "transcending," "defamiliarizing," "subverting," or "resisting" the system. In this approach, the methods should be understood as citational practices that have an outcome of differing from dominant expressions; they may have become favored performatives of authorship for subjects in minority-subject positions. For example, Claire Johnston proposed in the mid-1970s that Dorothy Arzner as a female director in Hollywood used disruptions of certain sorts as a feminist strategy to criticize patriarchy (Grant, 2001, 115–16); Judith Mayne additionally considers Arzner as fashioning herself in her own clothing and life-style as lesbian and extending that self-fashioning into her attention to those matters in her films.[62] In an authorship-as-technique-of-the-self approach, critics would describe Arzner as making performative statements through her handling of scenes and mise-en-scène.

It would be important to consider whether, in fact, it is primarily individuals with minority selves who make such citational practices (and, if so, what explanation exists for so doing) or whether the methods of critical analysis have led scholars to seek such deviations, ignoring normative statements by minority individuals and deviant statements by dominant individuals. As Bordwell remarks, in symptomatic criticism, the pattern has been for scholars to claim that dominant-authored texts subvert themselves without the knowledge of the authors but minority-authored texts do it intentionally (1989, 101–2). Other cautions exist. Bordwell also points out the fallacy of assuming filmmakers' statements about their work are obvious (and don't require the same sort of textual attention as texts such as their films). After all, they are part of the authors' techniques of the self. Cook notes, too, that a tendency exists to look at marginal filmmakers and declare that they stand for their variant group as a whole (Cook, 1999, 313). Essentialism also is possible. Andy Medhurst states the problem well: for example, a presumption exists in "gay male subcultures that the homosexuality of an individual will reveal itself primarily through matters of taste—not good or bad taste but *particular* taste" (198). And it is way too easy to assume that one aspect of an individual is all of which the individual speaks. Because someone is Asian American, that is not all that individual is. Such a fallacy produces a monoglossic subject. Finally, at least for this list, membership in a particular minority-self grouping by no means ensures any political membership (e.g., conservative or progressive). Still, this sort of approach to authorship has great potential in my opinion.

notes

1. Histories and analyses of this include Walter Benjamin, "The Author as Producer" [1934], in *Reflections: Essays, Aphorisms, Authobiographical Writing*, trans. Edmund Jephcott (New York: Harcourt Brace Jovanovich, 1978), 220–38; André Bazin, "On the *Politiques des auteurs*" [1957], trans. Peter Graham, reprinted in *Cahiers du Cinéma: The 1950s: Neo-Realism, Hollywood, New Wave*, ed. Jim Hillier (Cambridge, MA: Harvard University Press, 1985), 248–59; Stephen Heath, "Comment on 'The Idea of Authorship,'" *Screen* 14, no. 3 (Autumn 1973): 86; Michel Foucault, "What is an Author? trans. James Venit, *Partisan Review*, 42, no. 2 (1975): 603–14; Graham Murdock, "Authorship and Organisation," *Screen Education*, no. 35 (Summer 1980): 19–34; Manuel Alvarado, "Authorship, Organization and Production," *Australian Journal of Screen Theory*, no. 9/10 (1981): 18–19; these and other sources are hereafter cited in text.

2. A smart analysis of the author-function in new Hollywood is the collection of essays: *Directed by Allen Smithee*, ed. Jeremy Braddock and Stephen Hock (Minneapolis, MN: University of Minnesota Press, 2001).

    As noted above, textual criticism does not need authors or theories of causal production. Much of the last half of the twentieth century has witnessed attempts to do away with authors within textual criticism, starting with the Russian Formalists and the new American critics—although both schools of criticism did recognize individuals as causal sources for the texts they studied. For example, W. K. Wimsatt, Jr., and M. C. Beardsley in their famous 1946 essay, "The Intentional Fallacy," write that although a poem comes from a "designing intellect," the *cause* of the poem should not be the reason for studying it nor should any supposed authorial intent be the basis for critical judgment: "Critical inquiries are not settled by consulting the oracle." *Sewanee Review* 54 (1946): 487.

3. Roland Barthes, "The Death of the Author" [1968], trans. Stephen Heath, reprinted in *Image, Music, Text* (New York: Hill and Wang, 1977), 142–48. This disagreement may miss the mark as Barthes's point is not so simple nor is it clear that what he is explaining is the cause for a text. Rather, his essay is a gesture toward discussing the possibilities of its reception.

4. Roland Barthes, *The Pleasure of the Text* [1973], trans. Richard Miller (New York: Hill and Wang, 1975), 27.

5. Thomas Elsaesser, 1979 prefatory remarks to "Vincente Minnelli" [1969], reprinted in *Genre: The Musical: A Reader*, ed. Rick Altman (London: Routledge & Kegan Paul, 1981), 11.

6. Adrian Martin, "Sign Your Name Across My Heart, or 'I Want to Write about Delbert Mann,'" *Screening the Past*, no. 12 (2001), www.latrobe.edu.au/www.screeningthepast (accessed March 9, 2001). Others expressing this general desire for author studies are Dudley Andrew, "The Unauthorized Auteur Today," in *Film Theory Goes to the Movies*, ed. Jim Collins, Hilary Radner, and Ava Preacher Collins (New York: Routledge, 1993), 77–85; a special issue of *Iris*, no. 28 (Autumn 1999); and Dana Polan, "Auteur Desire," *Screening the Past*, no. 12 (2001). Polan's essay is a nice survey of authorship studies, but he never moves into theorizing why people desire auteurs except as an example of "collecting," which he writes "replaces history with classification."

7. David Eng and Shinhee Han, "A Dialogue on Racial Melancholia," *Psychoanalytic Dialogues* 10, no. 4 (2000): 667–700.

8. The first four of these approaches and examples as noted are derived from lectures by David Bordwell, Lectures in Critical Film Analysis, October 1977, but have been revised and redefined by me; I have added the last three approaches. Additional surveys of authorship are Pam Cook, *Cinema Book*, 2nd ed. (London: British Film Institute, 1999), 235–314; Stephen Crofts, "Authorship and Hollywood," *Wide Angle* 5, no. 3 (1983): 16–22; Stephen

Crofts, "Authorship and Hollywood," in *American Cinema and Hollywood: Critical Approaches*, ed. John Hill and Pamela Church Gibson (New York: Oxford University Press, 2000), 84–98; Robert Lapsley and Michael Westlake, *Film Theory: An Introduction* (Manchester, England: Manchester University Press, 1988), 105–28; and Polan, 2001.

9. Scott S. Derrick points out that authorship as a profession developed in the United States from the 1830s, and some authors became celebrities. This extra value to their name produced a strategy in the late 1800s of commenting on authorship within their own works to establish greater authority and profit. See *Monumental Anxieties: Homoerotic Desire and Feminine Influence in 19th-Century U.S. Literature* (New Brunswick, NJ: Rutgers University Press, 1997).

10. David Bordwell, *Making Meaning: Inference and Rhetoric in the Interpretation of Cinema* (Cambridge, MA: Harvard University Press, 1989), 53–4, 65–8.

11. Terry Eagleton, *Literary Theory: An Introduction* (Minneapolis: University of Minnesota Press, 1983); Cleanth Brooks, *The Well Wrought Urn: Studies in the Structure of Poetry* (New York: Harcourt, Brace & World, 1947).

12. Also see W. K. Wimsatt, "Genesis: A Fallacy Revisited," in *The Disciplines of Criticism*, ed. Peter Demetz, Thomas Greene, and Lowry Nelson, Jr. (New Haven, CT: Yale University Press, 1968), 210.

13. In this original version, the phrase is "a standard for judging the success." In 1968, Wimsatt revised the phrase to "a standard for judging either the meaning or the value"; I am using the latter version here.

14. Pauline Kael, *The Citizen Kane Book* (New York: Bantam Books, 1971), 45. Example from Bordwell, 1977.

15. David Bordwell, "*Citizen Kane*" (1971), reprinted in *Movies and Methods*, Vol. I, ed. Bill Nichols (Berkeley: University of California Press, 1976), 273–90.

16. David Bordwell, *The Cinema of Eisenstein* (Cambridge, MA: Harvard University Press, 1993); David Bordwell, *The Films of Carl-Theodor Dreyer* (Berkeley: University of California Press, 1981); David Bordwell, *Ozu and the Poetics of Cinema* (Princeton, NJ: Princeton University Press, 1988).

17. M. M. Bakhtin discusses this approach in "Forms of Time and the Chronotope in the Novel" [1937–1938], in *The Dialogic Imagination: Four Essays*, trans. Caryl Emerson and Michael Holquist (Austin: University of Texas Press, 1981), 257. Bakhtin writes, "if this image [of the author] is deep and truthful, it can help the listener or reader more correctly and profoundly to understand the work of the given author." Thus, Bakhtin assumes that knowledge of the author will lead to a better interpretation of the text.

18. Catherine Belsey, *Critical Practice* (London: Methuen, 1980), 7–15.

19. M. H. Abrams, *The Mirror and the Lamp: Romantic Theory and the Critical Tradition* (New York: Oxford University Press, 1953).

20. Michael Moon, *Disseminating Whitman: Revision and Corporeality in* Leaves of Grass (Cambridge, MA: Harvard University Press, 1991), 3–4.

21. Bordwell (1989, 43–48) provides the best history, although other sources contribute significant commentary and cover gaps in his account. Also see Donald E. Staples, "The Auteur Theory Reexamined," *Cinema Journal* 6 (1966–67): 1–7; Peter Wollen, *Signs and Meaning in the Cinema*, rev. ed. (Bloomington: Indiana University Press, 1972), 74–115; Raymond Durgnat, *Films and Feelings* (Cambridge, MA: MIT Press, 1976), 61–68; John Hess, "*Auteurism* and After," *Film Quarterly* 27, no. 2 (Winter 1973–74): 28–37; John Hess, "*La Politique des auteurs*," part 1, *Jump Cut* 1 (May–June 1974a): 19–22; John Hess, "*La Politique des auteurs*," part 2, *Jump Cut* 2 (July–August 1974b): 20–22; Edward Buscombe, "Ideas of Authorship," *Screen* 14, no. 3 (Autumn 1973), 75–85; Thomas Elsaesser, "Two Decades in Another Country: Hollywood and the Cinéphiles," in *Superculture: American Popular Culture and Europe*, ed. C. W. E. Bigsby (Bowling Green, OH: Bowling Green University Press, 1975), 199–225; Crofts, 1983; Janet Staiger, "The Politics of Film Canons," *Cinema Journal* 24, no. 3 (Spring 1985): 4–23; Jim Hillier,

"Introduction," in *Cahiers du Cinéma: The 1950s: Neo-Realism, Hollywood, New Wave*, ed. Jim Hillier (Cambridge, MA: Harvard University Press, 1985), 1–5; Lapsley and Westlake 1988, 106–8; James Naremore, "Authorship and the Cultural Politics of Film Criticism," *Film Quarterly* 44, no. 1 (Fall 1990), 14–22; Cook, 1999, 235, 240–55; Crofts, 2000, 87–9.

22. As I shall discuss below, French authorship study had several varieties. Usually *Positif* is linked closely to surrealist influences (see Bordwell, 1989 and Elsaesser, 1975). However, Naremore argues that *Cahiers du Cinéma* critics had more of a "quasi-surrealist view" than a romantic one (17–18). Yet Naremore makes this claim primarily on the basis of one essay by Jean-Luc Godard; thus, further research is needed to resolve this question.

23. For a discussion of the conjunction between the exhibition of art cinema and discourses on authorship see Janet Staiger, *Interpreting Films: Studies in the Historical Reception of American Cinema* (Princeton, NJ: Princeton University Press, 1992), 178–95.

24. Andrew Sarris, "The World of Howard Hawks" [1962], reprinted in *Focus on Howard Hawks*, ed. Joseph McBride (Englewood Cliffs, NJ: Prentice-Hall, 1972), 63.

25. Janet Staiger, "*Theorist*, yes, but what *of*? Bazin and History," *Iris* 2, no. 2 (1984): 99–109.

26. Alexandre Astruc, "The Birth of a New Avant-Garde: *La Caméra-Stylo*" [1948], trans. Peter Graham, reprinted in *The New Wave*, ed. Peter Graham (Garden City, NY: Doubleday & Company, 1968), 17–23.

27. Gilles Deleuze, *Cinema 1: The Image-Movement* [1983], trans. Hugh Tomlinson and Barbara Habberjam (Minneapolis: University of Minnesota Press, 1996), xiv.

28. Bill Nichols, "Introduction," in *Movies and Methods*, Vol. I, ed. Bill Nichols (Berkeley: University of California Press, 1976), 306.

29. Lotte Eisner, *The Haunted Screen* [1952, rev. 1965], trans. Roger Greaves (1969; rpt. Berkeley: University of California Press, 1973), 98.

30. François Truffaut, "A Certain Tendency of the French" [1954], reprinted in *Movies and Methods*, Vol. I, ed. Bill Nichols (Berkeley: University of California Press, 1976), 224–37.

31. Hess (1974a) provides two important differences. For one, Bazin is concerned with people in their relations in the world as a means to access divine revelation while auteurists were "concerned with transcendence and salvation of the individual" (20). Additionally, Bazin considered the world as providing "correspondences," whereas auteurists were "less metaphysical" (21). Durgnat also holds this view of Bazin (67–8). Although I would not agree totally with the characterization of Bazin's views, Hess's observations are still significant. Also note that Hess disagrees with Graham Petrie's criticisms of French auteurism, arguing that Petrie's characterizations of the strand of authorship are not accurate for French auteurism but may be for the U.S. and British versions promoted by Sarris and Robin Wood (28–33).

32. See Durgnat, 61–75; John Caughie, "Preface" and "Introduction," in *Theories of Authorship*, ed. John Caughie (London: Routledge & Kegan Paul, 1981), 48–50; Bordwell, 1989, 50; Naremore, 22, n12; and Cook, 1999, 264–76, for excellent details.

33. Andrew Sarris, "Notes on the Auteur Theory in 1962," *Film Culture*, no. 27 (Winter 1962–1963), reprinted in *Film Culture Reader*, ed. P. Adams Sitney (New York: Praeger Publishers, 1970), 128, and *The American Cinema* (New York: E. P. Dutton & Co., 1968), 19. Buscombe, 1973 is particularly useful in distinguishing Sarris from French critics.

34. Pauline Kael, "Circles and Squares," *Film Quarterly* 16, no. 3 (Spring 1963): 12–26.

35. Charles Boultenhouse, "The Camera as God," *Film Culture*, no. 29 (Summer 1963), reprinted in *Film Culture Reader*, ed. P. Adams Sitney (New York: Praeger Publishers, 1970), 136–40.

36. Lauren Rabinovitz also notes the influence of auteurism on how avant-garde filmmakers are studied. See her *Points of Resistance: Women, Power and Politics in the New York Avant-garde Cinema, 1943–71* (Urbana: University of Illinois Press, 1991), 16–17.

37. Jack Smith, "The Perfect Filmic Appositeness of Maria Montez," *Film Culture*, no. 27 (Winter 1962–1963), 28–32; David Ehrenstein, "An Interview with Andy Warhol," *Film Culture*, no. 40 (Spring 1966): 41. Perhaps the Godard review of Sirk discussed by Naremore might also be thought of in this context. Naremore does mention as well that the British auteurists were youth who enjoyed the culture of "mass media—films, comics, records, and so on" (15–16, 21, 22, n12). Perhaps retrospectively some of the "fun" has been lost in reviewing the past.

38. A strong criticism of some authorship work as ignoring production information was Graham Petrie's "Alternatives to Auteurs," *Film Quarterly* 26, no. 3 (Spring 1973): 27–35.

39. Jon Halliday, *Sirk on Sirk* (New York: Viking Press, 1972), 9. Also see V. F. Perkins, *Film as Film: Understanding and Judging Movies* (Middlesex, UK: Penguin Books, 1972), 184–86 in particular.

40. Thomas Elsaesser, "Vincente Minnelli" [1969], reprinted in *Genre: The Musical: A Reader*, ed. Rick Altman (London: Routledge & Kegan Paul, 1981), 12, emphasis in original.

41. Colin MacCabe, "Walsh an Author?" *Screen* 16, no. 1 (Spring 1975): 128–34.

42. This is the vocabulary usually used in sociology for the two approaches.

43. Paul DiMaggio and Paul M. Hirsch, "Production Organizations in the Arts," *American Behavior Scientist* 19, no. 6 (July–August 1976): 735–52; Paul M. Hirsch, "Occupational, Organizational, and Institutional Models in Mass Media Research: Towards an Integrated Framework," in *Strategies for Communication Research* (Beverly Hills, CA: Sage Publications, 1977), 13–42; Joseph Turow, "Unconventional Programs on Commercial Television: An Organizational Perspective," in *Mass Communications in Context*, ed. D. Charles Whitney and James Ettema (Beverly Hills, CA: Sage Publications 1982), 107–29; Joseph Turow, *Media Industries: The Production of News and Entertainment* (New York: Longman, 1984); Robert L. Carringer, *The Making of "Citizen Kane"* (Berkeley: University of California Press, 1985); Robert L. Carringer, "Collaboration and Concepts of Authorship," *PMLA* 116, no. 2 (March 2001): 370–70; Janet Staiger in *The Classical Hollywood Cinema: Film Style and Mode of Production* by David Bordwell, Janet Staiger, and Kristin Thompson (London: Routledge & Kegan Paul, 1985); Janet Staiger, "Introduction," in *The Studio System*, ed. Janet Staiger (New Brunswick, NJ: Rutgers University Press, 1995), 1–14.

44. Polan discusses this using the examples of work by Thomas Schatz and George Custen. See, respectively, their *The Genius of the System: Hollywood Filmmaking in the Studio Era* (New York: Pantheon, 1988) and *Twentieth Century's Fox: Darryl F. Zanuck and the Culture of Hollywood* (New York: Basic Books, 1997). In my view, Custen's construction of Zanuck escapes the problem of the "great man" because Custen is very careful to write about him as a conflicted, socially determined subject.

45. Also see Staiger, 1995.

46. See Charles Eckert, "The English Cine-Structuralists" [1973], reprinted in *Theories of Authorship*, ed. Caughie, pp. 152–65; Brian Henderson, "Critique of Cine-Structuralism," part I, *Film Quarterly* 27, no. 1 (Fall 1973): 25–34; Bordwell, 1989, 78–104; Cook, 1999, 282–87, 294–99; and Crofts, 2000, 89.

47. Geoffrey Nowell-Smith, *[Luchino] Visconti* [1967] (Garden City, NY: Doubleday & Company, 1968), 10.

48. Peter Wollen, *Signs and Meaning in the Cinema*, rev. ed. (Bloomington: Indiana University Press, 1972), 74–115. Lapsley and Westlake discuss Wollen's mid-1960s work as having elements of auteurism within essays he

wrote under the pseudonym Lee Russell and that Wollen shifts from terminology of "personal vision" to "structure" between the editions of *Signs and Meaning* (1988, 109–11). Also see Buscombe, 82–84; Henderson, 31–2.

49. Geoffrey Nowell-Smith, "Six Authors in Pursuit of *The Searchers*," *Screen* 17, no. 1 (Spring 1976): 30. Bordwell (1989) also discusses authorship as a set of assumptions that permits interpretations to occur.

50. John Caughie, "Teaching Through Authorship," *Screen Education* 17 (Winter 1975): 76, quoted in Alvarado, 24.

51. See Caughie, 200.

52. Paul Willemann, "The Fugitive Subject," in *Raoul Walsh*, ed. Phil Hardy (Colchester, England: Vinegard Press, 1974), 63–98; Stephen Heath, "Film and System: Terms of Analysis," part I, *Screen* 16, no. 1 (Spring 1975), 7–77, and part II, *Screen* 16, no. 2 (Summer 1975), 91–113.

53. Tom Gunning, *The Films of Fritz Lang: Allegories of Vision and Modernity* (London: British Film Institute, 2000). See a similar analysis of the problems in Gunning's method in Polan, 2001.

54. This is a classic "structuring absences" declaration featured prominently in the methodology of Macherey, the *Cahiers du Cinéma*, and comes from Jacques Derrida. Kaja Silverman's discussion of Jean-Luc Godard's *JLG/JLG* also indicates that Godard may be attempting to write his own authorship within this approach. See Kaja Silverman, "The Author as Receiver," *October*, no. 96 (Spring 2001): 17–34.

55. Pam Cook, "The Point of Self-Expression in Avant-Garde Film" [1977–1978], reprinted in *Theories of Authorship*, ed. Caughie, 272.

56. Nancy Hartsock, "Foucault on Power: A Theory for Women?" [1987], reprinted in *Feminism/Postmodernism*, ed. Linda J. Nicholson (New York: Routledge, 1990), 163–64.

57. Catherine Grant, "Secret Agents: Feminist Theories of Women's Film Authorship," *Feminist Theory* 2, no. 1 (2001): 121.

58. Nancy K. Miller, "The Text's Heroine: A Feminist Critic and Her Fictions," *Diacritics* 12 (Summer 1982): 53, quoted in Rabinovitz, 22. Also see Andy Medhurst, "That Special Thrill: *Brief Encounter*, Homosexuality and Authorship," *Screen* 32, no. 2 (Summer 1991): 197–208, who lists among the complainers bell hooks, Paul Hallam, and Ronald L. Peck, and Naremore, 21.

59. Michel Foucault, *History of Sexuality: An Introduction*, Vol. I: [1976], trans. Robert Hurley (New York: Vintage Books, 1980); *The Use of Pleasure: The History of Sexuality*, Vol. II [1984], trans. Robert Hurley (New York: Vintage Books, 1986); *The Care of the Self: The History of Sexuality*, Vol. III [1984], trans. Robert Hurley (New York Vintage Books, 1988).

60. Judith Butler, *Bodies That Matter: On the Discursive Limits of "Sex"* (New York: Routledge, 1993), 13. She is working from J. L. Austin, *How To Do Things with Words*, 2nd ed. (Cambridge, MA: Harvard University Press, 1975).

61. Susan Martin-Márquez (and quoting Carol Watts) quoted in Grant, 123. On this matter also see Rabinovitz, 21–23.

62. Judith Mayne, *Directed by Dorothy Arzner* (Bloomington: Indiana University Press, 1994).

part two

authorship

and

identity

in

hollywood

the auteur

theory

three

michael curtiz,

and *casablanca*

peter wollen

In his classic guidebook to auteurism, *The American Cinema*, Andrew Sarris characterizes Michael Curtiz as a director who "perhaps more than any other . . . reflected the strengths and weaknesses of the studio system."[1] As Sarris put it, "when one speaks of a typical Warners' film in the thirties and forties, one is generally speaking of a typical Curtiz film of those periods" (1968, 175). That is to say, Curtiz, in his many films, expressed the studio rather than himself. After 1951, with the collapse of the studio system, and "the bottom dropping out of routine film-making" (176), Curtiz's career "went to the dogs"(175). "If many of the early Curtiz films are hardly worth remembering, none of the later ones are even worth seeing" (1968, 175). However, as we all know, "the director's one enduring masterpiece is, of course, *Casablanca*, the happiest of happy accidents, and the most decisive exception to the auteur theory" (176). Or, as Sarris's great rival, Pauline Kael, put it, somewhat less charitably, "a good hack job."[2]

To Hal Wallis, however, Curtiz's producer on *Casablanca* (1943) and a number of other films, Curtiz "was a superb director with an amazing command of lighting, mood and action. He could handle any kind of picture: melodrama, comedy, Western, historical epic or love story."[3] Curtiz's peer, Billy Wilder, observed that "every director must admire Curtiz because there was no big fancy talk, no deep searching for the reason for certain actions. He was a good soldier. He clicked his heels and did it, and he did it as well as anybody in the world could have."[4] Nick Roddick, in his history of Warner Bros., *A New Deal in Entertainment*, goes as far as saying that in *The Adventures of Robin Hood* (1938), Curtiz "tends to tip the balance" in his own preferred direction, but then quickly steps back to add that "this is not to say that Curtiz was an auteur working against the system, merely to identify him as its most skilled practitioner."[5] Roddick goes on to note that *The Adventures of Robin Hood* "shows the system working at maximum efficiency, both in the sense of perfectly capturing audience requirements and in the sense of providing the best framework for the skills of producer (Wallis), director (Curtiz), writers (Raine and Miller), art director (Weyl), composer (Korngold), and star (Flynn)" (241).

Another "good hack job"? Or another "triumph," to use Roddick's word, another "masterpiece"? And, if so, who takes the credit? The consensus seems to be the studio system, with its discipline, its routine, its standard code of practice, and its teams of professional employees. Of course, not everybody considers *Casablanca* a masterpiece. François Truffaut, whose extravagant and vitriolic advocacy of auteurism first really put it on the map, was asked in 1975 whether he was interested in remaking *Casablanca* for Warners. He replied:

> It's not my favorite Humphrey Bogart film and I would place it much lower than *The Big Sleep* (1946) or *To Have and Have Not* (1945). So, logically, I shouldn't have any nervousness about the idea of directing a new version, and I haven't forgotten that the film has a French setting. But, I know that American students have a passion for the film and especially for the dialogue, every line of which they know by heart. This would be extremely intimidating for the actors, as well as for me, and, in the circumstances, I can't imagine Belmondo or Deneuve wanting to step into Bogart and Bergman's shoes.[6]

That is to say, auteurist to the end, Truffaut sees the two Howard Hawks films as the masterpieces he would be afraid to remake, while the Curtiz film is basically no more than a Bogart vehicle, but with memorable lines.

From the "Curtiz was a hack" viewpoint it seems that there is no problem in refusing him auteur status, as long as *Casablanca* is nothing special. A problem arises only if the films he directed, including *Casablanca*, really do stand out from the rest of the studio's output. I sometimes wonder whether Curtiz has been excluded from the canon precisely because *Casablanca* achieved its cult status through the public, rather than the critics, whereas *Vertigo* (1958) or *The Searchers* (1956) were made into cult films by the *Cahiers* team themselves. Was Curtiz really any more of a hack than Hawks or Alfred Hitchcock or John Ford, all of whom worked within the system for most of their lives, just like Curtiz? After all Hawks made *Sergeant York* for Warner Bros. in 1941, just one year before Curtiz made *Casablanca*. Wallis secured producer credit for both films. Although it is quite true that Curtiz worked solely for Warners from 1926 through to 1953, perhaps it was because he was happy there!

As for Hawks, Sarris observes that whether you "call it classicism or cliché, the fact remains that for a director whose credentials are so obscure to English-speaking critics, Hawks has retained a surprising degree of control over his assignments, choosing the ones he wanted to do, and working on the scripts of all his films" (Sarris, 1968, 53). But the very same thing could be said of Curtiz. Curtiz's loyalty to Warners suggests that he did indeed obtain "a surprising degree of control" over the films he directed. Nonetheless, although Curtiz held his own in comparison with other Warners directors, it was not until 1935 that his career really took off. In 1933 Alexander Korda's *The Private Life of Henry VIII* and Mamoulian's *Queen Christina*, with Greta Garbo, were huge hits, followed up at MGM the next year by Victor Fleming's *Treasure Island* and Reliance's *The Count of Monte Cristo*. Warners, struggling to compete, now decided to go ahead with a costume drama, a genre that they had previously assumed would be box office suicide. In March 1935, Warners announced that they would be producing *Captain Blood*, based on a Rafael Sabatini novel whose rights they already owned, and that Curtiz would direct.

Feeling that the climate had changed, as evidenced by the success of costume dramas made by other studios, Warners was now willing to risk a budget of $750,000, later reduced to $700,000. Casting differences between Jack Warner, Wallis, and probably Curtiz were finally resolved in April and production went ahead. Curtiz was determined, in James Robertson's words, "to stamp his personality all over it, evading most of Wallis's efforts at close supervision, as the film fell well behind schedule, particularly when Curtiz was filming the battle sequences."[7] Curtiz even interviewed every one of 2,500 applicants looking for work as extras. Toward the end of October, after two months shooting, Wallis closed the unit down. By this time, Curtiz had increased the cost of the picture to just short of one million dollars. He had also made both Errol Flynn and Olivia De Havilland into major stars, concentrating on Flynn's exuberance and athleticism and making sure he did justice, in his close-ups, to De Havilland's charm and vivacity. The film was an enormous success and Curtiz became the studio's leading director, just as Flynn became its leading star.

In 1936, the follow-up, *The Charge of the Light Brigade*, starring Flynn and De Haviland again, reinforced Curtiz's position as the studio's top director, making even more money than its predecessor. In 1937 the studio selected Curtiz to direct its first Technicolor showpiece, *Gold is Where You Find It.* The film was not a massive triumph, but it was enough of a success for Jack Warner to substitute Curtiz for William Keighley as director of *The Adventures of Robin Hood*, another swash-buckler, also in Technicolor, and a film that cost the studio over two million dollars, but made its costs back together with a handsome profit, becoming the studio's top moneymaker for the year. By now, Curtiz was plainly in a very powerful position within the Warners studio. In 1938 *Angels With Dirty Faces* became the most profitable James Cagney vehicle yet. Curtiz was nominated for an Oscar and had clearly achieved a status far beyond that of the studio's other directors, not only in artistic terms, but in financial ones too.

It is simply mistaken to believe that Curtiz was no more than a studio hack without authority over the films he made. It may be, of course, that tastes have changed, and westerns or gangster films, such as those of Ford or Hawks or Huston, are acceptable to the critics whereas swashbucklers are not, but if so, it would simply be a matter of opinion, casting very little light on Curtiz's role at a time when historical romances were extremely successful both with critics and at the box office. There has long been a tendency to consider auteurs almost as if they were a subset of genre, as defined by subject matter or studio. Thus the Ford western exists alongside the cavalry western, the Sergio Leone western alongside the bounty-hunter western, the Budd Boetticher western alongside the Ranown western. This phenomenon is particularly significant because the first major critique of auteur theory came precisely from the point of view of genre theory. This was André Bazin's essay, "On the Politique des Auteurs," published in *Cahiers du Cinéma* in April 1957, where Bazin takes issue with the auteurism of his younger colleagues, imposed during the previous three years. Of course, this debate is particularly relevant to the specific question as to whether Curtiz is best seen as an auteur or as a genre specialist.

Bazin deploys a number of arguments, but ends up with what he regards as his "most serious" complaint against auteurism, its refusal to recognize the role played by what we would now call "popular culture" and, in particular, genre. Genre, Bazin argued, citing the American comedy, the western, and the gangster film, develops "in wonderfully close harmony with its public," which is precisely what gives genre films their "vigour and richness." Bazin complains that an Anthony Mann western could be reviewed in the *Cahiers* without any concern about genre, which has its own implications for "a whole collection of conventions in the script, the acting and the direction."[8] He goes on to ask, "Well, what is *Stagecoach* if not an ultra-classical Western in which the art of Ford consists simply of raising characters and situations to an absolute degree of perfection" (257). In similar terms, of course, we might argue that Curtiz achieved for the historical romance what Ford achieved for the western, raising it to its highest possible level through his skills as a director, responsible for performance, camera work, design, and the tempo of cutting, albeit in collaboration with a group of extremely talented technical specialists—actors and actresses, cinematographers, editors, and so on.

Bazin argues that it was the centrality of genre that enabled directors in Hollywood to make their masterpieces, insofar as they did, and that it was genre, precisely because of its relationship with and reflection of the audience, that reveals "the genius of the system," which is more admirable than the "talent of this or that director" (258). In effect, Bazin saw Hollywood as an institution in which social myths and popular tastes produced works that might just as well be anonymous, like African masks or ancient Greek sculptures. If we want to identify auteurs, that is quite acceptable, but the genius of classical Hollywood cinema stemmed from its relationship with popular culture rather than the opportunities that it gave for personal self-expression, which were scant compared with literature or painting. We might say that popular culture, by definition, is repetitive, and the skill of the popular artist consists of fulfilling predictable expectations while introducing a renovatory degree of variation. By this definition, the auteur might almost be seen as the quintessential genre artist, accepting conventions and stereotypes while pursuing his or her personal predilections within the permissible constraints.

Bazin was suggesting, I think, that if the genre constraints were overlooked or brushed aside, the result would be a flawed film, whereas for the younger *Cahiers* critics, it would be an auteurist masterpiece. On the one hand, Bazin preferred *Citizen Kane* (1941), which, he agreed, had more of the studio, less of Orson Welles in it, rather than *Mr. Arkadin* (1955), which Eric Rohmer and others praised to the skies, precisely because it was all Welles. On the other hand, Bazin complained, when an auteur made a straight genre film, all the credit went to the auteur and not to the vigor and fertility of the genre. In the case of Curtiz, his reinvigoration of a genre brought him no credit as an auteur at all. The first problem with Bazin's argument, I would argue, is that Curtiz's most acclaimed film, *Casablanca*, is very hard to fit into a conventional genre schema. It seems to be a hybrid, combining the war propaganda film, the political melodrama, the romantic story of doomed love, the man-on-the-run film, and the wisecracking light comedy. Similarly *Mildred Pierce* (1945) was both a woman's film (now called melodrama) and a noir. *Yankee Doodle Dandy* (1942) was a war propaganda film, as was *Casablanca*, but also a musical co[mp...] a biopic. Robert Ray, in his discussion of *Casablanca*, even a[rg...] the film is a "displaced Western," comparable, for instance, w[ith] *Darling Clementine* (1946) or *Shane* (1953).[9]

In this context, it is significant to note that beside the five c[o...] romances or swashbucklers he made with Flynn and De Havilland

[*Captain Blood, The Charge of the Light Brigade* (1936), *Robin Hood, The Sea Hawk* (1940), *Elizabeth and Essex* (1939)] Curtiz also made three westerns [*Dodge City* (1939), *Virginia City* (1940), and nominally a western, *Santa Fe Trail* (1940)]. Of course, if Curtiz was basically a specialist in a single genre—the historical romance—it becomes tempting to see Humphrey Bogart in *Casablanca* as a kind of displaced swashbuckler, whose Flynn-like idealism is masked by a much higher degree of cynicism—i.e., he is an ambivalent, noirish Flynn, just as Doc Holliday in Ford's *My Darling Clementine* inflects that particular film toward a noir–western combination. This, in turn, could no doubt lead to an interesting discussion of the similarities and differences between the swashbuckler and the western: similarities in relation to heroism and energy and combativeness but differences in terms of history, geography, and style.

In *Casablanca*, Bogart's most decisive action is a nod. His most dramatic moment is one of abandonment and loss. Just like Jean Gabin in *Pépé Le Moko* (1937), Bogart misses the plane, loses the girl, is all washed up—but unlike Gabin, as Bazin notes, he is not meant to die, just to be stoical. Bogart was naturally noir, Bazin claimed, noir in himself rather than an actor performing noir roles, so that he has noir characteristics even when the film is not strictly noir itself. Ingrid Bergman, however, played a part that could easily be performed as noir—treacherous, cruel, gun-in-hand—but was acted in quite the opposite way by Bergman, who radiated sincerity, romantic love, good health, natural innocence, and so on. Ilse's "bad" qualities are concealed beneath the good, perhaps never fully revealed, only to be discerned when the viewer starts to think about the character and the implications of her role. The romance, the center of the film, is played criss-cross, with Rick hiding altruism behind a rough egotistic exterior, and Ilse, conversely, hiding egotism and narcissism beneath a sweet, submissive exterior. This is worth mentioning because the most interesting auteurist analysis of Curtiz I have read, in a communication from Jonathan Kuntz, stresses pretence and posing as key elements in Curtiz's oeuvre.

According to Kuntz and others, Curtiz's characters are riven by conflicts tearing them apart. Kuntz suggests a subtle reading of the idealism–cynicism double. On the one hand, the character needs "to pretend to be uncaring and unemotional" and, on the other, feels "the desire for true action to right an unjust world."[10] The characters try to appear uncaring, to be all business, to "stick their neck out for nobody," but their pose cannot be preserved. In the last scene of the typical Curtiz film, the hero (or heroine) drops his (her) pose at the price of presenting the moment of sacrifice as itself a pretence. That is to say, the characters "give up their social pose for a greater good, yet achieving this through a further, virtually Cukorian performance: 'Rocky Dies Yellow' in *Angels With Dirty Faces* [where tough-guy Rocky, played by Cagney, fakes cowardice as he goes to the chair so that he won't become a role model for the city's youth], Bogie at the airport, Mildred's phony murder confession. The electric chair, the walk into the fog, Crawford's facial expression, all acts that take the character to a new and unexpected level" (Kuntz). They perform an alternative self at the end of each story, each film.

Rocky puts on an act, faking it to appear cowardly, the very opposite of his true hard-boiled nature, ending his life with an act of self-sacrifice, whereas Rick acts the hero and the idealist, hiding his true feelings of loss and betrayal, concealing the world-weary cynicism he has previously shown. More surprisingly perhaps, even Flynn, in *The Charge of the Light Brigade*, deceitfully acts the part of hero—his heroic death is accepted as the result of his obeying battle orders, doing his duty, whereas in reality he has had the orders faked, after learning that De Havilland's character is really in love with his brother. The faked orders are destroyed, to preserve the illusion, by the only person who knows the truth. All three of these films, I should add, have different screenwriters. Should these endings be read as auteurist interventions by Curtiz? Probably not, but it seems quite possible that the director, seeing the potential of these moments, took special trouble to cash them at their maximum dramatic value.

Yet, these moments also seem to reflect the manic-depressive aspect of Curtiz's own character. On the set, as everyone stresses, he was manic, working as fast as possible, on one occasion finishing one-tenth of a feature film in just one day. Curtiz made more films than anyone else in Hollywood; 45 in his native Hungary, between 1912 and 1919, 15 in neighboring Austria between 1919 and 1925, 2 in Berlin in 1926, and then no less than 102 in Hollywood between 1926 and 1961, 87 of them before he left Warners and became an independent in early 1954. That is to say, nearly four a year over his entire career, nearly three a year in the United States, over three a year for Warners. Curtiz made an incredible number of films, even by Hollywood standards. His main fault, Wallis complained, was building up scenes by demanding more and more extras and additional sets—a form of manic activity that, paradoxically, sometimes counteracted his hectic work tempo, the ceaseless demands he made both of himself and his crew, constantly driving them to greater efforts. Looking at his films, the observant viewer must be struck by the way in which he keeps his camera constantly moving. If one word sums up Curtiz's work practice, it would probably be "energy," followed by "obsessive attention to detail."

Of all his films, Curtiz himself was happiest with *Yankee Doodle Dandy*, featuring one of Cagney's most manic performances, though not without its moments of depression. My own view is that *Mildred Pierce* is probably his best film, itself a portrait of a manic-depressive personality, as Mildred claws her way to the top through ceaseless hard work, while at the same time seeming incapable of enjoyment and rushing toward her own destruction, first unconsciously, then consciously.

Perhaps we can map this manic-depressive personality trait onto its idealist-cynical counterpart, which almost all Curtiz critics note: intuitively there seems to be an analogy between the two. The Flynn swashbucklers tend to set a manically active and idealist hero against a grimly depressing background: slavery, cruelty, slaughter. In *Casablanca*, however, the film looks like the classic portrait of a depressive. Rick hardly smiles, except stoically, from beginning to end. Victor Laszlo (Paul Henreid) could not understand how such a "crybaby" could be the hero. Bogart is at the other end of the emotional scale from Flynn (or from Cagney).

As Raymond Borde notes, there is something masochistic about Bogart: he wallows in suffering.[11] The film, of course, glosses over this with all the manic zip the Epstein brothers could bring to the script and all the manic energy Curtiz could bring to camerawork and editing—Curtiz was renowned for short takes that demanded rapid cutting. At the same time, Curtiz's heroes seem to adopt a pose, to be performers. Perhaps we should remember, as Kuntz reminds us, the psychoanalytic truism that manic activity is a cover, a defense against depression, against an inability to cope with separation and loss. The grim moments that Flynn or Cagney face are brushed aside in ceaseless activity, right up to the moment of death. In *Casablanca*, Bogart chooses loss and separation for a second time under the guise of being "noble." *Casablanca* is sometimes seen as an existentialist film and, indeed, it was made at the very time that Sartre was finishing *Being and Nothingness*, a book that stressed the need for authenticity and freedom during the German occupation of France. Publicly, Rick chooses freedom and commitment, but privately he chooses to accept fate, to retreat into a romantic acceptance of lost love, to be abandoned once again, to continue in mourning and melancholia.

Auteur theory necessarily poses a number of theoretical questions, stemming from issues concerning authorship, narration, and semiotic structure. Going back over thirty years now, I have to acknowledge my own share of responsibility for the first effort to theorize auteur theory, in an essay published in *Signs and Meaning in the Cinema*, written in 1968.[12] There I was already arguing for the auteur as an "effect of the text" when I talked about the critic "constructing" the auteurist film-text "a posteriori" as a Lévi-Straussian matrixes of differences and oppositions (78). Not until three years later, in the expanded second edition of the book, did I start talking carefully about "Hawks" and "Hitchcock" as textual structures that could be assigned *post factum* to the actually existing film directors, the walking, talking, living people in the studio, Hawks and Hitchcock (without quotes).[13] In this view, the critic delineated a coherent textual structure and simply assigns it to the concrete individual who, on empirical grounds, could be identified as the best available source of that coherence. The individual him—or herself—however, was not necessarily aware of this same structure. Auteurs were somehow like dreamers, films were like dreams, critics were like analysts. The object of analysis, however, was actually present in the film text.

In 1968, Roland Barthes published his now famous essay, "The Death of the Author," in an obscure journal called *Manteia*, a yellowing copy of which I may still have in some box or closet.[14] Looking back at this short squib-like essay, I realize that although written in Barthes's most provocative style (shades of Truffaut), it is not quite as earthshaking as I had remembered. Barthes asserts that the coherence of a text always comes from the reader, is always a posteriori, whereas the text is always multiple, plural, and hence incoherent, offering numerous different possible meanings. The author, it follows, cannot be located as the single prime source of the text's coherence. Barthes's title, however, was soon taken up as a critical slogan, with the implication that authorship, if it existed at all, was exclusively inherent in the text itself, as one of its rhetorical figures, or as an "author-function," in Foucault's phrase.[15] In this context, it seemed weirdly missing the point to specify a singular film auteur when the great majority of films were so obviously the product of collaborative work, a mish-mash of multiple private intentions.

Jack Stillinger, writer of *Multiple Authorship and the Myth of the Solitary Genius*, was quite correct when he argues that writing is always multiple—besides the denominated author there was always a preexisting source or series of sources, acknowledged or unacknowledged collaborators, publishers, agents, editors, censors, adaptors, revisers, influences, conscious or unconscious borrowings, and other generators of intertextuality.[16] Yet, although no such thing as a unique singularity of authorship exists, this does not imply that the very concept of authorship is consequently dubious or uncertain. It is simply much more complicated than we tend to assume. Stillinger's book actually has an entire section on film in which he considers both *Yankee Doodle Dandy* and *Casablanca*. He singles out these two Curtiz films as evidence for his dictum that "as a rule, the authorship of films is so complicated and diffuse as to be, for all practical purposes, unassignable" (174). In the cinema, he argues, because of its industrial character and work practices, authorship is much more dispersed than it is in literature, and so, rather than being a necessary but complex concept, "authorship" becomes a hopelessly vague term.

Stillinger also discusses the much stronger claim made in relation to Welles, using Robert Carringer's *The Making of Citizen Kane* to argue that Welles was not "the sole author" of *Kane* (179). He assigns Welles a much greater role than Kael has claimed, but much less than was suggested by Peter Bogdanovich, a follower of Sarris. Stillinger tries to assess authorship by looking at what happened in the studio and on the set rather than looking for patterns of repetition and variation within the corpus of a director's films. He rightly notes that film authorship is linked to issues of control—many recognized auteurs were writer-directors or writer-producers or are in a position to get their own way, as Curtiz was, because of their prestige, obstinacy, negotiating skills, or capacity for intimidation. Stillinger is right, however, to link film authorship to issues of control—many recognized directors are writer-directors or producer-directors or are in a position to have their own way. They succeed not just because of their pivotal position in the production process, but because they fight, as Curtiz did, to exercise control over script changes, casting decisions, set design, editing, and even camera positions and shots.

In his essay, "The Noble Cynic: Michael Curtiz," Paul Leggett proposes twelve films as the core Curtiz corpus.[17] Eight of these are Flynn films, historical romances of one kind or another, included together with *Casablanca* and *Mildred Pierce*. This suggests, of course, that Curtiz should be counted as an auteur alongside Ford or Hitchcock, each of whom specialized in one particular genre—western, suspense thriller—although not exclusively. Once again, it seems auteur claims become mixed up with genre analysis. Hawks, after all, achieved auteur status as a master of many genres, all of which have a Hawksian twist. Sarris put it succinctly: "Hawks has stamped his distinctively bitter view of life on adventure, gangster and private eye melodramas, Westerns, musicals, and screwball comedies . . . that one can discern the same directorial signature over a wide variety of genres is proof of artistry. That one can still enjoy the genres for their own sake is proof of the artist's professional urge to entertain" (Sarris, 1968, 56). So, if Hawks, why not Curtiz, pigeon-holed as "lightly likable" rather than one of the exalted "pantheon directors"?

One of Hawks's advantages, Sarris points out, was that he worked on his own scripts, together with cronies such as William Faulkner and Jules Furthman. According to Robertson, Curtiz knew that he possessed serious deficiencies as a writer (139). However, he always studied the scripts, well before production started if circumstances allowed, and engaged on personal research into their subject matter when appropriate. In 1947 he observed that few if any of his scripts at Warners had been perfect and that much depended on his treatment of the story in production. Curtiz never treated any script as sacrosanct and almost always altered scripts on the set as well as receiving and acting on advice from his wife, the former screenwriter Bess Meredyth. A number of studio producers were openly supportive of Curtiz and, as Robertson puts it, "so long as Curtiz's films fared well at the box office, the studio overlooked his idiosyncrasies, and in consequence it is often difficult to know within individual films whether he was subordinate to the studio or the system to him" (Robertson, 139). Frequently it was the latter—Wallis was often exasperated by Curtiz's shooting of unauthorized material. As for editing, Curtiz tartly observed that "a right director cuts on the set, instead of in the cutting room. His individuality should be on the film, not the individuality of a cutter" (139).

When he made *Casablanca,* the best documented of his films, Curtiz was certainly much more than a "hack" with no control over the script. Early versions of the screenplay were submitted to Wallis who then made notes and suggested changes before sending the script to Curtiz for further comment. A memo from Wallis to Curtiz, March 30, 1942, read: "Attached is my copy of the CASABLANCA script with notes. I have edited this carefully and have eliminated about 10 pages, and made other changes. I wish you would go over this in detail with the Epsteins this morning, the three of you can tell me with which of my notes you agree. . . . At the same time, you can discuss with them the next portion of the story so that when we get together this afternoon after lunch, we can proceed" (cited in Harmetz, 45). Clearly this was not a director who was left out of the loop. In fact, the Epsteins' script was changed a great deal, as a result of comments not only from Wallis and Curtiz but from other writers, such as Howard Koch, Casey Robinson, and Lenore Coffee, who all worked on the script even after production had started. The evidence refutes the often-made claim that Curtiz was uninvolved. After all, he had worked with the Epsteins on five of his previous films. Moreover, Meredyth was an old friend of Wallis's wife, Louise Fazenda. We know that Curtiz often telephoned Meredyth from the set. Julius Epstein observes that "When we had a story conference, and Mike came in the next day and made criticisms or suggestions, we knew they were Bess Meredyth's ideas and not his. So it was easy to trip him up. We'd make a change and say, 'What do you think, Mike?' and he'd have to go back to Bess" (Robertson, 123). It was with Meredyth's assistance that Curtiz had become Warner's most consistent moneymaker.

Curtiz's own strengths, of course, were as a director. He had enormous experience, he was completely dedicated to his art, he was a perfectionist on the set, he was inventive, and he was open to advice from those he trusted. Nonetheless, some crucial questions still have to be answered before Curtiz's claim to auteur status is finally decided. However, these are not questions about Curtiz and his role as director on the set, about which we know a great deal, nor, primarily, are they questions about aesthetic judgment and evaluation, important though these are. The fundamental questions that we need to pose are questions about the "auteur theory" as such. What kind of "theory" is it? At the most basic level, these questions involve the following: What is the source of this film? Who is sending this message to us? Who is telling us this story?—and, most crucial of all, Where does the meaning of this film come from? From its makers? From its status as language? From its viewers? These kind of questions were not seen as immediately relevant during the stage when auteur theory was effectively developed as a polemic weapon, devised for use in a struggle to change French cinema. Only much later was there any serious attempt to give auteur theory a genuinely theoretical foundation, form, and status. My own auteurist reappraisals of the sixties, writing as "Lee Russell," were largely dependent both on my reading of *Cahiers du Cinéma* and on the availability of films in retrospectives at both the Rue d'Ulm in Paris and the National Film Theatre in London. Later the Edinburgh Film Festival played a similar role in promoting, for instance, through a retrospective, the critical boom in the films of Douglas Sirk, a new auteur, which later broadened out, in conjunction with feminist film study, into a boom in melodrama as a genre—a genre in which Curtiz's *Mildred Pierce* played a central role.

It is important to recognize the role played by film buffs and cultists in the construction of auteur theory. In fact, many important critics have emerged from the ranks of cultists—the *Cahiers* critics were nurtured in the cine-clubs of the Left Bank, which they attended in virtual gangs. In America, Sarris even published a book called *Confessions of a Cultist: On the Cinema, 1955–1969*,[18] and, in constructing his Pantheon, drew on the taste of a cultist *sang pur*, Eugene Archer. Cultists play an apparently disproportionate role precisely because they care deeply (obsessively) about the films they love and constitute them spontaneously into a kind of "cult canon." Sometimes the line is hard to draw: are *The Wizard of Oz* (1939) and *Casablanca* cult classics or mainstream masterpieces? And are *Now Voyager* (1942) and *Mildred Pierce* feminist "cult films" or counterparts and rivals to the auteurist "classics," *Red River* (1948) and *The Searchers*? Cultists, of course, are also idiosyncratic in many judgments, often disagreeing violently with each other, as demonstrated by the gulf between the *Cahiers* critics' praise of Hawks and *The Big Sleep* and their contemptuous dismissal of Curtiz and *Casablanca*. However, why didn't the rediscovery of *Mildred Pierce* prompt a new interest in Curtiz and his elevation to auteur status?

The process of cultural negotiation among so many gatekeepers of taste results not only in the surface phenomena of lists and polemics, but also in the crystallization of an aesthetic paradigm at a deeper level. It is the task of theorists and historians to codify evaluative shifts in terms of aesthetic theory and historical periodization. Thus, when we look at the history of film we can see three contending phases of aesthetic theory-making: first, the "Seventh Art" theories, which grew up around silent cinema and stressed *photogénie*, montage, or filmic pantomime. These, in turn, were locked into certain exemplary auteurs: D. W. Griffith, Sergei Eisenstein, and Charlie Chaplin. Silent film theory fought a long rearguard action through the 1930s and was not really challenged until Bazin launched his countertheory on the basis of Jean Renoir, Orson Welles, William Wyler, and Roberto Rossellini. Bazin, however, was rapidly overtaken by his own heirs—the *Cahiers* group—who updated his preferences in favor of late films [*The River* (1948), *Arkadin*, *Viaggio in Italia* (1953)] and pivoted their own canon around "Hitchcocko-Hawksianism."

Casablanca, I might add, has much in common with *Rules of the Game* (1939). Both films mix social comment, romantic melodrama, and wild farce. Both films also feature Marcel Dalio, although in two rather different roles. Yet, one of these films is generally regarded as a masterpiece and the other as merely a cult film. Similarly, Renoir is regarded as an auteur and Curtiz merely as a cult favorite. Why is this? Partly, I have no doubt, it depends on the overall reputation of the two directors concerned—Renoir the auteur, Curtiz the hack—but other issues are involved too, issues that ought to provoke a reformulation of debate about the auteur theory, both in relation to the process of canon formation and to the Kantian question of aesthetic judgment. Genre studies also play an important part in the critical process, as one genre comes to be favored over another, a complex process that can suddenly foreground a film like *Mildred Pierce*, as the woman-centered melo-drama gains ground, while relegating Curtiz's swashbuckling romances as outdated and irrelevant. In this context, I would like to pay further attention to the whole issue of genre and, in particular, their associa-tion not only with Curtiz but also with Flynn and De Havilland—although Bette Davis should not be forgotten, despite her much more troubled relationship with the director.

Between 1935 and 1942 Curtiz directed five swashbuckling romances with Flynn, three of them with De Havilland, one with Davis dominat-ing De Havilland, whom she gets to call a "shameless hedge drab," and one with Brenda Marshall, after De Havilland had turned down the part, following her success in *Gone With The Wind* (1939). De Havilland had also appeared with Flynn in *Gold Is Where You Find It, Four's A Crowd* (both 1938), and *Santa Fe Trail*. Part of Curtiz's problem, it seems to me, stems not so much from his concentration on just one genre during this period, as from the continuity of the casting and, indeed, the status of his two leading stars, Flynn and De Havilland. In contrast, Davis made a film with Curtiz every year from 1932 through 1939, except for 1936; increasingly dissatisfied, she made her last film for Warner Bros. in 1943. The Davis films, however, never had the same kind of success as the De Havilland films, except for *Elizabeth and Essex*—a romantic swashbuck-ler, starring, of course, Flynn, but Davis became not simply a bigger star than De Havilland, but a much more admired and respected actress, with a much stronger artistic reputation.

Curtiz, however, was unable to benefit on his own account from Davis's success because the films that he made with her were, for the most part, considered to be minor works. In the end, Curtiz's reputa-tion depended entirely on his own achievements, rather than upon the genre or the casting, both of which were basically studio decisions—although I suspect Curtiz had a lot to do with the appearance of so many European actors and actresses in *Casablanca*. The art of the cin-ema, Sarris has written, "is not so much *what* as *how*. The *what* is some aspect of reality rendered mechanically by the camera. The *how* is what the French critics designate somewhat mystically as *mise-en-scène*" (Sarris, 1968, 36). That is to say, "auteur criticism is a reaction against sociological criticism that enthroned the how against the what. The whole point of a meaningful style is that it unifies the what and the how into a personal statement." On this basis, I would suggest there is no problem in proposing that Curtiz was an auteur. Of course, the *what* in his work varied from film to film, genre to genre, and, consequently, so did the *how*, as each genre required its very own appropriate style. Thus *The Mystery of the Wax Museum* (1939, the subject of a brilliant essay by Raymond Bellour)[19] demanded a very different stylistic treatment from *Cabin in The Cotton* (1932, the film that made Bette Davis a star). Similarly, *The Adventures of Robin Hood, Yankee Doodle Dandy, Casablanca,* and *Mildred Pierce* all required quite different stylistic treatments, ranging from action spectacle to noir.

The case for Curtiz as an auteur rests on his incredible ability to find the right style for the right picture. If he shows a thematic consistency across several genres, it is in his consistent preference for stressing the struggles of the rebel and the downtrodden against the entrenched and powerful. This theme is found throughout the series of swashbuckling romances—*Cabin in The Cotton*, a film about the exploitation and revolt of workers in the cotton plantations; *Black Fury* (1935), the saga of a miners' uprising against the coal companies; *Captain Blood*, the story of an Englishman sold into slavery and leading a slave revolt; *The Adventures of Robin Hood*, the story of an outlaw pitted against the king and the forces of order; *Angels With Dirty Faces*, the story of a hoodlum who redeems himself by his conduct in the death chamber; *Sons of Liberty* (1939), which dramatizes the Jewish contribution to American independence; the antifascist *Sea Hawk* and *Yankee Doodle Dandy*; *Casablanca*, of course, with its clear anti-Vichy and pro-resistance message; *Mission to Moscow* (1942), another explicitly anti-Nazi film; *Passage to Marseille* (1944), about escaped criminals who join the Free French; *Mildred Pierce*, the story of a single mother repeatedly betrayed by men, struggling to rise from a job as a waitress to running her own business; *Young Man With A Horn* (1950), the story of a jazz musician's comeback after a slump into alcoholism and depression, based upon the life of Bix Beiderbecke.

Although these films all favor the underdog and frequently portray resistance against cruel or corrupt authority, they nonetheless cover a wide variety of different genres, all of them with a single constant theme, the story of an underdog who refuses to be beaten down and throws in his or her lot with the struggle against corrupt and oppressive authority. In part, this trend reflects the stance taken by Warners during the New Deal period and, of course, the war years. But I think it is clear that it also reflects Curtiz's own instinctive sympathy with underdogs who resist the power of authority in a number of different forms, ranging from mine and plantation owners to feudal lords and contemporary fascists. It is not clear exactly what Curtiz's own politics were—although in Hungary, in his youth, he appears to have worked

Image from *The Sea Hawk*

with the revolutionary Bela Kun regime and he clearly supported both Franklin Delano Roosevelt, lovingly portrayed in *Yankee Doodle Dandy*, and the socially progressive concept of the New Deal.

In his introduction to his ranking of directors in "The American Cinema," published in *Film Culture* in 1963, Sarris begins by noting that

> the need for a systematic reappraisal of the American cinema, director by director and film by film, has become more pressing in recent years. The standard historical texts, outdated, outworn, or both, are no longer adequate references for specialists in the careers of individual directors. If Howard Hawks had been left to the tender mercies of the official historians, most of his films would still be moldering in the vaults. However, one coup does not constitute a successful revolution in taste. The resurrection of Hawks, like that of Lazarus, is still more the exception than the rule. The excavations and revaluations must continue until the last worthy director has been rescued from anonymity.[20]

It is exactly in this spirit that I would like to resurrect Michael Curtiz, to reevaluate his career, to look more closely at his relationship with Warners, with the swashbuckler, with his stars, and with *Casablanca*.

Curtiz was more—much more—than a studio workhorse. He was a director of enormous experience and drive, determined to get his own way in the face of studio pressure—often succeeding, often failing. Curtiz was, however a director who rose to the occasion, who could wring unexpected meanings from a script through his direction of actors

75

and cinematographers and his confident sense of style, in composition, in performance, and in editing. In the introduction to his book, *The American Cinema*, an updated new edition of *Film Culture*, no. 28, published in 1968, Sarris coins the phrase "the doctrine of directorial continuity" to describe the essence of auteurism (Sarris, 1968, 16). Recently I came across yet another piece of evidence relating to Curtiz's continuous insistence on supporting the underdog. In a memo to Curtiz during the filming of *The Sea Hawk*, Wallis noted that "I noticed when the sailors cheer for any reason, that a great many of them use a clenched fist in what is really the Communist salute. This is very noticeable, and I don't understand why you allow the people to do it."[21] I rest my case.

peter wollen

notes

1. Andrew Sarris, *The American Cinema* (New York: E. P. Dutton & Co., 1968), 175.
2. Pauline Kael, *I Lost It At The Movies* (New York: Holt Rinehart, 1982), 81.
3. H. B.Wallis and Charles Higham, *Star-Maker: The Autobiography of Hal Wallis* (New York: Macmillan Publishing Co., 1980), 25.
4. Quoted in Aljean Harmetz, *Round Up The Usual Suspects: The Making of Casablanca, Bogart, Bergman, and World War Two* (New York: Hyperion Books, 1992), 183.
5. Nick Roddick, *A New Deal In Entertainment* (London: British Film Institute, 1983), 133.
6. Antoine de Baecque and Serge Toubiana, *Truffaut* (Paris: Editions Gallimard, 1996), 452 [author's translation].
7. James C. Robertson, *The Casablanca Man* (London: Routledge, 1993), 34.
8. André Bazin, "On the politique des auteurs" [1957], trans. Peter Graham, in *Cahiers du Cinéma: The 1950s: Neo-Realism, Hollywood, New Wave*, ed. Jim Hillier (Cambridge, MA: Harvard University Press, 1985), 248–59, 257.
9. Robert Ray, *A Certain Tendency of the Hollywood Cinema* (Princeton, NJ: Princeton University Press, 1985), 65.
10. Personal communication with Jonathan Kuntz.
11. Raymond Borde et Etienne Chaumeton; *Panorama du Film Noir Américain, 1941–1953* [1955] (Paris: Flammariòn, 1988).
12. Peter Wollen, *Signs and Meaning in the Cinema* (Bloomington: Indiana University Press, 1969).
13. Peter Wollen, *Signs and Meaning in the Cinema*, 3rd ed., rev. and enl. (Bloomington: Indiana University Press, 1972), 168.
14. Roland Barthes, "La Mort de l'auteur," *Mantéia* 5 (1968): 12–16.
15. Michel Foucault, "What Is an Author?" [1975], *Foucault Reader*, ed. Paul Rabinow, trans. Josué V. Havari (New York: Pantheon Books, 1984), 105.
16. Jack Stillinger, *Multiple Authorship and The Myth Of The Solitary Genius* (Oxford: Oxford University Press, 1991), 163–81.
17. Paul Leggett, "The Noble Cynic: Michael Curtiz," *Focus on Film* no. 23 (Winter 1975): 15.
18. Andrew Sarris, *Confessions of a Cultist: On the Cinema, 1955–1969* (New York: Simon & Schuster, 1970).
19. Raymond Bellour, *Le Cinéma Américain: Analyses de films*, Symboliques 2 (Paris: Flammariòn, 1980), 184–93.
20. Andrew Sarris, "The American Cinema," *Film Culture*, no. 28 (Spring 1963), 1–51.
21. Rudy Behlmer, ed., *The Sea Hawk* (Madison: University of Wisconsin Press, 1982), 34.

i hear music and . . .

four

darryl and irving

write history with

alexander's ragtime

band[1]

george f. custen

If you could find the Negro and he had another hit like "Alexander" in his system, I would choke it out of him and give him twenty thousand dollars in the bargain.

—Irving Berlin

Give Alexander credit for every innovation that has been given to bands in the last couple of decades.

—Darryl F. Zanuck

Irving Berlin, of Tin Pan Alley (and Mohilev, White Russia), first encountered Darryl Zanuck, of Hollywood (and Wahoo, Nebraska),

---

1. It is regretful that the Estate of Irving Berlin refused permission to quote lyrics from "You're Just In Love," which I intended to use in the title of this essay. I chose the lyrics because they identified the central theme of this piece: the production of music within the absence—or elimination—of an identifiable author of that music. For the full lyrics that would have appeared in the title, the reader is referred to *The Complete Lyrics of Irving Berlin*, ed. Robert Kimball and Linda Emmett (New York: Alfred A. Knopf, 2001), 452.

when Zanuck, as producer of *The Jazz Singer* (1927), substituted Berlin's "Blue Skies" for the number Al Jolson had previously recorded, "It All Depends On You."[1] It is unlikely that Zanuck knew his last-minute change continued a tale inaugurated with Florenz Ziegfeld's musical, *Betsy*, the previous December. The story goes that hours before the show was to open, its star Belle Baker was worried that with words and music by relative newcomers Richard Rodgers and Larry Hart, *Betsy* didn't have "a Belle Baker song." Could her friend Irving help out? Perhaps. The opening night audience greeted Berlin's hurriedly scribbled reply with a demand for twenty-three encores, never dreaming that Berlin had written "Blue Skies" only twelve hours before. When a dazzled and disoriented Baker momentarily forgot some of the lyrics, Berlin "shot to his feet" from his first row perch and performed the twenty-fourth (and last) encore before "the enraptured crowd."[2] Curtain.

This Runyonesque tale of Broadway—triumph and rescue-at-the-last-minute—reminds us that at times film history tends to be theatrical. But even if Zanuck didn't know the "Blue Skies" story, he shared a belief many Americans held since the time of the composition of "Alexander's Ragtime Band": when you wanted to say something with music (and you needed a surefire hit) you turned to Irving Berlin. The question of whether the "Blue Skies" story is a fable or an accurate report of events is unimportant; what matters is how the legend of Berlin has been constructed—by both himself and others, such as Zanuck. This analysis, which lets us have a glimpse backstage at a different kind of performance, in fact, is what we need to gauge better the part Berlin played in one particular area: the struggles over the attribution of authorship for ragtime and other popular musical forms. Those who wish to study authorship would find a large number of films that might be useful as a point of entry into one or more of these topics that have adhered to film. Indeed, studying individual and what I call "cultural" authorship is profitably realized through an analysis of the history surrounding the production of *Alexander's Ragtime Band* (1938). The making of this film suggests that in addition to cinematic and biographical conventions largely determined by the culture of Hollywood, factors in Berlin's and Zanuck's identities produced variant versions of the story, variants all too obvious when comparing Berlin's and Zanuck's preferences about telling the narrative of the rise of American music. Moreover, because Zanuck held control over the final narrative, *Alexander's Ragtime Band* may display more of Zanuck's hand than Berlin's, even though the story is supposedly that of Berlin's life, and Zanuck had given him the unusual opportunity to write the synopsis for the movie.

On the one hand, Zanuck modeled the film along the lines of Hollywood musical biopics, a genre that he shaped first at Warner Bros. and later Twentieth Century-Fox.[3] In dealing with musicians or entertainers, the biopic explored the nature of creativity as well as the relationships of individuals to those people and institutions that determine the conditions of authorship. For Zanuck, *Alexander's Ragtime Band* would, as a musical biopic, join his previous nonmusical examples in that genre—*Disraeli* (1929), *I Am a Fugitive From a Chain Gang* (1932), *The House of Rothschild* (1934)—in playing a part in his evolving master narrative whose subject was nothing less than the symbolic environment created by the nature and function of American popular entertainment.[4] This purpose—Zanuck's ongoing construction of a supertext across his body of films as whole, a text that interrogated film's role in American popular culture, is a significant factor that determined what kind of musical history he would let the film tell. On the other hand was Berlin, Zanuck's collaborator on the film—in fact, the reason Zanuck wanted to do this film. As America's most famous popular songwriter whose stature enabled him to secure substantial input into the screenplay as well as the music, Berlin had much at stake in this story.

One of the most basic assumptions in the Western tradition of literature is the lone author's claim of a special relationship to what he or she has created. But another tradition is that of a community, rather than an individual, as being the point of origin of individual works, or, as is more often the case, the site whose conditions enabled the development of a school or genre of music, or performance, or reception style. In such conditions the totality of what is unique to a people or place invests the experience there with a particularly coherent quality such that one can speak of the "culture" as having been the author. These conditions offer a kind of joint or communal author, a situation that is particularly common in music that involves transmission via live or oral performance traditions rather than notation systems, recording, and copyright laws. The cases of blues and jazz and ragtime fit within what I have just described.

Yet Berlin—who was credited with "discovering" ragtime a decade after its appearance in a number of black American communities—not only refused to deny that he was the sole or most important point of origin but, given the chance, would reiterate a claim to authorship. Moreover, black influences were not part of the story he told, although within "Alexander's" lyrics he does indirectly credit Stephen Foster ("And if you care to hear the 'Swanee River' played/ in Ragtime"). In interviews and his proposed history for *Alexander's*, Berlin erased all black presence in a film that he claimed told the true story of the history of American popular music. This raises the issue of Berlin's (and Hollywood's) relations with black artists and black culture, particularly over the issues of the provenance and mainstreaming of music idioms created within black artistic communities, but that most often became popular (and lucrative) only after white-controlled institutions such as Tin Pan Alley and Hollywood vetted them for the larger (read "larger white") audience.

Eventually, Berlin believed that he had to set the record straight, insisting that "Songwriters don't steal. At least those of reputation don't."[5] It is precisely because his provenance to the song "Alexander's Ragtime Band" was useful as a means of securing his reputation and identity that, although Berlin was not guilty of theft, his refusal to share credit with others over ragtime—for which "Alexander's Ragtime Band" stood in—had an impact on black artists almost identical to what would have resulted if Berlin actually had stolen the music. To give him credit, Berlin's stance was an extension of the culture of Tin Pan Alley where it was not at all unusual for a publishing house "to purchase a song outright for a lump sum payment and give the creator no credit, a practice particularly harmful to black songwriters, such as Fats Waller and Andy Razaf" (Furia, 49). Thus, the continuation of this practice of cultural elision in the film *Alexander's Ragtime Band* is a specific instance showing that every new American medium of communications (as well as the forms of popular culture so dependent on them) have long been what historian Carolyn Marvin forcefully asserts, "a series of arenas for negotiating issues crucial to the conduct of social life; among them, who is inside and outside, who may speak, who may not, and who has authority and may be believed."[6] Berlin's synopsis offered him a very large and public forum in which he would assert the historic, almost genetic, originality of his contribution to American music, claims that could only be made at a high cost to others whom his narrative either eliminated or displaced. Moreover, it offered him an opportunity to declare his own "belonging inside": Berlin would transfigure his Russian Jewish immigrant status to become just like all "good" Americans—middle-class and ethnically assimilated.

becoming white through authorship

Berlin's liminal social status—he was a Jew and an immigrant—combined with the controversial place popular music held in American culture in the first two decades of the century made him a target for accusations of plagiarism. Just as Shakespeare had his Marlowe, similar specters haunted Berlin. People wondered, How could anyone produce so prolific and varied a body of work without some kind of unacknowledged assistance? For years, a rumor circulated that "a little colored boy" composed the output attributed to "Irving Berlin" (Bergreen, 69). A particular fanciful variant credited the ambitious Berlin with "a secret Harlem office with an entire staff of ghostwriters" (Furia, 49). Berlin told his accusers that if they could produce the "Negro and he had another hit like 'Alexander' in his system, I would choke it out of him and give him twenty thousand dollars in the bargain" (Bergreen, 69). The rumors and, ironically, Berlin's response, which both focused on allegations of African-American sources for his music, conveyed a clear message: the only people from whom a musically illiterate Jew would steal were of even lower status than he. This was not lost upon Berlin, who, as a result, never stopped insisting that America's greatest composers "are not negroes" but rather were like him, "of Russian birth or ancestry." Most important, "all of them are of pure white blood" (Furia, 49).

Why did Berlin continue to believe this when his own eyes and ears told him it wasn't true? Berlin's posture of defensiveness was not uncommon for successful people with little education who work in fields in which the norm is a great deal of education or special training. In part, anger and pride "prompted his unfortunate denials that ragtime was not the indigenous music of African-Americans" (Furia, 49). Nevertheless an analysis of Berlin's output shows that for all his denials, not only had "Berlin cast his lot with black music," but also that in songs such as "Puttin' On the Ritz" (which suggests that blacks, rather than whites, are the only people able fearlessly to experience the pleasures new music can offer) something else is visible: "his unconscious identification with . . . black musicians" (Bergreen, 56). Berlin acknowledged these links only (and then, often ambivalently) in his lyrics. Buttressed by borrowed musical forms (though Berlin was one of popular music's great innovators) and at times articulating the originality of his work through a number of minstrelized ethnic voices ("That's just the bestest band what am/Honey Lamb"), Berlin's relation to the black sources of his work took the form of the songwriter as the leader of an ethnographic field trip, in which he invited white Americans to tour and to take a gander at an exotic, alien black culture realized through his lyrics and melodies.[7]

In alleging that Jews sided with whites against blacks—as Berlin did by continuing the tradition of making fun of black mores as they related to music and entertainment in his songs—Berlin thereby joined a sad, but familiar dynamic of cultural "elevation" through the displacement of others. As Noel Ignatiev observes a similar transformation by an earlier "lowly" immigrant group (the Irish), Jews soon discovered "To enter the white race was a strategy to secure an advantage in a competitive society."[8] If some academics and critics "were inclined to recognize the contributions of black musicians, Berlin was quite certain that his group deserved to be center stage, not Blacks" (Bergreen, 121). Thus, in discussing the film version of his life, Berlin told Zanuck "We can make this man [Alexander] a combination of Paul Whiteman, George Gershwin, Irving Berlin."[9] On this important point about commercial popular culture the men were in perfect harmony. Because the world of their work was organized so they and not other people had both the authority that comes with power and the legitimacy to claim authorship that comes with control, they knew they could make the character of Alexander, in Berlin's words, "anything that we want" (TCF Brief, 42). Anything, that is, except black.

If the 1911 song "Alexander's Ragtime Band" was the moment when Irving Berlin, American, was born (and Izzy Baline, immigrant, faded away), then twenty-seven years after managing this first all-important breach into the mainstream, the film *Alexander's Ragtime Band* was again offering a way for Berlin to maintain that identity. Berlin knew that beyond the significance this one hit had in securing his status as America's foremost songwriter, whoever held the authorship rights to the tune generally deemed to have signaled the arrival of modernity to American popular music possessed something even more precious: the means by which a racially ambiguous Jewish alien could transform himself into a certified white American. Thus, Berlin wrote a story transforming his own biography into the tale of an identity he deeply desired.

controlling the authorship deal

After a successful Fox debut with *On the Avenue*, people wondered what Zanuck (always interested in playing with genre conventions) had in mind as a follow-up. Zanuck decided that Berlin's next effort would be the first Hollywood film whose score offered a mix of new and old works by a single composer. But *Alexander's* most interesting feature came about because Zanuck suggested that in addition to contributing songs, Berlin would write the short story that would serve as the basis for the film's screenplay. Asking America's preeminent popular songwriter to try his hand at screenwriting was both unusual for the film industry and certainly atypical of Zanuck, for whom control over story and reliance on a staff of seasoned "pro" writers (such as Nunnally Johnson or Lamar Trotti) was everything (Custen, 1997, *passim*).

Zanuck let Berlin write the story because, from the first, *Alexander's Ragtime Band* was meant to be a biopic of the composer. Let other studios hire Berlin for his music alone. Zanuck wanted nothing less than the rights to showcase Berlin's music within a full-scale biography. A Berlin biopic seemed like a brilliant idea, and, along with the lure of his songs, that Berlin was going to create his own story would give the film the imprimatur that justified Zanuck's insistence that all Fox advertising must refer to the film as "Irving Berlin's *Alexander's Ragtime Band*" (Bergreen, 266).

Asking Berlin to write the story served another function: it showed Zanuck's respect for a songwriter whose previous encounters with Hollywood had not always been pleasant. In 1930 United Artists cut all but one of Berlin's twelve songs from *Reaching for the Moon*.[10] Asking Berlin to write the story was Zanuck's way of reassuring the songwriter that this affront would not be repeated at Fox. But the man who liked control of his music also wanted control over any depiction of his life and herein lay a major problem, for even with uninterrupted success, Berlin was pathologically insecure about his standing in the field of popular music.

His peers revered him, echoing composer Jerome Kern's assessment of Berlin's place in American music: "Irving Berlin has no 'place' in

American music. He *IS* American music" (quoted in Furia, 1). Thus, Berlin's insecurity about whether he was perceived as American was compounded by anxiety about his status as a "real" musician or composer. When compared to "rivals" (most notably, his friend George Gershwin), Berlin thought himself to be at a distinct disadvantage. Where Berlin was a self-taught "hunt and peck" pianist who played in one key—F sharp major—Gershwin was, in comparison, something of a piano virtuoso. Where Berlin had studied on the streets of New York and in Bowery saloons such as "Nigger" Mike's Pelham Cafe, Gershwin had absorbed modernism's lessons at the feet of no less a figure than the legendary composer Nadia Boulanger. Like Berlin, Gershwin wrote popular songs. But, unlike Berlin, Gershwin was at home in prestigious high art forms—operas, symphonies, and pieces for large orchestras— that Berlin (save for a few parodies like his 1909 "That Mesmerizing Mendelssohn Song") simply couldn't manage (Bergreen, 304–5). In contrast to his own trio, Zanuck's new partner was a man extremely sensitive to criticism, and so in large part to spare himself from this, Berlin "aggressively opposed . . . nearly all investigative efforts by would-be biographers, critics, and cultural historians."[11] Though he made an exception in 1924 and cooperated with his friend Alexander Woolcott's study, Berlin was adamant that there would be no biopic of his life. It appeared as if the men had reached an impasse, for as Zanuck diplomatically put it, "he [Berlin] did not feel that it would be proper or good taste to present his more or less colorful life on the screen."[12] If *Alexander's Ragtime Band* was ever to see life, it would be in another genre.

But what Zanuck wanted, Zanuck usually got. What could have been a standoff between two self-made, stubborn men was, in the end, gracefully resolved to their mutual satisfaction. As he had done with Jolson's life in *The Jazz Singer*, Zanuck made *Alexander's* a Berlin biography manque that "would be the basis for a tremendous musical" that Zanuck would do "without violating [Berlin's] professional life" (Behlmer, 13). In following this tack, Berlin, Zanuck said, would simply "invent a fictitious story [that would nevertheless] include certain definite incidents from his life" in such a way that viewers would know whose life they were watching anyway (Behlmer, 13). Once at sea, Berlin now found himself on solid ground in the midst of Zanuck's favorite territories: Tin Pan Alley and its culture of vaudeville. And within this terrain, Berlin agreed to write.

authoring america's culture

But if this explains the history of how Berlin became a screenwriter, judgments about what he and Zanuck accomplished in *Alexander's Ragtime Band* remain more problematic. By 1938, the title song by now was a kind of lynchpin whose continued existence made a certain

83

view of cultural history possible. Its establishment as the originary site and moment for both Berlin and American popular music illustrated popular culture's first principle in action: "American" means "white American." The movie's fanciful version of this cultural history is thus itself part of a complicated set of discourses produced and seen in the media, then circulated and debated face to face in various forums. Thus, his breakthrough hit of 1911 becomes more than a musical landmark. It is a floating cultural signifier hovering over America's cultural terrain. If we wish to understand *Alexander's* take on authorship, we need to uncover each man's separate (though not necessarily contradictory) motives, as well as what each thought he could achieve by writing a certain version of musical history.

For Zanuck, *Alexander's* allowed him to play in the musical field as an equal with older studios that had bigger stars while furthering his argument about where film was positioned in some entertainment superculture. For Berlin the film offered a means of not only controlling his public image but also serving as a source of ongoing present publicity. It gave Berlin the means by which he could try and articulate the very particular version of history upon which his posterity would rest. The film's "cavalcade" format would assert his high place in the pantheon of popular composers and define musical history so that Berlin was present at every juncture and change of styles. Thus, Berlin's musical authorship and the history of American music in general would be identical.

In several music conferences in Zanuck's office, Alfred Newman, head of the studio's music department, divided (for narrative purposes) American music into three periods: the Ragtime Period (1911–1917), the War Period (1917–1920), and the Jazz Period (1920–1923). Using this as a kind of loose chronology, Zanuck told writers Lamarr Trotti and Kathryn Scola, "we want to introduce as many varieties of entertainment as we can to put over our songs in a sock fashion. Each time lapse should introduce something new."[13] This chronology had an added benefit for Berlin. The film would prove that his preeminence first announced with "Alexander's," and since that time resecured with over 500 published songs (an astonishingly large number of which were popular hits), had not been usurped by one of the "younger" rivals, Gershwin or Rodgers. By using twenty-four of Berlin's songs (including four eagerly awaited new titles), the film would demonstrate that being well known and well established was not to be confused with being well past your prime or old-fashioned. Berlin's desire in the synopsis was "simply to see whether there is anything to this [musical] angle on the story," and he told Zanuck "I have made no effort to cue any musical spots other than the old songs that are tied up to the story."[14]

Unfortunately, his talent, so prodigious in popular song, did not extend to screenwriting. Berlin's synopsis turned the drama inward, refracting the history of American popular music through his fears and insecurities. Zanuck was so upset by Berlin's work that he scrawled, in pencil, on the story's cover, "When you strip a story like this of all atmosphere, music, color it seems flat and dull. . . .The detail made the drama in the original—this seems a flat narrative—uninspired—have we lost it?"[15] Berlin's approach foregrounded the composer's interests at the expense of Zanuck's first rule: story development. Zanuck wondered, after all, if there might be *too* much Berlin in the film: "Maybe our trouble is that we are trying to tell a phase of American musical evolution instead of a story about two boys and a girl. The story of these three is our main plot: the other, [will function as] the important [musical] background. . . . We don't have to be EPIC in the old sense of the word: the epic quality should come out in ENTERTAIN-MENT."[16] Though disappointed, Zanuck followed his experience (and Hollywood's conventions) on how to picture the ages of man, a template more important to him than the musical events of Berlin's life.

Alexander was thus pledged from the start to live by the boilerplate *quid pro quo* clause found in the contract of all movie achievers. Thus, Berlin's story and the many versions of the screenplay thus all contained notable biographical glosses, substitutions, and startling omissions that departed from the known facts of Berlin's professional and personal life: the Lower East Side and Tenderloin districts of New York where Berlin had his start became San Francisco's colorful Barbary Coast; Berlin, the one-finger piano player, became, in succession, a clarinetist and then a classically trained violinist. Russian Jewish immigrant Izzy Baline was (in both Zanuck's and Berlin's versions) a WASP. Echoing his own ambivalent competition with friend George Gershwin, Berlin named his amanuenses George Stephenson, which Zanuck (perhaps in deference to Gershwin's recent death) promptly rechristened to Roger Stephenson. The biggest change was that Berlin's working-class protagonist was transformed into a socialite so that Zanuck's favorite theme could clearly emerge, the struggle for dominance between high art and popular art as these are fought out in front of American audiences.

Like *The Jazz Singer*, *Alexander's Ragtime Band* thus frames its characters' motivations within the fluidity of each generation's ascendant forms of popular entertainment by suggesting that the "natural" alignment of taste cultures to class are sorted out not by experts in the field but by an infallible panel of judges: the good common sense of the American people such as *Alexander's* love interest, Stella Kirby. In other words, in joining a rather large group of films Zanuck shaped at Warner Bros. and later at Fox, the script shows that American popular entertainment is not only egalitarian and accessible, its popular forms evolved organically from the same principles that comprise American participatory democracy. Here was an argument beloved of many media moguls, and Zanuck's assertion that no institutions were as democratic as the movies were echoed by broadcasting mogul William Paley who claimed, "he who attacks the fundamentals of the American system" of broadcasting aimed their missiles at "democracy itself."[17] Zanuck's master narrative of American entertainment suggested that the American character could be seen through struggles of performers and impresarios to find stories and players who articulated the country's (and the men's) ideas about evolving modes of popular entertainment.

Here, Zanuck embodied it in the tension-filled romance between high born Alexander and earthy saloon singer Stella whose arguments—over musical arrangements and style, over ambition, over wooing the girl—enacted what Zanuck saw as America's most significant cultural struggle: the perpetual wars of the high and low, of the classical versus the popular. Just as vaudeville and the movies would in their own times each claim to be the art of "all" the people, in the nineteenth century the theater "was a microcosm [which] housed both the entire spectrum of the population and the complete range of entertainment."[18] In the end (and continuing the line of this logic), Zanuck links his hero to democratic instincts by having Alexander renounce his aristocratic past and (after some rough sledding) embrace (and be embraced by) popular culture and its citizens. The film's moral is that Alexander can succeed only through this kind of class apostasy. Zanuck's manipulation of *Alexander's* along these lines fits the peculiar American tendency exhibited in our entertainment in which we see "anything even bordering on unpatriotic or aristocratic behavior was anathema" to American audiences (Levine, 60).

Thus, like the rest of America's entertainment ecology, *Alexander's* creates a pentimento of "American" art composed of overlapping fragments that blend (and confuse) material from a number of sources: the "good," the popular, the democratic are all conflated as a foil to the aristocratic and elite. In the age of the fragmented, class-, race-, and gender-divided audiences that were characteristic of entertainment in the age of mechanical reproduction, the linking of the popular to the democratic was the only way some kind of common taste culture was possible.

Zanuck believed that America's surest cultural prophylaxis predated Hollywood. Popular culture was in fact the very thing that the nation had used to set itself apart from the ways of the Old World. Although marriage can resolve this class problem for a feuding couple, Zanuck had to find a way to merge *Alexander's* dissonant musical human analogues into the great middle territory of the inclusionary folds of American democracy. In understanding why this was important beyond the solution it offered to a particular movie plot, film historian Gerald Mast points out, "*Alexander's Ragtime Band* is the first film musical to realize that the history of American popular music is the history of America. Irving Berlin is an historian; to hear his songs is to read that history."[19] Having changed the film's focus—from a plodding history of songwriting to a heterosexual romance uniting disparate classes through popular music—Zanuck turned to casting, and after toying with nonsinger (but certified urbanite) Barbara Stanwyck as Stella, who would be Alexander's (Tyrone Power) romantic foil, Zanuck cast Alice Faye. Highborn Power's elegance and breeding would clash with lowborn Faye's more direct manner. When Zanuck read Berlin's treatment, he immediately believed that Berlin had not factored in all these variables including the actors and audience sympathies, for "[t]he character of Alexander is completely wrong. He is conceited and egotistical—bad mannered, unsympathetic all because of wrong motivation."[20] Zanuck wanted the screenwriters to make certain not to repeat this error. The class conflict between Stella and Alexander (which would extend from their romance to all questions of style, particularly in the music) was the film's main thrust. Making film in a land that claimed to have few social distinctions, Zanuck was very concerned that the tensions arising from those that somehow survived must be drawn just right. As he bluntly told the writers, "We are lost unless the difference in class and viewpoints between Alexander and Stella comes through with great humor and lightness."[21]

The problem at the moment was not lightness, or light, but Power or, rather, Power's beauty. In this film and others [notably in *Nightmare Alley* (1947)] Power's looks added a hint of feminine allure beneath the carapace of his conventional matinee idol masculinity. This combination seemed to encourage writers to create characters largely motivated by their selfishness, and Zanuck found that early on "Alexander was drawn too priggish." Let the writers "retain all the things he does and practically everything he says but give him a sense of humor—in other words, let his hair down a little and be careful that he never appears stuck up."[22] Zanuck had to protect his star investment, and although writers could make Alexander brash and egocentric, he must also be basically likable.[23]

While the teams of writers continue to work on the screenplay, Zanuck completed the casting by adding also-ran Don Ameche as Alexander's amiable buddy Charlie. To make sure the class struggle did not overshadow other interests, Zanuck resorted to a favorite plot device: two male buddies vying for the same girl. Thus with Faye joining the duo Power/Ameche [as she had in a previous hit, *In Old Chicago* (1938)], the ballast that supported almost all Hollywood fare—heterosexual romance in the form of the men's struggle to win a girl—shifted the film's main thrust away from Berlin's self-interested musings. Anchored by this much-used "Coney Island" plot (named for the Zanuck film that best embodies its principles), *Alexander's* docked into familiar Zanuck territory, the land of star/genre formulations.

Seen within the contexts of the Zanuck supertext and the authority star and genre formulations had in the studio era, Alexander and Charlie's fight for Stella's favor is thus also a battle to mold Faye's performance style to better ally her with one male influence over the other, and one theory of social value, rather than its opposite. Zanuck needed a scene that would neatly embody this dynamic, and he came up with a situation in which Alexander tries to dress Stella in what he considers a more refined manner. It is a good scene, because it works to establish the class difference between the two lovers with a vengeance . . . but also with comedy. Charlie (being Charlie) is happy to leave Stella just as she is. Alexander, the hero, cannot. He has a vision. He wants to dignify Stella, tone down her image, remove a few feathers from her wonderfully vulgar boa here, and a ruffle from her dress there, so she is fit to perform his music in the image he deems most appropriate. At one point, he is so exasperated by her refusal to heed his sartorial advice that he baits her: "You're not dressing for your sailor friends now. This isn't Dirty Eddies. I'm trying to build a band with class and distinction, and I'm beginning right now." He doesn't want her to look like "a common valentine," a Production Code euphemism with unmistakable connotations of prostitution.

For the well-bred Alexander, the damning focus in his critique of Stella's style is the emphasis he places on the word "common." Even if ragtime is "of the people," if it appeals only to what Alexander views as the lowest element from which Stella draws her inspiration and style, he will never be able to fulfill his goal: to integrate it into mainstream musical culture. *Alexander's* makes it clear that although Stella has talent and (being played by Faye) a great, warm heart, she does not possess the genius that enables her to truly share in Alexander's musical and cultural obsession. Quite simply, she thinks all the fuss Alexander is kicking up about her dress and the band's image is a smokescreen for what she senses is the real issue: the war between the classes. If Stella is a valentine, then Alexander is, in her terms, "a two by four snob." She returns his fire by baiting him with class-conscious nicknames: "Mr. Asterbilt," "Fancy Pants," and the most damning judgment that can come from her direct, honest milieu, "stuck up pain in the neck."

As Bernado Bertolucci's cinéaste observes in *Before the Revolution* (1965), an implicit moral system underlies the operation in which an agent or author chooses one stylistic variant over another.[24] In this case, each artist views the interpersonal style of the other as proof that only he (or she) can truly understand the new music they have, by accident, jointly introduced. For Alexander, Stella's robust style of singing is "shouting." This judgment forces Stella to play her trump card of class. Even with his conservatory training, she insists she is more in touch with the new music than he could ever be: "Well maybe I don't know the tripe they play up on Snob Hill [*sic*], but I know what they like down here, and that's more than you'll ever know." To Alexander's annoyance, she proves her point. Dressed as she intended, Stella performs the number, "The International Rag," to great acclaim. As she twirls the offending boa in Alexander's face, she bites out the words that will tell this dense man the point he seems to be missing about this music.[25]

Her performance underscores the lesson she can teach: the down and dirty style is precisely the point of this music. But as Hollywood was a cinema of compromise, each will move a little. She sees what he does not: that the extreme end to which Alexander wishes to take the concept of dignity is at odds with the music's stated *goals*. But as the film progresses, it also becomes increasingly clear from her more refined style of dress that any hopes for a big time career are linked to heeding Alexander's advice on the strictures of middle-class deportment. If the musical linked democracy to the alleged taste-making power of the everyday audience, in Zanuck's biopic, democracy enters and stays in the frame because the hero's inevitable triumph is explicitly shown as possible only after he is a surrogate for the people whose will he expresses (Custen, 1992, 188). The opposition to these people's taste culture (in *Alexander's* represented by the horror and scorn expressed by the privileged upper-class members at the prospect of everyday Americans enjoyment of ragtime) is always depicted coming from figures so faintly ridiculous (and sometimes even malevolent) that Gramsci may have vetted them himself. These individuals seldom come armed with weapons—such as valid arguments—that might prove useful in their struggles with the hero. Instead they come loaded with other ammunition: pince-nez, upper crust or foreign accents, morning coats and bustiers, and highly developed senses of outrage and shock. Although it is better plotwise if such forces possess wealth, status, and power, their struggle against progress and innovation is ultimately rendered useless by the very thing their elite status is thought to preclude: the democratic values alleged to undergird America's class structure and, recapitulating this, the movies themselves.

Like other Zanuck biopic heroes, Alexander's support of jazz (after ragtime) had to be imbricated in an issue larger than mere personal success, or vindication, and Zanuck shared his classic formula for the biopic (in which one critical incident, very early in the film, establishes character motivation and serves as the basis for the audience's understanding) with his writers: "We need just one good episode to establish our boy [Alexander], and then start building him up as quickly as we can."[26] Thus, one of the main hurdles was how to link Alexander to the song whose name the leading character (and the film) would bear. Zanuck did not want to follow Berlin's lead by merely having "Alexander's Ragtime Band" appear from an unknown source, for such a plot might make the film's hero a passive recipient of Berlin's off-screen genius. What Zanuck preferred was an active, key rooting interest in which Alexander would be formed as the kind of visionary Zanuck's great men tended to be, and in the script of October 18, 1937, next to the scene where Alexander and his music professor part ways over his love of ragtime, Zanuck noted in pencil the word that, in the right proportion, would explain this character, "prophet."[27]

Thus, when a friendly bartender passes music to Alexander (who needs it for his audition, because Charlie left the band's charts behind), Zanuck has Alexander unknowingly "steal" the music from his love interest, Stella. Zanuck may have intended Alexander's theft to parallel other acts of selfishness in which Power the charming heel, as the Hollywood man with vision, sometimes found himself engaged. But, intended or not, in this situation the quasitheft functions ironically as a way of acknowledging other, unseen hands. Alexander's "theft" starts the action moving, links the music and romantic plot lines, and illustrates each character's motivations. Having seen Stella enter with the music, the audience sees that the credit Alexander takes is somewhat undeserved. Thus, Zanuck's move shifts the victim to the woman and away from the real life story of Berlin's own failed acknowledgments of borrowing from black cultures. From Berlin's synopsis, which wipes out all traces of this music's black roots, to a later verse in "Alexander's," which refers to the clarinet as "a colored pet," in different and sometimes unexpected ways, the act of theft and connections to black music and community authorship seem forever associated with writing this song and making this picture. Authorship that insists on its own disassociation from context shows its hand in other places.

At one point Berlin's story line further emphasized the egocentricity of a person such as Alexander, a man so wrapped up in his own sense of importance that not only does he fail to acknowledge that the music was Stella's, but he doesn't let his feelings for Stella stand in the way of his musical mission or his career. When he hears Stella intends to perform "his" number on a vaudeville bill, having the clout that comes with stardom, he takes "Alexander's" away from her and scores a hit with it himself. If Stella is surprised, Berlin was not. For taking a page from his own book of relations with his peers, his synopsis notes, "She doesn't know Alexander. He raises hell about it, and being the headliner, he naturally is the one to use the song for the week."[28] Zanuck found a use for Berlin's episode, and what might have been just another installment in the love-as-battle motivation that ran through the film became a key link connecting the creation of music with the making of the couple: "We should have," Zanuck said, "a definite tie-up ahead to give the Carnegie Hall finish some motivation. The aunt's ambition [for Alexander's classical career] is not enough. Try and get a link to this."[29]

Zanuck found the link. As it did for other great men, Alexander's belief in ragtime supplied a "rooting interest," stressing that what was most worthy about his crusade was the fact that this was *American* music, a belief Zanuck enunciated with an almost mystical fervor. Berlin in real life was no less sincere on this, telling an interviewer in 1915: "The reason our American composers have done nothing highly significant is because they won't write American music. They're as ashamed of it as if it were a country relative. So, they write imitation European music which doesn't mean anything. Ignorant as I am from their standpoints, I'm doing something they all refuse to do: I'm writing American music!" (quoted in Bergreen, 127). With Zanuck adhering to his biopic the particulars of a key moment in Berlin's actual musical life—the composition of the title song—would not so much have been erased as absorbed into a larger strategy by which Zanuck intended to secure audience approval for his most important goal: a master narrative about the function of American entertainment.

Even with the shield of democracy in front of him, the songwriter still had demons troubling him. Perhaps the clearest expression of the feelings Berlin wished to exorcise with this film was one repeated desire: Berlin wanted to conduct an orchestra playing his own work. Unlike Gershwin and Whiteman, he thought he "had been denied this honor" (Bergreen, 360). Berlin's treatment (and Zanuck's film) offers that Fitzgeraldian second act Americans are allegedly denied in real life when Whiteman arranges for Alexander to play Carnegie Hall. Can Berlin (in his fiction) pull off a feat he would never be able to accomplish in real life? The house is packed. Frightened Alexander "looks at a piece of manuscript on the leader's stand." Looking down he sees sheet music before him: "It is a copy of 'Alexander's Ragtime Band' as originally published in 1911. He raises his baton and begins to direct. Before the orchestra has played a few bars he takes them in hand and a miracle happens. He really directs them."[30] After more than a quarter of a century as America's most prominent musical figure, the man who once admitted "You know, I never did find out what ragtime was" (quoted in Bergreen, 70) finally makes the ragtime composer the equal of his jazz-oriented, symphonic peers: through Hollywood (and Power) Berlin played Carnegie Hall.

It is fitting that the final denouement, in which self-effacing Stella (who has even changed her name to "Lily Lamont" so she can obliterate her identity with Alexander) is reunited with the selfish man who finally comes to realize her value, takes place at the temple of musical value. In a move Faye would repeat in *Tin Pan Alley* and other films, she resurfaces at the last minute, here at Alexander's triumphant comeback at Carnegie Hall. High above the action on the stage, seated in an expensive box, Aunt Sophie and Professor Heinrich enthusiastically applaud Alexander's success. Good fellow Charlie, true to Zanuck's narrative, has made sure that Stella is there to share the moment with Alexander. An improbably precise newspaper headline spells out the significance of what we are about to see and hear: "Alexander and His Ragtime Band to Give Swing Concert at Carnegie Hall: Popular Music Out to Win Highbrow Recognition."

Berlin used Alexander's triumph at Carnegie Hall as a kind of vengeful but wishful movie voodoo cast against real and imagined rivals who had all played that hall. To Zanuck, staging the finale at the grand bastion of New York's classical musical culture was not an act of revenge, but a means to tie the lovers together, thus showing the inclusionary, rather than the exclusionary, participatory power of all "good" music. With Professor Heinrich, Aunt Sophie (for once, displaying wisdom that lives up to her name) even tells him to "just think how proud the Professor and I are." Perfect symmetry is achieved when the Professor feeds Alexander one of his own lines. Alexander confesses he is nervous about conducting at Carnegie Hall, but Heinrich tells his pupil his triumph is assured because the music is "Something you believe in." Like the best popular entertainment—in fact, like the movies themselves—Alexander's music bridges all cultures. For the film's last scene Stella is brought out from the wings to join the triumphant conductor. The film ends as it began, with Stella and Alexander united through Berlin's "Alexander's Ragtime Band." Alexander's triumph is certainly Berlin's revenge, for the audience in the film is told that the title song is "the first and best of all the swing songs," a Heraclitan reference with which Berlin, "The Ragtime King," tried to deftly dispose of one last rival, "The King of Swing," Benny Goodman. If Berlin had his revenge, Zanuck had the last laugh, for the film proved that he had been right from the start. For all its problems, *Alexander's Ragtime Band* was the studio's biggest grossing film that year.

crude fiction

The making of *Alexander's Ragtime Band* shows ways that the creative process in collaborative social enterprises such as commercial film differ in significant ways from processes of creativity in which a lone author works largely outside a group. The history of this film illustrates the ways an individual (here, either Zanuck or Berlin) working within a media organization can still use the authority and power that comes with being a kind of legitimated author in that specific setting so that his, rather than someone else's, goals or visions for a text are to be realized. After a number of experiences working in Hollywood, Berlin had learned what Zanuck had long known. If movies offer the viewer one kind of truth, recorded twenty-four times a second, Hollywood's mechanically reproduced epistemology is unstable and susceptible to any number of changes, particularly at the level of reception. But at the production level, only those with the power could create truths, or perhaps merely the desire, to do so. Berlin's stature and his control of all musical rights to his work gave him the leverage to attempt to be this figure. Zanuck's position as Vice President in charge of production certified that his editorial authority extended to all areas.

Because popular songwriting is in some sense analogous to Hollywood's enterprise, in showing how Tin Pan Alley and vaudeville altered American culture even before there was a Hollywood, the strategies the movies inherited from these institutions are demonstrated in this film. Zanuck and Berlin both worshipped vaudeville, and the way variety dealt with topics such as race exerted an enormous influence on their thinking about the function of entertainment. In an increasingly multicultural America, variety operated as "a kind of theatrical laboratory for experimenting with the new culture that clashed with Victorianism."[31] Nowhere was this more evident than in the way popular culture was used to identify what was acceptable and typically right for an American. These acts of "pointing out" and hiding, of letting in or limiting, found in the vaudeville skit, and the laughter greeting these explosive confrontations, couldn't disguise the damage after leaving the theatre of realizing that when funny things happened, it is at the expense of a selective pool of victims. The main lesson both men learned from vaudeville, and which we see applied in the way the film told the story of the development of American popular music, offers one of the century's transformative facts: popular culture, not just the news media, has long played a role as a powerful cultural agenda setter.

Last, an ironic footnote raises what heretofore has been an implicit point: how musical authorship was determined for America's popular songs. Berlin (who could neither read nor write music) was dogged by persistent speculations that questioned the legitimacy of the cultural claim granted to him (or taken by him) as the "owner" of ragtime, and the creators of *Alexander's Ragtime Band* became embroiled in their own authorship squabbles. Upon the film's release, an unhappy (and ultimately unsuccessful) plaintiff alleged that Berlin and Zanuck had "stolen" her songs and story ideas for use in their film. The stature of the two defendants made such accusations almost surreal, and although the outcome of the litigation proved to be a trivial, but costly, nuisance common in commercial entertainment, Zanuck's and Berlin's sworn testimony about the history of American music was not trivial, at all. In preparing arguments to clear their clients of the charges of plagiarism, Fox's lawyers had been told that although the film's "characters and their romances are fictional" nevertheless "the basic outline of the motion picture" was "historical." For both men, "the basic purpose of the motion picture 'Alexander's Ragtime Band' was to reveal" the teleology of American music using "this same historical development of jazz as shown in the lives of Whiteman, Berlin and Gershwin." Berlin claimed *Alexander's* story "is factual," although he and Zanuck "obviously . . . tried in a very crude way to fictionalize it" (TCF Brief, 13). And although they claimed the materials of the story were "historical," drawn (as they could prove) from actual case studies or incidents in the lives of famous musicians, it is curious that neither man thought that the screenplay should tackle the important issue that had long followed Berlin and "Alexander's Ragtime Band" around: the question of creative paternity, or authorship. But if the film ducked the first question regarding the authorship of this emblematic song, on another issue— Who should be credited with innovating ragtime music?—both men and their film were very clear. Whites, they said, had invented jazz.

The lesson of "Alexander's Ragtime Band" or *Alexander's Ragtime*

Band is that this most American of songs produced within the matrices of our culture industry was never really intended for the ears of people who might have most liked to listen to it, if for no other reason than for the pleasure one derives from associating with something of value that you have had a part in creating. The film's palimpsest of fact and fiction is less a representation or telling of history than it is a part of the process of making the history of music itself. Song and singer are irrevocably intertwined within the complex mediated and interpersonal chords by which entertainment performs our past while serving as a means Americans used to negotiate the present meanings of race and ethnicity. Berlin's actors are figures in a shadow play whose scripted and inspired *melos* remain, as they were from the start, haunted by ghosts audible, yet invisible. Along with Berlin and his protean talent, their presence can also lay legitimate claim to being the creators of this musical tradition. Although we rarely saw them on the screen in this role, the continued viability of the music as entertainment and as a source of debates about its meaning and use suggest that, like Berlin, these other creators too live in the imaginative acoustic spaces we inhabit on and off screen.

The real history told by *Alexander's Ragtime Band* is not concerned with who did or did not write this particular song. Rather, its cavalcade opens up (but also closes or obscures) an important issue: how the race and ethnicity of Jews and blacks, working together and against a common goal, molded the status of their identities and determined the nature of and possible range of authorship in trying to lay claim to creating American culture.

notes

1. Robert Carringer, ed. *The Jazz Singer* (Madison: University of Wisconsin, 1979), 17. I would like to thank David Gerstner and Janet Staiger for editorial advice.
2. Laurence Bergreen, *As Thousands Cheer: The Life of Irving Berlin* (New York: Viking Press, 1990), 276–77.
3. See George F. Custen, *Bio/Pics: How Hollywood Constructed Public History* (New Brunswick, NJ: Rutgers University Press, 1992).
4. See George F. Custen, *Twentieth Century's Fox: Darryl F. Zanuck and the Culture of Hollywood* (New York: Basic Books, 1997) for a detailed analysis of Zanuck's working method.
5. Philip Furia, *Irving Berlin: A Life in Song* (New York: Schirmer Books, 1998), 49.
6. Carolyn Marvin, *When Old Technologies Were New: Thinking About Electric Communication in the Late Nineteenth Century* (New York: Oxford University Press, 1989), 4.
7. For the full lyrics, see Berlin, "Puttin On the Ritz," in Kimball and Emmett, 262–63.
8. Noel Ignatiev, *How The Irish Became White* (New York: Routledge, 1995), 2.
9. "Brief for Twentieth Century-Fox Film Corporation, Defendant-Appellant," Civil Action No. 13, 121, in the *United States Circuit Court of Appeals for the Eighth Circuit*, "Twentieth Century-Fox Film Corporation, Defendant-Appellant, vs. Marie Cooper Oehler Dieckhaus, Plaintiff-Appellee" (hereafter TCF Brief).

10. Almost thirty years later, Berlin was still upset. "This [movie] was after the stock market crash. Musicals were the rage out there and all of a sudden they weren't. Out went the songs. I developed the damnedest feeling of inferiority." After this, Berlin understood that in the future, he would either have to find a way within the studio system's model of authorial power to exercise greater control over the way his music was used, or give up this lucrative market. Berlin had already tried to control his music by forming as early as 1914 the Irving Berlin Music, Inc., which provided rights' control to him (Kimball and Emmett, 266).

11. Josh Rubins, "Genius Without Tears," *The New York Review of Books* (June 16, 1988): 30.

12. Darryl Zanuck quoted in Rudy Behlmer, *Memo from Darryl F. Zanuck* (New York: Grove Press, 1993), 13.

13. Story Conference, June 7, 1937, 4, *Alexander's Ragtime Band* files, Twentieth-Century Fox Collection, University of California, Los Angeles (hereafter TCF/ARB).

14. Berlin Treatment, nd, TCF/ARB, 10.

15. Zanuck notes on Second Treatment, April 3, 1937, TCF/ARB.

16. Story Conference, September 8, 1937, TCF/ARB (emphasis in original).

17. Quoted in Robert W. McChesney, *Telecommunications, Mass Media, and Democracy: The Battle for the Control of U.S.. Broadcasting, 1928–1935* (New York: Oxford University Press, 1994), 251.

18. Lawrence W. Levine, *Highbrow/Lowbrow: The Emergence of Cultural Hierarchy in America* (Cambridge, MA: Harvard University Press, 1988), 56.

19. Gerald Mast, *Can't Help Singin': The American Musical on Stage and Screen* (Woodstock, NY: The Overlook Press, 1987), 229. Berlin's retributive history seems to derive its notions of biography from Oscar Wilde's Judas, a fact Mast either ignores or wasn't able to see. Ignoring any critique arising from the problematic kind of history Berlin was trying to write, his conclusions never-theless are I believe solid when he states of Alexander's that "No previous Hollywood musical demonstrated a closer bond between social history and cultural artifact" (Mast, 230).

20. Story Conference, June 7, 1937, 2, TCF/ARB.

21. Story Conference, September 1, 1937, 1, TCF/ARB.

22. Story Conference, September 14, 1937, TCF/ARB.

23. Zanuck later observed of the star "code" by which he guided Power's career that "In Alexander's they accepted him because he was redeemed by the war and because it was obvious that he was very much in love with the girl. Story Conference, April 30, 1940, "Tin Pan Alley" File, TCF.

24. See Robin Wood's essay, "Bernado Bertolucci," in which he locates the Godardian reference to cinematic style as a "matter of morality" in the film *Before the Revolution*. In *Cinema: A Critical Dictionary*, ed. Richard Roud (New York: Viking, 1980), 126.

25. The reader is referred to the lyrics for Berlin's "The International Rag" (1913) in Kimball and Emmett, 76.

26. Story Conference, June 7, 1937, 3, TCF/ARB.

27. Draft of Screenplay, October 18, 1937, 21, TCF/ARB.

28. Berlin Treatment, 5, TCF/ARB.

29. Story Conference, September 8, 1937, 7, TCF/ARB.

30. Berlin Treatment, 10, TCF/ARB.

31. Robert Snyder, *The Voice of the City: Vaudeville and Popular Culture* (New York: Oxford University Press, 1989), 132.

stepping out from behind the grand silhouette

five

joan harrison's films

of the 1940s

christina lane

Joan Harrison is not very well known, but she is best known for her collaboration with Alfred Hitchcock. She developed and cowrote six of his films in the 1930s and 1940s, and later co-produced the Emmy award-winning *Alfred Hitchcock Presents* televisions series in the 1950s and 1960s. In 1943, however, Harrison struck out on her own to forge a career as an independent film producer. She chose to parlay her association with Hitchcock into a more visible and autonomous role in the production of suspense thrillers. This meant that she also faced the difficult task of distinguishing herself from the "master of suspense."

Harrison's first solo venture was as the screenwriter of *Dark Waters* for United Artists in 1944. After experiencing a total loss of control over *Dark Waters* and seeing numerous speculative screenplays languish, she reached the conclusion that to produce would offer her the best strategy for holding the authorial reins of her projects. She told the *Los Angeles Times* in 1944, "You see before you a thwarted writer."[1] To break the cycle, she told the newspaper, she had responded to Universal's invitation to write *Phantom Lady* with a request to associate produce the film noir instead. By her third independent film, *The Strange Affair of Uncle Harry* (1944), she was a full producer associated with Universal. As an independent producer, Harrison survived on short-term studio contracts that financed and distributed her projects on a film-by-film basis. After *Uncle Harry*, she would go on to produce six more features, including *Nocturne* (1946), *They Won't Believe Me* (1947), *Ride the Pink Horse* (1947), *Once More, My Darling* (1949), *Your Witness* (1950), and *Circle of Danger* (1950).

With these mystery films, Harrison sought to draw on the genre conventions of her former mentor Hitchcock while extending them in a different direction. She displayed an interest in many similar themes such as the female investigation of threatening patriarchal structures or the questioning of coupling and happy endings. Yet, she often placed these preoccupations in a different context, pressing them further, especially through the use of "last minute" twists or unexpected gender-role reversals. Although Harrison was not the first woman to appropriate the "male" genres of suspense and film noir, she was the only one who rose to the position of Hollywood producer during the classical era. In her attempts to push the boundaries of "acceptable" behavior on the part of both her female and male characters, Harrison faced constant struggles with both studio executives and the Production Code Administration (PCA). Because she tended to attach herself to material that featured adultery, illicit sexual behavior, vulgar language, hints of nudity, and alcoholic enjoyment, she repeatedly found herself in the position of having to defend the integrity of her films to Joseph Breen's office. The struggles she faced in bringing her productions to the screen illuminate the producer's status as both insider and outside to the industry. More specifically, they capture Harrison's dual roles as consumer of the Hitchcock oeuvre (and the related thriller genre) and producer of a particular brand of feminist-inspired noir.

For the most part, traditional film histories remember Harrison as Hitchcock's protégé. Although Donald Spoto's biography of the director, *The Dark Side of Genius: The Life of Alfred Hitchcock* (1983), has by no means been received by film scholars as an ultimate authority, the role of the cool, unattainable blonde in which Spoto cast Harrison continues to shape her historical legacy. According to Spoto, the twenty-six-year-old reporter Harrison responded to a *London Times* advertisement for a "director's assistant." While waiting in Hitchcock's outer office, she crossed paths with Madeleine Carroll, who was auditioning for the part she would eventually play in *The 39 Steps*. Harrison, who like Carroll was "another blonde, and just as handsome," would face an audition as well. The director reportedly put the hopeful employee to the test with his off-color humor and was won over by her charismatic refusal to be shaken.[2] Spoto postulates that Hitchcock took Harrison under his tutelage because she embodied the cool, unflappable blonde figure over which he would obsess in his films for the next forty years.

She was, for Spoto, the real-life motivation for Hitchcock's numerous versions of the fantasy woman.

This interpretation of the Hitchcock/Harrison collaboration places Harrison squarely in the role of specular object, however. What was it like to see through the eyes of this "cool blonde"? How did her particular interests and concerns influence Hitchcock's work? At what points did she rewrite the director's narrative contributions and at what points did he rewrite hers? Given the creative process by which he worked, in which he relied heavily on the development work of brainstorming and free association with his writers, Harrison's role as facilitator should not be underestimated. John Houseman has said, "Working with Hitchcock really meant listening to him talk—anecdotes, situations, characters, revelations, reversals" (Spoto, 262). From there the screenwriter would organize and shape the director's "talk" into a coherent, character-driven storyline. Hitchcock's films thrived on the basis of his writer's success at such transformation for, as Tom Ryall demonstrates, the director's films proved to be critically and commercially successful when he had a strong support team.[3]

Although Harrison's contribution to Hitchcock's oeuvre was unique and powerful, her institutional history goes well beyond her work with Hitchcock. Her independent films constitute a "producorial" oeuvre, providing insight into the styles, themes, and ideologies that consumed her. Up to this point in film scholarship, Harrison's career has been reduced to a scant footnote or sketchy anecdote. By placing her work in the multiple contexts of historical period, industrial environment, and authorship debates, this chapter will identify various textual points at which Harrison either did or did not have filmmaking agency. Hence, it will define what "agency" meant in her career. After a brief discussion of her collaborative experience with Hitchcock, this chapter will examine two of her films, *Phantom Lady* and *They Won't Believe Me*. As her contribution to these productions make clear, Harrison gauged her own power on the basis of her ability to transgress 1940s conventional norms not only of femininity but of masculinity as well in a way that perverted their supposedly wholesome relation to marriage and family.

the hitchcockian influence

One of Harrison's most formative influences took shape in her collaborations with Hitchcock from 1935 to 1943. It was during these years that Hitchcock specialized in films featuring female investigators and the gothic "femme noire" genre.[4] His British feature *The Lady Vanishes* (1938) helped launch this cycle, which would reach its pinnacle in his 1940s American films with David O. Selznick. Harrison, along with Hitchcock's wife Alma Reville, carried out much of the development work in discovering and revising literary source material in which young, naïve heroines confront the dangers of romance and marriage in terms that are often life or death. As much as Harrison played a key role in shaping Hitchcock's narrative and cinematic interests, the director helped initiate her into the conventions of the suspense thriller and the gendered connotations of looking, knowing, and surviving within its hermeneutic structure. Her work on *The Lady Vanishes*, *Jamaica Inn* (1939), *Rebecca* (1940), *Suspicion* (1941), and *Shadow of a Doubt* (1943), in particular, proved to be an important training ground as she cultivated her story selection skills and experimented with various ways of conveying identity crises and the interiority of female psychological space.

Harrison joined Hitchcock as a secretary during the production of *The Man Who Knew Too Much* in 1934. As various reports indicate, she was not very skilled at menial office labor, and she found more motivation in learning about film production through generalist eyes. In 1945, Harrison reflected on those early years with the following assessment: "I am probably the worst secretary Hitchcock has ever had. I was too curious about all the departments with which, as a director, Hitch must deal."[5] She apparently thrived, however, when her duties shifted to reading potential source material and story conferencing. By *The Lady Vanishes*, she was writing short bits of scenario and dialogue, mentored not only by the director but also by Reville, who co-wrote the screenplay with Sydney Gilliatt and Frank Launder. A pivotal film in Hitchcock's career, it features a female investigative character who drives the narrative (at least until a point) and, as a result, activates a number of concerns regarding gendered looking relations and the illegitimate status of women's knowledge in relation to patriarchy. Margaret Lockwood stars as Iris, an ambivalent soon-to-be bride taking a train to her fiancé, who acquaints herself with a fellow traveler, Miss Froy, only to confront the woman's disappearance. The other passengers on the train, many of whom are "male experts," continually question her account of Miss Froy, nearly convincing her that she has lost her sanity, before Miss Froy is revealed to be a spy working against the Nazis. As Patrice Petro points out, *The Lady Vanishes* not only lends itself to a feminist reading that values female memory, vision, knowledge, and subjectivity, but it is also structured around a woman's search for a lost figure of female identification in a way that rejects the traditional Oedipal narrative of classical cinema. For Petro, the film registers a milestone in Hitchcock's oeuvre because "it leads [its heroine] to confront the patriarchal symbolic order and to refuse its definitions, which exclude a place for her identity, her experience, and her memory."[6]

Jamaica Inn would be the next film on which Harrison would work and although it does not foreground these issues as strongly as *The Lady Vanishes*, the female investigative role is still at work. *Jamaica Inn* has been excluded from the Hitchcock canon for its lack of sophistication and overall blandness, and I would make no argument against the film's negative reception. In the context of Harrison's professional growth, however, it had tremendous significance. As co-screenwriter with Sydney Gilliat, she "cut her teeth" on *Jamaica Inn*'s script, immersing herself for the first time in the writing process. The film introduces newcomer Maureen O'Hara, who plays a nineteenth-century orphan carving out a new home with her aunt and uncle on the Cornish coast. She soon discovers that her uncle is one of the ringleaders of a bandit crew that forces ships off course and then loots them. A plucky young woman, Mary continually stands up to the criminals and narrowly escapes being abducted into a life of sexual bondage by a delirious sadist played by Charles Laughton. Although the film spends much of its time following the criminals' escapades and one lawman's attempts to overrun them, Mary grapples with many of the issues raised in *The Lady Vanishes*, *Rebecca*, *Suspicion*, and *Shadow of a Doubt*. She confronts the image of her Aunt Patience (Marie Ney), who has lost her own identity as a result of subordinating herself to her husband's corrupt and violent ways, raising the question of how Mary will choose to perform mature femininity and domesticity.

This film also proved significant for Harrison because it inaugurated her correspondence with Daphne du Maurier who wrote the novels on which both *Jamaica Inn* and *Rebecca* were based. Though du Maurier was not very satisfied with the film adaptation of the *Jamaica Inn*, she agreed to sell *Rebecca*'s rights to Selznick for Hitchcock's first American production (Spoto, 202). The diligent work of Harrison and Kay Brown, who worked for Selznick, brought about the deal. Although Harrison plied the director with incessant enthusiasm for the book and made repeated contacts with du Maurier's agent, Brown provided the novelist with reassurances that her material would be respected.[7] The contribution of Harrison and Brown at the development stage cannot be underestimated, functioning as an important antidote to traditional auteur theory. As "D-Girls," or development executives, they were gatekeepers of material, making crucial decisions about which stories should be acquired and building substantial cases for their choices.

Rebecca comes closer to the gothic *Jane Eyre* formula than any other Hitchcock film, and it made an indelible mark on Harrison's creative development. This was Harrison's second screenwriting credit, earning her an Academy Award nomination along with co-writers Robert Sherwood and Charles Bennett. The film's protagonist (Joan Fontaine), who remains unnamed in both novel and film, undergoes an identity crisis as she falls in love with and marries the elusive, brooding Maxim de Winter (Laurence Olivier). When Maxim brings her to his ancestral home, she becomes haunted by the ideal image of his deceased wife, Rebecca, which propels her into an investigation of the true nature of her husband and the strength of their marriage. Highly regarded as one of Hitchcock's major achievements in developing modes of cinematic identification through point-of-view shots and subjective camerawork,

Rebecca demonstrates the director's adeptness in articulating women's troubled relationship to patriarchy even as it signals his own ambivalence toward femininity and feminism[8] (Tania Modleski, 1988; Mary Ann Doane, 1987).

Though one of Harrison's collaborators, Charles Bennett, has minimized her contribution, production files indicate that this was self-interested historical revision on his part.[9] One of Harrison's major responsibilities involved experimenting with ways of folding into the protagonist's psychological space "feminine" accouterments such as diaries, address books, and letters of personal correspondence.[10] In addition, much of Harrison's energy was spent finding concrete illustrations of the protagonist's identity crisis, especially as that crisis played out in relation to her idealized image of Rebecca and the socially prescribed role of wife. As a film, *Rebecca* compellingly engages concerns of female identity and identifications that the screenwriter was interested in taking even further and pushing in different directions. Many of the scenes she wrote that did not make it into the film dramatize the interior, psychological dilemmas of taking on the role of wife as an identity (*Rebecca* files, HRC).

As Harrison turned her attention to *Suspicion* and *Shadow of a Doubt* (for which she wrote some uncredited scenes) in the early 1940s, she continued to refine her interest in female characters who investigated the limits of their own agency within a patriarchal symbolic order. By this time, Harrison was beginning to extricate herself from the Hitchcock equation, however. She had apparently hit the top of her learning curve as the director's femme noire cycle itself wound down, and she was ready, in her own words, to "try my own wings" if she wanted to be regarded as "anything but a secretary" (Daggett, 22).

the "woman's angle": *phantom lady*

For Harrison's identity, agency, and authorship in the middle 1940s to be adequately theorized, her role as producer needs to be understood in multiple contexts, including but not limited to Hitchcock's influence. Each of her films was informed not only by her own status as a "Hitchcockian" writer but also by several influential genres ("wrong man" film, "working girl" drama, film noir) and two directors with whom she worked repeatedly. Robert Siodmak served twice as her director, for *Phantom Lady* (1944) and *The Strange Affair of Uncle Harry* (1945). The actor Robert Montgomery directed *Ride the Pink Horse* (1947) (in which he starred), *Once More, My Darling* (1949), and *Your Witness* (1950, UK). Indeed, one of the hallmarks of Harrison's authorial style was her tendency to form long-lasting male/female professional partnerships, suggesting that her agency lay, at least partially, in the collaborative process. She succeeded by virtue of her skills in conversation, brainstorming, and delegation. And, from her previous alliance, she knew the value of pooling resources with other powerful people in the industry.

Siodmak made a good fit with Harrison and her vision of film noir and melodrama. He brought to her productions a keen eye based in German expressionism, a gift for working with actors, and a reputation as a competent "assignment director."[11] The bulk of Harrison's contribution to *Phantom Lady* involved developing the adaptation of the William Irish novel with Bernard C. Schoenfeld, who earned sole screenwriting credit, though some accounts report that she co-wrote the script.[12] She was also instrumental in conducting negotiations with the PCA, casting talent, and coordinating production.

In choosing *Phantom Lady* as material, Harrison was both aligning herself with Hitchcock and staking out new territory. The story ostensibly focuses on Scott Henderson (Alan Curtis) as he attempts to prove that he is innocent of his wife's murder upon the disappearance of his alibi, an anonymous woman with whom he had shared an evening of theater. Toward the beginning of the film, however, the reins of narrative control turn over to his "girl Friday," Kansas (Ella Raines), who refuses to give up the search for proof of his innocence long after the "wrong man" has lost all hope. In supervising the adaptation, Harrison conducted a major overhaul of the novel, which follows two male characters, Scott's best friend and a police detective, in their collection of clues.

Given the similarities between Kansas and Harrison, who spent her pre-Hitchcock years indulging her interests in crime by sitting through various trials in London, Raines's character incorporates many of Harrison's characteristics and the "working woman's" world in which she lived. This film, and most of the producer's films to follow, contain threads of the "working girl" drama, a postwar genre that centralizes dilemmas between professional work and true love for women who have recently entered the public sphere.[13] It pays special attention to Kansas's relationship to her workspace and professional activities, especially such rituals as taking dictation and writing shorthand. Siodmak's biographer, Deborah Lazaroff Alpi, goes so far as to posit that Kansas was modeled after the producer (122). In this way, Harrison found a representational outlet for self-articulation by helping to construct the figure of the precocious secretary.

This relationship between biographical information about Harrison and her textual production is significant to the extent that it illuminates the producer's motivations and authorial focus. Certain aspects of her private life, especially her personal understanding of her position as a female role model in a male-dominated industry, prove relevant because she not only articulated them indirectly in films such as *Phantom Lady* but she also voiced them in the Hollywood press. For example, soon after this film's release, she described her decision to start working in the film industry in terms of her desire to avoid "settling down to a 'stifling' existence" with the boy next door in her birthplace in England. She remarked, "I wanted to write. I used to attend court sessions at the Old Bailey in London to learn about life. I wrote some short stories. I was eager to get into the cinema."[14] This self-positioning aligns her with the working women in her films who, like her, resist society's efforts to domesticate them.

In concentrating on Kansas, who was a marginal figure in the novel and would have been so in almost any other studio picture, *Phantom Lady* follows the investigation of a female protagonist in ways that are similar to the earlier femme noire cycle. The film is firmly rooted in Kansas's subjectivity, once she appears at its twenty-minute mark. And, once the audience learns halfway through the film that a man she thinks is her ally in the search for clues is actually the murderer, the central conflict becomes whether she will see the future of her victimization in time to stop it. *Phantom Lady*'s most powerful sequences consist of prolonged, silent encounters between Kansas and the suspects, such as her subdued provocation of the bartender in which she quietly stares him down and eventually tracks him to his accidental death. Even when he dies after stepping out into the path of an oncoming car, she doesn't flinch or react in typical "feminine" hysterics. In fact, she remains unflappable in the face of numerous outbreaks of violence.

In this and many other ways, Kansas functions as an assertive woman, refusing to step into the background of the investigation even when asked to by the police detective (Tomas Gomez). The film highlights several times the transgressiveness of her detective role, such as when Jack Marlowe (Franchot Tone) tries to dissuade her from pursuing the case, saying, "Look, this is a man's job." She replies, "I'm sorry but I can't just sit by." As Monica Sullivan puts it, "The secretary . . . places herself in one threatening situation after another as her employer awaits helplessly in prison. Hitchcock would have found some way to get the guy out, so that they could solve the crime together and fall in love."[15] Indeed, the film's decentralization of Scott's narrative crisis in favor of Kansas's singular storyline represents a departure away from such Hitchcock films as *The 39 Steps*, *The Lady Vanishes*, and *Saboteur* (1942).

Phantom Lady contrasts Harrison's previous work in the way that it counterpoints Kansas's agency and authority with Scott's. Not only is the male protagonist made passive through his imprisonment early in the film, he also suffers an illegitimate relationship to vision and knowledge. In essence, because the killer has bribed everyone who has seen the suspect with his alibi, Scott takes on the role of Iris in *The Lady Vanishes*. He tries to convince the police and, later, the jury that his version of the truth is correct; however, those on the side of law and order continually question his vision, memory, and experience. Kansas takes on narrative authority in two ways: she possesses the power and mobility to collect evidence and she *perceives* Scott's innocence when most others do not. She is, therefore, the "right" woman in contrast to the "wrong man."

In feminist terms, *Phantom Lady* is most compelling because its mystery hinges on a traditionally female object, a woman's hat. Kansas solves the crime by hunting down the missing witness's hat, a copy of a headpiece worn by nightclub entertainer Estella Monteiro (Aurora). Like those female accouterments in *Rebecca*, the hat takes on the significance of a symbolically charged object. This gendered artifact, along with several other feminine objects such as Kansas's purse, offer more than a mere backdrop to the film's world (though they do offer that). They provide the turnkey for unlocking *Phantom Lady*'s narrative and thematic secrets, which means that the film renews their value and insists on the fact that Kansas's identity as a woman is an asset.

Furthermore, the mystery culminates with Kansas's visit to the bedroom chambers of the phantom lady, Ann Terry (Fay Helm), in a moment of female friendship and mutual recognition that is rare in 1940s film noir. She gains access to Ann, who is experiencing a nervous breakdown, by virtue of her status as female, given that Jack (the murderer) is asked to remain in the foyer. (The medical doctor who bars him access and grants a visit to Kansas is a woman, a relative role reversal that defines even the mediated space between Kansas and Ann as female.) The meeting between the two women both incorporates and rewrites the tropes of the Gothic femme noire. Ann has become a "madwoman in the attic," after suffering the loss of her fiancé. She is not, however, a spectre of monstrous femininity—the insane and degenerate alter ego of the bride-to-be—and she neither frightens nor intimidates Kansas. Yes, Kansas bonds with her by identifying with her desire to be married; but this moment is less about subduing the female protagonist into submission to the patriarchal and heterosexual social order than it is about highlighting one version of women's connectedness to each other. The film's discourse on women's "knowingness" and their narrative value reaches a crescendo in this placid and contemplative meeting of two female minds. None of these events occurred in Irish's novel, which featured the phantom lady only as a corpse that Jack apparently discovers just moments after she has fallen off her balcony.

Although a number of *Phantom Lady*'s key elements do exist in the novel, and the contribution of Siodmak and Schoenfeld should not be ignored, it is important to understand Harrison's authorship within this feminist context. She exercised her authorial control, fundamentally, in reconstructing the source material so that it is driven by a woman's investigation and its destination is a woman's rematerialization. Told from the female secretary's point of view, with an emphasis on moments of female bonding, the story enables her to draw out female contours of film noir and refashion her professional reputation into one influenced by an amalgamation of Hitchcockian suspense, film noir, and the "working girl" drama.

The gender connotations and reversals in *Phantom Lady* were themes that Harrison was aware of and invested in publicizing. Implicit in a number of articles in the film's pressbook, all written by Universal's publicity department with input and approval by Harrison, is the angle that this film was a suspense thriller with a "gender twist." One article that prominently features Harrison, entitled "*Phantom Lady* First Mystery for Lady Fans," states that she found the film unprecedented because it "was a mystery story from the woman's point of view, a formula that had never before been translated for the screen."[16] The article goes on to explain that because the picture relied on "feminine psychology for its essential appeal," Harrison was brought on board to produce. It displays a certain self-consciousness about the use of charged objects discussed above, remarking, "It is mostly a story about a young woman and a woman's hat."[17] The hat, then, provided the female hook that made this film "different."

The publicity for *Phantom Lady* is important for two reasons. First, it demonstrates that many of the film's character, narrative, and genre attributes do in fact represent attempts to decode and recode the suspense thriller with gender ideology in mind *because* Harrison saw herself as speaking to a female audience. The "woman's angle" she often referred to in press accounts signified not merely a way of seeing but more importantly a tangible target, a market of female spectators who, like her, indulged in crime fiction and film noir and longed to be addressed directly. Second, the publicity indicates that she was quite willing to capitalize both on the essentialist discourse of women's "difference" from men *and* her association with Hitchcock. One piece of advertising copy starts off by announcing, "Joan Harrison, brilliant protégé of Alfred Hitchcock, is producer of new thriller."[18] Another item, "Lady Producer Gets Send-Off," focuses on the three-dozen roses that Hitchcock reportedly sent to Harrison to celebrate her new post as associate producer (pressbook). As this publicity suggests, she was more than willing to exploit her former professional relationship with the director and she sought to position herself as a "female Alfred Hitchcock."

Harrison effectively made the transition from writer to producer. She had succeeded, at least for a time, in claiming a good degree of power by forging a Universal contract that granted her more autonomy. Notably, though, in producing *Phantom Lady*, she found herself forced to contend with another unit of power, the Production Code Administration. Her encounters with the office were relatively minor skirmishes for this production, and she decided to go against its advice in at least one instance when she preserved several shots of Cliff (Elisha Cook, Jr.) who beats his drums in a sexual frenzy during the jazz jam session. One change to which she did submit involved a small piece of dialogue in which Scott describes his failed marriage to investigators. His declaration, "I don't believe in people remaining married when it just won't work," was deleted because, according to the PCA, it presented a threat to the sanctity of marriage.[19]

Phantom Lady did, in fact, open the door for some interesting inquiries into the limitations of marriage and the few available options for couples who had discovered that the institution just "wasn't working." Before the film leaves behind the unhappy coupling of Scott and his deceased wife in favor of a "who-done-it," it paints a convoluted picture of their stalemated marriage. Although Harrison would give into pressure to minimize this aspect of the film this time around, the PCA's concern and her interest in confronting that concern would intensify very quickly and continue to define her authorial agency over the next decade. Scott's questioning of marriage might be seen as a precedental "hot spot" that would continue to surface, especially as Harrison attempted to step outside the confines of traditional marriage and family dynamics in her films.

marital woes: *they won't believe me*

As Harrison made clear in 1940s press coverage, she held unconventional views on monogamy and marital institutions.[20] As someone who deferred marriage until her late forties (marrying novelist Eric Ambler in 1958), she spoke out with pride about being single and maintaining an active social life.[21] She once remarked to the *New York Times*, "I'm not a great believer in marriage, as I see it today. Put it this way: I'm a great believer in marriage as it might be."[22] She saw mystery in cultural and societal pressure to marry and chose to investigate the process by which movie characters cracked under such pressure or violated the sanctions of matrimony. The films she produced after *Phantom Lady* showed evidence of her increased focus on the perversity of marriage, suggesting that she exerted considerable authorial energy to bring such stories into the public eye with as little recuperative institutional influence as possible.

The second film produced by Harrison, *The Strange Affair of Uncle Harry*, represented a move away from the female investigative thriller. Focusing on a male protagonist, this combination melodrama mystery looked underneath the facade of an upper-class, New England family to find incestuous ties and violent impulses. In this adaptation of a popular stage play, a middle-aged bachelor (played by George Sanders) finally falls in love only to confront his sister's toxic (and romantic) jealousy. In the original draft of the screenplay, he murders his sister (Geraldine Fitzgerald) by poisoning her hot cocoa. Harrison battled Breen to retain this ending, developing five different framing devices in an effort to find an acceptable compromise that would remain true to the story's blunt, taboo-breaking thrust. The PCA applied overwhelming pressure on Universal, though, which eventually led the studio to adopt a conclusion in which the murder is revealed to be a dream.

This film is important to Harrison's career for two reasons: (1) it signaled her preoccupation with the perverse and pathological implications of the "family romance," and (2) the confidence she lost in Universal's ability to back her creative decisions during the PCA disputes resulted in her resignation from the studio. She made a move to RKO, where she produced *Nocturne* (1946) and *They Won't Believe Me* (1947).

If *The Strange Affair of Uncle Harry* reveals the sexual and violent underbelly of middle-class family relations, *They Won't Believe Me* takes a drastic turn altogether away from institutional marriage and reproductive sexuality. This RKO film opens with the trial of Larry Ballantyne, a man accused of murdering a woman named Verna Carlson. His testimony unfolds throughout the length of the film, thereby framing the plot. Larry turns back the clock one year to begin his flashback. A New York City stockbroker who has married for economic security, he is having an affair with a magazine writer, Janice (Jane Greer). Just when they are about to run away together, his wife Greta (Rita Johnson) convinces him to stay, announcing that she has bought them a ranch in Los Angeles and arranged for his promotion. Upon relocating to the West Coast, Larry falls into a familiar pattern by becoming infatuated with his secretary, Verna (Susan Heyward). Larry believes he has finagled a way to obtain some of Greta's estate, and, after abandoning his wife, he and Verna drive toward Reno for a makeshift honeymoon. When a runaway truck hits their car and kills Verna, Larry realizes that Verna's remains are unrecognizable and tells detectives that it was Greta who died in the accident. When it comes to light Greta has committed suicide by jumping off of a cliff, Larry goes on trial for Verna's murder. Janice, who has helped in the investigation all the while milking the suspect's affections, becomes the film's moral voice and pronounces him innocent. As the jury files in to read the verdict, Larry makes an escape through the window, only to immediately be shot by policemen. The clerk then reads Larry's verdict . . . not guilty.

As such a plot summary belies, *They Won't Believe Me* trips up a number of feminist alarms and fails to conjure up much sympathy for any of its characters, male or female. Like a number of Harrison's late 1940s films, this one makes very little effort to present its story through a female subjectivity, suggesting, at least superficially, that the producer had indeed exploited the "woman's angle" as a way toward self-promotion and authorial differentiation during her career transition. However, *They Won't Believe Me* (and some of her other late 1940s noirs) needs to be seen within the context of Harrison's attempts to accomplish two goals. In the first place, she apparently wanted to show that as a woman, she could succeed at the same perverse permutations of film noir as her male counterparts. And, in the second place, her association with *They Won't Believe Me* underscores her feminist concern with coupling. The picture's promotional tagline was "Too Many Women Loved Him! When a man goes to the devil, he usually takes a woman with him . . . This man took THREE!"[23] As this allusion to "tradultery" suggests, Harrison was interested in subverting traditional expectations for the wrong-man genre as well as for the more transgressive noir films in which women and men are typically paired up and shown the path toward some semblance of sexual law and order.

Harrison fought hard to make *They Won't Believe Me*, waging a protracted battle with the PCA that in and of itself indicated her determination to bust through "appropriate" standards of gender and sexual behavior. After an initial story meeting with Harrison and producers Jack Gross and William Gordon at Joseph Breen's office on April 25, 1946, Breen submitted a memo to the files stating that the storyline violated the Production Code's clause that required that "the sanctity of the institution of marriage and the home shall be upheld."[24] Its plot and theme did in fact fly in the face of these tenets and, although Harrison and her team, composed of director Irving Pichel and Jonathan Latimer, made minor concessions, they persisted in bringing this story to the screen.

The film prompts its spectators to believe Larry's account of Verna's accidental death and Greta's suicide; but it more urgently asks them to weigh whether Larry should lay claim to any responsibility in their separate demises. After all, he devalues Verna's life to the extent that he is willing self-servingly to change her identity. And he indirectly causes Greta's suicide by leaving her in a cold and cruel manner. Though he may not be a murderer, he is a womanizing cad who is motivated by his wife's money at almost every plot turn. His judgment is ultimately pronounced by the audience's surrogate, Janice, whose moral perspective on Larry takes priority over that of the jury. Just before the clerk reads the verdict, Janice declares "I believe you, Larry," and implies that she would be open to a future with him if he is set free. It is not so much that she believes him as that she forgives his actions and, if she can, the film suggests, so should the audience. This scene also features Larry's penance, in which he finally acknowledges that he has treated the women in his life poorly. His apology is, however, downplayed so that it operates more as an aside than as a climactic self-transformation. And the likelihood that the couple might achieve a happy ending together, even if he is released, seems incredibly low.[25] As a result, Larry's multiple sexual liaisons and overall disrespect of the institutions of law and marriage linger, even after his death.

Janice represents one of the few nonperverse characterizations in *They Won't Believe Me* and her narrative position was actually one of the few changes that Harrison did make in response to the censors. In addition to toning down the sexual innuendo between Janice and

Larry as well as their alcoholic intake, she and Latimer reshaped the female character's perspective on her suitor in the second and third acts. In Breen's letter to RKO, he proposes that as a solution to the film's lack of "proper compensating moral values," Janice might function as a character who "slaps Larry down for his wrongdoing." Breen goes on to remind Harrison, Gross, and Gordon of their discussion about "cleaning up the character of Janice, and having her, as one of the major characters, act as a 'voice for morality.'"[26] As the RKO team took this suggestion under advisement, in a strategic effort to appease the PCA in certain limited areas, they turned Janice into less of a sexual predator and more of a moral compass. They rewrote some of her scenes so that she would at first resist Larry's attempts to seduce her sexually before, after extended bouts of protest, she would finally give into his cajoling. In effect, she was transformed into a good girl. More important to the story, Janice began to voice more judgmental pronouncements about Larry's cheap attitude toward relationships. Her character came to embody a concession for the more transgressive elements in the screenplay, circulating on an underlying level as an extension of the film's governmental and corporate arbiters of right and wrong.

The character of Verna embodied a much greater sexual and cultural threat than Janice in *They Won't Believe Me* throughout its many production stages, and PCA documents reveal that Harrison worked hard to keep as many of Verna's transgressive qualities as possible. Verna jeopardized the production code for two major reasons: she was sexually assertive and she held a relaxed view of monogamy and marriage. Though she does not fit into the classic femme fatale figure, she is a self-described golddigger who targets him unapologetically in her efforts to enjoy an extramarital affair. The changes requested by the PCA were numerous and Harrison's team satisfied a few of them. For example, in the original draft, Verna wears risqué clothing for her first date with Larry and during the swimming scene she boasts "a very scanty bathing suit" (PCA files, April 26, 1946, 4). In the final film version, Verna's style of dress looks conservative, and both characters don robes just after the swim. The robes were suggested by Breen and, it is worth noting, Harrison resisted the conservative use of bathing robes until a second letter urged her to heed Breen's recommendation (May 28, 1946, 2). Despite the changes, the swimming scene does not wholly retreat from pushing the Code's boundaries regarding "scenes of passion" and allusions toward adultery. Highly suggestive, the swimming scene goes against Breen's directive that "there should be no physical contact between these two people dressed in bathing suits" (April 26, 1946, 4).

Another contention between Breen and the Harrison team concerned a kissing scene between Verna and Larry during one of their first dates. Breen specifically stated, "Verna should not, even for a second, 'respond' to Larry's kisses" (April 26, 1946, 4). Initially, Harrison refused to placate the PCA, keeping Verna's receptive return of the kiss in the script. At this point, William Gordon of the Administration indicated dismay that the scene had not been revised. Gordon states, "As noted in an earlier letter, it is agreeable to indicate that Larry is forcing himself upon her" (May 28, 1946, 2). In other words, Verna's sexual desire was not permitted; however, her sexual victimization was encouraged. Harrison and Latimer managed this suggestion in what might be deemed silent rebuttal. They refused to shift the scene's terms into a moment in which Larry overpowers Verna. Instead, they deleted it and deferred the first kiss until the moment when he places the dime-store ring on her finger. Through such a revision, they accommodated the censors' concern about Verna's sexual receptivity by delaying it until an allusion to marriage dangled in the foreground. They managed, however, to hold onto her assertive "response" to the kiss and, simultaneously, they imbued the questionable swimming sequence with an added touch of eroticism (given that the kiss directly precedes the swim). All in all, the exchanges between Breen and RKO intimate that Harrison made a concerted effort to keep the moments of female sexual agency and controversial heterosexual relations in *They Won't Believe Me* for as long as possible. She also essayed to minimize their curtailment through tactical and strategic script changes, rather than forfeit such moments altogether.

The second major threat caused by Verna, embodied in her progressive politics of monogamy and marriage, also resulted in some subtle maneuvering by Harrison. Verna's disregard for Larry's married status placed her in an unconventional position. She consistently expressed little concern for his relationship with Greta or her own marital status, in early script versions and in the final film. Two specific dialogue lines, however, concerned Breen's office. In the original screenplay, during a conversation that takes place just after the swimming scene, Verna implies that they "don't have to" be married—she would be content with Larry's leaving his wife to live "in sin" with her indefinitely (April 26, 1946, 5). The second reference to cohabitation was more serious. In the original screenplay, Verna gives Larry an ultimatum, asking, "Are you planning to live with her or with me?" The PCA asked for the elimination of this line, given that it directly pointed to illegal conjugal relations (April 26, 1946, 4). The solution for Harrison and Latimer was to change the line so that Verna queries, "Which one are you going to be seeing, her or me?" As the scene builds to this question, the underlying meaning of her question remains; however, the rewritten line does soften the overt reference to extramarital cohabitation. All of these communiqués, and the resulting changes, insinuate that Harrison was attracted to the themes of adultery, bigamy, and unsanctioned sexual relationships. She negotiated this interest with the PCA, making the fewest concessions possible and submitting to alterations only when pushed repeatedly or when she could find a strategy for keeping the implication of her characters' transgressions in tact.

Even when it came to the character of the betrayed wife, Harrison, Pichel, and Latimer exhibited an investment in questioning the institution of marriage. Greta's relationship with Larry seems complicated and even when she shows an effort to make the marriage work, she does not call on tenets of true love or the legalities of marriage. One important speech was deleted in accordance with Breen's request. In the scene in which Greta confronts Larry on his relationship with Verna (and proposes that they move to Santa Barbara), she was originally given a monologue that concerned censors. Greta was to launch into a tirade in which she asked, "What does the outraged wife do?" For her to pose this question would be "offensive" in the PCA's view, because it hinted that divorce might be acceptable in some situations. As a solution, the speech was rewritten so that after an exchange with Larry that frames Greta as sympathetic, she explains, "I can make all the moves, except the one that counts. You'll have to make that on your own." This change allows her to express her lack of mobility, emotionally and institutionally, but it doesn't enable her to articulate fully the message from the "outraged wife" diatribe. Due to PCA pressure, the film could not directly address the fact that in the current social climate, Greta was permitted to respond to Larry's "outrageous" actions in only a very limited way. Nor should she call attention to her restricted range of response options. As a result, Greta's voice was silenced in much the same way as Janice's sexual agency was muffled when her character was rewritten into that of moral guidepost. I would suggest, though, that these "silences" need to be seen in tension with the changes that Harrison's team refused to make. After all, even in the final film version, Greta maintains a flexible view of institutional marriage. Except when she becomes truly possessive at the Santa Barbara ranch, she does not subscribe to romantic images of monogamy and marriage nor does she subscribe to ideal versions of the role of wife.

As Harrison's struggles with the PCA over *They Won't Believe Me* make clear, the producer demonstrated a vested interest in pushing the limits of her women characters' sexual and moral transgressions. She often failed to circumnavigate the pressures of the PCA when she attempted to bestow agency or self-expression on the film's female love objects. The evidence indicates that she did try, however. Even more obvious in *They Won't Believe Me* and other 1940s films such as *Nocturne* and *Ride the Pink Horse* was her investment in taking the sexual and moral transgressions of her male characters as far as she could. In helping to construct a set of values for the world of *They Won't Believe Me*, she made repeated efforts to punish Larry as lightly as possible and compressed his apology and the potential for his redemption down to the bare minimum. At the broad level, her authorial agency consisted of her ability to get the kinds of salacious stories that interested her into the production stage in the first place.

As *They Won't Believe Me* suggests, Harrison's authorship habitually dwells in the pathological and often violent underside of marriage and family. *Phantom Lady* exists as an aberration, in terms of its careful attention to female subjectivity, but it is important because it gave voice to her worldview as a working woman and it laid the groundwork for her later more rigorous investigations of happy endings and normative family institutions. In creating a Harrison film, the producer liked to ask taboo questions: Why can't an unhappy couple get a divorce? Why must someone have only one romantic partner? Aren't there sexual dynamics that underlie the nuclear family and the workplace? What happens to "normal" people when they acknowledge those dynamics? Why are men always the most likely suspects in their wives' murder?

Her authorial agency provides a much needed microhistory as a counterpoint to the imposing master-history associated with Hitchcock's legacy. She functioned as a significant literary influence on Hitchcock and her contribution to his films illuminates the valuable place of development, which is usual women's work, within the studio hierarchy. Moreover, she carved out a space of feminist independence in 1940s Hollywood, daring to exert her producorial control as a lone woman in the studio system and presuming to criticize norms of monogamy, marriage, and family.

Nocturne; *Ride the Pink Horse*; *Once More, My Darling*; and Harrison's other films of the late 1940s present fertile areas for further study. They help constitute a body of work that has been largely ignored by film scholarship. Their influences and implications might be more clear now that Harrison's role as producer-author gives them biographical coherence and political context. Another pressing area of study involves her contribution to the *Alfred Hitchcock Presents* (1955–1962) and *Alfred Hitchcock Hour* (1962–1963) television series at which point her dual function as a consumer and producer of the director's oeuvre intensified greatly. Especially given the uniquely "horrific" place the series took up within the supposedly domestic and domesticated new medium of television, Harrison's work as co-producer (with Norman Lloyd) served many of the same critical and cultural functions as her 1940s films. She had found a venue, a genre, and a collaborative team through which she could exert her authorial agency, an agency that continually surprised her audience with the criminality lurking inside family members and married couples.

113

notes

1. Philip K. Scheuer, "Producer's Spurs Won by Woman," *Los Angeles Times* (February 23, 1944): n.p., Margaret Herrick Library clipping files.
2. Donald Spoto, *Dark Side of Genius: The Life of Alfred Hitchcock* (New York: Ballantine Books, 1983), 162–63.

3. Tom Ryall, *Alfred Hitchcock and the British Cinema* (Urbana and Chicago: University of Illinois Press, 1986), 118.

4. Thomas Schatz defines femme noire as a subset of films within the film noir cycle. Films such as *Rebecca*, *Gaslight* (1944), *The Spiral Staircase* (1946), and *Notorious* (1946) provided a "female Gothic variation of the women's picture" that spoke to different ideological concerns than more male-centered noir films. See Schatz's *Boom and Bust: American Cinema in the 1940s* (Los Angeles and Berkley: University of California Press, 1997), 233.

5. Ann Daggett, "It's a Woman's World Too," *Modern Screen* (February 1945): 22.

6. Patrice Petro, "Rematerializing the Vanishing 'Lady': Feminism, Hitchcock, and Interpretation," in *A Hitchcock Reader*, ed. Marshall Deutelbaum and Leland Poague (Ames: Iowa State University Press, 1986), 131.

7. Rudy Behlmer, ed., *Memo from David O. Selznick* (New York: Viking Press, 1972), 198–203.

8. Tania Modleski, *The Women Who Knew Too Much: Hitchcock and Feminist Theory* (New York and London: Routledge, 1988); Mary Ann Doane, *The Desire to Desire: The Woman's Film of the 1940s* (Bloomington: Indiana University Press, 1987).

9. Charles Bennett, quoted in Patrick McGilligan, *Backstory: Interviews with Screenwriters from Hollywood's Golden Age* (Los Angeles and Berkley: University of California Press, 1986), 36.

10. *Rebecca* Production Files, Harry Ransom Humanities Research Center (Austin: University of Texas, 1939).

11. See Deborah Lazaroff Alpi's *Robert Siodmak: A Biography, with Critical Analysis of His Film Noirs and a Filmography of All His Works* (Jefferson, NC and London: McFarland & Co. Inc., 1998).

12. Daggett, 22; Monica Sullivan, "Joan Harrison," *Movie Magazine International* (September 7, 1994), http://www.shoestring.org.mmi_revs/joanharr.html (accessed November 25, 2001).

13. Schatz, 372–74.

14. Florabel Muir, "Joan Harrison Worrying about Butter," *Hollywood Citizen News* (January 16, 1946), n.p., Margaret Herrick clippings files.

15. Sullivan, http://www.shoestring.org.mmi_revs/joanharr.html.

16. This marketing ploy self-servingly elides the possible ways that earlier femme noire films offered female characters as protagonists.

17. "*Phantom Lady* First Mystery for Lady Fans," *Phantom Lady* pressbook, Universal Studios files (Los Angeles: University of Southern California Archive of Performing Arts, 1944).

18. "*Phantom Lady* provides a New Experience," *Phantom Lady* pressbook.

19. *Phantom Lady*, Production Code Administration files, Margaret Herrick Library (Beverly Hills, CA: Academy of Motion Picture Arts and Sciences, 1944).

20. Muir, n.p.; Daggett, 22; Jerry D. Lewis, "'Murder,' She Says," *Colliers* (August 10, 1943): 55; Barbara Berch, "A Hitchcock Alumna," *New York Times* (June 27, 1943), section II, 3.

21. When Harrison finally did marry at the age of forty-seven in 1958, she continued to present herself as a "working woman" first, someone who delighted in the fact that she had a low-maintenance husband with few domestic demands. In *The Hollywood Reporter*, she gave advice for hopeful women writers concerned about balancing professional life and marriage. Harrison proffered, "If you're smart, you'll be lucky enough to marry a writer. They make the best husbands for career women. They like to work alone and don't really care how the house is run." See Bob Hull, "Marry a Writer, Advises One Lady Producer," *Hollywood Reporter* (April 5, 1968): 1.

22. Gilbert Millstein, "Harrison Horror Story," *New York Times* (July 21, 1957): sect. 6, 44.

23. *They Won't Believe Me* pressbook, RKO (Los Angeles, CA: University of Southern California Archive of Peforming Arts, 1947).

24. *They Won't Believe Me*, Production Code Administration files, Margaret Herrick Library (Beverly Hills, CA: Academy of Motion Picture Arts and Sciences, April 26, 1946), 1.

25. Harrison actually proposed an alternative ending, in which Larry is found "not guilty" and he establishes a future with Janice. The PCA rejected such a conclusion, due to the fact that Larry's punishment needed to be either imprisonment or death. Such a proposal on Harrison's part is interesting, though, because it betrays her own flexible moral perspective on monogamy, marriage, and reproductive sexuality while also revealing that his womanizing did not bother her to the point of making recuperation necessary.

26. *They Won't Believe Me*, Production Code Adminstration files (April 25, 1946), 2.

authorship

and identity

near and

far from

hollywood

intentions and

mass culture

oscar micheaux, identity,

and authorship

hugh bartling

In the spring of 1927, the *Frankfurter Zeitung* published a series of essays by cultural critic Siegfried Kracauer exploring the ways mass society consumed the growing body of spectacular entertainment that characterized contemporary cinema. Beginning his first essay with the proclamation that "films are the mirror of the prevailing society," Kracauer expressed the sentiment that however revolutionary or subversive the intentions of the particular filmmaker were, the product and reception of her or his work would undoubtedly be rendered ineffectual from a political standpoint because of the structural realities informing its production: "either such rebels are simply tools of society, unwittingly manipulated yet all the while believing they are voices of protest, or they are forced to make compromises in their drive to survive."[1]

During precisely the same period, on the other side of the Atlantic Ocean, one of these cinematic "rebels" was in the midst of controversy surrounding public reaction to his films. In the decade following the release of *Within Our Gates* (1919), Oscar Micheaux, a former frontier homesteader and budding cultural producer, occupied an important role in the production of so-called "race films" in the United States, where the Hollywood interests overseeing a segregated film industry rendered dominant images of African Americans through the lens of objectification and shallowness. Micheaux, through cinematic and literary productions, attempted to provide cultural expressions that subverted dominant racial images and represented African Americans in a full and human way. As might be expected, the consumption of these films by both black and white audiences did not proceed without contestation and protest. In an era of intense and often violent oppression of African Americans, Micheaux's attempts at disrupting "the color line" were not always held in high esteem. White audiences and censors often found his bold portrayals of blacks threatening in the context of institutionalized white supremacy.[2] Black audiences often considered some of Micheaux's portrayals of African Americans as replicating the worst racial stereotypes that were prominent in the white Hollywood films of the time.[3]

The divergent views from heterogeneous populations characterizing the response given to Micheaux's work are indicative of the complexities inherent in comprehending a particular cultural producer and the society in which he produces. This chapter seeks to take preliminary steps at understanding these complexities. At issue, for me, are the ways Micheaux, the producer and consumer of culture, is implicated in a presentation of (to use Kracauer's phrase) the "mirror of the prevailing society." I am simultaneously interested in how Micheaux functions as an author and the particular context that made (and still makes) the authorship of his "race movies" politically important.

To explore these issues, I will focus on the nexus between Micheaux's (auto)biography, the consumption/production dynamic of Micheaux's "race movies," and the politicized expression of race that informed the context within which Micheaux's movies were produced and consumed. The three spectra of consideration illuminate the complexities inherent when dealing with the interpretation of authorial intention, reception, and social significance of cultural articulations. The conclusions drawn and new questions that emerge from considering this nexus will be situated in a discussion of the continued relevance of a discussion of the authorship of "race movies" and their reception in our contemporary era.

In my discussion regarding agency, Micheaux, and intentions, I will discuss the efficacy of self-portrayal in his autobiographical fictions and the cinematic presentations within the context of a burgeoning "mass culture." As other scholars have discussed, Micheaux's vision of the world and his experiences encompassed a living example of the "rugged individualism" that has been a central part of the "American myth" since Alexis de Tocqueville. Because of the peculiarities of the African American experience in the United States, however, the deployment of the individualist impulse takes on an important and unique politicized function. The case of Micheaux offers an explicit example of politicized oppositional cultural expression that simultaneously resisted dominant representations of the black experience while engaging in a process of presenting counterimages that were seen in many quarters of urbanized African American communities as essential to improving the black condition. The extent to which his filmmaking was efficacious from the standpoint of political transformation will be discussed in light of the inchoate nature of the burgeoning apparatuses of mass culture.

The experience of Micheaux and "race films" problematizes negative critiques of the culture industry such as those offered by the Frankfurt School. For, if in their estimation, the technology and substance of mass culture shed any liberating potential when it takes the form of a commodity, Micheaux's case offers a compelling counterargument. Many African Americans saw the vehicles of mass culture—such as film—as offering positive opportunities for self-definition. Micheaux's cultural output can be understood as an important effort in civic definition that served the political purpose of asserting the need for African American cultural and social agency.

This moves me to the second aspect of my inquiry, which explores the tensions between the messages set forth in Micheaux's films and the ways the larger public consumed them. In keeping with Kracauer's suggestion that "society is much too powerful for it to tolerate any movies except those with which it is comfortable" and Walter Benjamin's contention that the role of the progressive author is to come to terms with his or her position in the production of culture, I will focus on the problems faced by Micheaux as an independent black filmmaker outside the Hollywood system and as a self-conscious producer of black culture.[4] Reliant on mass consumption of his product to perpetuate his ability to engage in cinematic expression, I talk about how the effort towards "massification" of the African American experience was an urgent and explicit task for African Americans at the time.

The final line of inquiry—that of the political economy of race in the 1920s and 1930s—provides the most important discussion for situating and understanding the productive and consumptive aspects of Micheaux. The interwar period in the United States brought a large number of African Americans from the southern U.S. to the industrial cities of the North. Contradictory impulses characterize urbanization under regimes of capitalism. On the one hand, the alienation that accompanies changes in the productive processes of industrialization has a counterpart in the anonymity, impersonality, and dynamism of the city. On the other hand, urban areas become spaces for the redefinition, remaking, and revitalization of identity. Cities such as Chicago, New York, and Kansas City became centers for black opportunity and cultural creativity. These trends did not go unnoticed by dominant forces of the burgeoning industrial capitalism prevalent in U.S. urban centers. Urban industrialists utilized black labor in place of white in an effort to streamline fiscally the laboring body and encourage working-class fragmentation. As the contradictions of industrial capital became more apparent in the years following World War I, industrial cities were fraught with race riots, lynchings, and other unrest. Although a significant number of black people experienced relative prosperity in urban America, many were concomitantly living under the constant terror of racist acts and economic insecurity. Micheaux's films, being directed at these newly urbanized African Americans, were produced and consumed under these general conditions. The reaction of audiences and the controversy surrounding Micheaux's message can be understood only with these conditions highlighted.

I conclude the chapter by attempting to draw the trajectories together with a general consideration framed around the following question: What is the function of understanding Micheaux as an important author for our contemporary era? To answer this I situate the invocation of Micheaux as the "father of black cinema" within a discussion of contemporary Hollywood and, in particular, the subject of race. I argue that Micheaux is particularly interesting today as a historical example of an oppositional filmmaker engaging in a seemingly counterhegemonic project of rewriting images of race. Revisiting Micheaux is important at this precise moment because the way that race and difference have been coopted into the cultural products of Hollywood has made what seems oppositional and rebellious into a commodity for global capitalism. Put another way, the opposition in which Micheaux was engaged is compelling precisely because the material relations of our contemporary sociocultural dynamic make opposition extremely difficult. If Spike Lee is our Micheaux, what does it mean that Lee is a major Hollywood director? The opposition has been mainstreamed. The intentions of a film such as *Bamboozled* (2000) are occluded in its commodity form. The author-function of Micheaux represents a nostalgic discourse striving for opposition in a culture in which such opportunities currently appear severely limited.

authorship and the invention of the "mass"

The emergence of efficient and expansive methods of cultural articulation and dissemination that accompanied industrialization in the nineteenth and twentieth centuries played an important role in the processes of identity formation and social interpretation. For the first time, the social production of people as masses is possible.

Karl Marx recognized the process of "massification" as indicative of the capitalist regime of production. Under capitalism, human labor is conceived as one of a number of inputs in the production process. In this way labor becomes an object of value, distanced from workers. Individuals are transformed into labor, implying an interchangeability and homogeneity that is associated with abstract value. The mass is objectified human labor, constituting a defining variable in capital's perpetuation and a subsuming of human freedom.[5]

Frankfurt School theorists provided a cultural corollary to Marx's conception of the creation of "masses" under capitalism. Theodor Adorno and Max Horkheimer, for example, argued in *The Dialectic of Enlightenment* that the technology of film and radio and its control by oligopolistic forces ensure that spontaneous and autonomous consumption and production are replaced with control and domination.[6]

For Marx and his latter day interpreters, authorial intent and cultural agency in general are dismissed. Individual consciousness arises in conditions of such disparities in power that autonomous existence is better understood as "mass deception." The abstract rationality that informs the production of culture stifles "organic" expression as the dictates of mechanistic-inspired productive paradigms predetermine the substance of cultural articulations. The realm of consumption that promises satisfaction, liberation, freedom, and identity is simultaneously a process of domination, homogenization, and subjugation. In short, the mass has come to be the determinant and constituent force producing the individual.

The power of these negations begs important questions for notions of authorship and intention. Can authors create counterhegemonic work given power discrepancies? Are the social structures so intractable as to militate against any oppositional and critical messages? What is the value of (auto)biography in a set of conditions that questions notions of autonomy? Does the author as a consumer of ideologically coded cultural products preclude critical expression? Can "mass" media be used for anything other than the reproduction of "masses"?

These questions are particularly important when considering a non-mainstream filmmaker such as Micheaux. By virtue of his very position as a self-consciously African American producer in an era in which the white-dominated "culture industry" presented limited, caricatured, and overwhelmingly derogatory understandings of the black American experience, Micheaux's productions were, by default, outside of the realm of hegemonic cultural institutions. Yet, as I will argue below, the dominant debates surrounding what should constitute African American and American identity infused his artistic output. As such, Micheaux was a diligent consumer of the culture industry in an age of mechanical reproduction. His position as cultural consumer must be read in light of larger forces in which his creative expressions were enmeshed. *Contra* the Frankfurt School, Micheaux produced oppositional messages that worked within established conventions. In fact, the central counterhegemonic strategy perpetrated by Micheaux was to embrace the notion of the "mass" that was able to emerge via the techniques of mechanical reproduction. Although the dominant culture industry during Micheaux's career retained the financial, distributive, and ideological power to propagate deleterious images of African

Americans, the contributions of blacks themselves to counteract dominant characterizations through the assertion of an alternative "mass" identity necessitates a sober assessment of the efficacy stemming from these endeavors. Rather than arguing that oppositional art cannot exist within the confines of the mechanistic culture industry, the experience of Micheaux and debates among African American cultural commentators during the 1910s and 1920s suggest that the creation of a unified mass vision of African American life was integral toward effecting social change and that the consumption of ideas and ideologies inherent in dominant cultural expressions was a central component of this endeavor.

consumption and oppression: practical strategies of uplift

Prominent debates in the burgeoning and vibrant black press (in which Micheaux was enmeshed as a participant, subject, and observer) show the urgency with which identity formation was addressed. Indeed I will argue that Micheaux's films can best be understood as responses to the evolving tenor of this established debate. Furthermore, the deliberate strategy of revisioning and reconstructing an alternative notion of the African American experience utilizing film as a mass medium was essential to Micheaux's perceived prospects of success. Thus, the prospect of mass representation is revealed less as a constrictive category of dehumanization than as a practice of *rehumanization*. The efficacy of this prospect is another matter, which will be taken up in the concluding section of this chapter.

Although a critic such as Walter Benjamin is ambivalent regarding the prospects of mechanical reproduction, his discussion of authorship reveals a more sanguine disposition. In his essay "The Author as Producer," he takes issue with the idea that tendentious content solely determines progressive authorship. Seeing art as being produced within the context of social relations, he is less concerned with the artist's work as either being supportive or resistant to forces of domination. Rather, he is interested in the practical activities and processes that the author embodies as she or he addresses relations of production. Having the "right" message, in this regard, is not enough. One must *act* and *produce* in a critical and progressive manner. Evoking the Soviet writer Sergei Tretiakov, Benjamin shows how "functional transformation" can be realized as the writer is simultaneously the organizer utilizing new technologies to articulate a transformative vision of the world. The author needs to avoid "supply[ing] a productive apparatus without . . . changing it."[7]

Oscar Micheaux, as an oppositional filmmaker, illuminates both the insights and pitfalls of the critical-theory approach to the role of culture in capitalist societies. He represents the complex position in which the oppositional producer is found when faced not only with inequitable class dynamics, but also with a historical legacy of racial and ethnic oppression that abuts the spaces for hope carved from what W. E. B. Du Bois referred to as "the greater ideals of the American Republic."[8] Put more simply, Micheaux's experiences exhibit the possibilities and obstacles endured on that indeterminate road toward being "a co-worker in the kingdom of culture."[9]

The legacy of racial and ethnic oppression in North America, of course, can be traced to the first instances of European presence. But the period encompassing the first half of the twentieth century represented an important era in the African American struggle for civil rights and social acceptance in American society. During this era, black migration from the southern United States to primarily northern urban centers increased dramatically. As Du Bois pointedly demonstrates in *The Souls of Black Folk*, the Reconstruction and post-Reconstruction South failed to ensure social, economic, and political security for African Americans. Jim Crow laws legitimized institutional discrimination and systematic social exclusion and violence contributed to an atmosphere of terror.

Simultaneous with these conditions in the black South were larger economic and political changes. The lure of urban areas that attracted not only blacks, but also immigrants from throughout the world, stemmed from the prominence of industrialization and the concomitant need for wage laborers. Industrial capitalism needs labor concentrated in urban spaces to realize its efficiency, and the uncertainties and inconsistencies associated with agricultural production make urban migration attractive to rural populations. With the ascendancy of urbanization comes a transformation of the human condition.

The peculiar characteristics of urban industrialization were understood early by the Chicago School sociologists who recognized the need for a systematic, empirical study of the city. As opposed to rural or village life, which was marked by communal empathy, social intimacy, and sentimentality, the developing city was better understood as impersonal, rational, and dominated by bureaucratic institutions.[10] According to Robert Park, "the modern city . . . is primarily a convenience of commerce and owes its existence to the market place around which it sprang up."[11] Park emphasizes that for city residents, these market relations privilege their identities as members of an occupational category. These market relations were but a component of the new urban subject: a whole host of different ways to think about the "self" was also emerging. The complexity of industrial city life is structured upon the mobilization and expansion of such reified categories as worker, consumer, client, employer, and patron. The anonymity and insecurity inherent in rapidly growing cities led, in this sense, to a crisis in subjectivity. It is no coincidence that many different authors have recognized the political contestation inherent in attempts to define subjectivities in the modern era. From Michel Foucault's concern with disciplinization to Jurgen Habermas's discussion of the development of "public opinion," from Stuart Ewen's depiction of the rise of the advertising industry to Alan Trachtenberg's rendering of the naturalness of the corporate ideal in America, each of these diverse efforts describes the imperative of fixing identities in an increasingly complex and anonymous world.[12]

For African Americans involved in the Great Migration, the turmoil of "identity fixing" took on an especially significant character. The legacy of slavery and its aftermath was rife with attempts to fix blackness for the purposes of oppression. Du Bois's powerful metaphor of the "veil" was a way of describing the power of inscription to denigrate the humanity of African Americans. Although recent scholarship has shown that the spectator, or consumer of culture, has the capacity to resist and reformulate representations, the power of representation should not be underestimated given the context of inequitable social, political, and economic relations.[13] Seen from the standpoint of the emergent political economy of fixing identities, Micheaux's cultural work must be understood as emerging out of an urgent need to develop alternative renderings of black identity in response to a craving for stability on the part of an urbanizing African American mass and the simultaneous hijacking of racial identity by forces steeped in the discriminatory history of white treatment of black Americans.

Although the emergence of mass culture may have had the effect of disciplinization and domination, it also provided opportunities for self-definition. One component of the mass media that served as an arena for exploring African American self-definition was the black press. As African Americans moved north and developed populations of scale in urban areas, newspapers emerged to serve these populations. Communications and transportation technologies became more efficient and expansive, and these periodicals were distributed to areas beyond their cities of origination. Papers such as the *Chicago Defender* had national readership and prominently featured discussions and stories about the systematic civil and social discrimination of African Americans (particularly in the South), the promise of northern urban areas, and efforts at self-definition for blacks in a society seemingly hostile to their ambitions.[14]

Micheaux, as an ambitious and socially concerned African American, was a consumer and follower of these debates brewing in the black press and they had formative effects on his cultural output. In his autobiographical novel, *The Conquest*, which depicted his time as a homesteader in South Dakota, he notes that as one of the only African Americans homesteading in his region, he was relatively isolated and his "closest companion was the magazines [*sic*]."[15] This is particularly important in the context of his narrative as this statement is immediately followed by the thought that "this brings to my mind certain conditions which exist concerning the ten odd millions of the Black race in America; and more, this, in itself had a tendency to open wider the gap between a certain class of the race and myself."[16] That a discussion of his digestion of periodicals would "bring to mind" the varying conditions of African Americans suggests that the debates regarding the black experience were of immense interest to Micheaux.[17]

The texture of these debates contextualizes the substance of Micheaux's films and novels and speaks to his efforts toward influencing the portrayal of African Americans in light of the possibilities and obstacles inherent in the emergent film industry. A recurring theme of many of Micheaux's works is the promise of redemption of the race through the good deeds of extraordinary individuals. Whether it is Oscar Devereaux making good as a rugged homesteader in *The Conquest*, Sylvia Landry's effort to secure funds to keep the doors of a rural southern school open in *Within Our Gates* (1920), or Sidney Wyeth's determination to advancing discursive self-reflection among southern blacks in *The Forged Note* (1915), the heroes of Micheaux's works are determined individuals who overcome economic obstacles, racial discrimination, and the indolence of fellow African Americans who through their self-absorbed and languorous behavior are "keeping the race down."

Similar sentiments were evident in the black press whose mission to report the news affecting the black community was supplemented with suggestions on how to properly "represent the race." Proper decorum exhibited in the public space of the theater, for instance, was discussed in a May 1920 article in the *Chicago Broad-Ax*. Approving the recent integration of the Avenue Theatre, the article discussed mixed-race audience reaction to "two remarkable little plays" in which the actors "were engaged in enacting the most intense parts of the plays and pouring their souls and all of their life into their art or high-class acting." According to the anonymous black correspondent, "many of those occupying seats in all parts of the theatre who were dressed in the height of fashion laughed out loud, kept up a continual noise and applauded at the wrong time to the utter disgust of decent or half-civilized people." A white couple was described as restrained whereas, "on the other hand a Colored lady and gentlemen occupied seats right next to us and they spent most of their time in talking out real loud and laughing or giggling like unto silly or brainless creatures." In this article the desegregation of the Avenue Theatre is presented as positive, as people of all races were able to achieve equal accommodation. Yet, the mere fact of accessibility was not enough to "reflect the highest culture or refinement so far planted in the breasts or the minds or the hearts of the Colored people." Rather it led the correspondent to remark that "one of the most important things that the vast majority of Colored people are sadly in need of at the present time is self-control."[18] That the story of racial behavior in an integrated theater was front-page news of a major black newspaper speaks to the importance placed on the

127

need for the construction of a counterhegemonic black representation in a political and social context of racial discrimination. Although it may appear conservative or accommodative to regard the white couple's behavior as exemplary and the black behavior as "silly or brainless," a contextual reading makes this interpretation untenable. Situated on the same front page of this issue of the *Broad-Ax* were articles describing a militant N.A.A.C.P.'s probing questioning of United States presidential candidates, Pullman porters successfully defending themselves against belligerent white passengers during a train car brawl, and efforts of an Arkansas county to ban possession of the *Chicago Defender*. Thus, literally next to the discussion of inappropriate theater behavior were strong statements of appropriate actions by African Americans.

The contradictions described here in a specific page of the *Broad-Ax* were typical of the black press during the 1910s and 1920s. Seemingly conflictive messages of accommodation and resistance, compromise and protest, integration and separation speak not to inconsistencies in argument or disposition, but rather to the complex undertaking of identity construction made possible by the emergent technologies of mass expression. Micheaux, himself, recognized the challenges inherent in redefining African American identity. The protagonist, Sidney Wyeth, of his 1915 novel, *The Forged Note*, which is the story of a northern novelist and entrepreneur traveling to the South to sell his books and conduct research, consistently comments on the need for African American self-definition. Early in the novel Wyeth finds himself in "Attalia," "the greatest commercial city southeast of the Mississippi . . . a progressive journalistic city"(34) and confronts local black professionals while searching for office space. Learning that Wyeth is from the North, they query him as to his impressions of their southern city. Wyeth offers these gentlemen who "were distinguished looking, compared with the average Negro" that he has been "considerably impressed with what I have seen" and that the office building in which they met "is probably the most commodious structure owned and operated by our people, in any city."[19] He notes that the building is populated by professionals, occupations that "count for much in the solution of the race problem."[20]

For all of the praise bestowed upon the symbols of middle-class values evident in the city, Wyeth does feel compelled to offer pointed criticism. He stirs a "hornet's nest" by chiding the lack of readership of "*The Climax*, which is, as you know, published in New York, and edited by a man who used to be professor of sociology in one of your colleges."[21] Wyeth contends that the development of African Americans in Attalia will be stifled unless *The Climax* is "read in proportion to what they should" because "it's the only magazine edited by, and in the interest of this race."[22] Here Micheaux is proposing the importance of autonomous cultural practice in the construction of black identity. Simply "making good" by attaining "respectability" through the assertion of middle-class values and occupations was not unitarily sufficient for the project of racial "uplift." People literally had to "be on the same page" and participate in the development of group cultural identity through the consumption of mass media. In one sense, Micheaux's heroes in *The Forged Note*, Wyeth, and *Murder in Harlem* (1935), Henry Glory, represent the apotheosis of African American forthrightness, as they are simultaneously cultural producers and entrepreneurs. These "authors as producers" follow Benjamin's characterization to the extent that they are not merely presenting the "right ideas," but also, more importantly, they are engaged in a particular mode of authorial *practice* as budding entrepreneurs.[23]

Micheaux held steadfast to the need for autonomous authorial practice. As J. Ronald Green has pointed out in his study of Micheaux, Du Bois is later singled out in *The Forged Note* for criticism as a writer who failed to depict accurately the African American character in his fiction.[24] Instead of being forthright about displaying "the fact that the Negro possesses many vices,"[25] Micheaux's narrator contends that Du Bois dwells on the "evil of prejudice," which does nothing except "to prepare ourselves for eternal misery."[26] Because black audiences are already intimately aware of racial oppression "to dwell upon the white man's prejudice, we will surely become pessimists." For Micheaux this type of theme is self-defeating for "it is the purpose of the practical Negro to forget that condition as much as possible."[27]

Far from being the "black novelist as white racist" portrayed by scholar Joseph Young, Micheaux was intimately enmeshed within the urgent project of forging autonomous African American identity. The urgency of self-definition was a consistent theme appearing in the black press. The lead, front-page editorial from the April 17, 1920, issue of the *Defender* is an example:

> Few big things are there in this world today that do not owe their success to the pioneer work of the propagandist. It is vitally important to tune the public ear to the note that is to be struck, that it may sound pleasing and harmonious. Men and things many times ride into popularity not through worth and merit, but because advance agents, paid or otherwise, have prepared the public mind to receive them.[28]

Far from thinking of the propagandist in Engles's sense of being the perpetrator of "false consciousness," the function is presented here as being a "big thing" in its service to the African American social and political struggle. The content of the propaganda must represent the full spectrum of the African American experience but should concentrate by "begin[ing] to toot our own horn, [we] must bring to the public notice our best side, [we] must devise ways and means of offsetting the influences that are working for our overthrow."[29] The ways and means by which this is to be done are apparent as "there are those who have eyes yet see not . . . it is to these we must give our attention. On the stage, screen, through the press, from the pulpit, from the platform, our propaganda must find place."[30]

Micheaux agreed with these sentiments and addressed the issue explicitly in an article appearing in *Half-Century Magazine* entitled "The Negro and the Photo-Play." He recognized the portents of the politics of representation by recounting an experience he had with a white member of a film board of censors who had "prepared a Scenario concerning Colored people" for him to produce ornamented with the insulting title, "A Good Old Darkey." This "kindly disposed northern woman" represented for Micheaux the assumption that white impressions of blacks as dehumanized were so intractable that "it seems the white race will never come to look at us in a serious light."[31] In response to the reality of the situation, Micheaux argues that it is incumbent upon African Americans to engage aggressively in practices of self-definition: "men and women must write original stories of Negro life, and as the cost of producing high class photo-plays is high, money must be risked in Negro corporations for this purpose."[32]

cinema and self-definition

Through these statements the need for autonomous expression is considered both pressing and necessarily expansive. The cinema, in particular, held a unique position in this regard. Films, as general forms of cultural expression, were, from the early days of the commercial cinema, politically contested terrain. Local censor boards and the codified and informal self-censorship agreements adhered to by major production houses are evidence of this fact. For African Americans, as consumers and producers situated on filmmaking's margins, the power of the cinema as a representational force was intimately understood. Micheaux himself was constantly contending with censor boards that had objections to the character of his representations. However, much of the discontentment came from within the black community itself—especially from ministers. In Micheaux's case, the enmity of black ministers may have come from his rather negative portrayals of the black church.[33] But evidence also suggests that there was a wider distrust of movies as a form of expression. Jean Voltaire Smith speculates that some black ministers saw the movies as a competitor for the attention of the masses:

Long sermons against the movies, admonitions to stay away from them, seem to result in empty pews in the church and an augmented attendance at the picture show around the corner. The minister faces his tiny audience in despair while the long lines wait patiently for their opportunity to purchase a ticket from the pretty cashier at the nearby film theatre. While rain might cause half of the congregation to remain home, it has little or no effect on the movie crowd.[34]

Much of the clerical skepticism of moviegoing had to do not only with the prurient subject matter of early commercial motion pictures and their penchant for sensationalism or their luring of the church's audiences, but also with the general black absence as producers and actors in anything other than stereotypical roles. In defending the movies against ministers' disdain, Smith offers an alternative vision: "Would it not be better then, to encourage more of our people to produce pictures—films of the clean, helpful sort, that will uplift; urge them to build first class moving picture theaters, rather than discourage them from attending picture shows?"[35] An article from the *Half-Century Magazine* in 1919 expressed a similar sentiment and situated black cinema within the larger issue of the African American condition: "If our Colored people with interest of the race at heart, would pool their money, stop fighting each other, and get down to business, they would not only reap unlimited returns, but also do the race a great service."[36]

Black cinema production was only one aspect of the urgency of self-definition that was promoted in the black press. Positive consumption of films was also encouraged. In another article defending the movies from criticism by "distinguished ministers of the sacred gospel,"[37] *The Chicago Broad Ax* recognized the power of mass consumption to affect social change:

> Frequently pictures are shown that capitalize the Negro as a janitor, or some kind of monkey; this is merely a fill in, and should not be regarded seriously, but it is generally observed that when such pictures are shown a lot of vapory and ignorant Negroes laugh themselves shamefully at their own people. Some attention should be given to pictures of this character and especially in houses patronized chiefly by the race, the managers should be given to understand that we regard such pictures as a reflection upon the intelligence of the patrons, and they must cut all such pictures out if they wish the patronage and support we seem to be giving them.[38]

The power of the cinema is expressed here not in its capacity for representation, but in its form as a commodity. Urbanizing populations are asked to withhold patronage of facilities that play objectionable movies as an effort of asserting the autonomy of African American presence. Although the power of the consumer is certainly not tantamount to political or economic freedom, it is important to recognize its presence in association with a discourse of emancipative strivings.

These expressions of interest in the black press and Micheaux's consumption of and contribution to the debate of autonomous identity construction must be understood within the larger context of the emergence of a black "mass" that was considered necessary for the realization of African American political and social rights. Rather than "massification" being thought of as a mechanism of domination, the black press

131

set it forth as a strategy for continual emancipation. This is not to argue that African American commentators ignored the deleterious effects of mass representation. The defining of identity was looked upon as an essential political struggle. In a portentous commentary two months before Chicago's bloody race riots of 1919, the *Chicago Defender* responded to a series of reports undertaken by one of the city's major white papers on the "race problem." Instead of being a thoughtful exercise in reportage, the white reporter's representation of race relations was based upon the assumption "that the white man has some sort of a proprietary interest in the Negro. That he is a something to be disposed of as the whim or caprice of the ruling class may dictate."[39] The reporter also blamed African Americans for the city's crime, destitution, and insalubrious living conditions implying that decreasing the number of blacks in Chicago would result in the rectification of these urban problems.[40] To answer this misrepresentation, aggressive efforts toward self-defining the African American experience and its contribution to the city were needed:

> The public mind is very susceptible to suggestion, as evidenced by frequent race clashes and neighborhood disturbances that follow in the wake of newspaper discussion of the so-called race problem. It is also an undisputed fact that our white neighbors are largely influenced in their attitude toward us by what they read in the public press. If the newspapers wish to help us they can do us no greater service than by ceasing to magnify the evil that we do while minimizing the good. . . . Public sentiment is very much like fashions; it follows the vogue. If the Negro is constantly held up to ridicule in the press the fickle public will take the position that it is not fashionable to treat a Negro with human decency.[41]

Within this context the black press, along with conscious artists such as Micheaux, worked. The prominence of mass media's power to represent could not be discounted or ignored. Rather, it was an urgent effort of survival that motivated much cultural production and informed the content of its messages. Micheaux recognized what his contemporary John Robinson argued, namely that "the Negro problem is but a human problem, demanding human treatment."[42] His cinema and fiction both represent practical applications of the politics of humanization.

132

conclusion

A major contribution of Adorno and Horkheimer's *Dialectic of Enlightenment* was to demonstrate that modernity was composed of two simultaneous logics: that of human emancipation from myth and that of the devaluation of humanity. In their discussion of the culture industry, the workings of the latter logic are emphasized. The "economicization" of culture corresponds to the dominance of mass production whereby mechanistic models (re)present humans as workers, consumers, or producers. The very structure of capitalism's production of mass society inhibits any counterexpression. Its purview is expansive and impenetrable.

Certainly, in early commercial cinema—and in particular the representations of African Americans in white mainstream movies—the dominant representations are those that either reinforce or replicate societal relations. For African Americans, with the legacy of slavery fresh in recent memory and the reality of institutional discrimination and lynching immediately apparent, the dehumanized representations of black life were especially powerful. Yet, the emergence of cinema as a mass medium occurred during a particularly significant time. Intellectually, black thinkers as diverse as Booker T. Washington and W. E. B. Du Bois were attempting to connect theory with practice in efforts to forge a respected space for African Americans within American society. The power of industrialization, which fostered black migration and urbanization, presented new opportunities along with the perennial obstacles of racism.

Films, novels, and journalism were consistently touted as mechanisms of uplift precisely because, when these same technologies were used in the service of a dominant racist social and political structure, they had such dramatic force of manipulating public opinion in a way that served to continue racial oppression. In a counterhegemonic fashion, producers such as Micheaux tried to utilize and manipulate the forms at their disposal in oppositional ways. Green, for example, debunks portrayals of Micheaux as a simple accomodationist by showing how his much-maligned production values and melodrama constituted a simultaneous assertion of black identity and a reworking of dominant white values of individualism, class, and gender.[43]

Micheaux's significance lies in his embodiment of a decidedly counterhegemonic practice within the context of a concerted effort toward asserting black autonomy in a hostile environment. He was counterhegemonic to the extent that his personal experiences and cultural articulations appropriated themes and episodes that had previously belonged only to whites: homesteading, filmmaking, entrepreneurship, and presenting his race as having the full range of human emotions and dispositions. And, as seen from the discussion of the black press, Micheaux's efforts were ensconced within an important strategy of uplift that a newly urbanizing African American civil society saw as an essential component of the road toward the social acceptance of blacks in the United States.

Any materialist account of culture, however, can be assessed only by what Benjamin called the "process of production."[44] It is undeniable that Micheaux's content and his methods of production and distribution were oppositional. Whether this is because of his literal position

133

on the margins or because of deliberate political/authorial strategy is the subject of fascinating contemporary research.[45] He certainly was able, particularly in his early silent films *Within Our Gates* and *Body and Soul* (1925), to disrupt poignantly and forcefully dominant representations of African Americans. From the investigation of nascent African American views of mass culture presented above, I have shown he was part of a self-conscious movement of artists, intellectuals, journalists, and professionals who were interested in presenting a revised vision of the African American experience through mass media.

Nevertheless, the consequences of his oppositional production should be interpreted critically. It could be argued that the counterhegemonic black filmmaking of Melvin Van Peebles or, more recently, Spike Lee, is indebted to the pioneering work of Micheaux. These are filmmakers who have been able to provide alternative, thoughtful, political portraits of race relations in contemporary America. Lee, in particular, as discussed by Amiri Baraka, has wanted to establish an autonomous black presence in contemporary filmmaking.[46] Yet the specter of the Frankfurt School's trenchant critique still looms. As the culture industry has become further consolidated, as black cultural expressions in the forms of hip-hop music and style have become mainstream, images and representations stemming from the corporatized teleculture have continued to assert their primacy. When the inane caricatures of *Booty Call* (1997) overwhelmingly outperform Lee's incisive *Bamboozled* (2000) at the box office, what hath mass representation wrought? Regardless of the existence of counterhegemonic, politicized, and self-defining oppositional forms of cultural expression, the autonomy of the culture industry remains a formidable force, able to coopt, redefine, and refashion, rendering intentional expressions of resistance docile.

notes

1. Siegfried Kracauer, *The Mass Ornament: Weimar Essays* (Cambridge, MA: Harvard University Press, 1995), 291.
2. Charlene Regester, "Black Films, White Censors: Oscar Micheaux Confronts Censorship in New York, Virginia, and Chicago," in *Movie Censorship and American Culture*, ed. Francis G. Couvares (Washington, D.C.: Smithsonian Institution Press, 1996).
3. Pearl Bowser and Louise Spence, "Oscar Micheaux's *Body and Soul* and the Burden of Representation," *Cinema Journal* 39, no. 3 (Spring 2000): 3.
4. See Kracauer, 292, and Walter Benjamin, "The Author as Producer [1934]," trans. Edmund Jephcott in *Reflections: Essays, Aphorisms, Autobiographical Writing*, ed. Peter Demetz (New York: Harcourt Brace Jovanovich, 1978).
5. Karl Marx, "Results of the Immediate Process of Production," in *Capital, Volume One*, trans. Ben Fowkes (London: Penguin Books, 1976), 1062.
6. Max Horkheimer and Theodor Adorno, *Dialectic of Enlightenment* (New York: Continuum, 1991).
7. Walter Benjamin, "The Author as Producer," 228.
8. W. E. B. Du Bois, "The Souls of Black Folk," in *The Norton Anthology of African-American Literature*, ed. Henry Louis Gates, Jr. and Nellie Y. McKay (New York: W. W. Norton, 1997), 619.

9. Du Bois, "The Souls of Black Folk," 615.
10. The extent to which this romanticized formulation of rural and village life—especially for African Americans in the South—was verisimilitudinous is debatable.
11. Robert E. Park, Ernest Burgess, and Roderick Mackenzie, eds., *The City* (Chicago: University of Chicago, 1925), 12.
12. Michel Foucault, *Discipline and Punish* (New York: Vintage, 1977); Jurgen Habermas, *The Structural Transformation of the Public Sphere* (Cambridge, MA: MIT Press, 1991); Stuart Ewen, *Captains of Consciousness: Advertising and the Social Roots of the Consumer Culture* (New York: McGraw-Hill, 1988); Alan Trachtenberg, *The Incorporation of America* (New York: Hill and Wang, 1982).
13. For a dated, but comprehensive, discussion of the debates surrounding the author/reader dynamic see Pauline Marie Rosenau, *Post-modernism and the Social Sciences* (Princeton, NJ: Princeton University Press, 1992); on oppositional readings of *Birth of a Nation* see Manthia Diawara, "Black Spectatorship: Problems of Identification and Resistance," in *Black American Cinema*, ed. Manthia Diawara (New York: Routledge, 1993).
14. The *Defender* was such an influential force in redefining the black American experience that some southern counties made the distribution or possession of the paper a criminal offense. See "Enjoin Sale of Negro Newspaper," *Chicago Broad-Ax* (May 13, 1920).
15. Oscar Micheaux, *The Conquest* (Lincoln: University of Nebraska Press, 1994), 142.
16. Micheaux, *The Conquest*, 142.
17. Further evidence of Micheaux's consumption of the black press lies in his written contributions to newspapers such as the *Chicago Defender*. See Pearl Bowser and Louise Spence, *Writing Himself into History: Oscar Micheaux, His Silent Films, and His Audiences* (New Brunswick, NJ: Rutgers University Press, 2000). Micheaux as an irregular newspaper correspondent is particularly interesting in light of Walter Benjamin's commentary on the nascent Soviet press being a laudable example of dismantling the distinction between the author and the reader. "For the reader is at all times ready to become a writer, that is, a describer, but also a prescriber. As an expert—even if not on a subject but only on the post he occupies—he gains access to authorship. Work itself has its turn to speak." The black press in particular provided this emancipatory function and was essential in processes of African American self-definition in the face of white hostility. See Walter Benjamin, "The Author as Producer," in *Reflections*, ed. Peter Demetz (New York: Harcourt, Brace Jovanovich, 1978), 225.
18. "Many Colored People Attending the Avenue Theatre Conduct Themselves in a Noisy or Boisterous Manner," *Chicago Broad-Ax* (May 13, 1920).
19. Oscar Micheaux, *The Forged Note* (Lincoln: Western Book Supply, 1915), 64.
20. Micheaux, *The Forged Note*, 64.
21. The obvious reference is to W. E. B. Du Bois and *The Crisis*—the major periodical of the N.A.A.C.P.
22. Micheaux, *The Forged Note*, 65, 66.
23. See n. 18 and Benjamin, "The Author as Producer." Given his Marxist tendencies Benjamin probably would not have equated entrepreneurship with the "correct" form of authorial production.
24. J. Ronald Green, *Straight Lick: The Cinema of Oscar Micheaux* (Bloomington: Indiana University Press, 2000), 18.
25. Micheaux, *The Forged Note*, 443.
26. Micheaux, *The Forged Note*, 442.
27. Micheaux, *The Forged Note*, 442.
28. "Welcome Stranger," *Chicago Defender* (April 17, 1920), 1.
29. "Welcome Stranger," 1.

30. "Welcome Stranger," 1.
31. Oscar Micheaux, "The Negro and the Photo-Play," *Half-Century Magazine* (May 1919), 9.
32. Micheaux, "The Negro and the Photo-Play," 11.
33. On movie censorship in general see Francis G. Couvares, ed., *Movie Censorship and American Culture* (Washington, D.C.: Smithsonian Institution Press, 1996). On Micheaux's experience with censors see Regester, "Black Films, White Censors."
34. Jean Voltaire Smith, "Our Need For More Films," *The Half-Century Magazine* (April 1922), 8.
35. Smith, "Our Need For More Films," 8.
36. Juli Jones, Jr., "Motion Pictures and Inside Facts," *Half-Century Magazine* (July 1919): 19.
37. "The Movies Detrimental to the Negro Child," *Chicago Broad Ax* (January 24, 1920): 1.
38. "The Movies Detrimental to the Negro Child," 1.
39. "No Longer Chattels," *Chicago Defender* (May 24, 1919): 1.
40. "No Longer Chattels," 1. Interestingly, the removal of African Americans from Chicago was not a mere rhetorical suggestion. A week before this article appeared, the *Defender* reported that the Chicago Association of Commerce had sent a telegram to southern chambers of commerce saying that there was a large surplus of black labor in Chicago and that southern businesses were welcome to come to Chicago to recruit black workers. Many southern businesses advertised in northern black papers during the 1910s and 1920s for laborers. See "Labor Agents are Shunned in Chicago," *Chicago Defender* (May 17, 1919) and "Rainbow Chasing," *Chicago Defender* (April 10, 1920).
41. "No Longer Chattels," 1.
42. John W. Robinson, "Can the Negro Solve His Own Problem," *Half-Century Magazine* (June 1919).
43. Green, *Straight Lick*.
44. Benjamin, "The Author as Producer," 228.
45. See Green, *Straight Lick*, Bowser and Spence, *Writing Himself into History*, and Pearl Bowser, Jane Gaines, and Charles Musser, eds. *Oscar Micheaux and His Circle: African-American Filmmaking and Race Cinema of the Silent Era* (Bloomington: Indiana University Press, 2001).
46. Amiri Baraka, "Spike Lee at the Movies," in *Black American Cinema*, ed. Manthia Diawara (New York: Routledge, 1993).

cundieff's revision of masculinity in film, or, a "hard" man is not necessarily good to find

seven

jacqueline fulmer

"a zest for parodies and an impatience with sacred cows"[1]

Screenwriter/director Rusty Cundieff spent the 1990s jumping between film genres, from the critically acclaimed rap parody *Fear of a Black Hat* (1993),[2] to the urban horror anthology *Tales From the Hood* (1995),[3] to the romantic comedy *Sprung* (1997),[4] the last two co-written with Darin Scott. All three feature mostly African American casts, broad humor, and sociopolitical themes. Where their humor and themes intersect are revisions of stereotypes of African American masculinity. In examining Cundieff's productions over time, his authoring practices reveal what Henry Louis Gates, Jr., has called, "an awareness of previous black traditions" that artists such as Cundieff "self-consciously echo, imitate, parody and revise in acts of 'riffing' or 'signifying' or even 'sampling'" (Gates, 66).

Gates refers to Cundieff specifically as one of the "new artists" who comprise what "may truly be the renaissance to end all renaissances" (Gates, 66). The filmmaker represents one of those artists who, as

Gates sees it, displays "confidence in the legitimacy of black experiences as artistic material," is "more conscious of their cultural traditions," and "presume[s] the universality of the black experience" (Gates, 66). Whereas Gates refers to Rusty Cundieff as the impetus behind the movies directed and written under that name, I use his name to represent the productions attributed to him in the spirit of Janet Staiger's "authorship as technique of the self," which examines "authoring as an 'art of existence,'" as "a repetitive assertion of 'self-as-expressor' through culturally and socially laden discourses" (Gates, 66).[5] Cundieff's films not only express ideas he lays claim to in interviews, they also repeat African American "methods for self-expression" from folk culture, which enable Cundieff and company to perform a "'transcending,' 'defamiliarizing,' 'subverting,' or 'resisting'" of a white hegemonic system (Staiger, 52).

In this chapter, I will point out how Cundieff's productions strive toward all of the above by signifying on stereotypes of African American men in films. This resistance via signification takes its strength from an awareness of both "previous black traditions" and previous film history (Gates, 66). "Signifying" in this use derives from an African American tradition of word play, "a way of encoding messages" in which a speaker uses terms that initially sound familiar and non-confrontational to the listener, but actually undermine the listener.[6] "It can mean making fun of a person or situation," or can "stir up a fight," by using "great innuendo" "to talk around a subject."[7] Geneva Smitherman includes "signification" under the "folk-oral tradition of the black masses," describing it as "the act of talking negatively about somebody through stunning and clever verbal put downs" and may include "elements of sarcasm," "indirection, circumlocution . . . punning, play on words," and "introduction of the semantically or logically unexpected."[8] But the point of such "humorous, ironic," "teachy but not preachy" signification "is to put somebody in check, that is, make them think about and, one hopes, correct their behavior" (Smitherman, 1977, 120–1).

Cundieff's films signify by initially repeating African American images in ways that viewers may find familiar at first. However, they utilize elements of African American traditional culture, as filtered through the perspective of each film, to undercut viewers' assumptions and thereby to humorously put filmgoers "in check" and "make them think." "Black experiences as artistic material," as Gates describes them, in the areas of music, folk tales, and folk utterances bolster the Cundieff productions' subversion of gender as well as racial assumptions (Gates, 66). The films repeat familiar stereotypes, then undermine viewer assumptions with shockingly funny reversals or inversions. Ultimately, an emphasis on an individual's responsibility to community emerges as a major factor in male, or female, identity.

The overall approach of the films reflects a trickster-like duality, also

jacqueline fulmer

a quality that echoes African American folk tradition. The trickster "lives by his wits," often by camouflaging transgression with a mask of amiability.[9] "His behavior at odds with the cultural values that restrain him," tricksters in African American folklore embody elements of "wish fulfillment and role inversion" (Joyner, 150–1). Role inversions and hints of "correction," which appear in African American trickster tales and folk practices such as signification, lurk throughout Cundieff's films. Thematically, Cundieff and company's bawdy *Fear of a Black Hat* (hereafter referred to as *Hat*), morbidly comic *Tales From the Hood* (hereafter referred to as *Tales*), and light-hearted *Sprung* signify upon the music documentary, horror, and romantic comedy genres and upon African American inter- and intraracial relationships. The corrective, didactic element appears most prominently in the second film, though. Those characters who do not change in *Tales* die.

The folk influence alters from music and language traditions in *Hat*, to images and storytelling references from folklore in *Tales*, to folk utterances in *Sprung*. Geneva Smitherman and Alan Dundes, among other scholars, include among the "'original contributions' of the folk" "folk utterances, songs and tales of folk expression," "folk expressive rituals," "folk speech with special reference to traditional names and slang,"[10] and "important forms of traditional word play, e.g., of 'signifying' and 'playing the dozens,'" as equally vital to "folk" culture as folktales and legends (Smitherman, 1977, 103). Cundieff's productions utilize broad aspects of folk culture, though often cloaked in images and plot devices common to popular film. With that cloaking, which adds to the initial deception of his form of signifying, Cundieff plays upon African American and gender stereotypes in order to puncture them.

For decades, Hollywood has presented white male stars "as supreme icons and incarnations of the rootless, decultured 'individual' in industrial consumer society" whereas it has presented African American male characters as either passive bystanders or aggressive villains, but rarely as individual heroes who win in the end.[11] In answering those stereotypes, some African American filmmakers have depicted similar "individualist," and possibly "reactionary," male heroes who win the day (Guerrero, 96–7). Some filmmakers have compensated for previously desexualized "sidekick" African American male characters with emphatically sexual characters,[12] and some have compensated for weak, impoverished stereotypes with depictions of African American males as strong and economically powerful.[13]

In contrast, Cundieff presents characters who defy or ignore Hollywood's dominant white culture—and the characters in *Tales* do win their battles against oppression. At the same time, the films' characters reflect, then contradict, some of the responses of African American filmmakers to the dominant culture. By using related themes from African American popular culture and folklore, the movie interrogates the stereotype of masculinity as tied to power, whether physical, economic, or sexual. Masculinity, in whatever color, the movies seem to insist, does not have to be synonymous with power.

On the surface, then, the films begin with familiar movie types, then reverse them. In *Hat*, macho posturing turns homoerotic and musicians posing as *gangstas* turn childish.[14] In *Tales*, monsters turn out to be heroes of their people. In *Sprung*, "hard" men accuse other men of being too sensitive, effeminate, or "whipped." Because Cundieff has said that some viewers would describe his characters and themes as either "hard" or "soft," I will use those terms to show how his movies repeat then blur that distinction.[15] Ultimately, the "hard" men turn "soft," supposedly "soft" men redefine "hardness," and men and women begin to see possibilities for a relationship that does, indeed, go "way past whipped," as the *Sprung*'s tag line reads. All the movies here, despite the variety of genres, enact such blurring of categories.

origins of diversity in cundieff's films and the necessity of indirect approach

Cundieff has reflected on this variety of genres, and the explicitly cultural meaning he seeks in them, beyond his own desire for new filmmaking experiences. When comparing his films *Tales* and *Hat* to his later film, *Sprung*, Cundieff agrees that the first two have a "heavy socio-political subtext" (Abbott, 4). "But," Cundieff adds, "I've always got to do something that has some kind of value to me. Because if you have a forum, you might as well use it" (Abbott, 4). Elsewhere he addresses what Sean O'Neill calls his "genre hopping": "Some black directors enjoy doing that whole violent gang thing. . . . And there's nothing wrong with that." However, he prefers "telling stories from the black experience."[16]

In addition to his aesthetic goal of wanting to pull black and crossover audiences into the film, Cundieff feels pressure to create broad audience appeal (O'Neill, 4). He does this by employing familiar motifs, with "enough interesting stuff up front" (Abbott, 2). "Then," Cundieff adds, "maybe I can get a little reprieve from [the audience] when I switch over and take the comedy in a different direction." Cundieff must rely on repetition and revision as a strategy of indirect argument not only to carry out his sociopolitical themes, but also to appeal to different audiences simultaneously.

In discussing *Sprung*, Cundieff describes how he addresses gender role stereotyping as a specific area in which he must "switch over" his audience (Abbott, 2). When an interviewer mentions that some characters in the comedy caricatured "the hootchie mama and mack daddy that were prevalent in the late 1980s in films like *Strictly Business*," but "that they got to a point where they almost became the very thing" they parody, Cundieff answers that some of "the black audience," in his view, "wouldn't accept it automatically" as a mainstream love story (Abbott, 2). He believes that some audience members might have responded, "'This is weak, it's soft, it's not real, it's not hard.'" The term "hard" becomes pivotal in the characters' dialogue, especially in the arguments between the leading male character Montel and his best friend Clyde.

To question such viewer assumptions, Cundieff employs popular genres such as romantic comedy, horror anthologies, the "rockumentary" popularized on MTV, and the rap music industry. In *Hat*, though, Cundieff satirizes rap and music documentary genres to broach not just the topic of gender relations but also politics. Cundieff recalls that when the studio (ITC Entertainment Group) looked at the rushes, "They would say things like, 'You guys have got to stop all the Bush bashing.'"[17] They required cutting of segments critical of police officers and George Bush. He also admits that "A lot of the same thing happened with *Tales From the Hood* . . . it was a more polarizing film, so it also got more reviews where people just said, 'F—k you.' I think that had a lot to do with the political angles we dealt with" (Harris, 53–4).

The trickster-like quality of Cundieff's productions springs from the need to approach volatile topics such as politics, gender, and race indirectly, using ambiguity and humor to ease the audience, and studio executives, into accepting aspects of a film that may challenge viewer assumptions. This style approaches the "change the joke and slip the yoke" masking strategy described by Ralph Ellison as "a kind of jiu jitsu of the spirit, a denial and rejection through agreement."[18] Ellison depicts such indirection in African American writing as frequently accompanied by references to folk culture (Dundes, 1990, 63).

fear of a black hat: no smiling while making love— mimicking rap stereotypes

In *Fear of a Black Hat*, the parody is all up front. Going after rock documentaries and rap culture, the film had its start in Cundieff's fondness for the rock satire *This Is Spinal Tap* (1984) (Harris, 50). The title plays off the name of a rap album, *Fear of a Black Planet*, whereas the name of the rap group in the film, N—ers With Hats (NWH), plays off of the album's artists, N—ers With Attitude (N.W.A.). In the film, rap reflects African American folk culture in the form of music and language traditions.[19] Smitherman defines contemporary rap as a "musical style rooted in the Black Verbal Tradition—talk-singing, *signifyin*, blending reality and fiction," simultaneously a cultural "response to . . . disempowerment" and a "multi-billion-dollar industry based" on a form of "Black Language and Culture" (Smitherman, 1994, 190, 21). *Hat*'s political undercurrent reflects the point of view of many rap artists, but then includes the rappers themselves in the critique.

The name of Cundieff's character, Ice Cold, plays on real rappers of the 1990s Ice Cube and Ice-T; Tone Def (Mark Christopher Lawrence) plays on Tone Loc; and Tasty Taste (Larry B. Scott) echoes Flava Flav. The fictional documentary filmmaker Nina Blackburn (Kasi Lemmons) traces the rise, fall, and reunion of NWH through multiple managers (all die violently, much like the drummers in *Spinal Tap*), fights with other bands, and a breakup precipitated by a girlfriend's machinations.

Filming this band for her "Ph.D. in sociology," Blackburn claims a "strong attraction to their political stance." But upon every probe for deeper meaning to their hypermasculine "Hat Philosophy," the group reveals a disdain for women contradicted by the professional demeanor of Blackburn. Cundieff first repeats the macho images of rappers who present themselves as gangstas and great lovers. He magnifies the movie's testosterone level to ridiculous extremes, then undermines the male characters by contradicting their assumptions.

The hyperbolic sex and violence of NWH recall the blaxploitation era's "sexploitative, aggressive, black *macho* image served up for consumption by young, urban black audiences," seemingly to "repress and delay the awakening of any real political consciousness" (Guerrero, 92–3). Similar criticism has appeared in the wake of some African American popular music genres such as rap. Cundieff lampoons a few of these artists' attempts at political consciousness when Blackburn asks the group to explain its "Hat Philosophy." In the days of the plantation, they explain, the slaves had no hats to protect them from the heat of the sun. Today, "we got some hats," the rappers state. The limited social consciousness of some artists takes another hit when Ice Cold insists, "We anti-violence," and Tone Def swears, "I'd bust a cap in anybody . . . who says different."

The film links NWH's politics to its views toward women, for the group explains that they also convey their seriousness by not smiling. "Especially when making love," one adds. Why? asks Blackburn. Because if you smile, women get "ideas," presumably about romance or commitment. Blackburn asks them about their purported misogyny. Ice Cold protests, "We love women!" and Tone Def agrees, "It's our civic duty to bang the booty!"[20] Ice Cold hammers the nails into his own political coffin when he opines, "The Butt is like society . . . all we want is openness and expansion . . . while the white man's plugging it up . . . with [his] foot up the butt." In the background of such scenes, African American women echo Blackburn's occasional dismay with a weary shake of the head. They signal that in no way should the repetition of these phallocentric characters be mistaken as glorification.

The parody of "hardness" as a sign of masculine identity, and what appears to be Cundieff's criticism of that mindset, extends from the ridiculous—one scene implies that Tone Def is scratching a turntable with his penis—to the humiliating. After complaints of censorship, the group performs "Grab Your Stuff" under threat of incarceration if any of them says "penis" on stage. Ice Cold, performing the song, grabs his "stuff" with so much gusto that he crosses his eyes in pain, squeaks "My dick!," crumples onto the stage, and is carried out by the cops. When Ice Cold does do what his song suggests, the movie makes clear that the result is ultimately self-destructive to the owner of the phallus.

Not only are hard men "softened" up, *Hat* signifies, too, on the proposition that a mere reversal of stereotyping would suffice as resolution. In the first third of the movie, the group practices their stage show with a choreographer portrayed in full gay stereotype, which includes a stuffed crotch and a pass at one of the homophobic rappers. Following this scene, NWH promotes their "Kill Whitey" album with a cover of white "cops with their butts in the air." Is the movie implying that the rappers' fondness for the image may represent something more complex than their desire to humiliate white cops? Cundieff often leaves the audience with such ambiguity.

The most sexually ambiguous moment in the movie likewise combines humiliation with violence and sexual innuendo, this time toward two of the rappers themselves. A fight breaks out over Cheryl's (Rose Jackson Moye) management of Tasty Taste: "So what are you saying?" Taste warns. "Where is your wallet?" Ice taunts, knowing Taste's girlfriend Cheryl keeps it. One tells the other to drop all his weapons, and, in a secondary sight gag, more and more weapons fall out of their clothes. Next, they order each other to "remove the hats" with ritual solemnity. They strip in a furious build up to a "naked" fist fight until referee Tone Def blurts out, "You n—rs gonna fight or f—k?" The two stand still, half-naked and embarrassed.

With the breakup of the group imminent, a final fight occurs when Taste discovers Cheryl hiding under the bedcovers of her supposed enemy, Ice. If the movie's commentary on the confusion among sex, violence, and gender roles isn't yet apparent, when Ice pulls out his gun it has a condom pulled over the barrel. In a great absurd "climax," Marty Rabinow, manager number six (Barry Heins), walks in on Cheryl, Ice, Taste, and Tone with guns pulled, shakily draws his own gun (which he told Blackburn he bought to "bond" with the group), and ends up accidentally shooting himself. The rappers and Cheryl all say "Damn!" in unison, then continue their bickering. Blackburn's voiceover intones, "NWH was history."

The movie points out that mere reversal, whether in reference to politics, gender roles, sex, violence, or violence as sex, is no better than "hard vs. soft" heterosexual power plays. Scenes depicting Tone Def's (literally) rose-colored politics further emphasize this. He tells the interviewer, "I'm not black," because he doesn't "see color anymore." The interviewer indicates Tone's round rose-tinted lenses and asks, "Could that have anything to do with your glasses?" Tone Def's video features dancing flower children and the refrain, "I'm just a human." In

143

spite of this, a mob beats Tone Def, ignoring his argument that he's not black. Instead of criticizing the Bush administration's policies directly, Tone Def's mishap indirectly ridicules the country's insufficient progress toward equality.

Despite studio restrictions on some political jokes, the film's editorial content prevails, as seen in its parodies of both militant and pacifist members of NWH. By the time the other two rappers attempt to reconcile by Tone's hospital bed, Taste has a new video, too, called "Granny Said 'Kick Yo Ass!" Ice has followed his phallus/muse to a video called "Pet the P.U.S.S.Y.," which refers to another vaguely political/sexual mantra similar to his "the butt is like society" philosophy. Cheryl has left all of them for their rivals, the Jam Boys, and the end credits announce that Blackburn is "pregnant with Ice Cold's second child. They plan to marry." Even the more respectful depiction of women like Blackburn ultimately bows to the movie's all-encompassing satire.

The repetition, parody, reversal, then partial revision of the male and female rap stereotypes bloom in Cundieff's multilayered slapstick. The movie hints in its unresolved homoerotic-tinged fight scenes that any reversal of the "hard/soft" binary is still a binary. Likewise, Tone Def's rose-colored glasses indicate that the opposite of a "Kill Whitey" stance may be equally damaging to a black man in America. By poking fun at many angles of racial discourse, and by making sexist behavior appear buffoonish, the movie indirectly challenges a viewer's own racial and sexual assumptions.

tales from the hood: grandma meets the zombie

Gates cites Cundieff's *Hat* as an example of African American art that displays consciousness of previous traditions and confidence in the "legitimacy of black experiences as artistic material" (Gates, 66). I agree with Gates's assessment, and I think *Tales* takes it one step further. In *Tales*, Cundieff revises not only African American artistic tradition for the screen, he and his company attempt something more, by reworking stereotypes of African American masculinity. The significance of Cundieff's 1995 horror movie lies in the progress it makes toward eradicating binary gender depictions, at least from the genre of horror film. Some small progress comes from the movie's use of certain elements of folklore to question and complicate depictions of African American men in film. Specifically, themes from African American folklore that emphasize the individual's responsibility to the community, the weak overcoming the strong, and the wisdom of elders appear to have influenced *Tales*. Elements from conjurer or trickster stories, ghostlore, and enchanted objects, especially those tied to the theme of vengeance, also appear in *Tales*.

Cundieff's horror movie simultaneously rewrites some of the most common "plots" of both horror films and American inequality: zombie movies and police brutality; monster movies and domestic violence; ancient curse movies and white supremacy accompanied by cooption; mad scientist movies and gang violence as self-hatred. Through the use of sociopolitical themes, subtle direction, and folklore, Cundieff plays upon viewer expectations of horror. When he tells Erich Leon Harris about the genesis of *Tales*, Cundieff mentions that he had previously written *The Black Horror Show*, also titled *Blackanthrophy*, a one-act play punning on "lycanthrophy," the werewolf's disease. "It was a comedy about two black businessmen, one of whom would turn into a Black Panther during Black History Month . . . and he would spew all of this 'kill whitey' and 'burn, baby, burn' shit" (Harris, 56). After he thought about adding two more one-acts to "make it an evening of horror-oriented, black-themed pieces," he spoke to Darin Scott about turning it into "a little film—sort of like *The Twilight Zone* of black films" (Harris, 57). Cundieff made a list of "twenty social issues and concerns" he wanted to address in the film and ended up with four or five, "the best stories that we could tell" (Harris, 57).

This account demonstrates how horror, social issues, politics, "black-themed" references, and the age-old mandate for storytellers to tell the "best" stories shaped the writing of the *Tales* screenplay. But how does folklore enter this mix of commercial horror and social commentary? As Alan Dundes writes, "all folklore, no matter what genre, will exhibit 'multiple existence,' meaning that an item will exist in more than one time and place."[21] Audiences can experience familiar stories in myriad ways.[22] The movie itself, then, is not an example of folklore but a production in which people may recognize "bits of folklore in different guises" (Brunvand, 7–9).

As it reconfigures ever-changing, yet ever-familiar examples of African American folklore, *Tales* urges its audience toward an altered view of African American and male identities. The movie reinscribes folk culture's didactic use, as if Cundieff and his company were later day *griots*, trying to lead viewers away from stereotypes of African American men in film.[23] The movie's imitation of a traditional setting, which may be seen in its anthology format, also encourages a didactic reading. *Tales* contains one frame-story and four separate segments, all introduced by a "storyteller" mortician to an "audience" of young gang members. Taken together, these segments not only blur the boundaries between horror and comedy, they also muddy the distinctions one might make between "films" that invite contemplation of race and gender and supposed "teen flicks."[24]

Before observing these complexities, let me review the film's structure. The overarching plot introduces, links, and closes a set of five stories that all bear some thematic resemblance to each other. In the frame-story, "Welcome to My Mortuary," Mr. Simms (Clarence Williams III), an eccentric mortician, takes three teenage gang members through his mortuary, telling gruesome stories, as they hold a gun

145

on him and demand the shipment of drugs they think he is holding. He always agrees but puts off their demands with more stories, with hints that they should consider the outcomes of the stories' protagonists. All the frame-story characters are African American, and everyone in the mortuary, including the corpses, are male. The plots are as follows:

1. In "Rogue Cop Revelation," Clarence (Anthony Griffith), a young policeman, fails to help Martin Moorehouse, an African American activist (Tom Wright), when the rookie's white cohorts kill the activist and frame him as a heroin addict. The dead Moorehouse coerces Clarence into bringing the cops to his grave; Moorehouse then pops up and kills the officers in a move straight out of African American ghostlore.[25] When Clarence asks, irritably, if Moorehouse is satisfied, the zombie strangles the insufficiently contrite young man.

2. This makes the three young gang members in the frame-story only a little uncomfortable, so Simms reveals another corpse. In "Boys Do Get Bruised," Richard (Rusty Cundieff) worries when one of his students keeps coming to school with bruises. Walter (Brandon Hammond) draws for him the "monster" who did it. At the boy's home, Richard meets Walter's mother, Sissy (Paula Jai Parker), and Carl, her boyfriend (David Alan Grier). Carl appears soft-spoken and professional, in dress shirt and tie. However, when Richard leaves, Carl becomes the "monster," a domestic batterer. Richard hears, comes back, but is no match for Carl. Walter mutilates the picture he drew of the "monster," using the drawing as an enchanted object, and Carl's body changes to match the piece of paper.[26] The twisted corpse Simms displays in the beginning of the segment turns out to be Carl.

3. The mortician finds a wooden doll. The young men sneer at the doll so Simms answers their disrespect for it with another story. In "KKK Comeuppance," a politician and former KKK leader, Duke Metger (Corbin Bernsen) moves into a plantation house. An older man (Art Evans) warns that Metger is desecrating the memory of the slaves murdered there, whose souls inhabit wooden dolls (another example of enchanted objects) made by the late Miss Cobbs (Christina Cundieff).[27] After Metger's public relations expert Rhodie (Roger Smith), a young African American man, makes some racist jokes, Rhodie trips over Simms's doll, tumbles downstairs, and dies. Metger, who declares his unbelief in "voodoo," is later chewed by the dolls while Miss Cobbs watches placidly from her rocking chair.

4. Simms then leads them to another coffin, which holds a young man they know as "Crazy K." In "HardCore Convert," scenes with Crazy K (Lamont Bentley) alternate between a shoot out and an experimental prison. There, Crazy K disrespects an older African American woman, Dr. Cushing (Rosalind Cash). Presented with the apparitions of those whom he has killed, he claims he doesn't care if he is responsible, and that if he is a monster, society made him one. He turns down

Dr. Cushing's offer to help him change, takes her assistant hostage, demands release, wakes up at the shoot out, then dies. This segment, foreshadowing the outcome of the frame-story, emphasizes the didactic parallel between Simms and the three teens and the film and its audience. The stories leave the three teenagers even angrier with Simms. He tells them that they will get their drugs when they open three more coffins at the end of the hall. They open the coffins, expecting to see drugs, but instead they see their own bodies. Simms turns into a demon. As the floor emits flames and the mortuary fades away, the young men writhe in hell.

Like the rappers in *Hat*, the young drug dealers project a "hard" interpretation of their masculinity, as do the characters who die in *Tales*. All receive punishment for performing a "hard" version of masculinity, for showing aggression against those whom they perceive as "soft"—women, children, or the elderly. Popular-culture studies have addressed the "hard vs. soft" binary as it appears in horror film. "Man or mouse" representations range from art films to low-budget horror, but African American men have been placed "in the symbolic space of being *too* hard, *too* physical, *too* bodily."[28] In the postblaxploitation era, African American male directors have answered the white directors' stereotypes in ways that may, in reality, prolong their existence. Harry Benshoff and Kalamu ya Salaam argue that African American directors from the 1970s through 1990s have sometimes reinscribed the binary under a revolutionary surface, with male characterizations that internalize old stereotypes. Or else the writers and directors embrace the "monster" to make him a black avenger fighting the dominant culture (Benshoff, 37; ya Salaam, 9). Although both approaches challenge the soft/hard, innocuous/monstrous binary, in many ways they still limit black male characters to its confines (ya Salaam, 6).

Tales reveals "oppressors" beneath upwardly mobile exteriors and then punishes those characters for betraying their communities. The film goes beyond questioning images of the passive "nice guy" and the "monster" to critique the message ya Salaam sees in other African American-made films: "that you can't fight the system or that the rewards—money, power and, consequently, manhood—are achieved by joining the system" (ya Salaam, 9).

Although Richard (Cundieff) as the schoolteacher wears a shirt and tie, he maintains a non-status quo hairstyle of short dreadlocks, which signals a reference to African American folk culture.[29] His hairstyle could be the tip-off that Cundieff's own character will be the exception to the other evil "suits." Activist Martin may be a partial exception, for although he turns vengeful zombie, he does so as an honorable (dead) man seeking ghostlore justice. However, the uniformed Clarence betrays his community, and Carl, with his professional clothes and quiet demeanor, pummels Walter and Sissy, then dies a "monster." Rhodie's death provides the most ominous example, an enchanted object punishing the smooth P.R. man for laughing with a Klansman. These folk-tinged reversals seem like an answer to the "internalized oppressor," "hard" male roles described by ya Salaam.

As director and co-screenwriter, Cundieff avoids reinscribing passive or oppressive stereotypes by creating *Tales* within an older form of story-telling.[30] Comeuppance at the hands of seemingly "weak" or "soft" characters in *Tales* undermines any type of power-based view of manhood. Aggressive males both white and black receive punishment similar to that meted out on arrogant characters in African American ghostlore, trickster, and conjure stories. Each segment contains five elements that also appear in folklore: (1) a figure of oppression, either a white authority figure or a disrespectful young man; (2) "comeuppance" at the hands of an elder or weaker character who represents the larger community; (3) powers exhibited by the elder or weaker character coming from ghost, trickster, or conjure lore; (4) an enchanted object as a tool of vengeance; and (5) some didactic message.[31]

The structure of ghostlore and trickster tales often centers on a victorious "weak" or "soft" character and an arrogant "strong" or "hard" character. In *Tales*, in the first short segment of the frame-story, three teenage boys with guns disrespect a seemingly weak elder figure, Simms the Mortician. With his wild-eyed stare and eccentric, yet formal, dress, he displays the traditional unusual appearance of conjurers.[32] His playing along with their threat of violence also shows his more trickster-like qualities.[33] When they demand that he bring them the drugs, "Give us the sh—!" Simms laughs, "Oh, you'll get the sh—." His coffins turn out in the end to be enchanted objects used for vengeance, as well as props for his didactic tales.[34]

There is also a precedent for the trickster having a close parallel to Simms's true identity—the Devil—in some of the traditional "trickster-as-badman" stories.[35] Devilish characters who blur the boundary between enforcer and violator of cultural norms parallel Simms's instruction of, as he calls them, the "boys."[36] In this didactic sense, Simms runs along the continuum between tricksters as badmen and as conjurers.

Tales portrays a reversal of the real-life horror in wider society of teens preying on older, more frail neighbors, and an inversion of intraracial power relations. When Crazy K is held prisoner by his former prey, the cartoonish threat of castration by the young female nurses and older female doctor strapping Crazy K onto the "treatment" table signals the film's didactic question: Where does "real masculinity" reside? In upper-class power? In guns? In violence? In enforcing a never-ending contrast between women and men? Is there such a thing as "real masculinity"? The film's implied answer is, "If you seek a masculine identity in these props, regardless of your cultural group, you stand to lose your identity altogether." Gender, *Tales* seems to say, possesses more complexity and ambiguity than popular culture routinely depicts in its "hard vs. soft" binaries.

Tales attempts to change gender-role stereotyping with alternative images of African American women. The depiction of Dr. Cushing and the Miss Cobbs as dignified, even ordinary-looking, women of power counteracts what Benshoff describes as blaxploitation horror films' previous demonization and "scapegoating of strong women" (Benshoff, 40, 41). The women's actions would have indicated, in other horror movies, those of a mad scientist in "Hard Core Convert" or of a "voodoo priestess" in "KKK Comeuppance." However, these characters represent two of the most admirable figures in the movie. Miss Cobbs's supernatural act recalls folk accounts of women who seek graveyard justice for their loved ones.[37] Dr. Cushing's role in psychiatric (and perhaps divine) intervention echoes the role of female conjurers and medicine women in restoring health and balance in their communities.[38] In voice, appearance, and action, the depiction of Dr. Cushing and Miss Cobbs opposes the binary of "normal" vs. "monstrous," which Benshoff sees as progress.

Unfortunately, another way that popular art distinguishes masculinity, even if it lampoons male stereotypes, is by using some interpretation of the feminine cast as its opposite. In spite of Miss Cobbs's and Dr. Cushing's portrayal as noble authority figures, the brief appearances of young women in the film tend to appear sexist. Walter's mother Sissy is portrayed as ineffectual, and so distracted by the attractive schoolteacher at her door that her robe "accidentally" loosens. The nurses assisting Dr. Cushing wear short, fluffy skirts and tend to prance, rather than walk, around the operating theater. Cundieff and company may have intended to parody the objectification of young women in music videos, but the parody and the objectification resemble each other too closely to be certain of this.

On the other hand, Jeffrey A. Brown discerns a rhetorical trade-off in the "hard vs. soft and masculine vs. feminine" binary of some progressive comic books, which suggests that *Tales* may employ sexist imagery to gain a foothold with its audience (Brown, 41). For many viewers, this may not excuse sexism in the production, or for some, its exclusively heterosexual emphasis. None of the more sympathetic male characters, at least, engages in overtly sexist behavior. "Men," whatever viewers interpret those to be, the movie implies, do not gain anything and may, like Carl the batterer, lose everything if they abuse women.

Because horror may operate in a folkloric mode, *Tales* can act out issues of race and gender in ways that may be more persuasive to an audience than if it took a strictly dramatic route.[39] *Tales* weds some conventions of film and television media, particularly as related to the horror anthology, to similar conventions from African American folklore and can thereby convey something beyond entertainment. The soft vs. hard, innocuous/monstrous binary fades. "Internalized oppressor" and macho characters take a more direct hit (ya Salaam, 9; Benshoff, 37). Like *Hat*, *Tales* mimics the status quo, parodies these characters, reverses some of the representations (this time via borrowings from folklore instead of folk language), and revises masculine gender imagery. Richard, Walter, Miss Cobbs, and Dr. Cushing—characters favored by the narration—are presented as worthy of the audience's respect. By making these characters the winners in the movie's power struggles, *Tales* provides some alternative to the "hard" male ideal so heavily promoted in youth culture. As for whether one owes any responsibility to his or her community (an issue lurking behind Ice's and Blackburn's engagement), the question and answer come to the forefront in *Tales*: "Yes, you do." And, if you don't acknowledge that duty, the movie hints half-jokingly to its audience, another Miss Cobbs or Mr. Simms may be waiting for you.

sprung: repetition, parody, with less reversal or revision

The third of Cundieff's films, *Sprung*, tries to combine a parody of the "hootchie mamma and mack daddy" characters from predominantly African American comedies of the late 1980s with a romance (Abbott, 2). Though not as strong as *Hat* and *Tales*, *Sprung* aims to undermine "hard vs. soft" gender stereotypes within the context of intraracial relations, via romantic comedy and African American folk utterances and language practices. Signifying, the Dozens, and social code words from African American folk tradition tie the screenplay together. "Hard" characters, sex-obsessed Clyde (Joe Torry) and materialistic Adina (Paula Jai Parker), try to keep their gun shy but more idealistic friends Montel (Cundieff) and Brandy (Tisha Campbell) apart. The plot resembles the meet-lose-wed pattern, except at the end, in a move reminiscent of the main couple in *Four Weddings and a Funeral* (1994), the "hard" couple marry and the "soft" couple do not.

Cundieff admits that this movie is "the least obvious" of the three in sociopolitical themes (Abbott, 4). Cundieff adds, "I think there's probably a couple of little lines here and there." Although it lacks some of the originality of the previous films, *Sprung*'s "little lines" give the clearest confirmation of the filmmaker's concerns. Cundieff even states, in character, his concern with gender stereotyping. The theme is tied to race early when Clyde, dressing for a dance, compares his masculinity to Montel's: "I'm more black and more hard . . . we dark brothers aren't like you yellow-bellies." Clyde delivers this in the manner of traditional signification, not intended with malice (Smitherman, 1977, 119). Later, in a restaurant, Clyde chides Montel's romance, "I'm still hard and on my own." Montel this time answers that what he does is "harder": loving with his head and heart, as well as with his male organ. Standing up, as a nearby table of women form an "amen corner," Montel shouts, "It don't get no harder than that!" (Smitherman, 1994, 47).

These scenes feature "in-group" terms, which connote cultural ties between the characters (Smitherman, 1977, 63). "Hard" can mean "a person who is tough, hardened by life and experience," or, as in the phrase "hard leg," simply "male" (Smitherman, 1994, 131). Two more terms appear in important scenes. "Yellow" stands for Clyde's ambivalence toward those with European ancestors, and both Clyde and Andina take turns calling each other "triflin": "inadequate, lazy" (252, 227). The title itself comes from a folk utterance, as "sprung" means "hopelessly in love; out of emotional control," and therefore, to Clyde and Adina, "soft" (213). Adina and Clyde themselves reflect traditional folk tricksters, with their machinations and wit (Joyner, 150).

Sprung's effort to undermine "hard vs. soft" gender and intraracial stereotypes appears so far below the surface of the story that it may go unnoticed, or, as in the scenes above, it stands out in the open. When Cundieff introduces elements of African American folk culture, though, with "terms rooted in the black cultural experience," he places more layers of meaning onto the term "hard," incorporating the semantics of the immediate linguistic and sociohistorical context (Smitherman, 1977, 62).

The movie's value to gender discourse appears when Cundieff's character tries to redefine the masculine stereotype. It moves from repetition of caricatured male and female stereotypes to parody—sight gags of Adina's *Terminator*-style vision of the financial status of all the men at the dance, Brandy's visions of the men wearing dog masks, and Clyde's vision of all the women in thongs—then to partial reversals. That is, the plot still puts everyone in bed, just some more tenderly than others. The partial reversals finally end with Montel's declaration of (uncertain) sexual independence. I interpret the latter as a partial revision of gender typing because the character is still prompted to define his "manliness" within some paradigm of "hardness," in this case "independence" from women. Although Cundieff has his character insist that making love is more than sex to him, Montel and Brandy still follow the basic pattern of sleeping together, only with a modest waiting period. This still implies that deep male–female relationships cannot exist without intercourse.

Another revision follows a romantic sex scene, which resembles the pottery scene from *Ghost* (1990), except in front of a flash at Montel's photography studio. Immediately after, we hear a woman's voiceover, "We're blessed," then we see Montel photographing a customer's baby. Note the "we." The juxtaposition seems quite pointed here. Again, commitment and responsibility receive unusual emphasis in a Cundieff screenplay. During a humorous interrogation between the two heroes, Montel assures Brandy that he has left no babies or wives behind him. As the movie presents Montel and Brandy as admirable protagonists, the message comes in clearly: Making love equals (eventually) making babies and staying with them. If we tie this to Montel's previous declaration, then the corollary to that becomes: If a truly "hard" thing to do as a man is to make love, not sex, then being "hard" equals making

151

babies and staying with them. As *Tales* suggests, a "real man" is socially responsible. Even if Cundieff keeps within the "hardness" paradigm, this does lean toward a redefinition of manhood, especially in the realm of popular culture.

Cundieff's position, it seems, is that younger viewers should be reminded now and then that sex with commitment is romantic and more socially responsible than sex without. I'm not certain that *Sprung's* folk language practices camouflage this didactic content as well as the folk language and folklore imagery in *Hat* and *Tales*. *Sprung* at least demonstrates the Cundieff productions' ongoing commitment to exploring themes of race and gender.

Cundieff's more radical disruption of gender imagery in *Hat* and *Tales*, especially the sexual ambiguities of *Hat*, recall Judith Butler's observation that acts, gestures, and enactments "perform," or create, gender itself.[40] If the "gendered body is performative" and "has no ontological status apart from the various acts which constitute its reality," and if that function appears in a "decidedly public and social discourse," then Cundieff's productions have shown the intricacies of that function on film (Butler, 336). In some respects, *Sprung* continues what Butler calls an "illusion discursively maintained for the purposes of the regulation of sexuality within the obligatory frame of reproductive heterosexuality" (336–37). But the "fight or f—k" scene in *Hat*, as well as less obvious scenes, exemplifies a disruption of what she sees as the "regulatory fiction of heterosexual coherence" (336). This performance of "hard" male violence as an expression of homoeroticism pokes holes in the "construction of coherence" that "conceals the gender discontinuities that run rampant within . . . in which gender does not necessarily follow from sex."

In the end, though, Cundieff's early body of work comes closer to Brown's comics model that expands conceptions of gender and race "by incorporating previously disassociated concepts of softness with hardness, of mind with body," infusing these movies with "gentler, more responsible, and more cerebral qualities within the codes of dominant masculinity" (Brown, 41). The films may not rework or revise these concepts as far as many cultural critics would prefer. But I see their moderate success as doing more, through references to African American folk tradition, to alter popular conceptions than some arthouse films might be able to do with the youngest members of the audience.[41] "With the younger audience, if you don't catch 'em in the first five or ten minutes, you've lost 'em," Cundieff says. Caught between audience expectations of "Why did you go soft?" and "Why did you put in that triflin' hootchie stuff?" and studio demands to cut the "Bush bashing," Cundieff and company seek "a middle ground" to express their themes (Abbott, 3; Harris, 52, 56, 54). The films do find that middle ground, in *Hat* and *Sprung*, by incorporating folk utterances and language traditions, like those noted above, and in *Tales* by looking back to folklore and ghostlore for models of reversal, inversion, and subversion. In the end, a "hard" man may not necessarily be good to find, but Cundieff's movies are.

notes

1. Henry Louis Gates Jr., "Black Creativity: On the Cutting Edge," *Time* 144, no. 15 (October 10, 1994): 66; hereafter cited in text.
2. *Fear of a Black Hat,* prod. W. M. Christopher and Darin Scott, director and writer Rusty Cundieff, 88 min., Incorporated Television Company/Oakwood Productions, 1993, videocassette.
3. *Tales From the Hood,* producer Spike Lee, director Rusty Cundieff, writers Rusty Cundieff and Darin Scott, 98 min., Forty Acres and a Mule Filmworks/Savoy Pictures, 1995, videocassette.
4. *Sprung,* producer Darin Scott, director Rusty Cundieff, writers Rusty Cundieff and Darin Scott, 105 min., Trimark Pictures, 1997, videocassette.
5. Janet Staiger, "Authorship Approaches," in *Authorship and Film* (New York: Routledge, 2002); hereafter cited in text.
6. Claudia Mitchell-Kernan, "Signifying," in *Mother Wit from the Laughing Barrel: Readings in the Interpretation of Afro-American Folklore,* ed. Alan Dundes (Jackson, MS: University Press of Mississippi, 1990), 311.
7. Roger D. Abrahams, *Deep Down in the Jungle: Negro Narrative Folklore from the Streets of Philadelphia* (Hatboro, PA: Folklore Associates, 1964), 54.
8. Geneva Smitherman, *Talkin and Testifyin': The Language of Black America* (Detroit: Wayne State University Press, 1977), 103, 82, 121; hereafter cited in text.
9. Charles Joyner, "The Trickster and the Fool: Folktales and Identity Among Southern Plantation Slaves," reprinted in *The Culture and Community of Slavery,* ed. Paul Finkelman (New York: Garland Publishing, 1989), 150; hereafter cited in text.
10. Alan Dundes, *Folklore Matters* (Knoxville: University of Tennessee Press, 1989), xv.
11. Ed Guerrero, *Framing Blackness: The African American Image in Film* (Philadelphia: Temple University Press, 1993), 126; hereafter cited in text.
12. Donald Bogle, *Toms, Coons, Mulattoes, Mammies, and Bucks: An Interpretative History of Blacks in American Films,* 3rd ed. (New York: Continuum, 1994), 16. Also see Thomas Cripps, *Slow Fade to Black: The Negro in American film, 1900–1942* (New York: Oxford University Press, 1993).
13. Kalamu Ya Salaam, "Black Macho: The Myth of the Positive Message," *Black Film Review* 7, no. 1 (1995): 6–9; hereafter cited in text.
14. Geneva Smitherman, *Black Talk: Words and Phrases from the Hood to the Amen Corner* (Boston: Houghton Mifflin Company, 1994); hereafter cited in text. Smitherman defines "gangsta": "(1) used to refer to any event, activity, behavior, person, or object that represents a rejection of mainstream society's standards. (2) A rebellious, nonconformist person, a social 'outlaw' who refuses to buckle under to white authority and white norms and is thus revered. Both of these meanings reflect a resurfacing and extension of the 1960s and 1970s concept of gangsta, referring to street life and street culture" (119).
15. Spencer H. Abbott, "Rough Cut Q & As: Sprungtime—and Love's in the Air," in *Rough Cut* [electronic periodical] [Turner Network Television, (updated May 16, 1997; cited May 2, 2000)]; five screens; available from <http://roughcut.com/main/drive2_97may3.html>; hereafter cited in text.
16. Sean O'Neill, "'Sprung' Fever: Triple-Threat Rusty Cundieff Directs, Scripts and Stars in His Third Film, Trimark's 'Sprung,'" in *Boxoffice Online* [electronic periodical] (updated April 1997; cited March 3, 2000); two screens; available from <http://www.boxoff.com/apr97sneak3.html>; hereafter cited in text.

17. Erich Leon Harris, *African-American Screenwriters Now: Conversations with Hollywood's Black Pack* (Beverly Hills, CA: Silman-James Press, 1996), 52; hereafter cited in text.

18. Alan Dundes, *Mother Wit from the Laughing Barrel: Readings in the Interpretation of Afro-American Folklore* (Jackson, MS: University Press of Mississippi, 1990), 63; hereafter cited in test.

19. See Smitherman, 1994, 190.

20. Recorded as folk utterances in Smitherman, 1994, 52, 54, 66.

21. Alan Dundes, *International Folkloristics* (New York: Rowman and Littlefield Publishers, Inc., 1999), vi–vii.

22. Jan Harold Brunvand, *The Study of American Folklore: An Introduction* (New York: W. W. Norton, 1986), 8; hereafter cited in text.

23. In a similar vein, Ed Guerrero refers to the executive producer of *Tales From the Hood*, Spike Lee, "an African American filmic griot and storyteller of considerable ability," visualizing "the complexity and power of the African American oral tradition and its attendant matrix of musical forms and idioms" (Guerrero, 154).

24. Harry M. Benshoff, "Blaxploitation Horror Films: Generic Reappropriation or Reinscription?" *Cinema Journal* 39, no. 2 (2000): 45; hereafter cited in text.

25. Elliott J. Gorn, "Black Spirits: The Ghostlore of Afro-American Slaves," reprinted in *The Culture and Community of Slavery*, ed. Paul Finkelman (New York: Garland Publishing, 1989). See recorded folk analogues to "legends of avenging black spirits" in Gorn, 114, 121, 123–24, 127–28.

26. Ruth Bass, "Mojo," in *Mother Wit from the Laughing Barrel: Readings in the Interpretation of Afro-American Folklore*, ed. Alan Dundes (Jackson, MS: University Press of Mississippi, 1990), 388–96. Also see Ruth Bass, "The Little Man," in *Mother Wit*, 380–87. Bass describes similar folk enchantments in her articles "Mojo" and "The Little Man" in *Mother Wit*, 383, 395.

27. See Bass for folk analogues to the power of playthings in conjunction with death, "The Little Man," 395.

28. Jeffrey A. Brown, "Comic Book Masculinity and the New Black Superhero," *African American Review* 33, no. 1 (1999): 28 (italics in original); hereafter cited in text.

29. Smitherman describes dreadlocks as a "Black rejection of Western society and what journalist Kenneth M. Jones called . . . 'the walk of Black spirits reaching back to Africa'" (1994, 100).

30. *Tales* illustrates some elements of Manthia Diawara's black film aesthetic, which is "concerned with the specificity of identity, the empowerment of black people through mise-en-scène . . . rhythmic and repetitious shots, going back and forth between past and present. Their themes involve black folklore, religion, and the oral tradition which link black Americans to the African Diaspora. The narrative style is symbolic" (Benshoff, 43).

31. Jacqueline Fulmer, "'Men Ain't All': A Reworking of Masculinity in *Tales from the Hood*, or, Grandma Meets the Zombie," *Journal of American Folklore*, forthcoming (Fall 2002).

32. Leonora Herron and Alice M. Bacon, "Conjuring and Conjure-Doctors," in *Mother Wit*, 359–68. See folk analogues to "conjure doctors" telling "long, exciting tales" and punishing those who disrespect them in Herron, 360–61.

33. Langston Hughes and Arna Bontemps, eds., *The Book of Negro Folklore* (New York: Dodd, Mead and Co, 1966). Compare with trickster qualities noted in Brer Rabbit tales in Hughes, ix.

34. John W. Roberts, *From Trickster to Badman: The Black Folk Hero in Slavery and Freedom* (Philadelphia: University of Pennsylvania Press, 1989). See Roberts, with reference to W. E. B. Du Bois, 65. For masking operations of tricksters, also see Joyner, 235–36, 238.

35. For folklore analogues of the conjurer in "trickster-as badman" stories and as demonic, see Roberts, 201.

36. For folk conjurers and "badmen" as agents of justice and group values, see Roberts, 39, 104.
37. See similar recorded folk examples in Gorn, 123, and Hughes, 169.
38. For analogous characters in folklore, see Herron and Bacon, 360, and Roberts, 65.
39. Carol Clover, *Men, Women, and Chainsaws: Gender in the Modern Horror Film* (Princeton, NJ: Princeton University Press, 1992), 231.
40. Judith Butler, "Gender Trouble, Feminist Theory, and Psychoanalytic Discourse," in *Feminism/Postmodernism*, ed. Linda J. Nicholson (New York: Routledge, 1990), 336; hereafter cited in text.
41. Sean O'Neill describes *Tales* as a success, "whose gross doubled its modest budget" (O'Neill, 2).

john waters

goes to

hollywood

a poststructural

authorship study

w a l t e r   m e t z

In 1981, the Baltimore-based filmmaker John Waters, notorious for his underground cinema masterpiece *Pink Flamingos* (1972), released his new film *Polyester* through the fledgling Hollywood distribution company New Line Cinema. Partly an underground film featuring Waters's Warhol-like company of misfit actors, most notably drag queen Divine, and partly a mainstream Hollywood parody of Douglas Sirk melodramas, *Polyester* represents a pivotal moment in the evolution of the underground cinema in the United States. The film successfully negotiated the transition from midnight movie to conventional Hollywood product, allowing Waters to spend the 1980s and 1990s churning out slightly off-kilter Hollywood films in various traditional genres: the musical in *Hairspray* (1988), the juvenile delinquent film in *Cry-Baby* (1990), and the slasher film in *Serial Mom* (1994).

Such a progression could clearly be read as the all-too-familiar story of a radical independent artist ruined by the Hollywood machine. However, I will argue that two very recent Waters films—*Pecker* (1998) and *Cecil B. Demented* (2000)—beg for a different critical response, one that sees the preservation of the ethos of the midnight movie, allegorically and literally in the case of these two films, respectively. In *Pecker*, Edward Furlong plays a Waters-like Baltimore teenager who becomes famous among the New York avant-garde set for a series of scandalous photographs he takes of his friends and relatives. At the film's end, Pecker rejects his fame, returning instead to his life in Baltimore as a suburbanite. In *Cecil B. Demented*, Steven Dorff plays a Waters-like twenty-something filmmaker who kidnaps a Hollywood starlet and forces her to play the lead in his underground movie. At this film's end, the police trap the renegade film crew at a drive-in and kill them for their transgression.

In these films, two possibilities are embedded in Waters's relationship to Hollywood: retreat to obscurity in Baltimore or tragic martyrdom at the loss of the sensational underground cinema of the 1960s as made famous by Jack Smith and Andy Warhol. In particular, both of these films imbed the mythos of the underground movie into larger Aristotelian, and fully comprehensible, conventional narratives. Pecker begins his career as a professional photographer by stapling flyers for his art shows to people's car windows, a strategy Waters pursued two decades earlier in successfully filling rented churches for screenings of his own underground films such as *Mondo Trasho* (1969), *Multiple Maniacs* (1970), *Pink Flamingos*, and *Desperate Living* (1977). Demented's film crew is tragicomically committed to the underground and exploitation cinema, having tattooed the names of Warhol, Kenneth Anger, Hershell Gordon Lewis, and William Castle onto their arms.

This case study of Waters's cinema pursues an historical investigation of marginalized subjectivity and authorship as discussed by Kaja Silverman in her essay, "The Female Authorial Voice."[1] Silverman responds to the liberal feminist suspicion of the poststructural critique of the author. This critique, forwarded by Roland Barthes, Michel Foucault, and others—white male theorists one and all—worked to dismantle the importance of authorship, but precisely at the time women, gay men and lesbian women, and people of color were beginning to be recognized.[2] Liberal feminists recognized that such a critique did not necessarily forward the goals of political liberation for marginalized people.

As a response, Silverman builds a psychoanalytic model that uses poststructural tools to produce a negotiated model of authorship, one that assumes the power of social construction yet also believes that agency crystallizes around "nodal points" having to do with the historically and culturally specific experience of individual authors (218). Silverman theorizes these socially constructed, but still personally felt, experiences as they sediment in the text as the result of "the authorial fantasmatic," a "cluster of fantasies which structures not merely dreams and other related psychic formations, but object-choice, identity, and 'the subject's life as a whole'" (216). In particular, one compelling facet of Silverman's authorial fantasmatic is that it tends to be expressed in a particular film through an allegorical figure related to the author, whom she calls "the author inside the text" (196).

This essay proposes that Silverman's model of preserving the agency of marginalized author's voices within the terrain of the poststructural critique of identity is an extremely useful path for analyzing Waters's cinema. As a middle-class Baltimore teenager, Waters continued the project of the 1960s New York underground film movement (in the guise of Anger, Warhol, and the Kuchar Brothers) of queering mainstream Hollywood film representation. Waters began filmmaking as the ideological shifts of the 1970s undermined the possibility of a radical avant-garde cinema. As a gay filmmaker, Waters has found a way to import a queering method into the Hollywood cinema itself. Whether that project of importation can be anything other than cooptation is, I suggest, the crucial question for academic approaches to his work. *Pecker's* decision to return to obscurity in Baltimore and *Demented's* choice to immolate himself on the historical impossibility of independent cinema in the age of *Titanic* (1998) offer two authors-inside-the-texts that negotiate the possibilities of John Waters the queer filmmaker working in a most unqueer Hollywood.

introducing john waters's body

But first, an anecdote as to how a straight, middle-class critic like myself would come to know anything about the wonderful world of John Waters. In early September 2000, a student from the Montana State University lecture program called me to ask if I would introduce "the Pope of Trash" when he came to speak on the campus. I said yes, reluctantly, since it was not at all clear to me what a critical studies scholar teaching in a film production department could possibly say about a filmmaker who had learned to make movies entirely by intuition, and whose films were usually associated with "sleaze," "bad taste," and "trash."[3] Furthermore, Mr. Waters's star persona has not exactly made overtures to the academic community. In *Divine Trash* (1998), Steve Yeager's documentary about the making of *Pink Flamingos*, Waters tells the story of attending New York University for one day, leaving during a screening of *The Battleship Potemkin* (1925) due to its irrelevance to his life. In *Crackpot*, the second of his two humorous books about life and filmmaking, Waters explains his love for showmanship, unfavorably comparing Sergei Eisenstein with Castle: "Would Sergei Eisenstein have arrived [to his premiere] in a battleship? I think not. I hate that Sergei Eisenstein."[4] As I had just finished giving a lecture about Soviet silent montage in my "International Film History" course, this did not bode well.

Beyond that, Waters has, of course, done poor film history here, as

William Castle stole the idea for Percepto, electrifying people's butts with buzzers under their seats, for his film, *The Tingler* (1959), from none other than Sergei Eisenstein, another queer filmmaker who, not without a sense of humor, put firecrackers under audience members' seats to shock and please them. But it was Waters's seeming antiintellectualism that had me most on my guard. He begins *Shock Value*, the first of his books on filmmaking, with an act of hyperbole: "I hate message movies and pride myself on the fact that my work has no socially redeeming value."[5] While lecturing at a university in Germany, the students enthused about the political challenge offered by his films. He responded in *Shock Value* with a nonsensical antiintellectual dismissal, "I guess you can read anything you want into a screenplay" (220), something I certainly would not want reinforced in my already anti-critical film production students.

Given that *Multiple Maniacs* concerns a woman (played by Divine in drag) who becomes a Godzilla-like monster celebrating her anti-bourgeois depravity—"[I am] a monster now . . . [I am a] maniac who cannot be cured. I am Divine"—and then is hunted down and murdered by the National Guard on the streets of Baltimore, juxtaposed against Kate Smith's singing of "God Bless America," it is hard to imagine what Waters would imagine a political film might be. I was with the Germans on this one.

However, caring more for the possibility of self-aggrandizement than the certainty of humiliation, I pressed on in preparing for the big event. Having thus committed to saying something about Waters, I set myself the task of both producing intelligent commentary and at the same time not providing him with too much *Potemkin*-like ammunition for ridiculing my academic pomposity. At that point, I had seen only one Waters movie, *Serial Mom*, and hadn't remembered enjoying it much. So to correct my ignorance, I began systematically working my way through Waters's oeuvre of exploitation cinema. It was at *Polyester*, Waters's sixth feature (out of a current eleven), that his brand of satire turned me into a convert. For it turns out that Waters's cinema voices the same sort of ambivalence toward various forms of cinema as I do. Usually, film academics inhabit one of two broadly defined camps: a cultural studies-based defense of popular cinema or a critical theory-based defense of art cinema. I tend to appreciate both types of cinema in limited quantities, with roughly equal amounts of critical self-consciousness. For example, just this past week, I found myself defending to students both Sally *and* Harry Potter: the former the director of a brilliantly antipatriarchal feminist avant-garde film, *Thriller* (1979), the latter the fictional hero of the sexist and racist *Harry Potter and the Sorcerer's Stone* (2001), Chris Columbus's block-buster film version of J. K. Rowling's popular children's novel.

Waters's *Polyester* is a film that takes a similar stance toward its cultural and cinematic predecessors, appreciating intelligent criticism while simultaneously reveling in populist entertainment, like rock music and film itself. At once a parody of 1950s science-fiction films (it is shot in Odorama, providing audience members with scratch-and-sniff cards) and Sirk melodramas (it features drag queen Divine playing Francine, a housewife whose pornographer husband dumps her for his secretary), *Polyester* also debunks elitist European art films. Toward the end of the film, Francine has fallen in love with Todd Tomorrow (played via camp casting by 1950s movie star Tab Hunter), the owner of a drive-in movie theatre. However, his is the strangest drive-in in the history of film exhibition: it is screening a Marguerite Duras triple feature, "from dusk 'til dawn," and serving champagne and caviar at the concession stand. The funniest moment of the film involves a quick cut to Francine, with a priceless look of confusion, attempting to make sense of the latest issue of *Cahiers du Cinéma*. We learn that Todd is evil, not only for showing boring art cinema, but also because the drive-in is really a front for his cocaine distribution business. However, in *Crackpot*, Waters explains that this reference to Duras is not exclusively one of contempt: "Even though I believe pretension is the ultimate sin, Marguerite Duras has taken pretension one level ahead of itself and turned it into style" (110).

A humane and tolerant approach toward those victimized by the resultant social order tempers this confusing layering of comic indictments against stupidity and pretentiousness. At the end of *Polyester*, as at the end of Sirk's *All That Heaven Allows* (1956), the middle-class housewife is offered a chance for happiness. Francine is left to raise her two children in a world in which, as she mellifluously puts it, "Everything smells so much better," now that her husband and the deceitful Todd Tomorrow are dead.

My love of Waters's world was sealed forever because of such intellectual approaches to this comedic and melodramatic material. For despite his films' reliance on generic formulas, they are most heavily influenced by the radical 1960s American avant-garde cinema. His pre-*Polyester* features—from *Mondo Trasho* through *Desperate Living*—cannily use the techniques of the underground cinema to tell coherent and relevant stories about the American nuclear family's dysfunctionality. As one famous example, Waters draws directly from the avant-garde premusic video technique of Anger's *Scorpio Rising* (1963) in *Pink Flamingos*, the story about Divine, a mother who prides herself on being "the filthiest person alive," the dubious honor of which she defends at the end of the film when she eats freshly laid dog shit in one take for the camera.

Earlier in the film, Divine shoplifts a steak from a grocery store, placing it in her panties. Accompanying this sequence is Little Richard's song, "The Girl Can't Help It," one of whose lines is, "If she's smiling, beefsteak become well done." As in Anger's film, the pop songs are turned against themselves to produce social critique. Divine, dressed in black bra and stretch pants, cooks the steak for her children, Cotton and Crackers, telling them that she precooked it in "my own little oven." The steak referent is thus recontextualized such that it now refers, ironically, to an exemplar of maternal love, not a beefsteak-cum-penis joke, as it was earlier in the film and in Little Richard's song.

Forced by the changing economics of the blockbuster-driven American film industry, Waters began making more mainstream films, beginning with *Hairspray*, and continuing with *Serial Mom*, the film that received his most widespread release because it starred a major Hollywood star, Kathleen Turner, and was released through HBO's Savoy Films. Whereas the early features aggressively continued an underground cinema ethos—Divine is executed in the electric chair at the end of *Female Trouble*, for example—these later films mainstreamed the sex and violence, turning toward nostalgia, as in the 1950s teen-pic, *Cry-Baby*.[6]

Just at the moment when one would conclude another minority artist had been coopted by the Hollywood machine, Waters's last two films—*Pecker* and *Cecil B. Demented*—have invented an ingenious solution to the mainstreaming-of-radical-cinema crisis. These two most recent films are conventional narratives about an artist employing the radical underground cultural techniques of Waters's films from the 1970s. *Pecker* is a classically structured, realist film about a Waters-like photographer who takes close-ups of lesbian strippers' vaginas. *Cecil B. Demented* is about a Waters-like filmmaker who kidnaps a major Hollywood star, Honey Whitlock (played by Melanie Griffith), to make an underground movie about the evils of Hollywood; in the film's funniest scene, Honey is forced to act as a theatre attendant at a Pasolini film festival at which no spectators have shown up. In this way, the films can both receive funding and distribution in blockbuster-minded Hollywood while at the same time express the countercultural themes of Waters's early work.

After much fretting about what I might say about Waters, it turned out that his films, as much as those of any other contemporary American director, would allow me to discuss the pressing importance of film history on the process of film production. As I began finalizing my introduction, I became confident that I teach courses that Waters would *not* walk out of, despite the fact that I do love to show the Odessa steps sequence from *Potemkin*. After all, like Waters, I also analyze both the underground cinema of Anger and the radical Hollywood melodrama of Sirk. Herein lies the point of contact I will explore in this chapter: Waters found a way to make avant-garde melodramas within the Hollywood cinema at precisely the time—the early 1970s—the avant-garde cinema's parodies of Hollywood were losing their currency. To have succeeded at this method for 30 years and counting, Waters deserves more attention than he has heretofore received in film studies.

theorizing marginalized authorship within
hollywood cinema

The method that I will use to explore Waters's approach to the melo-dramatics of the American family is derived from Silverman's post-structural criticism. In "The Female Authorial Voice," Silverman builds a poststructural theory of authorship that attempts to resolve the political problematic of declaring the author dead at precisely the same time as marginalized authors—women, people of color, and sexual minorities—were beginning to be studied seriously within academia. Silverman suggests that we can privilege an author's body of work while still acknowledging the role of social construction by seeing that body of work as the result of socially constituted forces. Silverman chooses a psychoanalytic method, showing how the films of Liliana Cavani can be seen as a coherent corpus through the fantasy described in Freud's *A Child is Being Beaten*. The structure that haunts the author's work, what Silverman calls "the authorial fantasmatic," is in turn expressed by rec-ognizable "nodal points," which are recurrent plot points within the films themselves (218). Thus, in the films of Cavani, *The Night Porter* (1971) for example, the authorial fantasmatic is castration whereas the act of undressing is one of the nodal points.

I believe using Freud's essay, "Family Romances," to read Waters's films will provide a similarly productive solution to the poststructural crisis in authorship studies.[7] For Waters's films produce a queering of the American family that is consistent across the eleven features, and yet clearly this consistency has everything to do with the particular his-torical and cultural moment—the collapse of the American family in the wake of the late 1960s—in which these films are articulated. My argument here is that the conflict between children and their parents is the authorial fantasmatic of Waters's oeuvre, expressed in nodal points depicting the perversity of heterosexuality.

Turning to Freud to discuss Waters is not as bizarre a move as might first appear. In "Puff Piece (101 Things I Love)" in *Crackpot*, Waters writes of his love of Freud's examinations of abnormal sexuality: "For inspiration I flip through Freud's *Dora: An Analysis of a Case of Hysteria* and *Three Case Histories* (the Wolfman, the Rat Man and the Psychotic Dr. Schreber) and wish I was this 'gifted' at being neurotic. I get so excited, I start applauding the pages. As a matter of fact, I think I'll pre-tend I am the Psychotic Dr. Schreber for the next ten minutes" (59). My premise here is that Waters's conscious desire to rescue "abnormals" (or "freaks," as they often refer to themselves in his films), exposing the more serious abnormality of typical, bourgeois American life is best studied by his films' less superficial working through of the family romance as articulated by Freud. As Silverman argues, drawing from the postscript to Peter Wollen's *Signs and Meaning in the Cinema*, "the author 'outside' the text thus becomes a kind of projection of the author 'inside' the text" (196).

In this case, Waters's obsession with abnormal psychology is clearly projected into the text, but not necessarily in a one-to-one correspondence. Although Pecker and Cecil B. Demented are clearly such authors-within-the-texts, they do not necessarily directly correspond to Waters as the author-outside-the-text without many gestures of repression and dislocation. For example, Dawn's daughter Taffy in *Female Trouble* reenacts car crashes in her living room, which directly relates to Waters's childhood in which his mother would take him to junkyards to play in the wrecked cars. However, Taffy is by no means the author-inside-the-text of *Female Trouble*: much more likely it is Dawn herself, whose career trajectory is from juvenile delinquent to famous celebrity.

Freud's "Family Romances," of course, explores a child's conflict with his or her parents. Contrary to seeing the resultant rebellion as harmful, however, Freud argues, "Indeed, the whole progress of society rests upon the opposition between successive generations" (237). Similarly, Waters—after having made eleven features in which his heroes rebel violently and sadistically against their authority figures—tends to speak quite lovingly about his own parents. In an uncanny discussion that concludes *Shock Value*, his first book about filmmaking, Waters gives voice to the contradiction between familial conflict and harmony that it is the basic project of "Family Romances" to resolve. Deluged with questions from fans who cannot believe a man who makes such vitriolic family films actually has parents, Waters replies:

> Yes, I have parents and I love them very much. When I'm in Baltimore, I see them about once a week, and even though there certainly have been major disagreements over the years, I think we've managed to get along astonishingly well, considering all they've had to go through . . . . My parents are very straight, thank God. I've always felt extremely embarrassed for friends with parents who try to be hip . . . . I think it's healthy to see your parents often (sort of like a tune-up), but I think it's neurotic to actually hang around with them. No matter how hard you rebel against your parents, you always end up being exactly like them. (228)

In "Family Romances," Freud similarly theorizes away any contradiction between such angry cultural production and its loving child producer: "[T]hese works of fiction, which seem so full of hostility, are none of them really so badly intended, and that they still preserve, under a slight disguise, the child's original affection for his parents" (240).

In keeping with this affection, the narrative flow in a Waters film moves from familial conflict to harmony. The best example of the archetypal structure of Waters's family romance films is *Female Trouble*. In this film, a middle-class high school girl, Dawn Davenport (played in drag by Divine), begins the film in terrible conflict with her parents.

Hating school and acting as a full-fledged juvenile delinquent, Dawn gives her parents one last chance. She asks for a specific Christmas present, cha-cha heels, a particularly trampy form of foot covering for girls. When she receives sensible shoes instead, Dawn turns psychotic, pinning her mother under the Christmas tree.

In "Why I Love Christmas," originally published in the *National Lampoon* but reprinted in *Shock Value*, Waters explains that this story is actually based on a real-life event in which his grandmother was comically pinned under the Christmas tree. Furthermore, Waters uses the essay to parody the wholesomeness of the Christmas season as a time for family harmony, theorizing that Santa is responsible for heroin addiction because malevolent parents instill in their children a fantasy belief that magical pleasure actually exists (117). Waters especially loves slasher films such as *Christmas Evil* (a.k.a. *You Better Watch Out*, 1980) that use Christmas as an excuse for murderous mayhem (118). And finally, were one to receive a Christmas card from Waters—oh, how I wish it could be so!—it would feature Charles Manson's face placed awkwardly on top of the Virgin Mary's body (119).

After the Christmas tree incident in *Female Trouble*, Dawn runs away from home, screaming, "You're not my parents!," which is, of course, the mantra of the family romance. Freud argues that the child comes to separate herself from the family, making sense of this division through a belief she must have been adopted: "His sense that his own affection is not being fully reciprocated then finds a vent in the idea, often consciously recollected later from early childhood, of being a step-child or an adopted child" (238). I have replaced Freud's sexist use of "him" to describe the subject of "Family Romances," with "her," as the class, and not the gender, issues are at stake here. For those less politically correct than I, perhaps this egregious castration is attenuated by the fact that *Female Trouble*'s "she," Dawn, is of course played by Divine, a man wearing a "cheater," that is, a fake vagina. A propos of the impetus for this madness, the cha-cha heels incident, Freud argues that such criticism of parents often surfaces over minutia, not major conflicts: "Small events in the child's life which make him feel dissatisfied afford him provocation for beginning to criticize his parents, and for using, in order to support his critical attitude, the knowledge which he has acquired that other parents are in some respects preferable to them" (237).

This comparison between good and bad parents forms the cornerstone of most Waters narratives. In his early period, *Pink Flamingos* provides the archetype: David Lochary and Mink Stole play Raymond and Connie Marble, a couple who have so debased the family as an institution that they kidnap young women and impregnate them so that they can sell the babies to lesbian couples. This evil family is directly compared to the loving one of which Divine is the head, which also includes Divine's children, Crackers and Cotton, and her mentally retarded mother Miss Edie (who lives in a baby crib and eats eggs all day). Divine takes care of these children with love and tenderness. When the family succeeds in defeating the Marbles to retain the title of "filthiest people alive," they light out for the territory—Boise, Idaho, to be exact—to live in familial bliss in gas station lavatories so that they may increase their filthiness. Huck Finn had to leave Aunt Polly to find this sort of freedom; in Waters's world, the family of freaks remains the basic unit of survival.

This theme of an aberrant family being preferable to the seemingly normal bourgeois one is remarkably consistent throughout Waters's oeuvre. In *Cecil B. Demented*, Cecil and his Sprocket Holes, his production crew, have formed their underground cinema family using the model of Warhol's Factory, yet are constantly besieged by their biological parents. Cecil's father engages in the worst insult possible when he questions Cecil's ability to direct films. His mother chimes in with the mantra of apolitical mainstream society, "Repeat after me, it's only a movie." Knowing full well the power of his adopted family's ability to make underground cinema that rebels against bourgeois oppression, Cecil embraces the familial unit forged by cinema, not genetics: "Thomas Alva Edison was the only father I ever had."

More seriously, Cecil's disciple, Fidget, is a young boy whose mother hires a psychiatrist to rescue him from Cecil's cult. However, Patty Hearst plays Fidget's mother, she whose infamous kidnapping and brainwashing by the Sibonese Liberation Army resulted in tremendous personal tragedy. Fascinated by the Manson family, Waters is drawn to these psychologically unstable families as his conceit for expressing the danger of all family relationships. However, Waters films' hijack these horrific stories of families gone wrong to reconstruct families of misfits that are functional by film's end.

This healing of the communal family, at the expense of the biological one, is perhaps best expressed in *Desperate Living*. The film begins with a Sirkian middle-class household that has been stretched to the breaking point. Peggy Gravel has recently returned home from a mental asylum and cannot bear the absurdities of conventional bourgeois life. When her kids accidentally hit a baseball through her bedroom window, Peggy shrieks, exposing the American hypocrisy in desiring peaceful family life while causing death and suffering around the world: "It's like war. Don't tell me I don't know what Vietnam is like." Realizing that she cannot murder her children lawfully, Peggy shouts, "I hate the Supreme Court."

When she settles down enough to leave her bedroom, she encounters a Freudian primal scene in reverse. Her prepubescent children Beth and Bosley, Jr., are naked, playing doctor. Peggy reacts hysterically, shouting: "Sodomites. Caught right in a sex orgy. Is that what you learned in private school? You could be pregnant, Beth. And you, I never thought you would rape your sister. Oh God. The children are having sex!" Freud comments that parental punishment of the sexual naughtiness of children initiates the "Family Romances" scenario: "It is, as a rule, precisely these neurotic children who were punished by their parents for sexual naughtiness and who now revenge themselves on their parents by means of phantasies of this kind" (240). In *Desperate Living*, the children, with the help of scriptwriter Waters, achieve their revenge on Peggy when the film's heroes, a loving lesbian couple, Mole and Muffy, kill her.

When her husband tries to calm Peggy down after she sees the children, her maid, Griselda, sits on his face, appearing to have a bowel movement, but in fact suffocating him to death. In a bizarre precursor to *Thelma and Louise*, Peggy and Griselda hit the road to escape the police. They end up in Mortville, a surreal city of the damned, run by a fairy-tale queen gone horribly wrong, Queen Carlotta (played by Edith Massey, the favorite of the Waters's troupe). At the film's end, Peggy has turned evil, working as the Wicked Witch for Queen Carlotta, who is attempting to poison all her subjects with rabies, including Princess Coo-Coo her daughter, who has now sided with the heroes because her jealous mother has had her lover, Herbert the garbage man, murdered. Mole and Muffy lead a rebellion, and kill, cook, and eat Queen Carlotta like a Thanksgiving turkey. Peggy, the last remnant of the film's bourgeois family, is done away with as Mole sticks a gun up her ass, resulting in the establishment of a utopian community of lesbian lovers, consisting of the hyperbutch Mole, the hyper-femme Muffy (played by former burlesque queen Liz Renay), and the four-hundred-pound black woman, Griselda.

The central motif of Freud's "Family Romances," of course, concerns the psychic severing of biological connection with one's parents in order to escape to a higher class status: "[T]he child's imagination becomes engaged in the task of getting free from the parents of whom he now has a low opinion and of replacing them by others, who, as a rule, are of higher social standing" (238–9). Even though this precisely describes Waters's flight from suburban Baltimore to Hollywood stardom, his films take a more progressive track: his heroic characters, invariably "poor white trash" orphans and rejects, move not upward in class but toward antibourgeois liberation. Cecil declares the Sprocket Holes "orphans of cinema." In *Cry-Baby*, the juvenile delinquent Cry-Baby (played by Johnny Depp), orphaned when his father and mother are both executed in the electric chair, falls in love with another orphan, Allison, who is a square (slang for middle-class). Cry-Baby fights to win her acceptance and love, not to enter her world, but to welcome her into his: Turkey Point, a poor white trash utopia filled with unwed mothers, men who bathe outdoors in washtubs, and drapes (1950s Baltimore slang for greasers).

The literal story of the "Family Romances" process of familial dislocation, of course, is "Cinderella," a fairy tale that is complexly parodied in Waters's first feature film, *Mondo Trasho*. Here, the film's hero, the Bombshell (a parody of Jayne Mansfield, played by Waters's best friend, Mary Vivian Pearce) spends the first half-hour of the film in sexual ecstasy in the park, receiving a "shrimp job" (a man sucking her toes absurdly brings her to multiple climaxes). While we hear her moans of sexual pleasure, she has a dream in which she is relegated to a life on her hands and knees scrubbing kitchen floors. Her two wicked stepsisters gawk at how ugly she is. In a scene inspired by Jack Smith's *Flaming Creatures* (1963), she comes downstairs in a beautiful black dress, only to have it ripped from her body by the wicked stepsisters. Her happiness is assured when the Prince comes to try the slipper on, and it fits only her foot.

At the end of the film, the Bombshell becomes a conduit for applying the "Family Romances" to classical Hollywood cinema via *The Wizard of Oz* (1939). The Bombshell discovers that if she taps her feet together three times, she can magically teleport herself somewhere else, via the power of jump cutting. Leaving a farm where pigs copulate in the mud, the Bombshell arrives in a back alley. Men cruise her in a car, including Glenn Harris Milstead (the man who plays Divine), and then sexually harass her by mooning her. She clicks her feet together again, this time arriving on a street where two judgmental middle-class women try to decide what sort of freak she is. They cruelly suggest she is "a drug dealer, a communist, a lesbian, a beatnik, a junkie, a shit kicker, a Pollack, a warmonger, a dingleberry, a yippie, and a jetsetter," none of which is remotely accurate. The film ends with the Bombshell escaping altogether by clicking her heels together, departing for points unknown.

In the early Waters films, the direct depiction of a utopia to which the Bombshell or her equivalents could escape is not yet available. In these early films, the only escape from traditional familial oppression is oblivion: being hunted down and murdered by the national guard in *Multiple Maniacs*, fleeing to gas stations in Boise in *Pink Flamingos*, and going to the electric chair in *Female Trouble*. By invoking *The Wizard of Oz*, *Mondo Trasho* first expresses the contradiction at the heart of "Family Romances," that the horrible world parents have bequeathed needs to be transcended even though it is ultimately impossible to do so. For Dorothy's life in Kansas is horrifyingly bleak and conventional. Her arrival in Oz is met, not by a Waters-like love for the Wicked Witch, but instead a recoiling from the freaks, and an immediate desire to return home. Whereas the classical Hollywood film would have us believe the return to Aunt Em is a happy one, *Mondo Trasho* will have nothing of it; at best, the Bombshell can disappear into oblivion. However, in the later works, Waters imagines utopian solutions: the lesbian liberation of Mortville from the evil heterosexual queen in *Desperate Living*, the elimination of both evil husbands at the end of *Polyester*, the racial harmony of integration that ends *Hairspray*, the unification of drapes and squares at the end of *Cry-Baby*, the not guilty verdict that liberates *Serial Mom*, and the success of Pecker's bar.

For the child in "Family Romances" to successfully imagine his alternative parentage, he must believe his mother to be unfaithful to his father. As Freud describes, "The child, having learnt about sexual processes, tends to picture himself in erotic situations and relations, the motive force behind this being his desire to bring his mother (who is the subject of the most intense sexual curiosity) into situations of secret infidelity and into secret love-affairs. . . . He often has no hesitation in attributing to his mother as many fictitious love-affairs as he himself has competitors" (240). Such a scenario is exactly present in *Polyester* and introduces the key to Waters's queering of traditional Hollywood melodramatic representation: the emphasis on the perversity of heterosexuality.

In *Polyester*, Francine embodies this component of the family romance when she has an adulterous affair, first as a fantasy with the pizza delivery boy and then in reality with Todd Tomorrow. In a parody of *10* (1979), to the strains of Ravel's *Boléro*, Todd tells Francine: "Let's make love, you sweet little thing." In keeping with the necessity of this fantasy in the family romance, this development does not result in the ruination of Francine's children, Lulu and Dexter, but instead in their cure. For at precisely the same time that Francine meets Todd, Lulu's and Dexter's juvenile delinquency is cured. Dexter, previously a terrorist foot stomper (he attacks women by stomping their feet as a sexual fetish), returns home to paint and sculpt women's feet. Lulu, formerly a trampy juvenile delinquent having sex with Bobo (played by punk rocker Stiv Bators), now wears bourgeois clothes and does macramé.

In the last sequence of the film, Todd jackhammers away at Francine, in a typical Waters parody of heterosex. However, shortly after, it is revealed that Todd is really in love with Francine's mother, the kleptomaniac La Rue. Todd tells Francine, "Let's keep love in the family," resulting in a surrealist sequence of violence that ends in Todd and La Rue being run over by a car, resulting in a happy ending for Francine and her children.

This fascination with the grotesquery of heterosex is the cornerstone of Waters's queering of normalcy within the American film melodrama. The revelation of Todd's incestuous affairs with both Francine and her mother is merely a tame version of other Waters's flirtations with incest, most scandalously featured in the fellatio scene in *Pink Flamingos*. Underneath a poster for Elia Kazan's *Baby Doll*, the film Waters's Catholic nun teachers insisted he would go to hell for seeing, Divine concocts a scheme to ruin the Marbles' middle-class home. After licking their furniture, a curse in a John Waters film—Cecil for example licks the Panavision camera filming the sequel to *Forrest Gump* (1994),

Gump Again—her son Crackers enthuses, "The house will react, Mama." In a shocking sequence, Crackers and Divine kiss. Divine sacrilegiously pants, "Let Mama receive you like communion," as she pulls his pants down. Calling it "a gift of supreme motherhood . . . a gift of divinity," Divine gives her son a blow job. "This will ruin this house forever," Divine insists. Nonplussed, Crackers gives her advice, "Get my balls, Mama."

This sacrilegious strain of Waters's critique of heterosexuality is most clearly expressed in *Multiple Maniacs* in the infamous "rosary job" sequence. Mink Stole, known in the film as "the religious whore," enters a church where Divine is attempting to pray the Lord's Prayer, giving Divine a "lewdly religious stare." Intercut with this sequence is an outrageous parody of the death of Christ, narrated by Divine. Back in the Church, Mink sits in a pew directly behind Divine. Mink and Divine suddenly kiss as a disgusted couple flees the church. Divine narrates, "She kissed me as if Christ himself had ordered every movement of her tongue." Mink interjects comically, "Think about the stations of the Cross," as she sticks her Rosary into Divine's ass. Divine moans in ecstasy. As the Romans nail Jesus to the cross, Mink nails Divine with the Rosary. When they are done, the music on the soundtrack announces that "He's got the whole world in his hands," as Mink wipes the shit off of her Rosary.

When not explicitly anti-Catholic, Waters's films are nevertheless filled with attempts to reveal the everyday horrors of heterosexuality, thus queering middle-class taste and normalcy. In keeping with Freud's "Family Romances"—"This stage is reached at a time at which the child is still in ignorance of the sexual determinants of procreation" (239)—the films are deliberately ignorant of the mechanisms whereby heterosex results in pregnancy. In *Female Trouble*, Dawn (played by Divine) has sex with Earl (played by Glenn Harris Milstead, Divine's male counterpart). Thus, Dawn becomes pregnant by herself, thus again one-upping Catholicism, as Waters takes on the role of God, arranging his own immaculate conception. Dawn then proceeds to have her baby in a sleazy motel room, chewing through the umbilical cord and spitting it at the wall. This scene is surpassed in comic impact only by the childbirth in *Cry-Baby*, wherein Cry-Baby's sister has her child in the backseat of a car in the middle of the climactic game of chicken. *Rebel Without a Cause* (1955) it ain't.

The most explicit reversal of homophobia into heterophobia in Waters's oeuvre is to be found in *Female Trouble*. Dawn falls in love with Gator, a hairdresser, and they are about to marry. Gator's Aunt Ida finds this extremely disappointing because she is convinced Gator, because he is a hairdresser, must be gay. Trying to set him up with gay dates, Aunt Ida insists he must come to his senses: "I worry that you'll work in an office, have children, celebrate wedding anniversaries. The world of heterosexuals is a sick and boring life." Gator never does see her point, eventually moving to Detroit, "to find happiness in the auto industry."

Beyond more acts of incest—Bonnie auditions for "The Cavalcade of Perversions" in *Multiple Maniacs* by describing sex with her uncle, Taffy's father molests her in *Female Trouble*, Cherish describes being raped by her own family under the Christmas Tree in *Cecil B. Demented*—Waters envisions heterosexuality as a bizarre, aberrant form of human behavior, reversing all of the stereotypes foisted upon us by heterosexism. Rarely depicting straight, missionary sex except to reveal its horror—Queen Carlotta and Serial Mom both shouting the non-sensical "get it" as they are penetrated by their lovers—Waters instead invents absurd acts and descriptions for what straight people do for sexual pleasure.

The most bizarre is the "shrimp job," performed both by the evil Marbles in *Pink Flamingos* and the Bombshell in *Mondo Trasho*. Heterosex even sounds ridiculous in a Waters film, as the loveable Bonnie in *Multiple Maniacs* wants to please Mr. David by "performing acts 24 hours a day." What acts these are she never specifies. The cross-dressing butler, Chandler, forced to impregnate the girls for the baby ring in *Pink Flamingos*, so detests heterosex that he masturbates and then syringes his semen into the women so he doesn't have to touch them. When characters do have straight, missionary sex, Waters queers even that. In *Pink Flamingos*, Cotton has sex with Cookie, but must pervert it by sticking a live chicken in between them. Gator cannot have sex with Dawn in *Female Trouble* without using his toolbox, often sticking wrenches and hammers into her vagina instead of his penis.

But I would argue this is by no means merely an articulation of male sexism, for Waters's films more often identify *women's* repulsion from heterosex. In *Pink Flamingos*, *Desperate Living*, and *Cry-Baby*, women loathe being touched by men. In *Pink Flamingos*, Cotton can only become orgasmic only while watching Crackers have chicken sex with Cookie. As soon as he touches her, she cringes in horror. At the beginning of *Desperate Living*, Bosley tries to calm down his hysterical wife Peggy, hugging her while preparing her medicine. She screams, "Oh, you touched me. Now my flesh is rotting. . . . The touch of scum." She proceeds to smash a bottle over his head.

At the beginning of *Cry-Baby*, we know that Allison, even though a square, is alright, because when her square boyfriend Baldwin gives her a shoulder massage, she squirms, annoyed because "I can't think because you're always touching me." Her grandmother, Mrs. Vernon-Williams (played by Polly Bergen), seems to mainstream this by insisting a "young lady does not like to be pawed," but a shock cut to Milton and Hatchet-Face, two drape lovers in another car wildly pawing each other, denies the possibility of any such reading. In the wonderful world of Waters, people love each other, but not in ways prescribed by bourgeois normalcy. The rebellion implicit therein is rendered coherent by the "Family Romances" conceit, but applied historically to a culture in which middle-class heterosexuality comes to oppress everyone else who refuses to play along.

conclusion

After much fretting, I finally delivered my intellectual, but hopefully not too pompous, introduction to Waters's talk at Montana State University. I refrained from calling attention to the more infantile jokes of Waters's career, such as the decision to call the film *John Waters's Pecker*, to elicit, I assume, queries as to whether one had seen "John Waters's pecker." Less concerned with his pecker, I got to shake *hands* with John Waters after I introduced him. I sat down in my front row seat, remembering Marsha Brady's example to never wash her hand again, after Davey Jones of *The Monkees* had touched it, in *The Brady Bunch*. Was this the appropriate response to shaking hands with Waters, the most famous person I had ever met? After all, my newly identified national treasure was also the sleazy filmmaker who convinced his star Divine to eat shit at the end of *Pink Flamingos*, and while stoned, thought it would be a good idea to light Mink Stole's hair on fire, all for the greater glory of the cinema.

I have relied on personal experience to frame this chapter because it not only indicates my by now obsessive interest in Waters's films, but also sets up my concern with his body, his *authorial* body, that is. In an age of the poststructural dismantling of authorship, what does it mean to have been so upset, engaged, and fascinated by meeting the director of these films, to the extent that I have now worked out a system that places him at the center of a plan to save radical cinema from being consumed by the Hollywood blockbuster machine? Clearly at some level, I had formed a "prepoststructural," indeed Romantic, attachment to the author. It mattered to me very much that the real John Waters would be in the audience listening to what I said about him. Mostly, I was concerned that his quite profound satirical, and humiliating, skills would be directed at me, a position in which few poststructural critics seem to have found themselves. After all, did Foucault have to worry about William Shakespeare writing a play about him after being called merely an "author-function"? Of course not. I hate that Michel Foucault.

172

Furthermore, I was proud to have had a chance to *touch* the author, this figure Barthes so arrogantly declared dead in 1968, precisely at the time a disaffected middle-class gay kid in Baltimore was learning how to use a camera, and this disaffected middle-class straight kid was born in Philadelphia. I hate that Roland Barthes.[8]

Clearly, my belief in poststructural theory and my own emotional experiences were in direct conflict. I still very much believe in the notion of social construction, and its ability to describe how and why we tend to think and act similarly at particular historical and cultural moments. However, we also need to emphasize the ways in which we willingly and usefully participate in the romanticization of particular figures, especially of ourselves as critics with the authority to speak, as well as of the directors about whom we speak. And so, John Waters's body, and my contact with it, has served as the occasion through which I have critically explored his films as a body of work about the American family during the late twentieth century.[9]

The chapter has enacted a solution to the crisis of authorship studies in a poststructural theoretical world. Following Silverman, I have shown how the coherent body of work by a marginalized filmmaker could be driven by a psychological fantasy. The middle-class child's fantasy of being adopted and belonging in an upper-class family is queered in a Waters film such that communal radicals replace the nuclear family as the normative site on which narrative is built. Waters films celebrate the triumph of this utopian reorganization, largely as a way of expressing the author-outside-the-text's escape from suburban Baltimore into an adult world of urban guerilla filmmaking. As a critic who escaped a similar suburban life-style to be able to write about films depicting "rosary jobs" and "chicken fucking," I view that progression as nothing less than a heroic triumph.

notes

1. Kaja Silverman, "The Female Authorial Voice." *The Acoustic Mirror: The Female Voice in Psychoanalysis and Cinema* (Bloomington: Indiana University Press, 1988).
2. Roland Barthes, "The Death of the Author [1968]," *Image, Music, Text*, trans. Stephen Heath (New York: Hill and Wang, 1977), passim; and Michel Foucault, "What is an Author?," *Foucault Reader*, trans. Josue V. Havari, ed. Paul Rabinow (New York: Pantheon Books, 1984), passim.
3. Hal Erickson's "Biography: John Waters" on the Barnes and Noble website lists his "dubious titles" as "The Sultan of Sleaze," "The Baron of Bad Taste," and "The Pope of Trash." http://video.barnesandnoble.com/search/biography.asp? userid=1961I42I28&mscssid=6M09FW4X43CT9KS1Q232FB01M9SLES 4C&CTR=748213.
4. John Waters, *Crackpot: The Obsessions of John Waters* (New York: Vintage, 1986), 16.
5. John Waters, *Shock Value: A Tasteful Book About Bad Taste*, 2nd ed. (New York: Thunder's Mouth Press, 1995), 2.
6. For a very different interpretation of these middle period Waters's films, which I find the least interesting of his career, see Jane Feuer's reading of *Hairspray* and *Cry-Baby* as Brechtian musicals. For example, Feuer argues: "*Absolute Beginners* . . . , very similarly to *Pennies from Heaven*, resorts to a Brechtian version of the classic happy ending, as does John Waters's more avant-garde follow-up to *Hairspray*, the box office failure *Cry-Baby*. Each film ends with an abrupt transition from (racial) conflict or chaos to the traditional final embrace by the young couple. *Hairspray*, while fully 'culinary,' also deconstructs many of the building blocks of Hollywood musicals, especially in terms of racial, gender and body-image stereotypes. The heroine is a self-affirming fat girl, the triumph of entertainment includes black youths, and the usually puritanical parental figure is played by Divine in drag." Jane Feuer,

173

The Hollywood Film Musical, 2nd ed. (Bloomington: Indiana University Press, 1993), 136.

7. Sigmund Freud, "Family Romances [1909]." *The Standard Edition of the Complete Psychological Works*, Vol. IX, trans. James Strachey (London: Hogarth Press, 1959), 237–41.

8. Clearly, I am (trying to be) funny here. Foucault and Barthes, both gay men themselves, are particularly apt theorists for studying Waters. Furthermore, they really do not kill off the author, as I have assumed here, but instead merely complicate questions of authorship, positing authors also as readers. Barthes, in particular, constructs the author as the first reader of a text.

9. For Waters's perspective on speaking at universities, see his essays, "Singing for Your Supper" in *Crackpot* and "Sort-of-Famous" in *Shock Value*.

len lye

reading with

the body

r o g e r   h o r r o c k s

"It was the sinful thing we did, artists of one kind of another, to sneak
in to the movies in the afternoon instead of working," recalls
Greenwich Village writer Alastair Reid. "If the movie was a tear-jerker
of some kind, suddenly we'd hear the sound of someone not only sob-
bing but howling—'Hooooooo!'—and three people would stand up
and call 'Len!', and he'd say 'Here.' Len blubbed constantly at movies,
it was very endearing, and when we heard him we'd all go and join
him."[1] This was Len Lye, avant-garde filmmaker, painter, kinetic sculptor, and theorist of a new "art of motion." He would go on a work
binge for weeks in his West Village studio, but a day always came when
this "sucker for romantic movies" would again be lured to the cinema.
In the words of his wife Ann who usually accompanied him, "Len often
cried at movies, he'd bawl and people would turn around. Once when
we came in late, he started crying then turned to me and said, 'It
wouldn't be so bad if I only knew what it was about!'"[2]

Lye described Hollywood movies as "good folklore fun" in contrast
to the tradition of "experimental" or "fine art" films in which he

worked. Although he took little interest in their narrative aspects, the movies provided him with an opportunity for emotional release; and for a person who spent most of his life in the isolation of his studio and at the far edges of the counterculture, it was relaxing to return for a few hours to the mainstream, to the cultural landscape in which almost everyone has grown up. In Lye's words: "There's that horse galloping around, there's that chap going to hit that other chap, there's that dame sashaying along; you knew what you saw and felt at home with it."[3] Like other avant-garde artists he had also developed his own highly specialized method of reading Hollywood films,[4] deriving moments of "kinesthetic pleasure" from the body language of the actors or the movements of the camera.

These Hollywood habits and pleasures would not be surprising if Lye's public reputation were not that of a fiercely uncompromising avant-gardist, a member of many vanguard groups (including the Surrealist Movement with which he exhibited in the 1930s), and one of the few filmmakers to continue making experimental films for more than 50 years (from *Tusalava* in 1929 to *Particles in Space* in 1979). In a collection of essays on Lye published in 2000 by the Centre Pompidou in Paris, William Moritz summed up this body of work as "one of the most important achievements in the field of . . . experimental film."[5] Stan Brakhage described Lye's *Free Radicals* (1958, revised 1979) as "an almost unbelievably immense masterpiece (a brief epic)."[6] And Kathy Geritz introduced a recent Lye retrospective at the Pacific Film Archive in Berkeley with the comment: "Hailed as one of the most creative and inventive individuals ever, Len Lye was by all accounts an astonishing man."[7]

Lye made a place for himself in the history books as the pioneer of "the direct film," the film created without a camera by painting or scratching directly on celluloid. He was not the first to use the method but he put it on the map by demonstrating its potential in such a thorough, sophisticated way.[8] Others making films of this kind (such as Brakhage, Norman McLaren, and Robert Breer) have acknowledged Lye's influence and mastery. Direct animation can be regarded as the only form of filmmaking that *literally* fits the auteur theory as the touch of the artist is physically present in every frame, with a recognizable sense of signature. A critic seeking to claim Lye as an auteur can also cite the distinctive rhythmic vitality of his work (in the syncopated way it combines images with music), its quirky sense of humour (very different from the earnestness of much of the experimental filmmaking of its period), and its striking physicality (both in its "direct" engagement with the film medium and in its evocation of the human body in movement). Many who knew the filmmaker related those qualities to his own characteristic humor and physicality.[9]

Lye is as well known in the tradition of experimental film, particularly animation, as, say, a Martin Scorsese in the tradition of

Hollywood feature films. The gap between those two traditions reflects not only a disparity in public awareness and interest but also a history of bad blood between them. Although some Hollywood filmmakers (such as Scorsese, Francis Ford Coppola, and David Lynch) have taken an interest in experimental work, and only the most hard-line experimental filmmaker never visits a multiplex, feelings of suspicion and defensiveness are common. Every avant-gardist has encountered the industry attitude that experimental films are indulgent, made by and for pretentious intellectuals, or represent an unfortunate stage through which film students pass before learning to make grown-up films the public really wants to see. In return popular filmmakers are accused of prostituting their talents for a Hollywood salary and leaving the serious work of innovation to the avant-garde. Each of the various traditions of film has its own turf—for example, Hollywood films go to the multiplex; American "independent" features and European "art" films head for the art house or the film festival; and, at least in large cities, experimental films have their own cinemathèque-style screening venues (such as Anthology Film Archives in New York). But in some areas such as universities, film schools, and art museums the traditions overlap, collide, and jostle for space and resources. At such institutions the argument over priorities can be fierce.

Though Lye himself found points of interest in many types of film, he devoted most of his public statements to "fine art film-making," which he saw as the underdog. For example, in 1959, after a long period of frustration over his inability to raise production financing despite the major international award he had won for *Free Radicals*, he announced publicly that he had "gone on strike." This was a serious gesture on his part for he shifted most of his best energies over the next decade from filmmaking to kinetic sculpture and built a new international reputation for himself in that field. Lye provided a rationale for his strike in the essay "Is Film Art?" published in *Film Culture*.[10] One of the most passionate of polemics for avant-garde film, it acknowledges the existence of "great" commercial films but sees them as great only "in the folklore and nostalgic . . . .sense." Too much American cinema is "Coney Island" in its unsubtle roller-coaster effects. In contrast film as a fine art—as a medium whose potential lay in its "unique kinetic beauty"—was still "a cinderella . . . waiting for her glass slipper." Lye's essay was not a plea to show more charity toward neglected auteurs but an explanation of why the industry needed research and how the avant-garde could provide this. As examples of Hollywood borrowing he cited the title sequences of recent feature films and stylistic changes in popular animation.

Lye's outburst on behalf of his community is perfectly understandable in terms of the frustrations of his own career and the almost total absence of public funding for experimental filmmaking in the United States in the 1950s. Yet Hollywood films had always played a significant part in his own life and the complexity of his personal relationship with them makes an interesting study. It is not that Lye failed to practice what he preached, but like most artists he was happy to pick up ideas from any genre. He would look anywhere in his search for Cinderella, the "unique kinetic beauty" of the film medium, his ultimate aim being to offer her the glass slipper tribute of his own work. His quest was guided by certain innovative reading strategies he had developed, which worked equally for mainstream and minority forms of culture, and came consistently to inform both his production and consumption of films. The rest of this chapter will seek to track the development of those reading strategies and their functioning within the circuit of his own activities as viewer and filmmaker. Lye offers not only a remarkable life story but a reminder of reading interests that are seldom explored, i.e., wild emotion, "bodily sensation," moments isolated and enjoyed for their own sake, and other seemingly irresponsible habits. Also, the complex interweaving of popular and experimental films throughout Lye's life allows us to challenge common assumptions about both traditions and to reconsider authorship in the broader context that this challenge can open up.

Born in 1901 Lye spent his childhood in New Zealand in a situation of poverty—important contexts in terms of his later work. By the time he was eight his father had died of tuberculosis, his stepfather had been committed for life to a mental hospital, and he was being boarded out to various foster homes. In later life he believed he had taken up the hobby of drawing partly as a security blanket or escape, and he vividly remembered the afternoon he had taken it up seriously. He had been poring over magazines that contained pictures of "cowboys and goddesses" from the new medium of the movies. He was so struck by the aura of those faces that he found a pencil and began to copy them. He discovered that if he worked carefully enough he could create a spitting image of a black-and-white poster-style cowboy. Although his picture was merely the copy of a copy, the process gave him an uncanny sense of closeness to the world he was representing. He also lingered over the female stars, "the queens of loveliness," trying by his drawing to discover what it was he liked about them. Seeing a western film was a rare treat for Lye and for days he would reenact it, particularly the way its cowboy hero moved—"I walked with a waddle, as if I'd just got down from a duck!"[11] Now he could relive them in his drawings, which also served to affirm his own agency: "You looked at a finished drawing and saw the magic of your best powers of self staring at you."

By the time Lye was a teenager it was clear he had developed a passion for image making and a fiercely individualistic or maverick streak. As Lye put it, "I was stuck with this thinking bug."[12] He also displayed a strong interest in the physical side of life that made him an unusual mixture of intellectual and street kid. He had spent much of his childhood outdoors, including two years living at a lighthouse in landscapes as dramatic as any in Jane Campion's *The Piano* (1993). He was a tough, wiry teenager who played sport, and after lack of money compelled him to leave school at 14 he supported himself through working-class laboring jobs. Less typically in a society dominated by puritanical religion he was sexually active from an early age and seemed exceptionally at ease with his body.

The strength of his creative drive remains mysterious, but it is interesting to relate it to the fact that during this period New Zealand had an underdeveloped art scene and virtually no film industry. The domination of the cinemas of New Zealand by Hollywood created a situation in which its imagery was both intimately local (part of growing up) and profoundly alien (because most local viewers lacked any direct knowledge of American contexts or any possibility of ever becoming part of such a film). The domination of galleries and museums by British art created a similar disjunction. Such local art production as there was tended to be narrowly imitative; yet this colonial situation also had the potential to generate a radical response, a questioning of all the given forms of visual language, and Lye was quickly drawn to that challenge, first in painting and then in film.

Brakhage has said of Lye's remarkable self-education within this context: "The extraordinary modernism of the man really had to be scratched up out of his own imagination."[13] Yet he did have a source or catalyst—European modernism—that came to him in fragments of information gleaned from the public library. Lye was wildly excited by modernism because it matched his own maverick sensibility. The two aspects that interested him most were motion (as explored by the Futurists) and modernist primitivism, which led him to make a serious study of Maori, Aboriginal, and other indigenous forms of art, and eventually to jettison all the European representational skills with which he had won art competitions. He had absorbed a Romantic conception of the artist as a unique individual, but "primitive art" taught him to have an equal respect for work that was anonymous and in some cases collective. Throughout his career his thinking about art would oscillate between an emphasis on extreme individualism and an emphasis on discourse, process, or mode of representation.

Primitivism also turned him into a resistant reader of "cowboy and Indian" films and period dramas about the British Empire: "Another phase in the un-pigging of my chauvinism came at the movies when I saw 'our' side shown as heroic and the other side as stupid" (Lye, 1975). But like other modernist artists Lye welcomed cinema in general as a medium free from historical baggage, allied to modern technology and refreshingly vulgar. Early modernism had developed strategies for reading and enjoying popular culture. Lye shared the taste for slapstick but as yet had no access to modernist films (such as Fernand Léger and Dudley Murphy's 1924 *Ballet Mécanique,* which included a homage to Charlie Chaplin). The film that convinced Lye that his future lay in filmmaking was something very different—Frank Hurley's ethnographic film *Pearls and Savages,* which he saw in Sydney in 1923. At a time when "tribal dancing and the living conditions of primitive society had only been seen in the remoteness of the still picture," Hurley's film made a strong impression on audiences, offering images of Papuan culture such as masks, body painting, and dancing.[14] Lye was not impressed by Hurley's patronizing comments about "fuzzy-wuzzies," but he was amazed at the ability of the film medium to add immediacy and movement to the tribal art he had been studying. To most viewers the film must simply have offered an evening of exotic adventure framed by the civilized values of its explorer-commentator; but to Lye it provided news from the front lines, information about his counterculture heroes, and vivid glimpses of their art.

And so he went in search of a filmmaking job. He found one at Filmads Ltd. in Sydney, which produced animated advertisements for products such as cigarettes and beeswax that were screened in cinemas all over Australia (Horrocks, 55). At Filmads Lye learned basic animation techniques and in the process discovered film editing ("I suddenly realized that films had cuts and sequences").[15] He also made his first film experiments based on the scratches and other accidental marks he saw on leaders. He later described those experiments as his first taste of authorship: "I got my first real intensity out onto something [i.e., film images] that could reflect it back, at least to me—and that was plenty because no one had the least idea of what I was up to. . . . [It was] the exhilaration of discovering [my] own motion imagery. I can still feel the effect of that moment in my heart muscles somewhere."[16]

Restless, Lye went off to live in Samoa for a year, studying *tapa* patterns that were to have an influence on his subsequent film imagery. He met up briefly with Robert Flaherty who was on another island making *Moana.* Then Lye was expelled by the colonial administration, which disapproved of the extent to which he had gone native (Horrocks, 64–7). Although his version of primitivism involved some of the same dubious assumptions made by the European modernists, he was able at least to be directly involved with indigenous cultures in his region of the world. Arriving in London in 1926 he proceeded to make the first primitivist animated film, *Tusalava,* a myth about the beginnings of life. Lye sought to work from intuition rather than conscious calculation. He showed mysterious organic forms going through a continuous process of metamorphosis in a film that appeared to have no edits. Its Samoan title implied an endless cycle of sameness. The visual ingredients were not entirely original—they were drawn from Aboriginal, Maori, and modernist traditions—but their combination was unique. Although *Tusalava* puzzled many viewers because they had no context for it, *Close Up* ("The Only Magazine Devoted To Films As An Art") ran an enthusiastic review by filmmaker Oswell Blakeston who described Lye as "a great artist with great ideas" and expressed interest in his radical approach to editing.[17] A copy of the film circulated round the European avant-garde and made a deep impression on a few filmmakers such as Hans Richter. Lye felt his best return for the years he had spent on the animation drawings was the receipt out of the blue of an enthusiastic letter from Roger Fry, the well-known Bloomsbury art critic, who wrote: "I thought that you had seen the essential thing as no one had hitherto—I mean you really thought not of forms in themselves but of them as movements in time. I suspect it will need a new kind of imagination to seize this idea fully but you are the first as far as I know to make a start."[18]

When *Tusalava* required a certificate from the British Board of Film Censors in 1929, astonishingly the Board considered banning the film. The Censors had already refused a certificate to the French Surrealist film *The Sea-Shell and the Clergyman* (1928) on the grounds that "the film is so cryptic as to be almost meaningless" and "if there is a meaning it is doubtless objectionable."[19] They had the same reaction to *Tusalava* and demanded to know what this strangely physical film was about. Could Lye convince them that its images were not full of sex and violence? He explained to them in detail that the film "represented a self-shape annihilating an agonistic element." At that point the censors threw in the towel and issued a certificate (Knowles, 237).[20]

Since Lye's arrival in London his membership in the London Film Society had enabled him to see avant-garde films for the first time. Although enthusiastically championing all films of this kind he admitted that he seldom saw more than a few seconds he liked—but that was enough, even in his own films: "I can make kinetic effects last two seconds or three and, out of a five-minute film, I've got three moments that just hold me doped, emphatically *doped*, I'm *involved*, all my senses are completely *shot*, I'm tied in with this. . . . When you get a kick from a work of art, it's something that triggers you for an infinitesimal second but lasts a long time in your bones."[21] Lye was well aware of individual directors (such as Oskar Fischinger), but he had an overall sense of filmmaking as a collective project, an ongoing formal experiment to tap the energies of what was still a new medium.

Both as a filmmaker and as an individual Lye was regarded as extreme even by the standards of the London avant-garde. The painter Julian Trevelyan offered a typical description: "He was like a man from Mars who saw everything from a different viewpoint, and it was this that made him original."[22] Of course many aspects of his difference came not from Mars but from the South Pacific. Lye's habit of wearing a Samoan *lavalava*, his total contempt for the British class system, and the fact that he had stoked his way to London after buying ship's papers from a drunken seaman in a Sydney pub all contributed to his reputation as a wild man, a kind of Crocodile Dundee of the London art world.

Yet Lye also enjoyed Hammersmith and was eager to share the

life-world of his new friends. One way to do that was to go to the cinema, and movies (along with dances) were an important part of dating for him. Jane Thompson who became his first wife in 1934 recalls: "There was a fleapit along Kings Road [towards Chelsea] with ninepenny seats. If there was something Len was feeling very special about we would pay 2/6d and go up to the West End so we could see the new print before it got messed up. God, if you knew what excitement! We sometimes moved four times until we got dead center on the screen."[23] Thompson, who became a dancing instructor, shared his love of movement: "We both used to like westerns—all that galloping. We were mad about Gary Cooper, we were both shaken by his walk." Lye spoke of "the celery stick walk of that stick of celery, Gary Cooper."

Vanguard artists had developed various ways to read mainstream films that today are categorized as "surreal" or "camp" (Taylor), but Lye had formulated his own set of interests focusing on movement and the body. Apart from his tendency to cry at melodramas, his approach remained consistent whether he was watching an art film or a Hollywood musical. In the words of editor Paul Barnes, "There were bits he'd enjoy, always from an odd viewpoint. He'd enjoy the way a particular actor or actress walked, and he'd like the film whenever they were on the screen as he could study the way they were moving." Lye would affectionately describe the body language of actors as though they were cartoon characters—for example "the nifty Balinese hand motions of a James Cagney" or "the mollasses of a James Dean spreading his bodily attitudes all over the armchair" or (in the 1970s) "the knobbly cast of the star Elliott Gould, bemused, his mouth full of marbles, finally flapping his foot-flippers enroute insouciantly to some horizon or other" (Lye, 1975). These were moments of "kinesthesia" and they were as likely to turn up in an action movie as in an experimental film. When Lye watched a martial arts film, for example, he would take no notice of the plot but might get excited about the choreography of one of the fight scenes. Focusing on isolated moments can be a fruitful and liberating way to read films. It also matched his approach to filmmaking, which involved putting a film together from hundreds of small sequences a second or so in length. He became increasingly a perfectionist and as an animator he would draw dozens of versions of each one-second strip until he felt he had realized a particular kinetic effect.

182

Lye's filmmaking career took off in 1935. Prior to this he had tried unsuccessfully for several years to find sponsorship for a sequel to *Tusalava*. Then he had attempted to fund a "film ballet" (Horrocks, 129–32) and some puppet films (because puppets were among the few areas of animation not yet dominated by Walt Disney). His dealings with large film companies were so frustrating he decided he must somehow get back to a cottage industry situation. The film medium required money, technology, and teamwork, and each was likely to compromise the freedom of the artist. His solution was a brilliant stroke of lateral thinking—to bypass the camera by painting images directly onto plain celluloid. What had previously discouraged film-makers (apart from a few experimenters) from employing this "direct" method of animation was the jittery effect caused by the slight differences between one frame and the next. It took a special kind of artist to regard this jitter as an advantage, as a display of kinetic energy, and as a visual equivalent of musical resonance. Animators of all kinds from Walt Disney to the German abstract artists had sought smooth movement and maximum control. Similarly, the long tradition of tinting film and adding hand-painted areas of color (by both brush and stencil) had emphasized neatness and precision. Lye was well aware of these precedents but with years of experience as an abstract artist in using "doodling" and free forms of brushwork he preferred (as Malcolm Le Grice has put it) to work "with rather than against the 'imperfections.'"[24]

As the author of *A Colour Box* and his subsequent direct films, Lye needed only one assistant, his musical editor Jack Ellitt. Lye used popular dance music for the soundtracks, not because he was seeking a larger audience but because he genuinely liked the music and conceived of his visuals as a "vicarious form of dance." This was a demonstration of modernism's attraction to the energy of popular culture and its interest in an alliance of avant-garde and popular against the middle-brow. The imagery of the films was abstract but seldom struck viewers as pretentious. Laura Riding acknowledged this down-to-earth appeal when she argued in *Len Lye and the Problem of Popular Film* that this "unsnobbish" filmmaker had the ability to develop a new kind of popular film, neither crudely commercial nor grimly aesthetic. She added: "He has, in a more robust degree than anyone I know of, those sensibilities of social pleasure that in earlier times would have made the master of community ceremonies, and must now be the criterion for the film-master of public entertainment."[25] On the strength of his films of the 1930s Lye has been celebrated as one of the fathers of the MTV-style music clip, and today his films continue to be screened not only in art contexts but by MTV Europe.

Producer John Grierson knew enough about modern forms of art to understand the power of what Lye was doing, and he saw the possibility of using such films to liven up the General Post Office Film Unit's packages of black-and-white documentaries. He offered sponsorship on the condition that a discreet Post Office advertising message was included. Lye saw this as an unhappy compromise but agreed to accept it, thus finding himself in the unusual position of making abstract art films that were classified as advertisements and screened before Hollywood movies in mainstream cinemas. Cinema owners were initially nervous about *A Colour Box* both because of the experimental style and because patrons might view it as an attempt to sneak advertising into the program, but in the end so many British cinemas wanted to screen it that it came to be seen (as David Curtis has pointed out) "by a larger public than any experimental film before it and most since."[26] Not that it did not generate controversy—audiences were polarized, booing and clapping in equal strength. This generated a huge amount of press coverage, everyone wanted to offer an opinion, and the debate rapidly make the film and its director famous. Anthony Vesselo said of it in *Sight and Sound*: "The reinforcements of sound and color have stirred the abstract film to a new vitality." He saw *A Colour Box* as "more profoundly effective than a horde of vacuous feature films."[27] Nevertheless at the 1936 Venice Festival *A Colour Box* was "met with such loud condemnatory stomping that the screening had to be stopped before the film was over." The Nazi press gloated over the incident, and William Moritz has suggested it was stage managed by Nazi sympathizers who condemned the film as degenerate art.[28] Meanwhile *A Colour Box* rapidly gained cult status among the avant-garde in other parts of Europe (Horrocks, 140–41). Lye's new associations with advertising and popular cinema had not undercut his credibility in the world of experimental films, and his work became a frequent talking-point in discussions of film as art.

Frank Evans of the *Evening Chronicle* wrote in 1937: "In the cartoon field Disney has lost a good deal of his pre-eminence to men like Len Lye and George Pal."[29] This may have been true in terms of prestige among critics but the popular audience still associated animation with Disney. Yet the phrase "English Disney" continued turning up in reviews of Lye's work, often as a way of cheering on the local side as almost all forms of English filmmaking were engaged in a fierce, lopsided struggle with Hollywood.[30] Even the American magazine *Time* drew the Disney comparison though Lye's films were not eligible for cinema distribution in the United States because of restrictions on advertisements. *Time*'s enthusiastic 1938 story began: "Last week in London an original artist named Len Lye, working on a shoe string budget, crashed through with an animated movie called *Colour Flight* which previewers hailed as art, as entertainment, and as the freshest stuff of its kind since Disney arrived." The magazine went on to develop a vivid David and Goliath comparison between Lye and Hollywood: "The Disney *Silly Symphonies* are the product of a big corporation employing 75 animators, 150 copyists and a gang of gagmen, musicians and technicians. . . . Lye, however, paints or stencils his designs by hand."[31]

Disney is known to have taken an interest in Lye's films, and several moments in *Fantasia* reminded reviewers of those films, but Disney never offered him any work.[32] Within the British film industry Lye did receive occasional commissions for special effects. One of his notable clients was Alfred Hitchcock who asked him to do some hand-painting for the 1936 feature film, *Secret Agent*. Hitchcock admired Sergei

Eisenstein's surprise use of color in black-and-white films such as *The Battleship Potemkin* (1925) in which a new stage in the political situation was signaled by the hoisting of a red flag, or *The General Line* (1929) in which the success of a farm cooperative was celebrated by a hand-colored fireworks display. *Secret Agent* included a train crash, and Hitchcock and his collaborator Ivon Montagu asked Lye to paint scarlet and yellow flames directly onto the preview print to help "give a feeling of the complete, rending break that it [the crash] represented in the characters' lives."[33] Lye painted flames, then made it even more of a "hot shot" by adding the impression that the film itself had caught fire in the projector, "jerking off the screen and back on the melting emulsion," followed by a blackout.[34] At the preview his warning somehow failed to reach the projectionist. These were the days of highly inflammable nitrate film, and as soon as the sequence appeared on screen the projectionist shouted, "My god, the thing's on fire!" and threw the tripping device in a way that damaged the projector. Discovering his mistake, the projectionist stormed out of the box and threatened Hitchcock and Montagu with a punch on the nose (Montagu, 124). Meanwhile the audience assumed there was a fire and hurried for the exit. Because the film was about to go into general release, a special letter to projectionists was drawn up: "In reel five of this feature there is an effect of fire in the gate—it's just an effect—it isn't real—please be aware of this and don't turn your projector off." But the front office of Gaumont-British was not willing to run the risk of audiences panicking. Montagu wanted to make a stand, but Hitchcock was willing to bow to pressure (John Russell Taylor, 137). Montagu brought the bad news to Lye: "It's a great idea but it could cost the film industry millions of dollars!"[35] This was one of several occasions the film industry found Lye's appetite for experiment too much to cope with.

Jane Lye's assumption that one day her husband would be able to cash in on his innovations helped her to weather a decade of poverty. She finally accepted the futility of that hope in 1943 when a British company offered him a large-budget *Fantasia*-style feature film to direct, and he turned the project down because of its conservative flavor (it was based on the Bible). In her words: "I had long been accustomed to the fact that his work was the most important thing in his life, and I never raised a squeal about whether he was going to make a particular film or not. He had the tendency, if anything looked as though it were going to be a commercial success, he would be off it and on to something else."[36] Yet not all of Lye's problems were due to his selective attitude—work was generally scarce in the British film industry. Every national industry outside Hollywood tends to lead a volatile and anxious existence.

In 1944 Lye moved to New York to accept a directing job with *The March of Time* (the monthly cinema equivalent of *Time* magazine). His reasons were political—it was the only way he could get to the United States to follow up a personal invitation from Wendell Willkie. Willkie, spoken of as a strong contender for the American presidency, had expressed interest in sponsoring a film about certain philosophical ideas that Lye had developed during the war. The collective madness of Fascism and its censorship of modern art had strengthened Lye's commitment to the idea of individualism (though his way of formulating this concept was complex). Willkie's death before the end of the year brought the film project to an end, but the artist decided to stay in New York and take out American citizenship. He was exhilarated by New York's energy and modernity. Subsequently he married an American, Ann Hindle, and they based their ultrabohemian life-style in the West Village.[37] Lye was able to contribute to the development of an experimental film scene in the city, teaching a course organized by Richter and personally assisting filmmakers such as Arnold Eagle, Francis Lee, and Ian Hugo. In the late 1940s his old friend Stanley Hayter introduced him to the young painters later known as the New York School or the Abstract Expressionists. Screening his films for them at "The Club" on East 8th Street, he felt a strong affinity between his kinesthetic approach and the physical style of painting being developed by artists such as Jackson Pollock. Indeed, subsequent films by Lye such as *Free Radicals* (1958) have been described by critics as among the purest examples of an Abstract Expressionist aesthetic in film.[38]

Until the series came to an end in 1951 *The March of Time* provided Lye with a meal ticket. He did his best to adapt to its strict house style and production line methods, though his assistant James Merritt commented: "Sending Len out to direct ordinary newsreel footage is like using a race horse to pull an ice wagon" (quoted in Horrocks, 239). During the 1950s Lye made his own films when he could afford to do so, but even direct animation involved paint and processing costs, and he yearned to find another sponsor like Grierson. He sometimes told friends "he wished he could go to Hollywood, not to make story films, but to make feature films of movement and color in ways that hadn't been done before."[39] Occasionally he would imagine a project for which a particular Hollywood star had the perfect physical skills. An example was Gene Kelly to whom he sent letters and made telephone calls. Kelly was sufficiently intrigued by Lye's ideas for a dance film to invite him to visit his house in Los Angeles. Lye arrived by bus then walked round the area looking for the actor's house, but a police car picked him up as a suspicious character because "there were no sidewalks in the area and nobody was supposed to walk."[40] When Lye finally persuaded the police to take him to the right house "he and Gene sat out on the front steps and talked for half the day and they got on very well. They were both interested in each other's work, and Gene knew all about Len's films. But in the end nothing came of it" (Ann Lye, 1988).

Visits to the cinema continued to be an important social ritual for the Lyes, although orthodox film editing increasingly bored him. Talking to a group of New York filmmakers he made the provocative comment that "all film is D.W. Griffith."[41] He used Griffith's name as a shorthand for what he saw as Hollywood's classic narrative codes. He had always felt an outsider to the conventions of cinema, as he had to the conventions of painting, and he saw his film career as an ongoing search for ways to escape from the claustrophobia of those codes—by painting on film, new laboratory techniques, complex superimpositions, the application of cel animation methods to live action, and so on.[42] To his eyes the camerawork and editing of most films were simply not selective or inventive enough. The fluidity and freedom of early animation by artists such as Emile Cohl had been lost when Disney flooded the market with slick cartoons based on the Griffith conventions. Lye wanted the makers of both animated and live-action films to go back to basics by breaking motion down to its essential elements then building it up again "in cinema terms, kinetic terms" so the medium could recover a freshness of vision comparable to modern painting. He wrote polemic essays on the subject and extravagantly praised isolated moments in films and television programs that provided any hint of an alternative. His examples ranged widely from "a bridge convention" in *The Man from UNCLE* to Robert D. Cannon's animation effects in *Gerald McBoing Boing*.

Lye tried with only occasional success to offer his services to television and to advertising as a researcher and innovator. Then between 1966 and 1969 he accepted the position of "Master Artist" and lecturer in the new "Creativity Cross-Over Program" at New York University. This program grouped media with performing arts courses and encouraged students not only to learn craft skills but to develop their creative imagination in a broad and interdisciplinary way. One of Lye's students, film editor Paul Barnes, recalls that "The program was quite separate from the Film Department which looked on them as very bizarre and far out."[43] Teaching students on a regular basis encouraged Lye to articulate his approach to making and reading films in more detail. Before referring specifically to the film medium, he would lead his students through a series of general exercises, designed not to inculcate a particular style of reading but to help the student to discover his or her own potential. The "Sense Game" (which he said he had himself played since childhood) involved focusing for a whole day on one type of sensation: "Select one quality such as color, size, dimension, tactility, sound, smell, texture, weight, tension, stress, poise, balance, motion, etc. If it's a color day, your attention may start to stray from the orange's color to its tactility, shape, and taste associations, and so on—but don't allow this to happen." And: "Before you go to sleep, pick out the images or sounds you liked best that day. Develop your standards of selection and decide why this was better than that to you."

The "Moments Game" involved focusing in great detail on any moment of intense physical experience and/or heightened individuality. Then there was a plethora of motion exercises, starting with the study of movements in nature such as waves and tree branches in the wind, trying to identify what Lye called their "figures of motion" (like "melodic figures"): "Begin to look at things in terms of their oscillation, say, the branch swaying to extremes of its tensile periods of timing, and note the bounce in the extremities of all the other branches with their disparate timings, along with incidentally the flap and twist of the leaves." Or: "Try to draw the diagonal lines in flapping overcoats as they swing along or the criss-crossed lines formed on a skirt by the owner's walking motion." Or: "Study a door—the look of it, the motion, the sound. Imagine miming it on stage. Imagine how you'd film it." One of his film-making students, Erik Shiozaki, recalled: "When you set up a shot he would require you to get any motion thoroughly worked out, to think always in terms of camera and motion."[44] In all such exercises Lye emphasized the fact that the body as well as the eye was involved in reading movement. To watch an athlete is to be conscious of strain, weight, and balance, and often this makes one's own body tense. Such effects are similar to the implied sensations of touch in our eyes' recognition of texture (say, on a thickly painted Abstract Expressionist canvas). Lye developed a game of assigning particular types of motion to particular areas of the body. Observing the curling top of a wave, for example, he would imagine a similar movement in his shoulder. Watching a cat stretch its back he would try to transfer the feeling to the arched instep of his foot. And to remember the pitch and lurch of a boat's deck he would tighten his stomach muscles.

Aware that most of the teaching in the university focused on the development of the intellect, he sought to give equal emphasis to physical and sensory awareness and to practice the ability to talk about such experiences without overintellectualizing them. Such "kinesthetic" viewing lay behind Lye's heightened response to the body language of actors, and helped to explain the distinctive physical resonance of his own films. Abstract as they were, the images of *Free Radicals* seemed constantly to imply body movement as they danced to African tribal drumming.

Lye developed his own theories of art and individualism that he delivered at festivals or universities as a barrage of ideas, films, slides, and audiotapes. Like Charles Olson or Buckminster Fuller, he was one of the great idiosyncratic lecturers of the 1960s. Since the war he had emphasized radical individualism as the driving force of art. His conception of the individual was made complex, however, by his focus on the mind's relationship with the body. A former Surrealist, Lye developed a uniquely physical notion of the unconscious as "the old brain," finding confirmation in the contemporary scientific view that the human brain encompassed three systems, each corresponding to a different stage of evolution. The three systems operated together but the two older regions (the reptilian and mammalian) were responsible for the human body's basic functions and rhythms and were the source of the strongest emotions. Lye described those two regions as the "old brain," as the crossroads between the conscious mind (or neocortex) and the body. Here he was creating his own body-based version of C. G. Jung's idea of the "collective unconscious" that had had such a strong influence on avant-garde art in the United States in the 1940s.[45] Lye's version enabled his understanding of the reception and production of art to be based on a sense of extreme individualism and constant search for the new, while still retaining a sense of common humanity. Because we are all physical beings and products of human evolution, we can tune in to the most diverse forms of art and movement. Lye was fascinated by the subtle ways we read and respond to body language— our empathy for a dancer in a musical, a tennis player judging a ball, or a pedestrian slipping on an icy curb.

He considered the movement dimension of movies to be underresearched and overintellectualized by theorists, but remained optimistic about the general audience. Many viewers in the 1930s who were unfamiliar with modernism had still responded instinctively to the color and movement of Lye's animated films. One journalist reported for example that "the audience began by hissing, but caught up the rhythm as the film progressed, and ended by clapping."[46] Such experiences sustained Lye's hope that the walls erected between experimental and other forms of filmmaking could be broken down. He saw many examples of Hollywood borrowing new techniques from experimental films.

But did he, as an experimental filmmaker, ever borrow from Hollywood? It is hard to identify what exactly he took from a lifetime of cinema going for even his live-action films are so unusual it is hard to find any obvious examples of borrowing. Feeling the stifling weight of the "Griffith" tradition he strove constantly to escape its conventions. Yet he was always happy to watch films of any kind and to extract "moments" from them. "It's all I aim for . . . just a few moments of real kinesthesia—there's no other kick of its kind."[47] If any genre does seem to have left a mark, it is the Hollywood musical, that popular dating ritual in the 1930s for Lye as it was for millions of other cinema goers. Dancing was always one of his favorite activities and favorite metaphors, and suggestions of the dancing couple crop up in the most unlikely places—in sequences of his animated films and in his motorized sculptures (described by Dore Ashton as unique within kinetic sculpture because of their human quality and their erotic energy).[48] At the same time this possible link with Hollywood's great tradition of stylized mating dances operates only at a distance, pared down to abstract "figures of motion."

In conclusion, Lye provides an interesting historical case as a film-maker who appears to come as close as it is possible to come to the literal conditions of authorship by developing a new technique that minimized costs, gave him almost total control over the medium, and enabled him to align the role of the director more closely with the individualism of the painter. Yet authorship is never entirely pure. Lye was required to add advertising material and to enlist the help of a music editor, and there were times he needed expert advice on film stock and processing. (In his parallel career as a kinetic sculptor he was similarly frustrated at times by a lack of technical assistance, but another chapter would be required to document that story and to compare the complexities of authorship in the two fields.) On the whole, an auteurist approach continues to provide a valuable tool for the study of his work, particularly an approach able to take into account the social and regional contexts from which that work emerged. In his own theorizing Lye was fascinated by the concept of individuality. At the same time he had a complex understanding of subjectivity that valued forms of intuition ("the old brain") as strongly as conscious agency ("the new brain"). And his discussions of art always drew upon a variety of approaches, with his training in the study of "primitive" or tribal arts helping to ensure that general issues of discourse and representation remained as important to him as an individual authorship.

notes

1. Alastair Reid, November 4, 1988 (interview).
2. Ann Lye, November 4, 1988 (interview).
3. Adrienne Mancia and Willard Van Dyke, "The Artist as Film-Maker: Len Lye," *Art in America* 54 (July–August 1966): 105.
4. See Greg Taylor, *Artists in the Audience: Cults, Camp and American Film Criticism* (Princeton, NJ: Princeton University Press, 1999).
5. William Moritz, "Len Lye's Films in the Context of International Abstract Cinema" in *Len Lye*, ed. Jean-Michel Bouhours and Roger Horrocks (Paris: Centre Pompidou, 2000), 193.
6. Stan Brakhage to Roger Horrocks, September 2, 1980 (letter).
7. Kathy Geritz, *Film Notes* (University of California at Berkeley Art Museum and Pacific Film Archive) 25, no. 4 (July–August 2001): 14.
8. The Futurists Arnaldo Ginna and Bruno Corra had made a direct film in 1912 but this had been lost. Lye believed he was the first, and reviewers of the period shared his belief. See Roger Horrocks, *Len Lye: A Biography* (Auckland: University of Auckland, 2001), 141.
9. See comments by Lou Adler and Hamish Keith in Horrocks, 2001, 278 and 339.
10. Len Lye, "Is Film Art?," *Film Culture*, no. 29 (Summer 1963): 38–9, reprinted in *Figures of Motion: Len Lye Selected Writings*, ed. Wystan Curnow and Roger Horrocks (Auckland: Auckland University Press, 1984), 52–4.
11. Len Lye, "Somewhat Autobiographically," 1975, New Plymouth: Len Lye Foundation Archive.
12. "Ray Thorburn Interviews Len Lye," *Art International* 19 (April 1975): 64.
13. Stan Brakhage, "Len Lye," October 13, 1980 (talk at the Rocky Mountain Film Center, Colorado).
14. Rachel Low, *A History of the British Film 1918–1929* (London: George Allen

and Unwin, 1971), 289, and "Frances Calvert on Frank Hurley," *Metro* (Australia), no. 112 (1997): 14.

15. Joseph Kennedy, "Len Lye—Composer of Motion," *Millimeter* 5 (February 1977): 18–22.

16. Len Lyn, "A Kinetic Biography," no date, New Plymouth: Len Lye Foundation Archive.

17. Oswell Blakeston, "Sketches by Len Lye," *Close Up* 6, no. 2 (February 1930): 155–56. See also *Close Up* 6, no. 1 (January 1930): 74.

18. Roger Fry letter to Len Lye, December 3, 1929, New Plymouth: Len Lye Foundation Archive.

19. Dorothy Knowles, *The Censor, The Drama and the Film 1900–1934* (London: George Allen and Unwin, 1934), 237.

20. *Close Up*'s general summing up of the Board's activities was "Puritannia Rules the Slaves"! See the magazine's censorship issue: *Close Up* 6, no. 2 (February 1929).

21. Gretchen Weinberg, "Interview with Len Lye," *Film Culture* no. 29 (Summer 1963): 45.

22. Julian Trevelyan to Roger Horrocks, March 26, 1981.

23. Jane Lye, July 9, 1980 (interview).

24. Malcolm Le Grice, *Abstract Film and Beyond* (London: Studio Vista, 1977), 71.

25. Laura Riding, *Len Lye and the Problem of Popular Film* (London: Seizin Press, 1938).

26. David Curtis, *Experimental Cinema* (London: Studio Vista, 1971), 36.

27. "The Colour Box," *Sight and Sound* 4, no. 15 (Autumn 1935): 117.

28. *Film Kurier*, August 16, 1936, quoted in Moritz, 194.

29. Frank Evans, "Picking the Best Films of the Year," *Evening Chronicle*, January 1, 1937, clipping file, New Plymouth: Len Lye Foundation Archive.

30. The phrase is used as early as November 10, 1935 in the *Sunday Referee*, describing Lye as "the English Disney . . . a different Disncy, but with all [Disney's] genius," clipping file, New Plymouth: Len Lye Foundation Archive.

31. "Film Painter," *Time* 32 (December 12, 1938): 50–1.

32. The reviewers included Dilys Powell, "The New Disney," *Sunday Times*, April 27, 1941, clipping file, New Plymouth: Len Lye Foundation Archive. The Disney connections are documented in Horrocks, 163–64.

33. John Russell Taylor, *Hitch: The Life and Work of Alfred Hitchcock* (London: Faber and Faber, 1978), 137.

34. From Lye's annotations in the margin of his copy of Ivor Montagu's *Film World* (Harmondsworth: Penguin, 1964), 124.

35. James Manilla, July 22, 1980 (interview).

36. Jane Lye, June 25, 1980 (interview).

37. Jane Lye remained in New York, with principal custody of their two children. For her side of the story, and a general account of Lye's personal relationships, see Horrocks, in particular 225–29.

38. See, for example, Wystan Curnow's essay, "Lye and Abstract Expressionism" in Bouhours and Horrocks (eds.), 205–12.

39. Cecile Starr to Stan Brakhage, December 27, 1980.

40. Ann Lye, November 4, 1988 (interview).

41. "Len Lye Speaks at the Film Makers' Cinematheque," *Film Culture,* no. 44 (Spring 1967): 50. See also Lye's essay, "Television: New Axes to Grind," *Sight and Sound* 8 (Summer 1939): 65–70.

42. This chapter has focused on Lye's direct animation but his experiments with other techniques in films such as *Rainbow Dance* (1937), *Trade Tattoo* (1937), and *N. Or N.W.* (1937) are also important.

43. Paul Barnes, July 16, 1980 (interview).

44. Erik Shiozaki, February 11, 1981 (interview).

45. Lye acknowledged this parallel—"It's something like the Jungian mass

psychology theory"—in "Sight Sound Consanguinity," 1966, New Plymouth: Len Lye Foundation Archive.

46. "Where Children May Hiss," *World Film News*, May 1936, clipping file, New Plymouth: Len Lye Foundation Archive.
47. Len Lye to Wystan Curnow, September 1979.
48. Dore Ashton, "Vision and Sound: Today's Art at Buffalo," *Studio International* 169 (May 1965): 211–12.

roger horrocks

a lost man

willie varela and

the american

avant-garde

t e n

c h o n   a.   n o r i e g a

Since Luis Valdez's *I Am Joaquin* (1969)—widely identified as the "first" Chicano film—the notion of a Chicano cinema has been framed within the political discourse of the Chicano civil rights movement.[1] As such, in the 1970s, filmmakers and collectives worked within a binarism of reform and revolution: on the one hand advocating for access to U.S. television stations and film studios, and on the other hand theorizing their work as the "northernmost expression" of New Latin American Cinema.[2] In the same period, however, a different type of Chicano film practice was taking shape that neither sought access to the industry (reform) nor rooted itself in a radical national politics (revolution). Instead, these filmmakers produced low-budget films drawn from personal or local experience and situated within the context of the American avant-garde or "underground" film. Although this body of work is not as well known as the rights- and identity-based genre of "Chicano cinema," it is also much larger, affording an opportunity to examine Chicano authorship as an aesthetic or text-producing phenomenon with critical mass, rather than as a structured absence within the film and television industry.[3] Even so, some of the same exclusions are at work, albeit within a noncommercial framework.

Inspired by Sheldon Renan's *An Introduction to the American Underground Film* (1967) as well as regional screenings of avant-garde films, Chicanos were among the "fantastic numbers of people" who started shooting and screening their own underground works as personal expressions in the late 1960s and early 1970s.[4] But Renan and others rarely acknowledged racial minorities within this movement. The underground film has been faulted for its "repression of a materialist analysis of society and culture" in favor of disengagement. Nevertheless, it has generated alternatives to Hollywood and society at large, most notably in Beat subculture, Warhol's Factory, and the personal art films of Maya Deren, Stan Brakhage, and Jonas Mekas, among others (James, 99).[5] Given its antithetical positioning, as David James argues, underground film did not so much become an autonomous and authentic cinema as it did a "countercultural activity" engaged in "intertextual dialogues with Hollywood" and "vulnerable to eventual assimilation and commodification by the culture industries" (99–100). For Chicanos, however, things were not quite so simple, because *their* rejection of the commercial cinema would not be assimilated and commodified, whereas their participation within the avant-garde revealed the underlying limits of its stylistic and thematic hetereogeneity. In both directions, what Chicanos encountered was the fact of racial homogeneity within Hollywood and the underground. Perhaps for these reasons, then, Chicano underground filmmakers often registered a critique of the very styles they used: Severo Perez (the trance film), Ernie Palomino (Beat poetic narrative), and Willie Varela (the lyrical film).[6]

Of these filmmakers, Varela is perhaps the most prolific and well known, having produced nearly 100 films within the tradition of personal cinema since as early as 1971. But his emphasis on individual self-expression situates him within an avant-garde tradition that, by most accounts, ceased to be relevant within a mostly white counterculture by the mid-1970s. The Chicano civil rights movement necessitated a cultural politics over and against either individual or abstracted self-expression, setting cultural production within the terms of an identity-based integration into U.S. social institutions. In this manner, the mid-1970s marked a shift within avant-garde art from an existential subjectivity to an identity politics, and from the universal to the particular, while suppressing the connection between these two generations—an underlying liberal humanism—to posit an epistemological break. Rather than see Varela as atavistic, however, I want to argue that his development as an artist since the 1970s signals precisely what both Chicano cinema and the (decidedly non-Chicano) postmodern avant-garde had suppressed in order to constitute themselves: someone who wanted to be in both camps and for whom the personal was political because it was personal.

In what follows, I provide an overview of Varela's career as well as a related discussion of the personal and political in the history of U.S. avant-garde film. I examine in depth *A Lost Man* and how its representation of gender and genre provides a revisionist history of the personal filmmaker against the backdrop of the Americas and its two major alternative film movements: New American Cinema and New Latin American Cinema.

biographical history

Born in 1950, Varela grew up as a bona fide member of the television generation, albeit from the hybrid border culture of El Paso-Juárez where his childhood influences also included the strictures of Jesuit High School and the Catholic Church, Mexican telenovelas, and the cultural and economic conditions that gave rise to the Chicano student movement and La Raza Unida Party. In the late 1960s, Varela drifted in and out of college, eventually working on the 1970 census. At this point he stumbled across two publications that introduced him to film art: an interview with John Lennon in *Rolling Stone*, in which Lennon discussed his 8-mm home movies, and a profile of visionary filmmaker and polemicist Stan Brakhage in Renan's *An Introduction to the American Underground Film*. These two self-taught film artists—one a rich pop icon from the working class, the other a rugged individualist poised against popular culture—came to exemplify the urgency of personal vision as well as the inherent contradiction in the broader do-it-yourself movement. Did that movement represent an alternative space for public discourse or just another route to the mainstream? Positioned between Brakhage and Lennon, Varela's work emerged as a site of aspiration, struggle, and contradiction: "I wasn't looking for a filmic 'Spanglish,' but a visual language that would acknowledge the reality that a Chicano must always have one eye pointing north and the other pointing south, with the occasional luxury of both eyes actually gazing inward, to the *personhood* that minorities are usually denied, and that we often deny ourselves."[7]

Using the income from his census job, Varela purchased a Super-8 camera in 1971. Although the written word provided the *idea* of a practice, Varela was self-taught as a filmmaker; only with his return to college (1974) and the public exhibition of his own work (1978) did he begin to see the avant-garde films that inspired his own light studies, diaries, media appropriation, and straight documentation. Since 1974, he has directed nearly one hundred films and more than a dozen videos (remaining in low-end technology), and he has played a significant role as an advocate, writer, and programmer. In El Paso, for example, he founded two showcases for film and video exhibition: the Southwestern Alternative Media Project (also called SWAMP; 1978–1982) and Frontera Media Arts (1986–).

Varela's work as a programmer allowed him to meet and correspond with many of the central figures in the development of U.S. (and, to a lesser extent, Mexican and European) avant-garde film since the 1940s, including Kenneth Anger, Beth and Scott B, Bruce Baille, Su Friedrich, Peter Gidal, Raul Lopez Herrera, Jon Jost, Kurt Kren, George Kuchar, Danny Lyon, Jonas Mekas, J. J. Murphy, Carolee Schneemann, Paul Sharits, Chick Strand, and Woody and Steina Vasulka.[8] Like many filmmakers of the period, Varela exchanged his films with other artists, eliciting commentary. In particular, Brakhage served as Varela's mentor, initially gently chiding him for mastering technique over "style as soul" while encouraging him to let his filmmaking become "much MORE 'musical,' less socially (and especially less verbally) referential."[9] Brakhage repeatedly cited William Carlos Williams's dictum, "No ideas but in things," while directing Varela to look into himself and "go DEEPER, beyond any in-tension YOU (consciously) might have."[10]

Varela's use of different first names allows a critic to periodize his work within American cultural politics. Yet, his visual aesthetic is more closely related to changes in his geographic location. In the end, *pace* Brakhage, his style as "soul's-heart" did depend on where the home is.[11] In El Paso from 1974 to 1981, Varela explored light, color, and rhythm, alternating between the photographic technique of in-camera editing and a more painterly effect achieved by rapid, gestural camera movement: for example, *Moondance I & II* (1974), *Green Light* (1974), *A Neon Crescent* (1975), *Becky's Eye* (1975), *April 1977* (1977), and *Leaves of Grass* (1979). In 1980, however, this period came to an abrupt end following a bitter censorship battle over a weekly independent film series that Varela had initiated at the El Paso public library.

Varela had encountered censorship efforts before when he had tried to screen Carolee Schneeman's *Fuses* (1964–1967) at the University of Texas at El Paso while he was a student there in 1976.[12] Now, however, Varela found himself in the center of a political controversy that had both local and national implications in terms of arts funding and exhibition. In response to press allegations of an "erotic" film program that included George Kuchar's *Hold Me While I'm Naked* (1966) and James Broughton's *Erogeny* (1976), El Paso's mayor declared an all-out war on "pornography pollution," even joining an antipornography rally by a Christian alliance formed in response to Varela's program.[13] The library's board of directors briefly considered using the vice squad to evaluate the films, while SWAMP's state and federal arts funding came under question and was mentioned in almost all press coverage. In response, Varela reluctantly and angrily dropped the six so-called obscene films from the public library program, moving them to another venue—ironically enough a *church*, the Universalist Community Unitarian Church. The incident was one of the first censorship battles in what would become the "culture wars" of the 1980s, pitting Christian groups and politicians against state-supported art *that they had not even seen.* Varela responded to the attacks point by point, rallying the national media arts community behind him, while also drawing support from the National Endowment for the Arts. But, in El Paso itself, Varela was rather isolated.[14]

The experience led to a bitter three-and-a-half-year exile in San Francisco that marked a decisive change in the nature of his work. Nevertheless, Varela seems to have already begun a self-critique of visionary cinema for its willful inattention to the social environment and issues of class, cultural, and national identity. In *Stan and Jane Brakhage* (1980), for example, he documents a day trip to Juárez with the Brakhages. What emerges, however, is a telling contrast between Stan Brakhage and the Mexican urban poor. In several scenes, Brakhage stands in the foreground amid the crowded markets and streets with a far-off gaze, as if looking inward, as if absented from the scene around him.[15] The irony of Varela's critique is that he is left looking at Brakhage looking at himself. But rather than reject Brakhage's aesthetic and mentorship, Varela now found his own life as an artist and programmer to be socially referential in and of itself, something his exile in San Francisco would make even more pronounced and into which he would, indeed, "go DEEPER."

More than anything, San Francisco itself seemed to shift the focus of Varela's personal aesthetic from domestic spaces to public ones. As Varela himself explained, in contrast to El Paso, "San Francisco is a very public city—people's lives and dramas and problems and joys are really lived out in a very public fashion."[16] Between 1982 and 1984, his films became much more thematic and event oriented, dealing with the representation of sex and sexuality (*Fetish Footage*, 1981; *In the Flesh*, 1982), death (*Recuerdos de flores muertas*, 1982; *Forest Lawn*, 1982), and ironic social commentary (*Struggle in Futility*, 1983; *5th & Market*, 1983). Although these films place less emphasis on light, color, and editing than his earlier works had done, they also incorporate sound recording. Varela's new Super-8 camera with sound allowed him to add *nonvisual* commentary that encompassed the reflexive, documentarian, and didactic modes.

From 1985 to 1990, Varela's work became increasingly political and concerned with popular culture. For example, *Fearless Leader* and *In Progress* (both 1985) appropriate and manipulate television images of President Ronald Reagan, exploring issues such as the construction of public image and nuclearism. Although Varela chose to return to El Paso in late 1985 to raise a family, he maintains a "bemused detachment" about the region's poverty, conservatism, and military-dependent economy, noting that "I am *from* El Paso, but not *of* it."[17] His return presaged a renewed interest in domestic space (*A House of Cards* and *House Beautiful*, both 1988), but the home no longer served as the site of an abstracted personal vision. Instead, the public, private, and mass media began to intrude upon one another, leading Varela to explore aspects of a postmodern time (*January 8, 1988*, 1988), space (*Border Crossing, Version One*, 1988), and image culture (*Detritus*, 1989). As an exception, *Reaffirmation* (1990) returns to a nonnarrative visual pleasure, limiting itself to the anachronistic "painterly" techniques of the still life and the landscape. But it is an exception that proves the rule of the mass media because what the film reaffirms no longer constitutes a viable alternative. For the personal filmmaker, Varela seems to argue, you can never go home again.

personal and political

This is the standard history of a personal filmmaker. But Varela is a paradox for those who want a certain history confirmed as natural, inevitable, or, at the least, influential. Though he emerges amid the social upheaval of the 1960s—with its various movements and countercultures—Varela never seems to partake of its concerns or causes. In short, he became a personal filmmaker at a time when that aesthetic had been superseded, with its impulses divided between radical cinema and structural film, such that the personal was either political or irrelevant (James). And yet, even in Varela's earliest light studies and diaries, elements would later become more predominant: political critique, reflexivity, and an engagement with issues of ethnicity and gender. Even his formalist light studies contain establishing shots of the domestic environment, suggesting both continuity and contradiction among the public, private, and oppositional spaces that Varela occupies. Thus, rather than impose hard-and-fast periods, it makes more sense to see Varela's work according to shifting emphases among a set of socioaesthetic concerns, techniques, and thematics. But the question remains, can a personal (and anticommercial) filmmaker also participate in the political agenda of an ethnic or minority cinema? In two major works, Varela addresses this issue head on, redefining his career as a personal filmmaker in self-consciously gendered and cultural terms: *Making Is Choosing: A Fragmented Life: A Broken Line: A Series of Observations* (1989) and *A Lost Man* (1992).

In 1989, Varela completed a Super-8 feature film (104 minutes), *Making Is Choosing: A Fragmented Life: A Broken Line: A Series of Observations*, a nonnarrative, autobiographical "fiction" of a five-year period in his life that coincided with his self-imposed exile to San Francisco, the birth of his daughter, and the Varelas' eventual return to El Paso. The film also constitutes a summation of Varela's extensive short work in narrow gauge, whereas its feature length signals a new interest in both avant-garde duration and commercial cinema. The first part of the title suggests an aesthetic (*and very male*) response to the birth of his daughter. But, rather than making facile, romantic comparisons between art production and human reproduction, Varela's title postulates a politics of choice in both arenas where the three subtitles serve to fragment and particularize his authorial presence, shifting it from the terms of a modernist auteurism to those of postmodernist "situated knowledges."[18] As part of this shift, Varela juxtaposes domestic scenes with his own abstracted personal vision throughout the film. These different aspects of the "personal"—Varela as father and as filmmaker—are themselves intruded upon by images of a television set in the living room as well as by isolated or appropriated shots of different programs. The ubiquity of television in the film and in the home collapses the distinction between public and private spaces.[19]

It is, after all, this distinction that made the oppositional space of an underground cinema possible. Whereas Super-8 film practices had been theorized in opposition to Hollywood within these modernist terms, here Varela shifts to a postmodernist critique that situates his films *within* mass-media discourses. As Varela himself has noted, in contrast to the first generation of personal filmmakers who worked in a high art tradition, his influences came from popular culture itself—rock 'n' roll, television, Hollywood—even if he also placed his filmmaking in opposition to these forms on the basis of their commodity status. This conflicted orientation toward the mass media opens up a paradox in Varela's work that can be seen in the troubling, ambiguous presence of television in his earliest films. In *TV Playland* (1974), television distracts from his camera's exploration and manipulation of light, shapes, and color outside Varela's living room window. The camera literally turns away from the television set and chooses another window of perception, but in the process Varela both registers the television's presence and equates its realist codes with the middle-class, suburban domestic space in which the set is situated. In later films, such as *In the Flesh* (1982) and *Thoughts of a Dry Brain* (1988), the VCR and television monitor introduce both pornography and Hollywood action films into the home. Varela then appropriates and manipulates these genres in ways that call into question the representation and reception of masculine desire.

In either case, though, "television" constitutes a norm from which Varela deviates, and it is a norm that increasingly blurs the boundary between public and domestic. Varela's Super-8 films have, for the most part, been situated within domestic space, but they reject or, rather, refigure the quotidian concerns of that space (home, family) as well as the political debates of the public sphere. Neither personal nor political in the usual sense, Varela's films occupy the underground of both spheres, an underground that had become an ambivalent site by the late 1970s. In the midst of social unrest and nationalist politics, who were these personal films for, after all, and what function did they now serve?

For Varela, this question of audience would lead to an impasse in his work, especially with the decline of the institutional space for underground cinema, coupled with an historical and generational shift in the terms of both artistic identification and sponsorship—from the avant-garde to the media arts. Although this shift is often proclaimed to have taken place in the name of "feminism," "identity politics," and "postmodernism," on a material level it signaled the failure of film art to circulate as a commodity within the art world or as part of a film culture (as it had been advocated), and coincided with the creation of an independent sector financed by governmental and foundation funding sources and closely tied to the university and museum.

genre blurring, gender bending: *a lost man* (1992)

In the remainder of this chapter, I will examine Varela's *A Lost Man*, which represents a decisive break with his earlier Super-8 films insofar as it is his first narrative, first video, first use of professional actors, and first piece to explore (explicitly, thematically) issues of cultural and gender identity. In a sign of that shift, it is also the first work since 1982 in which he uses his "public" Anglo-American nickname (Willie) rather than his "private" Mexican-American given name (Guillermo), suggesting on one level a reconciliation with Varela's exile from El Paso. Thus, if *Making Is Choosing* suggests the limits of Super-8 by the late 1980s, *A Lost Man* represents Varela's belated and qualified acceptance of video and narrative as viable alternatives to and within television. In a sense, both works suggest a strategic desire on Varela's part for an audience constituted by the exhibition parameters for industry *products* rather than by the implied marketplace of film and media arts: *Making Is Choosing* conforms to the theatrical-release feature film, and *A Lost Man* remains with television's one-hour broadcast standard and has been shown on public television stations in El Paso and Corpus Christi.[20]

In *A Lost Man*, as the title itself suggests, Varela attempts to relocate himself within the post-Brakhage media arts, the postmodern condition, and postnationalist cultural and identity politics of his earlier work. But it would be wrong to look for Varela's "voice" in a literal sense—that is, to locate it as a stable, coherent point of articulation within the text—insofar as Varela remains true to the abstracted, existential subjectivity of his Super-8 films. If Varela now "speaks" within the conventions of narrative and subject matter, it is from the multiple perspectives of the entire text, and not at the level of character, plot, and story, let alone a "speaking subject" whose avowed multiplicity nonetheless produces a singular message. In the end, as the video poses in riddle form, perhaps he was never lost to begin with.

In one respect, the video serves to position his oeuvre at the border between two opposing systems of alternative textual production and reception in the Americas: New American Cinema (personal) and New Latin American Cinema (political). But although New American Cinema and New Latin American Cinema articulate quite different positions for the filmmaker and possibilities for cinema, both film movements developed in opposition to Hollywood, not just textually, but structurally, criticizing its role in monopoly capital, the state, and national culture.[21] Likewise, as a consequence, for both movements the "major determinant, both positive and negative, was Hollywood" (James, 24). In this respect, James's thesis about U.S. underground film can be expanded to account for both movements: "[alternative] codes emerged, then, as mutations and mutilations of industrial codes, and its practices were carried on either in the spaces between industrial practices or as modifications of them" (24).

Varela makes this point through the self-conscious use of two genres, one from Hollywood cinema and the other from Latin American television. To this extent, *A Lost Man* is similar to other Chicano works that draw upon two national aesthetic traditions, often one from Hollywood and another from culture- or community-based counter-genres that disrupt or demystify the Hollywood genre. *The Ballad of Gregorio Cortez* (1982), for example, operates simultaneously as both western and *corrido*, two opposing narrative forms for histories of the Southwest during the Border Conflict era (1830–1930). But, as I will discuss, Varela uses two commercial genres, film noir and telenovela, to establish a critical discourse that crosses and undercuts national frameworks. Film scholarship, however, tends to equate genre with the entire text (that is, as a way to classify the text), so that the appearance of multiple genres is treated as a singular "hybrid." In this approach, genre functions as a series of traits that organize expectations about how to read a text or how to find narrative coherence. Through an analysis of character types, themes, settings, plots, and iconography. In this view, genre operates within a stable set of relationships: between topic and treatment, text and genre, and genre and audience. In contrast to that critical method, I would like to explore the ways in which multiple genres are used to organize different levels of signification within the text, or expectations for the text.[22]

Multiple or concurrent genres have often been situated within theoretical discussions of postmodernism, as when Marjorie Perloff concludes that "Postmodern genre is . . . characterized by its longing for a both/and situation rather than one of either/or."[23] Postmodern genres are seen as upsetting usual or historical expectations, mostly through the juxtaposition of specific and nonspecific genres within a given medium. In "Blurred Genres," for example, Clifford Geertz points to "baroque fantasies presented as deadpan empirical observations" and "theoretical treatises set out as travelogues" as signs of a new way of thinking or of a new kind of social inquiry.[24] Such periodization of mixed forms, however, must be questioned, because—as Ralph Cohen notes—"The basis for a genre of mixed forms or shared generic features is as old as Aristotle's comparison of tragedy and epic. . . . And such mixtures were not isolated cases but rather a way of thinking, of assuming that genres, mixed or unmixed, were appropriate carriers of ancient knowledge."[25] In other words, genres do more than just establish a set of expectations to be fulfilled or manipulated; genres also function as a discursive element within a text, organizing and circulating particular kinds of knowledge, experience, or investigation.

Similarly, Varela mixes genres to organize and circulate seemingly opposed sets of knowledge, experience, and investigation, but he does so on a number of levels within the text: realist, autobiographical, and allegorical. This in turn produces three levels of investigation that question, respectively, (1) male–female gender relations and the ideology of heterosexual couple formation, (2) Varela's conflict between being a filmmaker and a father–husband–worker, and (3) the function of alternative cinema within the United States, as posed from the regional perspective of El Paso. In the end, he manipulates industrial genre codes to open up a space within the new terrain of narrative cinema and identity politics for the old existential notion of the personal as it operates within each of the above three levels.

In *A Lost Man*, a Los Angeles private investigator returns to El Paso in search of his lost father, only to confront his ex-wife instead. In his synopsis, Varela outlines a hard-boiled plot:

> El Paso native Adrian Juárez returns from Los Angeles to investigate the sudden disappearance of his father, whom he has not seen or spoken to for fifteen years. Since Juárez is a private investigator in L.A., he has been summoned by relatives in his hometown to solve this mystery. Juárez has been "hiding out" in Los Angeles, plying his craft, more an exiled Chicano from Texas than a true southern Californian. Reluctantly returning to west Texas, he has a series of tense meetings with his ex-wife, confronts his own mortality at his mother's grave site, and finally returns to Los Angeles without locating his father. Still, nagging questions revolving around identity and self-knowledge impinge on Adrian's consciousness. In the end, things simply end.[26]

As the synopsis should indicate, *A Lost Man* is proposed as a modern day film noir. In fact, the video begins with a noir voice over set against slow motion images of the underside of Los Angeles. The rest of *A Lost Man*, however, evinces the presence of another commercial genre, the telenovela, brought into high relief through "bad acting." But it is bad acting of a particular kind, the result of a shift in acting codes from cinematic realism to theatrical (and televisual) melodrama. The actors, whose experience is limited to stage productions and telenovelas, seem to overwhelm the intimate scale of Varela's gestural, hand-held cinematography, which privileges stylized medium shots of dialogue scenes over the usual close-ups in shot/reverse shot. The shift in acting codes, however, can be recuperated insofar as it reinforces or highlights rather than determines the interplay of the two genres and two media. In other words, it draws attention to a question of genre that exists within the very structure of the narrative.

The middle section of the narrative, which is set in El Paso, uses the telenovela codes as Adrian becomes trapped in quasidomestic spaces and moribund male–female relations: hotel rooms, apartments; ex-wife, dead mother. This correlation of genre and gender is explicit in a five-minute section that uses split screen. Adrian (in black-and-white) and Margie (in color) explain their situation and failed marriage in abstract, general terms. Both characters conclude that "the little things" in a marriage (albeit from different discursive paths and genre codings) prohibit a rapprochement. This irreconcilable difference is confirmed in a later scene when Adrian visits his mother's grave to ask for her help in finding his father. There, Margie and Adrian continue to talk past each other: she about their failed marriage, he about the significance of John F. Kennedy to the Mexican-American generation of his parents.[27] To punctuate the above dual-genre narrative structure, Varela quotes formalist shots drawn from his personal aesthetic as transitional segments between scenes: in particular, posterization, light studies, and single-frame photographic sequences. These segments isolate and foreground changes in scene, location, and genre, drawing attention to the construction of the narrative. But these segments can also be seen as an attempt to insert nonnarrative, nongenre experimental film as the essential backdrop to Varela's narrative—as that which peeks through the cracks of the two genres and the social issues addressed and resolved therein.

In U.S. film scholarship, melodrama and film noir tend to be compared in terms of their representation of gender. "In the classical Hollywood cinema," as Mary Ann Doane notes, "there are two types of films within which the contradictions involved in the patriarchal representation of woman become most acute—melodrama and film noir."[28] The two genres share several other similarities, not the least of which is their problematic status as genres. Both are often referred to as "visual styles" that predominate over narrative coherence and plot structure. *Mildred Pierce* (1945) presents a more extreme case, as both genres structure the narrative as "gender-inflected forms of discourse" that mark a struggle for textual-*cum*-patriarchal authority.[29] In contrast, as Lauren Rabinovitz has argued, Maya Deren and Alexander Hammid's *Meshes of the Afternoon* (1943) juxtaposes film noir and melodrama to critique "the cinematic structures of containment" for the female subject.[30] It is of note, then, that the film, often cited as the start of the American avant-garde,[31] locates itself in "Hollywood 1943" in the credits.

Although *A Lost Man* falls within the terms of the above genre comparisons, Varela's use of the telenovela rather than Hollywood melodrama for the middle section of the narrative remaps the genres and their gender dichotomies across two boundaries: medium (film and television) and geopolitical borders (Mexico and the United States). In these overlapping dichotomies, then, Varela weaves together an analysis of gender roles that must stand in relation to questions of mass media, postcolonialism, and cultural identity, all at the level of genre codes. In *A Lost Man*, each gender is positioned by way of one of these genres: Adrian with film noir and Margie with the telenovela. In the process, issues of gender and cultural identity are mapped onto the conventional markers for each genre: character type, place, location, narrational style, even the use of color or black-and-white images. These two genres, then, establish a dichotomy in which differences of gender, medium, and national culture are aligned!

Medium	Cinema	Television
Genre	Film Noir	Telenovela
Contry	United States	Mexico
Character	Male/Adrian	Female/Margie
Type	Antihero	~~Femme fatale~~ (film noir)
	~~Hero~~	Heroine (telenovela)
Relation	(Ex)husband	(Ex)wife
Location	Los Angeles	El Paso
Narrative space	Exteriors	Interiors
	Car/motel	Apartment
Search	Father	Husband
Narration	Voice-over and direct address	Dialogue
Style	Black and White	Color

This structure raises a question about what happens when Adrian and Margie confront each other in the narrative given that each character functions within the parameters of a different genre/medium/culture system. Posed another way, what happens when Adrian enters the domestic space of the telenovela, or, from another point of view, when Margie's apartment is intruded upon by a film noir character? In some sense, the answer is that *A Lost Man* disrupts the conventional formula for both genres, so that one genre is resolved according to the terms of the other, and vice versa. Let's consider film noir in the video. As Doane notes: "Film noir . . . constitutes itself as a detour, a bending of the hermeneutic code from the questions connected with a crime to the difficulty posed by the woman as enigma (or crime) . . . the femme fatale in film noir is characterized as unknowable" (Doane, 102). In *A Lost Man*, by shifting from film noir to the telenovela for the middle section of the narrative, the woman is refigured as the social salvation (heroine) rather than as the sexual threat (femme fatale). Thus, in the context of the film noir that frames the narrative, it is the male (Adrian) who becomes unknowable to himself, confronted—as Varela explains in his synopsis—by "nagging questions revolving around identity and self-knowledge." Varela's language in his synopsis and character sketches is instructive, insofar as it reveals "self-knowledge" to be an impulse outside of Adrian's profession (private investigator) and defining trait ("voyeuristic tendencies") and, hence, outside film noir and its location in Los Angeles. In describing Adrian, Varela notes: "He felt that the camera was an unwanted buffer in his direct visual experience of the empirical world. It was an unusual posture, but one that Juárez maintained, contradictions and all." In *A Lost Man*, the "nagging questions revolving around identity and self-knowledge" derive from non-"male" gender positions located in El Paso: the "nagging" man in the motel (identity) and the "nagging" ex-wife (self-knowledge). Thus, the video's film noir enacts a detour from a crime (missing father) to the woman (ex-wife), but its confrontation with the "unknowable" takes place within melodrama's "drama of recognition" as Adrian seeks an answer at his mother's gravesite. Melodrama's "drama of recognition," then, makes manifest the male Oedipal scenario, as Adrian must—as he puts it in the last scene—"come face-to-face with who you are and what you're running from." In the final analysis, the answer is one and the same: his father. The father was never found, as he informs Adrian in a letter at the end of the video, because he was never lost.

Although the video focuses on Adrian, it nonetheless refigures the role of women in both genres. In the shift to family melodrama, for example, Margie's "home" is not the usual domestic space, but rather an overlay of allusions to Virginia Woolf's *A Room of One's Own* and Jean Paul Sartre's vision of Hell as other people in *No Exit*.[32] Indeed, books, but no mirrors or windows are in her apartment (as in *No Exit*), in contrast to the mirror- and window-laden spaces of film noir— including the film noir portion of *A Lost Man*.[33] If, as Pam Cook argues, melodrama assigns "an unusual place to female protagonists,"[34] in *A Lost Man* that place escapes its usual narrative consequences, ensuring that Adrian's existential resolution is not at the woman's expense. For Margie, her apartment remains that of *A Room of One's Own*, and if her apartment is that of *No Exit* for Adrian, he nonetheless escapes. Margie's story functions as a progressive interlude within the entire narrative (which *is* Adrian's story), but it is neither reducible to nor subsumed within that function—it continues, albeit off-screen, on the same terms with which it began. In the process, however, Margie is cast more as an asexual antiheroine rather than as the "desiring" heterosexual and homosexual women of *No Exit* (and family melodramas). In contrast to *No Exit*, the homoerotic tension in *A Lost Man* emerges between Adrian and an intrusive drifter who follows Adrian from the motel lobby to his room.[35] Their tense and elliptical encounter can be read as a homoerotic one, which is then displaced or resolved by invoking *racial* difference within the social space of the video. In a rare and paradoxical expression of cultural identity, Adrian blames Columbus for the unwanted encounter after the drifter leaves, with the implication that Columbus somehow brought the European-descent man onto the scene, but not Adrian himself (as *mestizo*). As with his emphasis on "direct visual experience," Adrian's sexual and racial identity are "maintained, contradictions and all," largely through an act of disavowal. Ultimately, within the terms of the two genres, Adrian's encounters with both the drifter and Margie exile him from corporeal desire within rented domestic spaces (motel, apartment), in the end identifying him with scopophilia, the automobile, and the absent father. Meanwhile, Margie continues to live in a room of her own. Thus, in a twist on the conventions for both genres, Adrian and Margie remain "safely" outside the reach of the law and the home, although at the price of sexual desire whether it be within or outside of the companionate marriage.

Somewhat at odds with its realist discourse on the failure or limits of heterosexual couple formation, *A Lost Man* provides an "allegory of cinema" with emphasis on the role of genre in structuring an international perspective on Hollywood. Although film noir has been attributed to postwar pessimism, if not nihilism, in the United States, here the institutional gloss given by Mike Davis seems more appropriate: that film noir of the 1940s "expressed autobiographical sentiments, [and] became a conduit for the resentments of writers in the velvet trap of the studio system."[36] Thus, on one level, the genre's existential pose expresses a romantic vision of the film artist in society within the terms of New American Cinema, but not without ambivalence and irony. Indeed, in Adrian's photographic surveillance as private investigator a strong link occurs between watching and the avant-garde tradition from which Varela himself emerges. In this sense, Varela builds upon Brakhage's earlier theorization of the camera as an extension of the body and of life. As James explains: "Bridging the aesthetic and the existential, film became identified with his life and coextensive with it, simultaneously his vocation and avocation, his work and play, his joy and terror—as integral as breathing" (37). In *A Lost Man*, however, the autobiographical filmmaker is rendered through a symbolic displacement onto the figure of the private eye *cum* photographer. The contradiction that Varela examines lies in the investigator's simultaneous denial of "mediated experience" and the construction of "private" visual evidence as the product of his labors. In thus placing the filmmaker (as private eye) within the diegesis, Varela opens up a space for self-critique unavailable to the Brakhage aesthetic—a space between vocation and avocation.

206

To read this video as allegorical of Varela's own career, however, it is important not to limit the interpretation to a one-to-one correspondence that equates Varela with Adrian and Adrian's father with Brakhage, although that Oedipal dynamic does inform Varela's work and, more self-consciously, *A Lost Man*. Although Varela does not deny Brakhage's influences, *A Lost Man* suggests a more complex subject position for the filmmaker at the level of characters and genres, one that exceeds a simple location in Adrian and his love–hate relationship with his "lost" father, and thereby incorporates Margie as well. Here is where the telenovela provides a counterpoint to the film noir in the construction of autobiographical and allegorical accounts of alternative cinema. In contrast to the avant-garde, the telenovela provides another "alternative" model that contrasts with the auteurism, elitism, and masculine perspective inherent in much of New American Cinema and New Latin American Cinema, working instead through popular forms to address social issues, cultural identity, and gender politics for a *mass* audience.[37] The bulk of Varela's narrative takes place in Margie's space as telenovela. That Varela does not engage the aesthetic or textual dimensions of New American Cinema and New Latin American Cinema per se, but rather *invokes* them through industrial counterparts (film noir and telenovela, respectively), allows him to make these oppositional movements into icons of the political and personal without, at the same time, falling into the same traps that made them either ineffectual or easily coopted.

A Lost Man presents a nuanced critique of gender roles and marriage that would seem to fault Adrian, even as it seeks to understand his motivations, juxtaposing his existential solipsism with Margie's existential humanism. What is interesting, however, is how this reading provides an allegorical account of Varela as a "lost" man within the media arts in which Margie seems to represent cultural and familial redemption within the framework of identity politics (although it should be noted that such a position is mitigated by her existential premises). But even if Margie represents a form of redemption, Adrian nonetheless returns to Los Angeles alone, contented with his peculiar oppositional stance. In other words, such a reading rejects marriage as a metaphor for resolving the conflicting impulses of Varela as personal filmmaker and as father–husband–worker. Thus, the personal remains split between these two positions—vocation and avocation—with the domestic, familial, and affective correlated with labor within capitalist society. Personal, artistic expression, then, becomes the antithesis that establishes new terms for a dialectic rather than a transcendental gesture whose synthesis (vocation/avocation) elides the material conditions that make the personal a conflicted site rather than a safe haven. Likewise, the allegorical reading rejects marriage as a metaphor for a direct relationship between art and politics, signifier and signified, which can be seen as the underpinning of contemporary "identity politics" in the media arts. "Varela" was never lost between the personal and the political, the video argues, because "his" life and art embraced these contradictions rather than posit their symbolic resolution. Thus, if Adrian must admit that he is like his father, he is also quite unlike him—neither a father nor a husband. Likewise, "Varela" is both like and unlike Brakhage in ways that complicate the binary opposition that the latter's name invokes within the media arts.[38]

In *Allegories of Cinema*, James notes: "If the alternative cinemas were typically powered by obsessions with authenticity, they were as often steered by the perspectives allowed by the rear-view mirror of irony" (James, 28). Likewise, Adrian's desire for "unmediated experience" and to be left alone is steered by his awareness of the contradictions that make this "an unusual posture" that must be actively maintained. With no small amount of irony, *A Lost Man* ends with Adrian speaking into the rear-view mirror of his car, parked beside a movie billboard. Having rejected as useless any solutions that involve self-analysis and social engagement, Adrian proclaims that at least his existential isolation doesn't hurt anyone. The camera pans to the side and zooms in on a billboard for the Steve Martin and Goldie Hawn film *Housekeeper* (1992). In juxtaposing *A Lost Man* with a regressive Hollywood romantic comedy about a woman who intrudes upon a man's domestic tranquility, Varela's visual gag offers a revisionist argument for New American Cinema and the "film artist," one that relativizes their sins of gender/racial ommission and commission against those of Hollywood. But toward what end?

In Sartre's *No Exit*, to which the video alludes throughout, hell has no mirrors, just other people. Adrian is more comfortable speaking into mirrors (as well as tape recorders and phones) than to other people face-to-face. What is interesting about the penultimate scene of *A Lost Man* is that the viewer is unable to see Adrian's mouth reflected in the rear-view mirror. Here, in contrast to *No Exit*, mirrors and other people are not placed in opposition per se, but rather both are revealed as always incomplete and inadequate in their ability to reflect a coherent, unified self. There is no such thing as unmediated experience. But if so, Adrian's resolution nonetheless remains ambiguous in terms of its location in the text. Are his words the product of an internal dialogue, direct address, or voice-over? There is no single answer. As Varela notes in his synopsis, "In the end, things simply end." Or do they? If anything, the "rear-view mirror of irony" rests in the fact that although Adrian rejects self-analysis and social engagement, the video itself does not, and, in fact, cannot. In not confusing Adrian with either Varela or the video itself, I arrive at another conclusion wherein the "old" personal cinema enters into dialogue with "new" concerns over cultural and sexual identity—and form with content. In sharp and calculated contrast to Brakhage, the gestural camera in search of "unmediated" and transcendent visual experiences is revealed in *A Lost Man* as always an extension of a gendered and racial body within contending geopolitical, socioeconomic, and representational boundaries. If things simply end, they do not end simply, for making these boundaries visible cannot resolve or collapse the problematic spaces between genders and genres; or, in the video's implied pun on Adrian's last name, such a strategy cannot locate the man between Juárez and El Paso, even if he was never lost.

Varela's political and cultural concerns may now be more "explicit," but his *argument* is not, if indeed there is a single argument. Nor has Varela's work ever been a simple matter of posing visual riddles and puns, or of otherwise playing cat-and-mouse with the referential quality of film and video. Instead, Varela's editing privileges rhythm over direct associations and repetition over linear analysis. His emphasis continues to be on looking rather than on persuasion within the partisan categories of contemporary public (and policy) debate. To be sure, these positions or categories can be found in his texts, but process takes precedence over product, even in *The Bad Girl* (1994), which explores gender and narrative "manipulation" by recycling a Castle horror film. Thus, if Varela is a personal filmmaker, it is because the personal, like his native El Paso, functions as a crossroads for domestic, local, and national discourses.

notes

1. I am grateful to Lisa Cartwright and Kathleen Newman for their careful readings of earlier drafts of this chapter and to John G. Hanhardt for his generous support and encouragement. Portions of this chapter appeared in the program note for a retrospective on Willie Varela that I curated at the Whitney Museum of American Art, April 29–May 29, 1994. Ali Hoffman provided invaluable editorial assistance in the final stages of this chapter.
2. Jesús Salvador Treviño, "Chicano Cinema Overview," *Areito* no. 37 (1984): 40.
3. See Chon A. Noriega, " 'Our Own Institutions': The Geopolitics of Chicano Professionalism," in *Film and Authorship*, ed. Virginia Wexman (New Brunswick, NJ: Rutgers University Press, December, 2002).
4. The quotation is taken from Sheldon Renan, *An Introduction to the American Underground Film* (New York: E. P. Dutton, 1967), 18. According to Renan, "The underground film *is* a certain kind of film. It is a film conceived and made essentially by one person and is a *personal statement* by that person. It is a film that dissents radically in form, or in technique, or in content, or perhaps in all three. It is usually made for very little money, frequently under a thousand dollars, and its exhibition is outside commercial film channels" (17). See, also, Parker Tyler, *Underground Film: A Critical History* (New York: Da Capo Press, 1995 [1969]). For an excellent critical analysis of underground film, see David E. James, *Allegories of Cinema: American Film in the Sixties* (Princeton: Princeton University Press, 1989), 94–100.
5. The most influential account of this period remains P. Adams Sitney's *Visionary Film: The American Avant-Garde, 1943–1978*, 2nd ed. (Oxford: Oxford University Press, 1979). For a recent attempt to explore the confluence of the underground and gay subcultures, see Juan A. Suárez, *Bike Boys, Drag Queens, and Superstars: Avant-Garde, Mass Culture, and Gay Identities in the 1960s Underground Cinema* (Bloomington: Indiana University Press, 1996).
6. P. Adams Sitney defines the trance and lyrical films in *Visionary Film*: "The trance film was predicated upon the transparency of the somnambulist within the dream landscape. The perspective of the camera, inflected by montage, directly imitated his [*sic*] consciousness" (64). "The lyrical film postulates the filmmaker behind the camera as the first-person protagonist of the film. The images of the film are what he sees, filmed in such a way that we never forget his [*sic*] presence and we know how he is reacting to his vision" (142).

a lost man

7. Willie Varela, "Chicano Personal Cinema," *Jump Cut* no. 39 (1994): 96–9, see p. 96.

8. Varela's papers—including correspondence with over sixty avant-garde filmmakers and videomakers, advocates, and scholars—are archived in the Department of Special Collections, Stanford University Libraries, Stanford, California. (In my citations, I refer generally to the Varela collection, rather than to specific boxes and folders, as I saw the collection *before* it was catalogued. I appraised the material for acquisition by Stanford.) These files provide an excellent case study of the exhibition and social networks that sustained the avant-garde film community between 1976 and 1983. What is notable about the collection is that it covers the five- to seven-year period *after* the ostensible death of the film avant-garde in the mid-1970s, as related in most film histories. In 1981, Varela became the target of a much-circulated Gary Doberman tirade in which he called him the "CHICANO WHITE KNIGHT" for his defense of Brakhage et al. (Doberman did not mail the letter to Varela, however, who received it through an intermediary.) In the letter, Doberman identified Varela's programming efforts as "SUCKING UP . . . to garnish I.O.U.'s," trading liberally in racist name-calling: "Dear Wade-Back Varela: ...You refer to your ethnic group ad nauseum in attempts to gain undue advantage while societal dictates restrain me from stating that we know you're Chicano from the grease on the paper." In a later letter to Brakhage, Varela alludes to other racial slurs within the avant-garde, which Brakhage indirectly attributes to an endemic "meanness" in the field given the need to balance being "INDEPENDENT filmmakers" with making a living: "A no-win situation, for SURE!" Letter from Gary Doberman, April 16, 1981; Letter from Willie Varela to Stan Brakhage, May 1, 1984; Letter from Stan Brakhage, May 9, 1984. Varela collection.

9. Postcard from Stan Brakhage, November 16, 1979; letter from Stan Brakhage, June 29, 1977. Varela collection.

10. Letter from Stan Brakhage, November 20, 1979. Varela collection.

11. The phrase is from a letter from Stan Brakhage acknowledging that Varela's new work has "gone thru the rhythms of your 'heart' (soul's-heart . . . not some simple 'lub-lub' as is all rock-dominated-pop-people can imagine these days)." August 21, 1984. Varela collection.

12. Charles B. Taylor, "Film Controversy Percolates," letter to the editor, *The Prospector* (University of Texas at El Paso) (December 7, 1976): 9; Willie Varela, "Alive and Well: Censorship," letter to the editor, *The Prospector* (University of Texas at El Paso) (December 10, 1976): 11; and Jonas Mekas, "Movie Journal," *Soho Weekly News* (December 16, 1976).

13. See Terry Cannon, "Willie Varela: Deep in the Heart of Texas," *The Cinemanews*, no. 81 (1982): 75; and Gary Scharrer, "Christians Rally to Squelch Pornography," *El Paso Times* (May 18, 1980): 1-B.

14. For extensive clippings (mostly undated) and correspondence, see Varela the collection.

15. Interestingly, Jane Brakhage's response to the film points back to Varela's own dislocation within Mexico: "I got a sense from your films this time of the Mexican aesthetic. . . . Remembering what Becky said that walloped me at the time, 'I'm Aztec,' and something you said once about being a filmmaker, not a Chicano. Remembering then how you both stuck out in Juarez about as much as we did, all I can say is one's aesthetic must be in the blood." Letter from Jane Brakhage, July 1981. Varela collection.

16. "Willie Varela," interview by Terry Cannon, *Spiral*, no. 6 (January 1986): 52.

17. Willie Varela, "Art in Spite of El Paso," *MAIN: Media Arts Information Network* (June 1993): 4, 13.

18. Donna Haraway, "Situated Knowledges: The Science Question in Feminism and the Privilege of Partial Perspective," *Feminist Studies* 14 no. 3 (Fall 1988), 575–99.

19. Kurt Easterwood provides an excellent analysis of the film in a two-page

program note for San Francisco Cinematheque, dated, March 31, 1990. Varela collection.

20. In a 1986 interview, Varela described *Making is Choosing*, then a work in progress, as part of a new "trajectory" in his work: "I want more than anything else to make a larger statement . . . [that] . . . might even begin to approximate a narrative structure." In contrast to his shorter works, this film would be exhibited by itself. "Willie Varela," interview by Terry Cannon, *Spiral* no. 6 (January 1986): 51–3.

21. In some ways, these two movements developed simultaneously throughout the 1960s and early 1970s, although their historical determinants were quite different. The notion of a Third Cinema proposed by Fernando Solanas and Octavio Getino situates the auteurist "new waves"—the model for the New American Cinema Group—as a Second Cinema rooted in the bourgeois subject and an industrial mode of production and distribution. For an English-language version of their manifesto, see "Toward a Third Cinema," *Cineaste* 4 no. 3 (Winter 1970–71): 1–10. It should be pointed out, however, that a wide range of film practices has taken place under or alongside the names of these two movements.

22. Although he does not explore its ramifications, Rick Altman argues that his distinction between semantic and syntactic approaches to genre provides a model that can "account for the numerous [Hollywood] films that innovate by combining the syntax of one genre with the semantics of another." I argue that a more wholesale juxtaposition takes place in *A Lost Man*; and, in any case, I explore the use of Hollywood genres within the *experimental* mode. Altman, *The American Film Musical* (Bloomington & Indianapolis: Indiana University Press, 1989), 97.

23. Marjorie Perloff, ed., *Postmodern Genres* (Norman: University of Oklahoma Press, 1988), 8.

24. Clifford Geertz, "Blurred Genres: The Refiguration of Social Thought," *The American Scholar* 49 (Spring 1980): 165–66.

25. Ralph Cohen, "Do Postmodern Genres Exist?," in Perloff, ed., *Postmodern Genres*, 12.

26. Brief synopsis from "Film/Video Production Information," 38th Robert Flaherty Seminar, Aurora, New York, 1992.

27. His mother has an image of JFK's head etched into her headstone and the scene is letterboxed with quotations about death from JFK, Tom Stoppard, Emily Dickinson, and Gertrude Stein running along the bottom. Other than a brief reference to "Kennedy's head exploding" earlier in the narrative, this is the one scene to identify Adrian as part of the Chicano Generation that rejected the Democratic party after JFK's narrow election and subsequent failure to respond to the Mexican-American community that supported his candidacy.

28. Mary Ann Doane, *Femmes Fatales: Feminism, Film Theory, Psychoanalysis* (New York: Routledge, 1991), 103.

29. Linda Williams, "Feminist Film Theory: *Mildred Pierce* and the Second World War," in *Female Spectators: Looking at Film and Television*, ed. E. Deidre Pribram (London: Verso, 1988), 13. See also, Pam Cook, "Duplicity in *Mildred Pierce*," in *Women in Film Noir*, ed. E. Ann Kaplan (London: British Film Institute, 1978), 68–82.

30. Lauren Rabinovitz, *Points of Resistance: Women, Power & Politics in the New York Avant-garde Cinema, 1943–1971* (Urbana and Chicago: University of Illinois Press, 1991), 55–65.

31. See, for example, the first chapter of Sitney, *Visionary Film*.

32. Interestingly, the film makes an implied comparison between Virginia Woolf (alluded to with respect to Margie's apartment in El Paso) and Marilyn Monroe (in a shot of a Monroe mannequin in Los Angeles with up-blown dress). For an extensive discussion of this "monstrous doubling" between female icons of beauty/sex and intellect/power, see Brenda R. Silver, "Mis-fits:

The Monstrous Union of Virginia Woolf and Marilyn Monroe," *Discourse* 16.1 (Fall 1993): 71–108.

33. See Janey Place's discussion of mirrors in her article, "Women in Film Noir," in Kaplan, ed., *Women in Film Noir*, 35–54.

34. Pam Cook, *The Cinema Book* (New York: Pantheon Books, 1985), 74.

35. For an argument that gay characters "constitute a defining feature of film noir," see Richard Dyer, "Homosexuality and Film Noir," *Jump Cut* no. 16 (1977): 18–21.

36. Mike Davis, *City of Quartz: Excavating the Future in Los Angeles* (New York: Vintage Books, 1992), 38.

37. Ana López describes that paradoxical relationship between the telenovela and New Latin American Cinema, insofar as both are positioned against U.S. mass media, in "The Melodrama in Latin America: Films, Telenovelas and the Currency of a Popular Form," *Wide Angle* 7.3 (1985): 9.

38. In her insightful critique of this gender and generation gap, Laura Marks writes, "We assume that nothing good can come from the hermetic formal experiments of a buncha white men, a self-selected artistic elite who embodied experimental/avant-garde filmmaking in its formative years." Marks, "Here's Gazing at You: A New Spin on Old Porn Exposes Gender and Generation Gaps," *The Independent* (March 1993): 28.

grassroots authors

eleven

collectivity and

construction in

community video

cindy hing-yuk wong

Although many feature films and documentaries discussed in this volume celebrate their authors in credits, publicity, and even the critical legacy surrounding them, this does not mean that the concept of authorship takes the same shape, or merits the same accolades, across the complete spectrum of contemporary film and video production. Alternative works such as grassroots community videos offer a distinctive construct of what an author is or, indeed, of how the author and text take shape. Often, these videos espouse an oppositional stance toward the mainstream media that permeates the message of the video.[1] Yet, opposition imbues not only their texts but also the processes of production and reception that create and recreate these texts. Ultimately, as I will argue, such opposition also comments on the nature and implications of mainstream cinematic authorship itself.

Few viewers, whether producers, spectators, or critics, see community-based videos as works of art. These videos are narrowcast works made primarily by nonprofessional (noncareer) videographers working in groups that serve to convey arguments or information to a targeted audience rather than to evoke aesthetic or even narrative pleasure. Thus, they can be said to be works without an author in the common sense of the term. Yet, the complexities and even paradoxes of authorship become evident in both the organizational ideologies and practices of community creation that underpin them and the practices of exhibition and spectatorship intrinsic to narrowcast production. The diffuse and concealed authorships of community video come to embody alternative means of community building.

Moreover, activist alternative videos exist within social, historical, and political contexts, situations that illuminate these videos more effectively than any organizational or operational sense of an author. Therefore, exploring issues of authorship, antiauthorship, reading, and recreation with this genre is imperative to create a counterpoint with discussions emergent from mainstream media and public documentary.

In this chapter, I look at a group of thirty-plus grassroots videos made by Philadelphia community organizations under the aegis of Scribe Video Center's Community Vision Program in the 1990s. My methods are primarily ethnographic.[2] I first explain Scribe's objectives in instituting this program. The implications of its structure for the issue of authorship include understanding how collective authorship is constituted and how multiple authors come to decisions. My analysis of texts will focus on how authorship shapes and appears in these videos, with a close reading of one piece, *Face to Face: It's Not What You Think* (1996). Finally, this analysis will be linked to the reception of these texts to understand the authorial interaction between texts, specific audiences, and exhibition venues within a more general goal of democratic media literacy. In my conclusions, I underscore how collective and community-based authorship must be understood as a commitment withstanding challenges rather than a natural option.

Throughout this chapter, I will emphasize three central points about grassroots authorship. First, both the general producers and the community organization sponsoring the product see such authorship as collective rather than individual. This vision may be difficult and even disruptive to community building.[3] It conceals the pivotal roles of specific individuals within a collective, whether more highly trained professionals or those few who stay in Scribe's studios many late nights to finish editing. Yet, the commitment to collective authorship provides a foundation for texts and use (and for organizational reconstruction).

Second, and perhaps corollary, community video authorship remains subordinate to message. These videos emerge from the desire to communicate a message about an organization and its concerns. They are ultimately bound to the goals and uses of these organizations and may be used or discarded as these goals evolve. Authors are agents of an organization that promotes a cause in which it believes and the videomaking process is part of this agency.

Finally, and perhaps again corollary, authorship is intimately bound up with exhibition and spectatorship. Those who make the video may well be in the video, and those who are in the video may be, in turn, part of a targeted audience or at least the imagination of one. Alternatively, producers may act as live commentators and reauthors of a video's meaning in conversation with a viewing public. This immediate, intense, and embodied presence of authorship again distinguishes these products from mass media while redefining the implications of authorship.

searching for authors: an introduction to scribe

Louis Massiah founded Scribe Video Center in 1982. Its primary mission since that time has been to facilitate the making of small films and videos in the greater Philadelphia region. As its mission statement reads in part, "Scribe makes use of video technology to document issues and ideas affecting diverse economic and cultural communities; create media works that comment on the human condition and celebrate cultural diversity."[4] On his own, Massiah has been an active filmmaker whose commitment has been recognized with a MacArthur grant and whose own work has ranged from cooperation with Toni Cade Bambara on the documentary *Bombing of Osage Avenue* (1986) to *W.E.B. DuBois: A Biography in Four Voices* (1995). Under his leadership, Scribe, with its small and dedicated staff and its network of professional volunteers, offers videomaking classes, supports facilities and workshops with visiting artists, and fosters outreach programs with public high schools (such as the current Broad Street Oral History project) alongside other community projects. Street Video screenings around Philadelphia in the summer, for example, take independent issue-oriented videos into parks, parking lots, and other venues to create not only events but also conversations, a video-based public sphere. Scribe also supports local independent videographers who may in turn teach or facilitate for Scribe.

The Community Visions (CV) project thus represents only one of Scribe's projects for community and media. The CV project emerged from Scribe's search to attract people who would make videos that are more relevant to the various social and community issues of postindustrial Philadelphia. Unlike many other grassroots video projects, including Scribe's own classes, CV tries to locate people who are not necessarily aspiring videomakers and who are certainly outside the local film/video circuit of schools, professionals, and independent filmmakers. Rather than reproducing video professionals, CV has sought committed citizens who would use media as a democratic tool. Hence, in Scribe's 1990 proposal for funding for CV, Massiah stressed themes of community as alternative practice that already had emerged in Scribe's goals and operations:

215

With some notable exceptions, video producers remain predominantly white and almost exclusively college-educated. It has been our repeated experience at the Scribe Video Center that students who participate in our training programs are already in some measure video-literate. For the most part, grassroots organizations based in poor communities of color are not yet taking advantage of video. . . . By assertively engaging grassroots organizations in video production projects, we can take our skills to them rather than waiting for them to come to us.[5]

Scribe begins the Community Visions process each year by actively contacting groups. Scribe offers to help any organization "create your own videotape about an important concern in your neighborhood, an innovative approach to change, or an aspect of your community's cultural life."[6] The CV project is presented in terms of neighborhood culture, social change, community expression, and the rights for all to tell their stories. CV, then, is not about individual but about collective communication.

Community groups submit proposals to ask Scribe's help in the technical assistance in the design, production, and editing of a video of their choice. Scribe's initial questions delineate an expectation of communal authorship. These questions begin with the group itself:

—*The purpose of your group: What do you do?*
—*How long you have been in existence?*
—*Who is your constituency?*

Having identified the community (and its stability), the questions address the product:

—*What kind of video do you want to make?*
—*What is it about?*
—*What message do you want to deliver?*

At this point, Scribe defines those who will actually make the video solely as an autonomous, if not anonymous, collective and its message to someone. Only after clarifying the communicative mission of the organization and problem with which it deals is any functional concept of authorship addressed:

—*Who from your group will work on the video?*
—*Names of team members?*
—*Who will be the team leader?*

Finally, Scribe turns to audience and distribution as fundamental points that also sometimes escape a group making its first venture into the medium:

—The purpose of your video?
—How it will be used to reach and motivate your constituency?
—How you will distribute it?
—Who will use it?

To assess this project in a wider metropolitan context, Scribe also asks for letters of support from "other people or groups who would use your video," followed by an almost ironic question for new videographers: "Does your group/community have video screening equipment?" Overall, then, unlike other film grant proposals, especially those for creative works, the qualifications for CV are based more on the strength of the community organization and parameters of use of the product, rather than on any individual's past history or creative inspiration.

The CV selection process sets structural parameters of authorship. From the very beginning, these videos are not to be about individual creativity. Reading the proposal, the only person actually named is the *team leader*. Like everyday Scribe practice, this questionnaire emphasizes that a team, not any so-called auteur, should produce the video. Moreover, Scribe is interested in successful exhibition and social value before it allocates its limited funds to help any production.

Furthermore, Scribe does not simply want a team, but seeks people who work together in an egalitarian fashion. Community Vision envisions a production environment that differs from mainstream production with its strict division of labor and hierarchy. Videomakers must be part of the organization or the broader community the product/message aims to reach, not someone from the outside.[7]

Scribe's procedures and questions obviously adapt to different possibilities and groups. They provide the template for an idealistic exercise in videography. Yet, they also charter real practices of community and videomaking that temper and develop such ideal claims.

creating community behind the screen: the production process

Most CV projects take at least ten months to complete; some run up to two years. In the beginning, facilitators meet with the group to discuss the design of the videos. This includes choosing a theme, discovering formal elements, deciding on structures, locations, and production personnel, and choosing interviewees. These production meetings are always open to the whole team.

The process can be adapted to different groups and contexts. Asian American United (AAU), for example, met every Saturday for the first four months. One team leader, Julie (an AAU staff member), ten youths, ages from fifteen to twenty, and two facilitators met for at least four hours at the organization's headquarters on the fringe of Philadelphia's Chinatown. The group members first sought to know each other as each individual shared what was important to him or her about the lives of Asian American youths. These discussions constituted a concerted effort to understand the common concerns of youths recruited from diverse neighborhoods and high schools so that they could become a more cohesive team in charge of their own project. Authorship evolved as the individual created a collective message by negotiating personal experiences within a wider, yet focused context.

One of the most difficult grassroots production tasks is to select a topic. Most CV videos fall into four major categories: (1) general pieces about the history, mission, and accomplishments of the organization, (2) issue-oriented presentations about themes for which the organization fights, (3) instructional videos, perhaps dealing with the work of the organization, and (4) fictional or personalized accounts of an issue dear to the organization. Obviously, these categories sometimes overlap. COMHAR, a community organization focused on mental health/support issues, for example, made a video explaining its different programs. Yet, it also highlighted interviews with relatives of clients to provide a multilayered history of the treatment of the mentally ill, from institutionalization to independent living. Similarly, Women Organized Against Rape (WOAR) incorporated powerful interviews with rape survivors into a tape for outreach or counseling. Good Shepherd, a mediation center, made a video explaining the steps and processes involved in mediation, using their own constituents as actors in a fictionalized story. By contrast, many youth-produced videos avoid organizational or pedagogical data to focus on stories of generational experiences or intersections with schools and police.

CV authors are not supposed to champion their own creative visions but to deliver a collective message to audiences who in turn would reshape their vision. Thus, the projected audience will also become authors of the videos as they take up the message in belief and action. For COMHAR, the imagined audience initially evoked potential clients and funding agencies; therefore the video was to explain the organization and how it works. WOAR, however, produced searing vignettes almost too powerful for a wider audience to watch but nonetheless extraordinarily meaningful in a one-on-one session counseling women dealing with rape. Good Shepherd, finally, conceived of their audience as the "other," those who had never heard of mediation. Consequently, they created a piece that was very pedagogical, including a fictional reenactment rather than "authentic" testimonies and strong symbolic representations of peace and fellowship.

In the case of AAU, the team chose to make an issue-oriented video with autobiographical foundations. For *Face to Face,* the youths eventually decided that it was more urgent to make a video that spoke to a larger audience of non-Asian Americans rather than an audience more like themselves. Hence, transnational intergenerational conflict was deemed too difficult to explain to non-Asian American audiences. The group also decided to drop that issue because they were not comfortable talking about this with their own parents in a video. By focusing on a wider audience, "difference" itself became a theme that permeates the entire video.

Collective effort also shaped the division of labor in the production process. In the case of AAU, the youths did not attend the production classes at Scribe; instead, the team leader did so and, with the two facilitators, shared the technical training with the group. This educational format meant that tasks were also shared in learning and action. Because production was one of the most exciting aspects of the project (a point endorsed in almost all youth projects), there was never a single camera person, writer, or editor. Each youth, at one point or another, became the camera, sound, or lighting person and interviewed or was interviewed by his or her fellow videographers.

In exploring the relationships between the filmmakers and their subjects, CV production differs from even reflexive and experimental nonfiction filmmaking.[8] The distinction between maker and subject is often blurred, for example. Because CV means making videos about your own concerns, the videos are intensely personal: the videomaker is on camera because he or she has something to say. Yet, unlike independent documentaries such as *Sherman's March* (1986), autobiography does not focus on one individual, but on collective experience and action. The voice speaks from shared experience to a shared experience—a relationship already posited in production. Moreover, during the taping, when the videomakers are not on camera themselves, their friends, families, colleagues, and peers are on camera. This creates a very open, fluid relationship between subjects and videomakers. The subjects are free to express themselves as they wish, except where technical requirements dictate certain choices in terms of shot composition, light, and sound. Yet, technical problems, too, became part of the explanation and cooperation necessary to tape—explaining why a scene had to be done over was a lesson for both videographers and subjects. In this sense, the subjects develop a great deal of control in how they want themselves to be represented, sharing some authorial authority, learning video literacy, and undercutting the power of the videomakers themselves. This, too, is part of a collective authorial relation and Scribe's goals in promoting democracy through media.

This came home to me when as facilitator I went with four youths to shoot some footage about South Philadelphia gangs. We went to a game and pool parlor where some twenty Asian American youths milled about. The AAU members knew some of them so videographers and subjects started chatting as peers as the AAU youths explained to the others that they were shooting a video about Asian American youths, including a section on gangs. The others proved extremely cooperative: some made gang hand signs for the camera or talked, while the rest continued their games, appearing extremely comfortable with the camera in the building. In many ways, these videomakers were documenting particular parts of their own lives, thus establishing a kind of authorship embedded in collective life experiences of particular constructed communities.

The AAU videographers also did many interviews and spoke on camera. One team member talked about how her brother became a gang member as a way to rebel against their parents. Other team members shared thoughts about identities, and still others talked about stereotyping in the media and schools. These interviews flowed into conversations with their friends; again, the distance between videomakers and subjects became moot. During this phrase of production, in fact, the authors of *Face to Face* used this experience of videomaking to cement relationships with their imagined community.[9] They asked their peers to share and express a projected common vision. This contrasts with authors who develop individual creative visions of certain subject matter or even pose questions as interlocutors in a documentary.

Absolute collective input and effort, of course, are the stuff of an idealized democratic model; as the project entered its later stages, some youths missed meetings and some individuals took up heavier portions of the work. The most important point about the production process, however, is that CV tapes become collective efforts despite the shortcomings of the production team itself. To make the process democratic and participatory, authorship has to be shared; to complete the project, everyone has to do almost everything at some point. In *Face to Face,* as I have noted, every team member contributed ideas, shot footage, or did sound. All of them were on camera, making the piece itself textually an ensemble piece. They also involved friends, family, and others in the production, renegotiating the project through the footage they assembled for a wider imagined audience. These characteristics of authorship, in turn, were reflected in the video itself.

faces: the authors in the text

The credits of many CV videos often lack familiar roles such as "director" or "producer," or, indeed, "one" of anything. Yet, this is not simply an artifact of the production teams. In classic authorship studies, one tends to look for a coherent style through a series of works done by the same director. In CV, this is not a possible approach, as most videomakers are first timers (or one-timers), lacking any comparative corpus of work. More important, because of the varied individual efforts of team members, many of the texts lack a single, coherent vision.

Nonetheless, the complete collection of CV works illustrates many common conceptual traits shared with other nonfiction films. Many of the videos are didactic, presenting needs in an expository voice and working toward a solution. Most texts offer collective discussion and affirmation of their issues or organizational information. Places become very important in these works; because these tapes are local, identification with the surroundings grounds the formation of communities. Place also refers to the identification of the organization by headquarters, projects, or field of action.

Textual traits also recur across multiple CV works, defining them as an ongoing conversation among groups, and between groups and the urban society in which they work. Most videos use multiple nonexpert talking heads, with a continual focus on people and stories, but without a single heroic, dominant voice. Materials from other media—old photographs, news stories, wedding videos—are also incorporated despite changes in quality of the materials. Despite training, production values of these tapes are low or perhaps secondary in comparison with mainstream models. Their techniques are not polished although many (especially youth) will play at some point with more complex effects, incorporation of music or graphics, and other characteristics of mainstream documentaries. Although no text is ever transparent, most CV works use fairly conventional methods to tell their story, which seldom invite attention to form or demand that the audience pay attention to a particular style, be it oppositional or conventional.

In the pieces that explore the history and mission of community organizations, for example, the texts often commence with segments explaining the foundation of the organization, mostly through talking heads and archival photos. As the tapes move to the present, mostly introduced by the same talking heads, visual materials of the spaces of the organization and its activities situate the audience in concrete relations with familiar realities. At this point, the text emphasizes the connection between projected audience and place, concretizing a spatial relationship around a problem or message rather than creating one between the creator/person of the tape and the audience. In the latest Scribe screening of "The Power to Change" (2001), made by Camden Churches Organized for People, for example, the tape opens with different talking heads and voices running over photographs of the old Camden, showing a vibrant city with happy families and residents walking in the streets. When the tape reaches the present, a worn and neglected Camden dominates the screen. These images, in turn, are interspersed with meetings of people in different locales, many of them churches, trying to resolve problems of the new city and, by implication, to recapture the values of the past one. The tape thus offers a very simple structure of past stability, the present problem, and the struggle to overcome these problems while engaging producers and viewers as citizens.

Face to Face also can be situated within subgenres of CV that have emerged around place and subject. In fact, Scribe's website stimulates this repetition of form by highlighting thematic categories as potential models for new applicants.[10] These categories are labeled HIV/AIDS,

Local Histories and Communities, Social Activists and Alternative Visions, Housing, Artists, Prison Issues, Women's Advocacy, and Youth Activism and Schools. The last, of course, situates *Face to Face* within a tradition of Scribe productions. Among earlier Scribe products available for AAU viewing, for example, was the 1993 *To School or Not to School,* produced by Youth United for Change of Woodrock. Subsequently, in 2000, other Asian youths dealt with problems of intergroup violence, while in 2001, two other videos joined the CV "school" group. One, *Fighting for Our Schools,* from the Philadelphia Student Union, deals with activities in local public schools. The second, *(((in stereo))) types,* presents multiracial lesbian and gay youth. In both cases, youths tackled critical and immediate problems of school, peers, race, and identity. In fact, many members of the Student Union were unable to attend the initial public screening of their work as they were preparing a massive rally to protest privatization of the city school system. Their video was both record and tool in that protest.

As the titles suggest, these "school" videos often share an "in-your-face" attitude of youth taking charge. They also share textual characteristics including flashy editing, enacted sequences, and creative forms such as poetry, music, and collective events as well as talking heads—obviously, these are generations shaped by MTV and other mass media as well as community concerns. In fact, by 2001, it became apparent that new generations of computer-literate youths could rival their older professional facilitators in adapting to the possibilities of computer editing. These are high-energy as well as highly pointed texts, designed to appeal to youth as well as speak for it.

Face to Face brings together, in fifteen minutes, many of the themes of other youth videos: schools, gangs, acceptance, and identity. Its multiple sections are framed by a prologue that addresses general issues of identity and a poetic epilogue that defies stereotypes and presents a positive and playful image of Asian American youth culture.

The tape starts with a youth walking toward the camera in a park, interrupted with rapid cuts of close-ups of Asian faces; the sound track carries a string of (constructed) racist slurs. This scene ends with the youth screaming at the camera, interrupting conservative frames for documentary by the vividness, directness, and emotional power of this act. A rapid collage of Philadelphia street scenes follows, gradually moving to Asian establishments in the city. Quickly, the tape has established its theme and place—Philadelphia Asian American youths and their problems—by juxtaposing faces, place, and its collage of racial slurs. It has also established a hip, defiant tone.

Three interviews on being Asian American close the prologue. Their voices convey to the audience that Asian American identities are sometimes invisible to other Americans where race often means only black and white. Meanwhile, they argue, Asian Americans can see themselves as bicultural.

The four internal sections deal with schools, stereotypes, police harassment, and gangs. Inserted into the video are film clips depicting Asian Americans stereotypes from Suzie Wong (*The World of Suzie Wong,* 1960) to the Asian "nerd" from *Sixteen Candles* (1984, an alternative reading of the myth of the "model minority").[11] On camera, students distort their own faces to show slanted eyes, juxtaposing this to statements of how these stereotypes feel. Although polemic, the tape also indicates that some other Asian Americans internalize racism. Hanyin, for example, explains that Asian Clubs in schools put on fashion shows. But Hanyin does not like the shows' Orientalist emphasis on traditional costumes, arguing that Asian youths actually wear baggy jeans and sneakers. These words resonate with images throughout the film of the videographers and subjects in jeans and sneakers.

The "Gang" section starts with gang members making hand signs in different locales. Unidentified gang members claim that "gang" is a label imposed on any group of people hanging out together. They also assert that in real gangs people treat one another as families and support each other. For example, a young woman recalls that her brother joined a gang because he could not meet the family expectations of earning straight A's. The tape does not provide a simplistic defense, however: this is a collective discussion, not a monovocal statement. Hence, another gang member poignantly confesses that he is tired of being in a gang and wants out. He has decided that "hurting your own brothers is stupid." Still another agrees that Asians are killing Asians and blacks killing blacks but argues the biggest gang is the one in "suits and ties, the President." No alternate voices of "expertise" are called in to support or deny these claims (which respond, nonetheless, to the off-screen presence of myriad television and newspaper stories worried about bad teenagers).

These sections use conventional documentary techniques: different levels of information are assembled to authenticate claims and substantiate an argument: hence, social statements to the contrary refute stock footage of Asian stereotypes. Still, "authoritative"/adult experts are notably absent. The video also poses complicated interpretations without a simple narrative resolution or documentary point. The video argues against stereotypes but acknowledges that some Asian youths internalize these stereotypes or find themselves trapped by them. In the "Gang" section, many opinions about gangs are crammed into three minutes of tape. Most betray a sympathetic attitude toward the gang experience, but the section provides neither endorsement nor rebuke. Although posing images of stereotypes and gangs oppositional to mainstream American culture, these segments also provide space to contest a one-dimensional positive or negative image *within* the Asian youth community, taking production debates into the text and, as I will show, into the audience.

The most interesting textual aspect of this video is how it presents itself as an ensemble piece. Without being formally reflexive, the tape gives the audience the impression that the youths who are the subjects of the video also made the tape. This occurs through many instances of direct eye contact between the subject and the camera. The relaxed attitude of the subjects in front of the camera further negotiates an inclusive empathy.

In *Face to Face*, even an individual artistic element, the closing poem that lasts for about two and one-half minutes, weaves producers and themes together. Leap recites her poem standing against a red wall. Entwined with it are short clips of the Asian speakers glimpsed earlier in the video, often now in family settings. This transformation stresses the human complexity of the roles and identities the people have spoken about on camera. This footage shows the youths in new guises—performing in front of the camera, waving hands, imitating kung fu, and making faces. Unlike actuality footage, these performances invite a dialogue between the subjects and the audience, with the statement, "Look at all that I am as I am talking to you." Although these textual strategies can be achieved by fiction film production, credits and multiple intertexts of stardom and criticism preclude this assumption in most viewing contexts.

Not all manifestations of collectivity need be seen as so textually empowering. The lack of a strong stylistic coherence may also attest to the difficulties of collective action and agreement in the CV tape. Overall, even *Face to Face* touches only superficially on many issues. In fact, it never really asks what Asian American culture "is" (if such an embracing category exists) or who Asian Americans are. Still, the teens were more than happy with their work. After the screening Julie wrote me that she hoped to see this film contributing to an ever-changing, diverse, yet inclusive definition of Asian American. Even this sense of a work in dialogue sets it apart from some other documentaries and returns us to the special questions of audience and authorship that this form of video raises.

readings: the audience as author

In the November 2001 presentation of new CV products, including the works by the Philadelphia Student Union and RAVE, both youth-oriented groups emphasized their "realness" in relation to potential audiences. The essential albeit circular claim was "We are youth so we know it will speak to youth because they are us and created this film." Such identification, although at first glance tautological and vainglorious, represents an important and illuminating claim about authorship.

From a variety of screenings and events I have attended over the past decade, it is clear that people who watch these CV videos do not come there looking for any specific author, director, or writer (although they do respond knowingly to familiar faces on screen). This does not mean that audiences do not look for some kind of authority behind the creation of the videos; in fact, they may presuppose an authorial role. Part of this implication of authorship, however, may be necessary for the purposes of the sponsoring organization.

Scribe lacks a very organized distribution system for CV works. After a group of tapes is finished, they will premiere in a local venue. The International House near the University of Pennsylvania hosted this premiere, but it has moved now to the downtown Prince Theatre near Philadelphia's new Avenue of the Arts. These events attract several hundred spectators although friends, families, and organizational affiliates of the groups presenting predominate. The premiere is an event for community groups, activists, and Philadelphia's independent video producers rather than for a general public. These events are not reviewed in local papers, for example.

Thereafter, both Scribe and the organization own the rights to the tape. In the past two years, Scribe has developed a more formal distribution list on their website, where most of the tapes can be bought. The videos are also screened on the local alternative public television station, WYBE: public television and public access are major issues of concern in many Scribe discussions.[12] Organizations also send their tapes to film and video festivals including the Philadelphia International Film Festival. Although this distribution may reach a larger audience, such opportunities are rare enough to make apparent that these venues are not the focal audience for the groups.

The most important distribution channel for these tapes remains their use by the organizations themselves. Producers and managers know their constituents and the people they want to reach. In this sense, the audience requested by Scribe in its initial solicitation dominates distribution and exhibition and imposes an overarching authority in place of the individual author as auteur. Oftentimes, for example, these tapes are shown in different outreach programs of these organizations. In some cases, videos have been mailed out to organization members (*We the People*). They may even be supplied to antagonists. *To The Point*, produced by the needle exchange program Prevention Point, was distributed to police and police training units.

Because grassroots videos are narrowcast media, the producers also create concrete situations in which they can meet the actual audience, trying to exert control over the effects of their work. These events can also be both creative and reflexive. *Peace at Home*, which deals with domestic violence and restraining orders, became a basic tool for Women Legal Services, where it served to lessen the workload of its already harried staff. Over time, though, they have learned that its questions still demand answers, and it is never shown without someone from the group present. *To School or Not to School* (1993), which hopes to shows how to prevent dropouts, was later used by the producers as

225

an empowerment tool for inner-city youths, the original intended audience, in face-to-face group sessions. This use focused less on the original textual message than on what students as filmmakers and organizers can do (i.e., making this video) to deal with problems around them. Again, the producers, by witnessing a match between the intended and actual audiences, can use the video in new and unexpected ways to build relationships among a larger community of producers *and* audiences. COMHAR, for instance, has found that its tape is useful as an orientation tool for new staff members who are unaware of the personal history of the organization and the hopes it embodies. In these instances, recognizing an intertextual frame is very important to being an author. The audience, the producers, and the subjects in the tape all have either undergone or are knowledgeable about the particular experience. The tape is a catalyst that allows them to comment and build upon that implicit relationship, which also changes.

Audiences also bring and take more from screenings over time. Sometimes, this is difficult to elucidate, even after long-term relationships, as CV audiences are not trained as critics nor do they approach screenings with a critical reflexive goal. One of the most common—and valued—responses from audience members in screenings, for example, is a simple "I like it."

Yet these works evoke meanings from those who can relate to and comment on the content of the works because the content is supposed to be "real." Explaining how home movies have strong historical recognition and authenticity, Bill Nichols poses a paradox of time and distance with which we must grapple in terms of defining authenticity and authorship in these cases:

> Such material, often close to raw footage in its lack of expository or narrative structure, has clear documentary value for those of whom it offers evidence. Usually this is a family or a small circle of friends. . . . Nevertheless, in order to take on evidentiary value, the footage must be recognized for its historical specificity. The viewer who says, "Ah, that's me eight years ago!" has a radically different rapport with the footage than the viewer who has no inkling of who this figure in the image is. But were the viewer who only recognizes a human figure to recognize, subsequently, that this is a friend, to see not only general resemblance but an indexical bond stretching across eight years of time, the effect of discovery would be equivalent. (160)

226

Although it may be difficult for a general audience to identify with the subject of CV works, the targeted audience shares an intertextual frame with the videomakers and the subjects of these tapes and adds its authorship to the process of reading.

To understand reception for these works, I must reiterate the autobiographical underpinnings of these works. The authors are very often the subjects and members of a wider community as well; therefore, an audience's identification with the subject builds a bond between the audience and the author. However, given collective authors and/or a collective subject, the audience is asked to participate in a collective body rather than relating to a single, albeit outside vision. When collectivity speaks for and about a specific social group, whether students, Asian American youths, artists with disabilities, people who are fighting for equitable housing, or prisoners, the subjects and the audience of these tapes often share some social characteristics. Identification becomes based on a shared experience reconceived as a shared destiny (a theme that evokes reading of authorships in situations of group or national identity).[13]

CV producers, in turn, impose heavy responsibilities on a participatory audience of social actors who share similar concerns. They consider their mission a failure if this intended audience does not grasp the intended message of the video, or provides an aberrant reading of the text (much less rejecting it). Indeed, the desire for this identification with the organization they represent often makes it hard to evoke an elaborated reading. They aim for people to say, "Yes, that's what we meant," rather than saying "the jump cuts were an effective device for me in communicating the fragmentation of ethnic identity I feel in the postmodern world" or "I want to grow up and have a wedding like Willie and Varee" (the conclusion of *New Faces of AIDS*). They seek assent, not deconstruction.

The grassroots frame also encompasses intentions: how producers want the work to influence the audience or how the audience should use the work in society. Again, these are not isolated points in a process: the videographers and organization conceived of these uses before beginning productions, and, although these may evolve, they presuppose a continuing intimacy of production, text, and use. This leads to patterns of audience and use reminiscent of those Eric Michaels explored in his work on Australian Aboriginal video practices. For example, the video *The Fire Ceremony* was produced for present and future generation of Australian Aboriginals, to ensure cultural reproduction for traditional oral societies. The producers—the Warlpiri at Yuendumu in Northern Australia—wanted to make a tape of a seldom-performed rite to ensure the reproduction of the ceremony among an imagined audience of Warlpiri who have little recollection of the ritual. Other Aboriginals constituted wider audiences; cultural patterns of distribution meant the nearby Willowra community received this tape as a medium of exchange.[14]

Yet, at the same time, producers as collective author(s) worry about being displaced entirely, about an audience who imposes its own meaning. Recognition that videos do not speak for themselves remains a problem facing Scribe, which has discussed study guides, a speakers bureau, or other devices to build bridges between authors and audiences

227

as shared communities. Here, visions of collective authorship pose problems as concrete and complex as those of individual authorship or auteurism.

final notes: contesting and constructing authorship

Obviously, in dealing with alternative production the danger of idealizing process and product must always be kept in mind. Even in an ethnographic inquiry such as this, the ideology of collective authorship represents a shared commitment rather than an automatic patterning of behavior. Some final questions of individual authorship that emerge within these collective settings illuminate both the tensions and commitments of grassroots cinema and the reverberations of these issues for classical visions of cinematic authorship.

In fact, tensions over other possible readings of authorship can emerge within production, text, and audience. Within production, for example, despite the premise of learning democratic models of videography, facilitators who are also video artists may be torn by their feelings. Checks and balances within the system prevent any "hijacking" of the video. Nonetheless, both professional and proprietorial feelings exist as videos show up on resumes and as facilitators themselves worry about exposure. As one said in passing, "I did a lot of work with that group and the video got a lot of play. It's good for me that it's out there." I would stress, though, that even this tension is bounded within an initial commitment to community-based filmmaking that separates many of these people from independent artists who also use Scribe facilities.

Those within community production also take on unequal responsibility and control. This becomes especially evident in long nights of editing when one person makes choices, even with the acquiescence of the group. The need to add segments at a late phase of production to fill out a loosely conceived video can also add more autobiographical elements such as monologues or artistic products as parts within a larger collective. For example, in many teen videos, elements of acting—skits, parodies, poems—often highlight the individual as artist even within a collective piece. Yet, this is part of the theme I have emphasized throughout: who will recognize themselves in the behavior of others of their peer groups.

Within the texts, one scarcely deduces the hand of a potential Alfred Hitchcock or Akira Kurosawa. Yet, the process of modeling new generations of community video on past efforts can produce the invisible hand of authorship shaping exposition, music, and framing. Although this influence from the past is not a question I have addressed specifically to production groups, I can see the process from my own work as facilitator in choosing CV products, talking about them, and shaping a final product. Although not equating this to authorship, such an

228

invisible hand seems to be a critical component of comparison with mass media production in which authors are hidden by formal repetition or rapid production.

Challenges to collective authorship in the realm of audience seem more elusive but also illuminate the paradoxes of the author–audience relationship in grassroots video. Insofar as these are texts produced to be mediated, by teachers, spoken introduction, commentary, or even reflections, the appropriation of the text in public settings may permit the emergence of an authorized and authentic voice. Here are echoes in the legitimization so often given documentaries by the presence not only of filmmakers but even subjects who can explain the "reality" behind the text to the audience. Such an authorial claim is echoed potentially when a teen videographer takes his or her work into school, or an organization such as Good Shepherd stops, pauses, and fast-forwards a video to incorporate it as a tool into a mediation class. Yet, the alternative, an audience who would read into a video a completely different message (as did my students at one collegiate institution who read *To School or Not to School* not as a plea for help but as a story of losers)—seems to threaten the mission and collective authorship of CV itself in uncomfortable ways.

Such tensions in authorship can become tensions in the social construction of organization and community itself. Yet, potential tensions also reveal how CV processes and community organizations themselves work to impose collective authorship on a complex process. Neither institutional support, nor text, nor reading, for example, will ever say "a video by x" and designate a single person as a responsible author. Scribe itself would have intervened before this in the production phase (if not in original selection) and would certainly avoid such labeling on any work. Moreover, the video is always the goal and property of an organization. Hence, it is more likely that CV videos will credit an organization in which people may change and the organization retains ownership of the video after personnel are gone and even forgotten. Alternatively, as has happened in some cases, the video can be forgotten while the person continues in nonmedia roles. It will not figure as a personal oeuvre or even in succession or development; the sequel is another film by the *organization-as-author*, not by an individual artist, auteur, or production team.

Scribe does not evoke a "natural" absence of individual author but instead has constructed an insistent challenge to this idea in the name of social values. As I have suggested through ethnographic analysis of process and products, this sense of authorship is not "accidentally" different but intentionally and collectively constructed as different at several levels. In analyzing this process, therefore, we can come to understand both the range of meanings of authorship in contemporary grassroots video and the depth to which "alternative" may be a meaningful interrogation of mass media and their assumptions.

notes

1. See, for example, Deidre Boyle, *Subject to Change: Guerilla Television Revisited* (New York: Oxford University Press, 1987); Dee Dee Halleck, "Deep Dish TV: Community Video from Geostationary Orbit," *Leonardo*, no. 5 (1993): 415–20; Alexandra Juhasz, *AIDS TV: Identity, Community, and Alternative Video* (Durham, NC: Duke University Press, 1995); Robert W. McChesney, *Corporate Media and the Threat to Democracy* (New York: Seven Stories Press, 1997); Robert W. McChesney, *Telecommunications, Mass Media, and Democracy: The Battle for the Control of U.S. Broadcasting, 1928–1935* (New York: Oxford University Press, 1995); Annabelle Sreberny-Mohammadi, *Small Media, Big Revolution: Communication, Culture, and the Iranian Revolution* (Minneapolis: University of Minnesota Press, 1994); Don Hazen and Julie Winokur, eds., *We the Media: A Citizens' Guide to Fighting for Media Democracy* (New York: The New Press, 1997); Patricia Zimmermann, *States of Emergency: Documentaries, Wars, Democracy* (Berkeley: University of California Press, 2000).

2. In the early 1990s I worked with Scribe as both facilitator and investigator, participating in the Community Visions project with several groups as well as interviewing others about their experiences, drawing on models for the ethnography of media as diverse as Wilton Martinez, "Who constructs anthropological knowledge? Toward a theory of ethnographic film spectatorship?" in *Film as Ethnography*, ed. Peter Crawford and Ian Turton (Manchester: Manchester University Press, 1992), 131–64; Sara Dickey, *Cinema and the Urban Poor In South India* (Cambridge: Cambridge University Press, 1993); Eric Michaels, *Bad Aboriginal Art: Traditions, Media and Technological Horizons* (Minneapolis: University of Minnesota Press, 1994); Susan Ossman, *Picturing Casablanca* (Berkeley: University of California Press, 1994); Purnima Mankekar, *Screening Culture, Viewing Politics: An Ethnography of Television, Womanhood, and Nation in Postcolonial India* (Durham, NC: Duke University Press, 1999); and Cindy Wong and Gary McDonogh, "The Mediated Metropolis: Reflections on Anthropology and Communication," *American Anthropologist* 103, no. 1 (March 2001): 96–111.

3. Vicki Mayer, "Capturing Cultural Identity/Creating Community," *International Journal of Cultural Studies* 3 (2000): 57–78; Robert Putnam, *Bowling Alone: The Collapse and Revival of American Community* (New York: Simon & Schuster, 2000).

4. Scribe Pamphlet 2001. See further, Cindy Hing-Yuk Wong, "Community Through the Lens: An Ethnographic Study of Grassroots Video" (Unpublished Ph.D. Dissertation, Annenberg School for Communication, University of Pennsylvania, 1997).

5. Community Vision Funding Proposal to William Penn Foundation, March 1990, Scribe Archive (hereafter SA).

6. Solicitation letter, March 19, 1990, SA.

7. In the mid-1990s, for example, a group applied for a CV grant; however, the proposal seemed to suggest that a videographer outside the organization would be the team leader. Louis and I, as a prospective facilitator, held a meeting with the leader of the organization and the team leader. The team leader was a professional artist/videographer who would assume a directorial mode in the production of the video. She already had determined ideas about the video, without any apparent input from the constituents of that organization. This kind of authorship worked against the objectives of CV and this project was not selected.

8. Bill Nichols, *Representing Reality* (Bloomington: Indiana University Press, 1991), 69–75.

9. This is in a literal sense Benedict Anderson's mediated term in *Imagined Communities: Reflections on the Origin and Spread of Nationalism* (London: Verso, 1983).

10. See http://www.libertynet.org.scribe.
11. Gary McDonogh and Cindy Wong, "Orientalism Abroad: Hong Kong Readings of *the World of Suzie Wong,*" in *Classic Hollywood, Classic Whiteness,* ed. Daniel Bernardi (Minneapolis: University of Minnesota Press, 2001), 210–44 .
12. Laura R. Linder, *Public Access Television: America's Electronic Soapbox* (Westport, CT: Praeger, 1999).
13. See Juhasz, Sreberny-Mohammadi, and Mankekar for relevant discussions.
14. See further, Michaels, 116–24.

part four

the

author-function

reframing a biographical legend

twelve

legend

biographical

style, european filmmakers,

and the sideshow cinema

of tod browning

matthew solomon

Unlike perhaps any other filmmaker past or present, the films of Tod Browning seem to invite a peculiarly biographical form of commentary. In striking contrast to the critical discourse on other film directors, discussion of Browning often turns to what he did before making films. The impulse to correlate the diegesis of several noted films with certain features of the director's precinematic résumé has become a characteristic trope of Browning scholarship. In particular, many who have written about Browning mention that he began his professional career working in a sideshow. It is often suggested that these early life experiences had telling effects upon a number of his later films, including *The Unholy Three* (1925), *The Show* (1927), *The Unknown* (1927), and *Freaks* (1932), all of which center on the lives of characters who perform in the circus, sideshow, or dime museum. In a recent chapter devoted to *Freaks*, for example, Rachel Adams comments, "That a circus is the mise-en-scène for Browning's most memorable work is unsurprising, since he often recalled his youthful experiences as a carnival performer as a source of inspiration for his films."[1]

This chapter, however, treats Browning's association with the circus sideshow as a critical and biographical cliché that requires further interrogation. Browning's relation to the sideshow, I argue, is a biographical construct that crystallized during the 1920s, when Browning was directing a series of sideshow films for Metro-Goldwyn-Mayer. Although this particular biographical construct informs most contemporary studies of Browning's films, it is but one of many that could be productively applied to the director's work. In this chapter, I foreground another set of biographical factors that are obscured by a more metonymic version of Browning's biography. Reframing the "biographical legend" of Browning with respect to a particular international film historical context does much to illuminate his work. Although Browning's sideshow films seem to proffer traces of his own biography, these films may also be read to yield more indirect evidence of Browning's aesthetic engagement with contemporaneous European cinema. Placed within a much larger complex of biographical determinants, Browning's identification with the sideshow is seen less as a series of straightforward recollections than as a self-conscious strategy for authoring Hollywood films. Attention to the style and settings of Browning's sideshow films suggests that this strategy bears an important relation not only to Browning's precinematic biography, but also to the filmographies of several of his European contemporaries at MGM—most notably, Victor Sjöström and Benjamin Christensen.

French critic Patrick Brion argues that Browning's biographical association with the sideshow is the central feature of what he aptly describes as the "Browning legend."[2] The legend conflates art and life, Brion suggests, substituting the uncanny mise-en-scène of films such as *Freaks* and Edmund Goulding's later *Nightmare Alley* (1947) for the milieu in which Browning himself entered show business: "The legend, readily maintained by the interested, insists that Tod Browning had a passion for the universe of the circus since childhood. . . . Not the more prestigious American circuses, but the traveling shows which showed bizarre creatures, Siamese twins, bearded ladies, and magicians from town to town. An often sordid world, where one found the inevitable *Geek*, a half-savage man who devoured raw meat. . . . A bizarre world, on the margins of traditional American society, which the fascinated Browning would eventually enter" (Brion, 84, my translation). Browning's association with the sideshow has further been cemented by the publication of David Skal and Elias Savada's biography, *Dark Carnival*, which posits the shady realm of the American tent show as the definitive metaphor for Browning's life and work.[3] Within critical circles, the increased attention accorded to *Freaks*—along with the belated critical rediscovery of *The Unknown* and *The Unholy Three*, together with diminished interest in *Dracula* (1931) and the status of *London After Midnight* (1927) as a lost film—has also helped to promulgate this legend, effectively deemphasizing Browning's relation to the gothic and melodramatic traditions.[4]

In his account of the "biographical legend" of Carl-Theodor Dreyer, David Bordwell says, "we can situate a filmmaker's work in film history by studying the persona created by the artist in his public pronouncements, in his writings, and in his dealings with the film industry."[5] The "biographical legend" of Dreyer, Bordwell claims, helped to position his films—though made within an industrial system of commercial mass production—as semiorganic works of art modeled upon the principles of Naturalist theater (Bordwell, 9–24). Similarly, as Robert Allen and Douglas Gomery emphasize, the "biographical legend" of F. W. Murnau was part of a larger set of discourses on cinema as art that ascribed privileged aesthetic status to German cinema of the 1920s.[6] Although the "Browning legend" focuses not so much on his career as a filmmaker as on his professional beginnings in the realm of the circus, I posit that it can be analyzed along the lines of these other, roughly contemporaneous, "biographical legends." Surveying the enthusiastic critical reception that greeted such German films as Murnau's *The Last Laugh* (1925) and E. A. Dupont's *Variety* (1926) in the United States, Allen and Gomery ask:

> Something in the German films was obviously viewed as "aesthetic," but what was it? In America, the term "German cinema" came to mark out an aesthetic space, if you will, somewhere outside the normative boundaries of conventional Hollywood style. At issue was how far outside, and whether this aesthetic distance from the Hollywood cinema constituted a positive or negative aesthetic difference. Discussions of individual films tended to be framed by three aesthetic criteria, each having both a positive and a negative dimension: spectacular/excessive, complex/elitist, and artistic/self-indulgent. The closer the individual film came to being described by the first term in each pair, the more its difference from Hollywood films was regarded as "innovative" and hence positive. A film defined by the latter terms, however, was seen as too different and hence too "strange." (Allen and Gomery, 95)

This schema helps to explain the varied critical responses to Browning's films during the 1920s, yet it also provides a useful matrix for consideration of Browning's "biographical legend." During the early 1920s, a number of film directors were touted as artists through reference to their precinematic careers in the traditional arts, including Hugo Ballin (painting), Penrhyn Stanlaws (painting), and Rex Ingram (sculpture). The emergent Browning legend suggests a distinctively lowbrow attempt to negotiate several of the aesthetic binaries that Allen and Gomery find in critical writing about German cinema. By historicizing the "Browning legend" and juxtaposing his sideshow films with the work of a number of émigré directors, I argue that Browning's links with the circus sideshow should be placed in relation to the critical caché of Scandinavian cinema during the late 1910s and 1920s.

Given the absence of memoirs or surviving personal papers, Browning's life is known almost entirely through a collection of biographical anecdotes culled from newspapers and periodicals of the 1910s, 1920s, and 1930s. One of the earliest articulations of the narrative appears in a 1914 fan magazine, published while Browning was performing as a comedian in one-reel comedy films produced by D. W. Griffith. The article begins with the following story of Browning's professional origins: "The show business got into Tod Browning's blood with the lure of the sawdust. He was sixteen when he ran away from Louisville, Kentucky, and joined a circus."[7] A 1920 biographical sketch, published after he had become a successful director for Universal with the films *The Virgin of Stamboul* (1920) and *Outside the Law* (1920) to his credit, contains a slight elaboration of the same basic story: "Tod had a rather exciting sort of life in his early youth. He found the confines a trifle irksome, so at an early age he ran away and some time later became a ballyho-artist [*sic*] with the Manhattan Fair and Carnival company."[8] By the late 1920s, such details were no longer merely a quasibiographical aside, but had in fact become a relevant preface to the discussion of Browning's apparent predilection for the sideshow milieu. As one often-quoted fan magazine article asserts, parenthetically: "Browning came to Hollywood and pictures from a long experience as an actor on the vaudeville stage and a 'barker' in a circus. (He admits to drawing on this colorful background for many of the characterizations and incidents in his pictures.)"[9]

Such sources help us to outline some of the features of Browning's professional life, yet they should also be seen as a seminal part of the "Browning legend." Skal and Savada claim:

> Since almost all accounts of Browning's entry into show business originated with himself, or with studio publicists in the ballyhoo-heavy 1920s, they need to be evaluated with a certain skepticism. . . . According to the legend, as put forth in friendly newspaper interviews in the *Louisville Herald-Post* and in studio handouts, a street fair came to Louisville in 1898 and Browning fell under the spell of one of the dancers. The show left town, and so, supposedly, did Tod. When his parents next heard of him, he was a ballyhoo artist, or spieler, with something called the Manhattan Fair and Carnival Company. (Skal and Savada, 22)

Acknowledging the clearly fictionalized nature of most of these stories—a number of which seem to echo the narrative of James Kaler's popular nineteenth-century novel, *Toby Tyler; or, Ten Weeks with a Circus*—Browning's biographers conclude, "In short, most of the 'record' of Tod Browning's early career cannot be confirmed by documentary evidence, and is likely an uneasy amalgam of truth, half-truth, embellishment, and, in some cases, outright fabrication. Obviously, show business pulled Browning powerfully, and from an early age, but the full nature and extent of his apprenticeship is far from clear" (Skal and Savada, 29). Despite Skal and Savada's probing research, we still know relatively little about what exactly Browning did during fifteen years of adult life before becoming a film actor in 1913, although "documentary evidence" allows them to reconstruct parts of a theatrical career that included performances as a blackface performer, magician's assistant, and vaudeville comedian—as well as the relatively mundane details of Browning's earlier employment with a Louisville railroad company, saddle merchant, and amusement park (Skal and Savada, 24–36, 331–33). The blurring of filmography and biography that underpins the "Browning legend" has its origins in the publicity discourse of the studio system during the 1920s and 1930s. Indeed, a brief biographical text (dated 1932) circulated by MGM emphasizes: "His experience with the traveling carnival has been vividly reflected in 'The Unholy Three,' 'The Show' and 'Freaks.'"[10]

Whether or not the mise-en-scène of such films truly "reflects" Browning's life experiences, the carnival—and entertainments of its ilk—had certain definite connotations during the early twentieth century. A 1908 article published in *Show World* (one of a handful of periodicals, along with *Billboard* and *Variety*, in which the history of American itinerant amusements is chronicled) asserts: "We all know that the carnival business has lost considerable prestige during the past few seasons, that it has fallen in the estimation of the general public. . . . It—the carnival business—has been condemned by the clergy, the press and the public. . . . The average carnival company of today is made up of a set of cheap 'hold up shows' and grafters."[11] The sideshow was a similarly marginalized form of entertainment in American culture. Within the circus, the sideshow was situated at some distance from the center ring(s), and its personnel were strictly segregated from other performers by the rigorously demarcated geographies of circus life. Janet Davis describes the organization of the turn-of-the-century American circus as an elaborately segregated "caste system" that sharply differentiated between groups in the circus hierarchy.[12] The sideshow staff was at the bottom of this hierarchy, and included not only the "freaks" who were often its primary draw, but also a variety of close-up performing artists (sword swallowers, fire eaters, snake charmers, tattooed persons, knife throwers, contortionists, mind readers, magicians, ventriloquists), as well as the "talkers" who ballyhooed the attractions for spectators perambulating the midway, the ticket sellers, and the musicians of the sideshow band (who were typically African American).

The "Browning legend" allows a vague notion of the sideshow or carnival to stand in for much of Browning's early career, but additional biographical information discovered by Skal and Savada and a more richly detailed picture of American itinerant amusements indicate that Browning was ensconced in a much more varied set of occupational

239

and professional circumstances. He likely worked in a number of different cheap entertainment venues (circus, carnival, amusement park) and played a range of different roles in several distinct types of popular theater (vaudeville, burlesque, magic, blackface minstrelsy) in addition to jobs in retail and the transportation industries. Elsewhere, I have argued that evidence of Browning's professional associations with magicians Leon Herrmann and Chung Ling Soo (born William Ellsworth Robinson) points to an entirely different context in which to consider his films—that of theatrical magic.[13] Magicians and illusionists are, of course, prominent characters in *The Show*, *West of Zanzibar* (1928), and *Miracles for Sale* (1939), but, more generally, Browning's films tend to inscribe the structure of dis/belief specific to stage magic. As Jacques Goimard contends, "far from believing that reality is an illusion, it [the cinema of Browning] would lean for the idea that illusion is a reality."[14] Charles Tesson, noting the ways that films such as *The Thirteenth Chair* (1929) and *Mark of the Vampire* (1935) deal with "the perception of things and the comprehension of inexplicable phenomena," argues, "the cinema of Browning, unique in its kind, rests on the constant affirmation of a veritable denial of belief that must not be confused with disbelief."[15]

Although an emphasis on *Freaks* has tended to equate Browning's work with the freak show's sheer display of malformed bodies, his films often seem more concerned with laying bare elaborate performed deceptions. I would also contend that blackface minstrelsy—in which the tacitly acknowledged identity of the performer is as important as the grotesque burnt cork mask that only partially conceals it—potentially suggests an equally fruitful intermedial paradigm for considering Browning's work. One could also certainly find a compelling biographical impetus for several key Browning themes in the horrible physical and emotional trauma suffered in a 1915 automobile accident that partially disfigured Browning's face, leaving him bedridden for several months, and killed passenger Elmer Booth, the actor who had played the Snapper Kid in Griffith's *The Musketeers of Pig Alley* (1912) (Skal and Savada, 47–50).[16]

The crucial aspect of the "Browning legend" is the continuity it implies between Browning's early sideshow experiences and a subsequent series of feature films. Attempting to render the director's films legible biographically removes attention from the stylization of the films themselves and the complex set of aesthetic choices involved in each. The legend sanctions a neat biographical-critical narrative in which Browning's cinematic oeuvre becomes a belated response to his personal participation in the world of late nineteenth- and early twentieth-century popular entertainment. Read alongside Peter Wollen's version of the "auteur theory," this narrative implies that Browning is the ultimate *metteur-en-scène*, responsible merely for "transposing into the special complex of cinematic codes and channels a pre-existing

240

text"[17]—in this case, the cultural "text" of the American circus. By attributing the creative essence of such films as *The Unholy Three*, *The Unknown*, and *Freaks* to the director's previous life experiences, this biographical-critical narrative implies, in Wollen's terms, that "the meaning—semantic, rather than stylistic or expressive—of the films of a *metteur en scène* exists *a priori*" (Wollen, 78). A related consequence of the biographical impulse has been author studies of Browning that tend to privilege—again in Wollen's terms—the project of "revealing a core of meanings, of thematic motifs" with little stress upon the related area of "style and *mise-en-scène*" (Wollen, 78).

A contrasting approach to Browning is found in the perspicacious criticism of Richard Watts, Jr., longtime film critic for the *New York Herald-Tribune*. In a 1927 review of *The Unknown*, Watts identifies "preoccupations with sideshow freaks" as one feature of "Mr. Browning's methods of picture making," but links this recurrent theme with such formal and narrative choices as Browning's "avoidance of exteriors and sunlit scenes" and "love for the Grand Guignol manner in story telling"[18]—rather than to the tales of Browning's purported sideshow experiences then being circulated through articles in the popular press and MGM studio publicity. Noted as one of the few critics to review favorably Erich von Stroheim's *Greed* (1924) upon its initial release, Watts's reviews evince a protoauteurist attempt to define the styles of individual directors through mise-en-scène. In a 1931 article, Watts classified Browning as one of the few "directorial stylists" of the early sound film (along with Josef von Sternberg and Griffith), pointing to lighting as one of the hallmarks of Browning's style: "Perhaps the most characteristic feature of Browning's films is their hatred of sunlight and the open air. Grim, murky interiors where sinister shadows play menacingly and some haunting suggestion of unknown, impending doom ever is present in the form of shadows and rodents of equally macabre aspect—these are the chief materials from which he manufactures his ghostly, evil, slightly unhealthy and decidedly Poe-like narratives."[19]

Watts's conception of the film director belongs to a critical tradition that identified stylization primarily with European filmmakers; Wollen points out, "For years, the model of an author in the cinema was that of the European director, with open artistic aspirations and full control over his films" (Wollen, 77). In a 1927 article, Watts identified Browning as "an original of the cinema," favorably juxtaposing Browning's films with those of such celebrated film stylists of the 1920s as Stroheim, Ernst Lubitsch, and James Cruze:

> It has been one of the less desirable results of current cinema development that the individuality of directors is suppressed before the standardization of picture making. Lubitsch's once individual comedies are so constantly imitated that they become merely a type of film; the realistic intensity of

241

Stroheim is reflected into channels of slightly mature, but inherently conventional, romance; the gift for believable small town comedy of Cruze is wasted in routine chronicle films of the "Old Ironsides" school. Only Tod Browning stands for the moment aloof from the blandishments of imitators and the bludgeons of those who would change his intent.[20]

Placing Browning's *The Show* in a class with such examples of Continental stylization as Stroheim's *The Merry Widow* (1925), Lubitsch's *So This is Paris* (1926), and Cruze's *Beggars on Horseback* (1926), Watts positions the director—and Browning, in particular—as an individual bulwark against the standardization and imitation that characterized the studio system. Watts continues to describe Browning's originality as a function of the ways that he perverts the typical formulas of Hollywood storytelling:

> Not only in atmosphere and story, but also to a high degree in characterization, does the director's originality manifest itself. His heroes invariably break every convention of cinema virtue. In "The Show" Mr. John Gilbert beats women handily, takes money from them, is disrespectful of feminine goodness and almost strikes a blind man. He is a thief, an ingrate, and so far as you can discern, he is not especially averse to murder. And at the end, when the reform wave hits him, you can see the director standing off at one side signaling to you not to believe it. (Watts, 3)

Watts continues, "It is pleasant to note that there is no reason to think Mr. Browning is in immediate danger of becoming a director of clean-limbed photoplays" (Watts, 3), pointing to the director's plans to adapt his own original story, "Alonzo the Armless," and Tod Robbins's "Spurs" for the screen—films that would be released as *The Unknown* and *Freaks*, respectively.

As Watts suggests, the *style* of Browning's films invites comparisons with films made by European directors. Bordwell includes *The Show* among Hollywood films of the late 1920s that "dramatically use high and low angles," he says, "probably as a result of the influence of certain German films."[21] A possible relationship with Weimar cinema is also mentioned by French critic Jacques Brunius, who noted in 1929, "even when making box office pictures for the average cinemagoer he [Browning] does not conceal the fact that he is influenced by German romantic-expressionism" (quoted in Skal and Savada, 166). After completing *The Thirteenth Chair* in 1929, Browning visited Europe, where he is said to have attended the premiere of Fritz Lang's *Woman in the Moon* (1929) and visited the set of Josef von Sternberg's *The Blue Angel* (1930).[22] With its evocations of F. W. Murnau's *Nosferatu* (1922), *Dracula* is perhaps the Browning film most clearly "influenced" by German cinema. According to Edgar Ulmer (who worked with him), "Browning had been perhaps the first to see what were called, at the time, 'Fantasy' films, which were made in Germany and in Sweden."[23] Thus, Browning's possible familiarity not only with German cinema, but also with Swedish cinema raises interesting questions about another axis of influence that may have shaped the style of his films. By privileging German national cinema and the so-called "expressionist" style, film historiography has underestimated the impact that Swedish and Danish filmmakers had on American cinema of the 1920s.

The *setting* of Browning's sideshow films suggests a connection to the work of several Scandinavian filmmakers. *The Unholy Three*, *The Show*, and *The Unknown* are sometimes paralleled with Browning's early biography, yet these films might usefully be placed in historical relation to a contemporaneous cycle of Hollywood circus films that was largely the work of European directors. Graham Petrie points to Sjöström's *He Who Gets Slapped* (1924) and Christensen's *The Devil's Circus* (1926) as key films in this cycle of émigré-directed films, which involve "a vulnerable heroine, sexual jealousy and a climactic moment in which the circus props . . . are used to settle accounts with sexual rivals."[24] Both *The Show* and *The Unknown* clearly fit Petrie's description, and both were produced at MGM around the same time Christensen and Sjöström were making films for the studio. Like *Freaks*, both films are conspicuously set not in America, but in Europe. According to the recollections of Mrs. William S. Hart, Sr. (one of a small group of people who claimed to have known Browning well), Browning and Sjöström were fairly close friends during the time Sjöström lived in Hollywood.[25] The cycle described by Petrie could be expanded to include other émigré-directed circus films, including Michael Curtiz's *The Third Degree* (1926), Herbert Brenon's *Laugh, Clown, Laugh* (1928), and Murnau's lost *Four Devils* (1929). Unlike such films as Griffith's *Sally of the Sawdust* (1925) or Charles Chaplin's *The Circus* (1928), which depict the canvas-enclosed realm around the big top as a benign refuge for the individual social misfit, in this "foreign" cycle, the circus is a hazardous place that offers no possibility of social redemption.

The affinities between Browning's sideshow films and the work of several European filmmakers suggest another means of reframing the "Browning legend." In an analysis of the careers of European émigrés who worked within the American studio system, Thomas Elsaesser emphasizes the ways that their identities as filmmakers were constructed along specific lines: "Other directors of European origin also promoted themselves as more or less subtle versions of national stereotypes. One thinks of Chaplin or Hitchcock, and in a lesser register of Dieterle, who affected the wearing of immaculate white gloves on the set during the shooting of his 1930s films. The Hollywood publicity machine ensured not only that the private self could be consumed as myth, but also that it was a highly coded and thus immediately recognizable myth."[26] This self-conscious and readily identifiable notion of "the European" extended also to the settings and themes of their films, as Elsaesser points out:

> Once arrived in the United States, Lubitsch, along with other "name" émigrés who came to Hollywood with an international reputation, realized that for the New World, they were representative of the Old World. They found Hollywood hungering for images of a Europe fashioned out of nostalgia, class difference, and romantic fantasy. Obliged to recreate and imitate a version of the world they had left behind, directors found their previous work in Germany little help in fashioning an American career. In this context, Vienna became an important reference point, the master sign and key signifier of "Europe" to America, comparable only to the function of Paris in this regard. (Elsaesser, 111–12)

Elsaesser argues that quasifictional settings such as "Vienna" and "Paris" were especially congruent with the mythmaking of the American cinema: "The secret affinity that existed between Hollywood on one side and Vienna or Paris on the other was that they were societies of the spectacle, cities of make-believe and the show" (Elsaesser, 112). Given this claim, one might treat Browning as an "émigré" whose identity as a filmmaker was constructed around his origins not in another country, but instead in a parallel (and more exoticized) form of entertainment—the sideshow. The highly constructed image of Browning as a former tent-show entertainer dovetails nicely with the mise-en-scène of some of the films he directed at MGM during the 1920s and early 1930s. Like the personas adopted by a number of European émigrés, this identity provided a certain critical distance from the Hollywood system. By being *of* the "sideshow"—and not *of* "Hollywood"—Browning could freely call upon elements drawn from the former realm of spectacle in reorienting the narratives of his Hollywood film productions.

The apparent symmetry between Browning's biography and filmography—along with the sheer paucity of reliable biographical information about the director—has drawn considerable attention to Browning's early professional life in itinerant entertainment. The "Browning legend" tends to try to resolve the critical enigmas posed by Browning's films with select biographical details from Browning's early professional life. It is these former critical enigmas that demand further—and more nuanced—attention both to Browning's biography and the form and content of his films. What, for instance, was Browning's relation to particular European filmmakers such as Sjöström, and to European cinema more generally? What do the surviving films like *The Wicked Darling* (1919) and fragments of *The Exquisite Thief* (1919) reveal about the roots of Browning's unique approach to lighting? What elements of his film practice might Browning have derived from Swedish and/or Danish cinema of the

Teens? What do films such as *West of Zanzibar* and *The Thirteenth Chair* indicate about Browning's relation to Broadway? What impact did a 1929 visit to Ufa have upon Browning's filmmaking style? What do lost films such as *Puppets* (1916) and *The Big City* (1928) suggest about Browning's relation to modernist movements in theater and dance? What do such international and intermedial contexts add to an understanding of *Freaks*? These and other questions point to alternative ways of combining aesthetic analysis with biographical research, and thus productively reframing the "Browning legend."

notes

1. Rachel Adams, *Sideshow U.S.A.: Freaks and the American Cultural Imagination* (Chicago: University of Chicago Press, 2001), 65. I would like to thank David Gerstner, Janet Staiger, and Oliver Gaycken for their helpful comments on this chapter.
2. Patrick Brion, "Une vie dans le fantastique," *Cahiers du Cinéma*, no. 550 (October 2000): 84–5.
3. David J. Skal and Elias Savada, *Dark Carnival: The Secret World of Tod Browning, Hollywood's Master of the Macabre* (New York: Anchor Books, 1995); hereafter cited in text.
4. On Browning's relation to melodrama, see Oliver Gaycken, "Tod Browning and the Monstrosity of Hollywood Style," in *Screening Disability: Essays on Cinema and Disability*, ed. Christopher R. Smit and Anthony Enns (Lanham, MD: University Press of America, 2001), 81–3.
5. David Bordwell, *The Films of Carl-Theodor Dreyer* (Berkeley: University of California Press, 1981), 9; hereafter cited in text.
6. Robert C. Allen and Douglas Gomery, *Film History: Theory and Practice* (New York: McGraw-Hill, 1985), 93–104; hereafter cited in text.
7. The Biographer, "The Personal Side of the Pictures," *Reel Life* (July 25, 1914): 19.
8. "Tod Browning," *Motion Picture News* 23, no. 1 (December 25, 1920): 212.
9. Joan Dickey, "A Maker of Mystery: Tod Browning Is a Specialist in Building Thrills and Chills," *Motion Picture Classic* 27, no. 1 (March 1928): 80.
10. Personality files, Film Department, Museum of Modern Art, New York.
11. A Carnival Man, "Graft Death-Blow to Carnivals," *Show World* 2, no. 22 (May 23, 1908): 1.
12. Janet M. Davis, "'Instruct the Minds of All Classes': The Circus and American Culture at the Turn of the Century" (Ph.D. dissertation, University of Wisconsin, Madison, 1998), 61–73.
13. Matthew Solomon, "Stage Magic and the Silent Cinema: Méliès, Houdini, Browning" (Ph.D. dissertation, University of California, Los Angeles, 2001), 188–230.
14. Jacques Goimard, "Le jour où les maudits prirent la parole," *L'Avant-Scène du cinéma*, no. 264 (March 15, 1981): 6, translation mine.
15. Charles Tesson, "Le monstreux sentiment de l'espèce humaine," *Trafic*, no. 8 (Autumn 1993): 58–9, translation mine.
16. Perhaps intoxicated, Browning was driving the vehicle when it collided with a railroad car in the middle of the night. See also "Investigating Ride to Death," *Los Angeles Times* (June 17, 1915): sec. 2, p. 1 and "Real Tales About Reel Folk," *Reel Life* 4, no. 24 (August 29, 1914): 18.
17. Peter Wollen, *Signs and Meaning in the Cinema*, 3rd ed. (Bloomington: Indiana University Press, 1972), 78; hereafter cited in text.
18. Richard Watts, Jr., "Mr. Tod Browning Continues His Grand Guignol Exploits," *New York Herald-Tribune*, (June 19, 1927): n.p., clipping, Billy

Rose Theatre Collection, New York Public Library for the Performing Arts.

19. Richard Watts, Jr., "The Directorial Stylist—Has He Passed from the Picture?" *Motion Picture Classic* 102, no. 13 (March 28, 1931): 95.

20. Richard Watts, Jr., "A Glance at Tod Browning, An Original of the Cinema," *New York Herald-Tribune* (March 20, 1927): sec. 6, p. 3; hereafter cited in text.

21. David Bordwell, "The Classical Hollywood Style, 1917–1960," in *The Classical Hollywood Cinema: Film Style and Mode of Production to 1960* (Routledge & Kegan Paul), 7.

22. "Mystery Film Director," *New York Times* (November 24, 1929): sec. 10, p. 8.

23. Edgar G. Ulmer, "Entretien avec Edgar G. Ulmer," interviewed by Bernard Eisenschitz and Jean-Claude Romer, *Midi-minuit fantastique*, no. 13 (November 1965): 10, translation mine.

24. Graham Petrie, *Hollywood Destinies: European Directors in America, 1922–1931* (London: Routledge & Kegan Paul, 1985), 197.

25. Vivian Sobchack, "Tod Browning: Raising the Dead, or the Film Historian as Archaeologist" (unpublished paper, University of California, Los Angeles, 1974), 28, 38, citing author's interview of Mrs. William S. Hart, Sr., May 13, 1974.

26. Thomas Elsaesser, "Ethnicity, Authenticity, and Exile: A Counterfeit Trade? German Filmmakers and Hollywood," in *Home, Exile, Homeland: Film, Media, and the Politics of Place*, ed. Hamid Naficy (New York: Routledge, 1999), 113; hereafter cited in text.

robert stigwood

producer, author, text

m i c h a e l   d e A n g e l i s

> Called the Ultimate Hollywood Party, it was a super-bash of such propor-
> tions that it may never be equaled, even in a bigger-than-life town known
> for always trying to outdo itself. . . . Like the movie itself, it was a party for
> young and old alike. At one point, pop superstar Peter Frampton could be
> seen dancing near ex-vaudeville star George Burns.[1]

With over 100 past and present stars of the music industry attending
and participating, all of whom were flown to Hollywood for the occasion, the $500,000 megaevent described above set the stage for the final
scene of *Sgt. Pepper's Lonely Hearts Club Band*, an elaborate narrative
fantasy rendition of the Beatles classic starring current recording superstars Frampton and the Bee Gees. Premiering on American screens in
the late summer of 1978, the $12–million production demonstrated,
among other things, the superlative tendencies and marketing savvy of
megaproducer Robert Stigwood. For the past 15 years, Stigwood
proved himself to be an enterprising and trendsetting force in the
British and American popular culture industries, through his early

associations with Beatles' manager Brian Epstein, sole management of the 1960s groups Cream and the Bee Gees, sponsorship of glam rocker David Bowie in the early 1970s, and producer of the original stage productions *Hair, Oh! Calcutta!, Pippin,* and *Jesus Christ Superstar.*

Besides the success of such past projects individually and collectively, Stigwood had also become a master of finesse in effecting the concept of what the 1970s press would describe as "crossover," a synergistic (and, at the time, fairly recent) phenomenon in which the success of a project in one media form could function as tried-and-true promotional hype for another version of the same project in a different medium. If the strategy worked well in *Jesus Christ Superstar* (1973) and *Tommy* (1975), it catapulted in 1977 with *Saturday Night Fever.* A month before the film's Christmas release (which preceded the *Sgt. Pepper* party by a few months), one of the original Bee Gees musical compositions and the film's soundtrack double-record set were already in the top 10. This success was so unprecedented that it permitted Paramount Pictures to entice theater owners into extended booking agreements six months in advance of the anticipated release of Stigwood's next project, *Grease* (1978).[2]

Although historically the concept of film "authorship" has been applied most often to directors whose accumulated body of work evidences distinctive stylistic, formal, or thematic traits, the case of Robert Stigwood provides an insightful opportunity to analyze the workings of authorial "name brand" recognition in the realm of media production.[3] Such an analysis harbors distinctive resonances within the historical framework of the American film industry in the 1970s, when a generation of film-school-trained New Hollywood directors were earning the same status of cinematic auteurs with which *Cahiers du Cinéma* critics of the 1950s had marked earlier generations of Hollywood directors working under the studio system. As the present work will demonstrate, the mark of distinction behind the cultural force emerging from the name of Robert Stigwood operated through a subversion, effacement, and redefinition of the signatorial identity usually assigned to the director. The producer whose initials comprised two-thirds of his company name, and whose "trademarks" were amalgamation and hybridity, earned and sustained his reputation not through the development of any distinctive "style" that emerged in spite of the constraints of industry in which he worked. Rather, Stigwood became prominent as an influential media force by sustaining his ability to work within a set of prevailing industrial practices, and by carefully managing the perceived visibility of his considerable influence upon the products that would bear the stamp of his organization's name.

It was this very ability to regulate his own visibility that made Robert Stigwood and his organization so successful in the realm of another prevalent and equally well-publicized "crossover" phenomenon of the 1970s. During this period, America witnessed the increasing influence of a more visible gay culture upon the consumer behavioral patterns of the mainstream, straight-identified public. By the middle of the decade, the crossover from gay to straight culture was recognized to such an extent that advertising agencies and public relations firms could deliberate the management of a "gay style" phenomenon in terms of marketing strategy. As they did so, what they discovered to be most effective was the promotional strategy that either disavowed or effectively disguised the affiliations of specific products with their gay cultural roots.[4] With his pivotal role in converting disco into a mainstream cultural staple, and the prevalence of vulnerable masculine protagonists in the films that he produced, Stigwood directly participated in the promotion of "gay style" in the 1970s. He developed ways to structure textual ambiguities such that mainstream audiences could distance themselves from the gay origins of the products they were appropriating, while simultaneously offering reading strategies that would allow gay audiences a sense of validation and identification. He actively participated in the production of gay texts through the most viable means of demonstrating "intentionality" accessible during this historical period, structuring ambiguity in his industry products in the same way that he maintained the opacity of his own sexual identity in the eyes of the mainstream public.

Stigwood's publicly circulated professional identity emerged in sharp relief against the backdrop of new and prevailing trends in the film industry during the 1970s. Beginning in the 1960s and continuing into the next decade, declining box office receipts and rising production costs were making the major Hollywood studios increasingly vulnerable to takeover by conglomerates in order to avoid bankruptcy. During this period, executives who were fronting the money and monitoring the budgets for new film projects often had no prior affiliation with the film industry.[5] Much to the dismay of film exhibitors who were in the process of dividing up their large-screen houses, the studios were producing and releasing far fewer films than ever before, and relying upon the anticipated returns from a handful of blockbusters with larger and larger production and marketing budgets. Providing justification and momentum to the logic of this strategy was the unprecedented success of *Jaws* (1975) and *Star Wars* (1977), both of which encouraged the conglomerates to repeat the formula through sequels.[6]

By the mid-1970s, the Robert Stigwood Organization (RSO) had developed as a production company that, like the studios, was financed by conglomerates (specifically, Polygram, under the umbrella of Dutch and German conglomerates), but that operated outside of their influence, largely because of Stigwood's proven successes in the music and theater industries. The fact that the producer had sufficient funds to be able to exact "final-cut privilege" for his film productions placed him in a position of control greater than that of the studio production executives who hired him for projects.[7] The media frequently portrayed the conglomerates who owned the film studios as big-name entities who "pulled the strings" from invisible positions and consequently remained anonymous, but the name of "Stigwood" was afforded a much more personal form of reference and resonance not only because it alluded to a man behind a name, but also because of the very "human" qualities that *this* man came to embody.

A world apart from the image of the cutthroat corporate entity caught up in a seemingly endless cycle of takeovers and mergers, hirings and firings of top management, and myopic worship of the almighty dollar, Stigwood was portrayed as a skilled businessman whose concern over profits and losses would never make him lose sight of ethics and professionalism. For example, after experiencing an uncharacteristic flop with the Broadway musical *Rachel Lily Rosenbloom . . . And Don't You Ever Forget It* in 1973 (closed by Stigwood during previews), he repaid investors $650,000 "even though he was under no legal obligation to do so. He explains: 'I want to maintain credibility in the money market.'"[8] Equally crucial to his image is the notion of the "self-made man" who never compromised his ideals or his integrity to please more powerful or influential figures in the industry; among the list of celebratory appositives featured in a 1978 *Newsweek* cover story of Stigwood is "an I-did-it-my-way independent in the era of conglomerate drones."[9]

Stigwood's handling of RSO's infrastructure and his management of human resources also served to distinguish this ethical company leader from corporate anonymity. As the press would have it, Stigwood was not a bureaucratic tyrant who made (or forced others to make) rash and impulsive top-level decisions without regard for his employees. Stigwood valued trust and ran RSO "like a family firm . . . [with] a small, closely-knit team of co-workers to whom he is sugar daddy, best friend, guru and toastmaster" (Ansen, 1978, 45). If it might be inferred that such "family values" are incongruous with the role of a Hollywood "supermogul," popular press articles emphasized that Stigwood is neither a product nor an emblem of Hollywood. Instead, he developed the image of an outsider who maintains residences in a number of cities worldwide (including Beverly Hills), preferring to call home his multi-acre estate in tax-free Bermuda: "his very elusiveness—his air of mystery—may be a source of his success" (Ansen, 1978, 45).

The star discourse surrounding the name of this influential producer equally emphasizes the congruity between his treatment of company employees, his work ethic, and his decision-making practices: the common elements are sharp instinct and intuition, the ideal qualities of a leader. Accordingly, when Stigwood makes deals that might provide fodder for other less visible and more anonymous corporate heads to be labeled instantly "ruthless" or "cheap," his actions simply attest to a business savvy that ultimately permits him to conduct his own proceedings without yielding to the influence of others.[10]

Stigwood's finesse in business handlings is nowhere more evident than in his radical transformation of a genre that by the end of the 1960s had appeared to be on a permanent decline. In fact, the very unsuccessful attempts to repeat the success of the early 1960s film musical (especially *The Sound of Music*) drove studios such as Twentieth Century Fox and MGM into further financial debt and made them ripe for corporate takeover. The box office failure and universal critical invective launched at the 1973 remake of *Lost Horizon*, with original score and all-star cast, provided even greater disincentive to experiment further with the genre.[11] Using an already proven success record with pop-music management and a very reliable sense of the direction of popular musical tastes and trends, Stigwood was elevated from nameless to "signature" status by producing and promoting musical vehicles with an already demonstrated popularity geared toward a target audience through one media form. In this way, he strategically widened the audience base through a crossover transformation to film that resulted in something more than just another version of the same experience. In so doing, the producer consistently foresaw potential markets for audience expansion, as he did with the film version of *Jesus Christ Superstar* in 1973, the stage version that had initially brought his name to the attention of the American public in 1970.[12] Such a strategy was even more profitable with the narrative version of *Tommy* in 1975, which retained the entire soundtrack of The Who's hit double-album rock opera.[13]

The cinematic transformation of the stage musical *Grease* and the Beatles' *Sgt. Pepper's Lonely Hearts Club Band* were yet more intricate. Working with the nostalgia for the 1950s already evidenced in early 1970s American popular culture with *American Graffiti* (1973) and the TV sitcom *Happy Days* (1974–1984), and that was sustaining the Broadway stage version of *Grease* in a record-breaking, multiyear run, RSO significantly altered *Grease's* original musical score to include songs and narrative elements that neither required nor presupposed the audience's familiarity or experience with the historical period that provided its setting. By adding John Travolta and the hot contemporary vocalist Olivia Newton-John, the film version symbiotically drew upon and rejuvenated the success of the still-running Broadway musical.[14] According to Maxine Fox, co-producer of the musical's Broadway version, the film was "less satirical and more overtly romantic than the show"; her co-producer Ken Waissman was "relieved that the film is different. Audiences can attend the show and not feel they're seeing a carbon copy. We know from the boxoffice treasurers that people who've seen the movie are coming right over to the show."[15]

Sgt. Pepper's Lonely Hearts Club Band, RSO's second musical of 1978, synthesized the production and promotional strategies of *Tommy* and *Grease*. Like *Tommy*, it used only materials written by its primary musicians (actually, several of the Beatles later albums were represented in the soundtrack), included almost no unsung dialogue, and gathered an even wider variety of cinematic and musical performers into the mix. Like *Grease*, *Sgt. Pepper* relied on universal themes (here, the triumph of good over evil, the value of tradition, the eternal nature of love) that broadened the material's appeal in the crossover from original to film adaptation. Rather than an updating of a highly innovative musical-aesthetic artifact from the previous decade, the result was an amalgamated media product that seemed unstuck in time—except, perhaps, for its at-times psychedelic visual design, which was perfectly appropriate to the film's attempt at fantasy. "If the two irreconcilable poles of '60s movies were 'The Sound of Music' and 'Easy Rider,'" David Ansen argued, "in today's mass market the two have merged. Call it the Easy Riding Sound of Music, or 'Sgt. Pepper's Lonely Hearts Club Band'" (Ansen, 1978, 43).

"He doesn't want to make a movie for a movie's sake," explains Stigwood executive Kevin McCormick. "He's only interested in things that are commercially viable" (Schwartz, 40). Such pronouncements certainly do not represent the perspective of the American auteurs who were becoming more prominent as the 1970s progressed. Many of these, like Robert Altman, had experienced one or two noted financial successes (in Altman's case, *M*A*S*H* in 1970 and *Nashville* in 1975). Such successes, however, were interspersed with a much longer list of titles with great critical acclaim but lukewarm box office response [*Brewster McCloud* (1970), *Images* (1972), *California Split* (1973), and *Buffalo Bill and the Indians* (1975)]. Even as theories that qualified or challenged the notion of the director-as-auteur were beginning to take shape in critical and academic communities, the names of Altman, Scorsese, and Coppola rose to "author" status for their seeming adherence to a unifying and coherent vision. Their perceived demonstration of distinctive formal/stylistic traits and their indifference to the formulaic blockbuster mentality were becoming more firmly entrenched in the conglomerate studio consciousness as the decade progressed. Stigwood's professional identity as producer (even as "independent" producer) might have disqualified him from any considerations of auteurist practices in the first half of the 1970s, even if the works that he produced had been deemed worthy of critical consideration in the first place.

Indeed, the producer received little attention in any publicly circulated discourse aside from trade publications until he "made it big" with *Saturday Night Fever* in 1977, and the semibiographical pieces devoted to Stigwood in the later 1970s are teleological constructions that center primarily upon the notion of the self-made man, all of whose past exploits point unidirectionally to the independent, multimillionaire status that he has attained. The eighty-page "Collector's Edition" *of The Official Sgt. Pepper's Lonely Hearts Club Band Scrapbook* offers one among several indications that by the late 1970s Stigwood and RSO were strategically using their six-figure party and eight-figure production budgets as marketing tools, with little objections from the popular press in publications such as *Newsweek*, in which David Ansen described *Sgt. Pepper* as "a multimillion-dollar [$12–million, to be exact] home movie."[16]

At the same time that other filmmakers of the 1970s were making their mark as film-director artists, Stigwood demonstrated his talent by his "instinctive" ability to gauge emerging public consumption trends rather than by any inherent or extrinsic aesthetic predisposition. That signatorial identity could be assigned to a producer on the basis of such instinct—at least, as long as the ultimate success of the product justified describing it retroactively in terms of "instinct"—attests to the various and often conflicting ways in which the "name" was circulating and functioning in 1970s popular culture. As Foucault explains in his analysis of authorial functions, the "aspects of an individual which we designate as making him an author are only a projection, in more or less psychologizing terms, of the operations that we force texts to undergo, the connections that we make, the traits that we establish as pertinent, the continuities that we recognize, or the exclusions that we practice."[17] Although "success" of some kind remained a universal criterion for assessing authorship potential, film discourse in the 1970s clearly tolerated more than a single prescription for how success could be attained or demonstrated in culture. The public notation of Robert Stigwood's success indicates, however, not only the breadth and elasticity in this notion of "tolerance," but also a subversion of the very processes used to obtain signatures.

In all three of the musicals that RSO produced in the mid-1970s, success is intricately interwoven with the management of the "visibility" of directors and performers. It is hardly an exaggeration that by 1977, with final-cut privilege and the ability to assemble creative teams according to his own specifications, Stigwood enjoyed much more freedom and control over film projects than most of the emerging or established directorial auteurs. Yet this liberty never dovetailed into any sense of the coherent "vision," nor did it ascribe to any single individual in the production team a primary agency of creative genius. In fact, after working with noted director Ken Russell on *Tommy* in 1975, Stigwood actively resisted hiring directors who had already established critical reputations on the basis of their stylistic distinctiveness or their thematic successes in past endeavors. Immediately after John Avildsen received an Academy Award nomination as best director for *Rocky*, Stigwood fired him from *Saturday Night Fever*—not, apparently, because Stigwood felt at all upstaged by the director's accomplishment, but because, according to *Newsweek*, Avildsen was "reshaping the script too much like a dancing 'Rocky'" (Schwartz, 40).

Stigwood replaced Avildsen with the relatively unknown John Badham, who until then had worked in the television industry, and whose only other film directorial credit was *The Bingo Long Traveling*

All-Stars and Motor Kings (1976). After Stigwood and Allan Carr repeated the same strategy for *Grease* in hiring Randal Kleiser, a 30-year-old who had worked only in television (most recently, with John Travolta in the 1976 made-for-TV film *The Boy in the Plastic Bubble*), Stigwood turned to an only slightly more experienced director for *Sgt. Pepper's*: Michael Schultz, who had worked primarily in the television and theater industries.[18]

Sometimes naive and misguided, Stigwood's strategy derived from the conviction that the individuals best suited to the position of director would be those most willing to defer their own personal visions to the already inherently hypervisible aspects of performance embedded in the musical narrative. According to this logic, style (personal or otherwise) is not something to be imposed from outside of the performance by someone with whom the audience will not directly engage as they watch the film or discuss it after leaving the theater; rather, style arises organically from specific aspects of the musical form and genre, its expression is the job of the performers, and the director's role is primarily to facilitate the performance. "There's been a lot of conjecture as to why such a relatively untried filmmaker was chosen for such a plum assignment," *Film Comment* suggests in an article on *Grease*. "Someone in the Paramount hierarchy told me that above all, [co-]producer Allan Carr wanted someone who was malleable and could work smoothly with Travolta, the prime ingredient of the package."[19] Similarly, the "prime ingredients" of *Saturday Night Fever* were Travolta and the Bee Gees. Indeed, the experience that the audience was most prompted to remember was a crowded dance floor being cleared for John Travolta to perform his elaborate disco dance to original Bee Gees tunes.[20]

If effecting such strategies undoubtedly required a high degree of maneuvering and orchestration on the part of the producer, the promotional and publicity discourses in anticipation of the films' release deflected any suspicions of production micromanagement by engaging Stigwood's devotion to experimentation, his established trust in the team he has assembled, and his belief in the values of collaboration. The *Film Comment* piece never assumes a tone of cynicism or disbelief as it assesses Kleiser's capabilities. Instead, writer Stephen Harvey highlights that the director's relaxed attitude in production allows the performers the creative freedom to develop their own styles without undue interference. Even in the case of *Sgt. Pepper*, in which the concept of "experimentation" was radically extended by the lack of experienced actors in the central roles, Stigwood's methods are portrayed as embracing, bold, and provocative means of facilitating creative collaboration. Discussing the production decisions in a *Rolling Stone* piece before the release of *Sgt. Pepper*, scriptwriter Henry Edwards explains that "the studios don't understand this picture. . . . Do you realize what Stigwood is doing? He's got a writer who never wrote a movie before. The director never directed a musical. . . . And the stars never acted before. Can you imagine what the people who produced *Earthquake* think about this?"[21] The daunting task that Edwards and director Michael Schultz faced in facilitating *Sgt. Pepper* is described as a welcome challenge and opportunity made more exciting because of how extensively it works against the grain of the production norm. Admitting that his assignment is an "impossible" task, Schultz affirms that "I am an optimist and a dreamer, and so is Stigwood. He's very *positive*, a person who believes in making magic, in making something happen out of nothing" (Zuckerman, 53). Edwards echoes this sentiment in explaining that "Mr. Stigwood eradicated the notion that there could be a 'wrong' solution. He felt he could stimulate good work by never displaying a disapproving attitude. Everyone working on 'Sgt. Pepper' felt this generosity."[22]

Audience response confirmed the accuracy of Stigwood's instincts in two of his three experiments with the musical genre in 1977 and 1978. Although *Sgt. Pepper* turned out to be a financial disaster, grossing less than $6 million in its initial 1978 run (covering barely half of its production costs), *Saturday Night Fever* and *Grease* each grossed over $30 million by the end of 1978.[23] These figures become even more noteworthy when one considers how extensively the public disavowed the reviews and critical responses, which grew less favorable with the release of each new film. In curious ways, however, even these responses reveal the integrity of Stigwood's strategic regulation of "visibility" in the production team, especially in the case of *Saturday Night Fever*. "I suspect the filmmakers didn't know exactly what kind of movie they were making," Ansen observes in his mostly favorable review of the film, "but you can bet they had a good thing going when they turned on the music and let Travolta loose. The man can boogie!"[24] If the reviews in *Time* and *The New Leader* are less forgiving of the film's flaws—especially regarding John Badham's direction—they are equally ecstatic about Travolta's accomplishments as a dancer and an actor.[25]

In the case of *Grease*, however, the strength of Travolta's performance becomes insufficient to offset the almost universal critical response that the production comprises a very weak assembly of discordant elements, none of which is effective in itself. Rather than noting how extensively Travolta stands out in the mix, the reviewers express blame, accusation, and forgiveness (or the lack thereof) for the resulting product. "One is inclined to absolve Travolta," Frank Rich decides, "since the rest of *Grease* offers abundant evidence that there was no one behind the lens capable of giving him any guidance."[26] Although the some film critics attribute its failure to the age of the performers (too old for high school students), the considerable limitations of Olivia Newton-John's acting abilities, and the weakness of the musical score, the most oft-cited flaws are the lack of a central, organizing presence and a clumsiness in visual design. Conforming to a logic that situates the role of the director as empowered *auteur* with control over the final product, the target of critical invective consequently and unsurprisingly becomes Randal Kleiser.[27]

Considering the high degree of publicity and promotion drawing attention to the producers' central role in the production process, the fact that Stigwood's name (and, to a lesser degree, Allan Carr's in *Grease*) is largely excluded from the network of responsibility for the quality of these musicals evidences the historical prevalence of a tightly closed system that intertwines the functions of critic and director. As Barthes explains, "To give a text an Author is to impose a limit on that text. . . . Such a conception suits criticism very well, the latter then allotting itself the important task of discovering the Author . . . beneath the work: when the Author has been found, the text is 'explained'—victory to the critic. Hence, there is no surprise in the fact that . . . the reign of the Author has also been that of the critic."[28] In the text of Robert Stigwood, however, authorial signature remains more complexly susceptible to erasure and reinscription, distinctively arranged as a curious game of hide-and-seek. His name appears primarily in discussions that mark him as profound and distinctive in his approach to the role of producer, especially when this approach ultimately yields profits, yet it disappears almost entirely in the discussion of the quality of the final work produced.

This facility to regulate one's own absence and presence clearly affords great cultural power and currency to the producer, who becomes, in effect, the author who cannot function as Author, and whose directors are rendered no more capable of assuming that function. Even the fact that most critical accounts of *Grease* and *Sgt. Pepper* ultimately "write off" the films as chaotic and incoherent texts reinforces the producer's power. Indeed, if the contributions of those involved in a specific production process are intertwined to the extent that the narrative text itself becomes indecipherable, this level of "noise" is taken to an extreme in Stigwood productions.[29] Here, the question becomes not what can be ruled out as noise that disrupts consistency and coherence in the encoding of meaning, but, rather, what specifically is *not* noise in the amalgamated production?

The emergence of the producer whose works are models of amalgamation and hybridity, and who has perfected an elaborate hide-and-seek strategy of manipulating authorial signature, thereby freeing himself from the burdens of intention and accountability in the production process, correlates directly with a cultural-economic phenomenon that was occurring at the same historical moment as this producer's greatest successes in the film industry—namely, the crossover of what contemporary critics would call "gay style" from the subculture into mainstream culture. By the mid-1970s, the fashion and recording industries were recognizing the seemingly unlimited marketing possibilities inherent in gay culture's potential and already demonstrated influence upon mainstream cultural tastes. At the same time, these industries came to acknowledge the considerable cultural and economic clout that gay consumers harbored. Careful to avoid any association with the still potentially alienating label of "gay," however, the culture industries developed elaborate strategies to mask any inherent or constructed notion of "gay origin" in their promoted products, preferring instead to introduce them in contexts with which straight-identified consumers would recognize and identify.

As early as 1975, American critics and historians had begun to notice an increased visibility of gay images and characterizations in the products of the Hollywood film industry as well, along with the narrative strategies that this industry was developing to avoid any accusations of alignment with gay culture. In this context, the problem of authors' "visibility" in the production process connects with a subculture's struggle to emerge from invisibility. As Alexander Doty notes, "For queer people on all sides of the camera . . . the problem of expressing ourselves from our positions as invisible and "oppressed" sexual cultures within a hypervisible straight culture offers a compelling parallel to auteurist notions that certain studio directors expressed their unconventional views by developing oppositional practices within conventional production and narrative models."[30]

Even if 1970s cultural discourse never situates Robert Stigwood in any fixed position within this historically specific schema of gay subculture's emergence, his manipulation of the "place" of the author correlates with a remarkable ability to disguise notions of sexual identity and identification. At the same time, the case of Stigwood illuminates the pratfalls inherent in any attempt to stabilize identity, intention, or influence in the production process, especially in 1970s popular culture. Certainly, biography and discourse about the author's "personal" life either identify Stigwood as "gay" or offer sufficient ambiguity to question that he was exclusively straight-identified. Arguing that "it was gay managers, and their friends in fashion and media, who were chiefly responsible for creating the image of British youth culture that was being sold around the world" in the 1960s, noted music-industry manager Simon Napier-Bell matter-of-factly includes Stigwood in a lengthy list of influential and successful gay managers of musical talent.[31] *Newsweek's* description of the man "who travels in circles of fashionable androgyny and pals around with rock 'n' rollers," and who "has assembled a small, closely knit team of co-workers . . . [who] tend to be young, attractive, and fanatically loyal," maintains the ambiguity in Stigwood's sexuality, even as it neglects to mention that all of these co-workers, in 1978 at least, were male (Ansen, 1978, 45–6). Tony Schwartz supports the ambiguity of the producer's sexual identity by explaining that Stigwood "has never been married and centers his social life around a surrogate family made up of those he works with" (Schwartz, 50). The most emphatic testament to a version of Stigwood as at least not-exclusively-straight-identified arises, however, not from biographical discourse, but from an unnamed RSO executive commenting upon the practices of his organization in 1975: "The

Stigwood Organization markets gayness, but the product it markets is a lot less gay than the Stigwood Organzation is. We know the secret of broadening gayness so that it sells to straights. And that's really what you're after, isn't it? How gayness is penetrating the marketplace in ways straights can't even identify. . . . Our productions do very well for the most part—we've helped put gays out there as a market like women and blacks now, but you can't say that yet."[32]

Various elements within the films clearly support the notion that RSO's productions strategically engaged in constructions of ambiguity that made "gayness" visible even in its unrecognizability. The most blatant cases of this phenomenon involve the objectification of the male body. Especially after the hero of *Tommy* emerges cured from his deaf, dumb, and blind cocoon, for example, the camera relentlessly seeks out new opportunities to reveal, survey, and scrutinize the contours of Roger Daltrey's firm, well-muscled, bare-chested frame as it climbs mountains, splashes in waterfalls, walks through fire, and dazedly alights from an LSD-injected sarcophagus. *Saturday Night Fever*, whose narrative trajectories are almost hyperheterosexual, reveals even more of the body of buff John Travolta, shown tight-underwear-clad in accentuating low-angle shots, or posing before his bedroom mirror in various states of dress and undress. In the opening third of the film, at least, Tony (Travolta) is defined by his obsession with personal appearance—an unashamedly narcissistic obsession with purchasing that perfect shirt and dressing himself up in napkins at the family dinner table to avoid unsightly spaghetti sauce stains. With respect to gender identification and desire, RSO productions provide equal-opportunity hero worship for their protagonists and their audiences. Full-color posters of Bruce Lee, Al Pacino, and Farrah Fawcett-Majors grace the walls of Tony's bedroom, and he fantasizes about his resemblance to Pacino. Tony himself becomes the idol of both the men and women in his cohort of friends that accompany him on pilgrimages to the discotheque.

If such narcissism and idolatry ever appear to push the narratives too dangerously close to the edges of "permissible" representation in a context that maintains itself as straight-identified, the effect is tempered, and paradoxically enhanced by less risky means, through constructions of male vulnerability. *Grease* distances itself from its own tough-guy references and excessive macho posing by presenting a lead character who always verges upon emasculation, aware that his persona is overly stylized and that his body is not as strong or pretty as the jocks who receive the bulk of the high school girls' attention. For all of his macho bravado and rhythmic prancing, *Fever*'s Tony is ultimately defined by his capacity to learn to be sensitive, or at least to be perceived as such in the eyes of Stephanie (Karen Lynn Gorney), the woman who agrees to be his first female friend.

In relation to facilitating multiple perceptions of its primary male protagonist's sexuality, *Saturday Night Fever* becomes most effective, if

258

most subtle, in its representation of the various stages of enlightenment that Tony undergoes. In addition to his increased sensitivity to women, Tony comes to accept and appreciate his brother's decision to leave the priesthood; he also demonstrates broadened perspectives on race and ethnicity, learning to understand the futility of the gang-war pranks that he has been accustomed to staging with his friends, and recognizing the talents of the Puerto Rican couple who, he decides, are more deserving of the first-place trophy in the dance contest than he and Stephanie. In the context of these transformations, the film's means of representing homosexuality are rather ingenious. That is, the only gay characters in the film are a couple of effeminate men who have the misfortune of crossing paths with Tony and his male friends on the street. They are greeted with jeers and insults from all except Tony, whose conspicuous silence and lack of participation enhance the sense that he has risen above the arbitrary pettiness that pits one group against the other. On the dance floor, however, the film extends this sense of acceptance of human diversity to groups that differ widely in age, race, and ethnicity, but not sexuality—in this local Brooklyn discotheque, men dance with women, except in Tony's case, in which a rehearsed perfection of style also permits him to dance alone. As such, for straight-identified audiences, the film disavows any recognition of the fact that the musical form it so strategically exploits holds its origins in gay clubs.[33] Still, this rather conspicuous omission becomes yet one more testament to the finesse of Stigwood and RSO, as the film's exploitation of the phenomenon sanctioned disco as acceptable for the straight-identified masses.[34]

It is perhaps most appropriate that a musical form representing the apex of amalgamation—in its sampling of other styles, and its use of the most hybridizing of all instruments, the synthesizer—should become the vehicle for the success of a producer who for over ten years had developed such skill at orchestrating, regulating, and displacing authorial signature in the production process. The accomplishment is yet more remarkable in light of Stigwood's ability to reshape into an almost universally acceptable musical phenomenon (until the "Disco Sucks" rallies later in the decade, at least) an aspect of the disenfranchised subculture with which he was provisionally aligned. In spite of his adherence to prevailing cultural attitudes regarding the status of this subculture, Stigwood proved himself able to define and rework the very strategies that rendered it invisible, shaping ambient noise into something quite harmonious, for accountants as well as audiences.

259

notes

1. Pressbook for *Sgt. Pepper's Lonely Hearts Club Band* (New York: Val Ventures, Inc., 1978), 14.
2. "Travolta's 'Fever' Infects 'Grease' Booking in May," *Variety* (January 25, 1978): 1.

3. Among the most notable book-length studies of producers as auteurs are George Custen's rich biographical work, *Twentieth Century's Fox: Darryl F. Zanuck and the Culture of Hollywood* (New York: Basic Books, 1997) and Thomas Schatz's groundbreaking analysis of production practices in an industrial context, *The Genius of the System: Hollywood Filmmaking in the Studio Era* (New York: Henry Holt & Company, 1988).

4. In the 1970s such strategies were described in terms of "window advertising." See Karen Stabiner, "Tapping the Homosexual Market," *The New York Times* (May 2, 1982): sec. 6. For a more extensive discussion of this phenomenon and its use in the film industry, see Michael DeAngelis, *Gay Fandom and Crossover Stardom: James Dean, Mel Gibson, and Keanu Reeves* (Durham, NC: Duke University Press, 2001), 131–46.

5. Although film trade publications, business weeklies, and popular news magazines explicated and bemoaned this phenomena throughout the early 1970s, a particularly enlightening overview and discussion of the transition from "movie mogul" to conglomerate enterprise can be found in Robert Lindsey, "The New Tycoons of Hollywood," *The New York Times Magazine* (August 7, 1977): 12–23.

6. By the end of 1977, 31 weeks after its premiere, *Star Wars* had grossed over $56 million for Twentieth Century Fox. The studio's second largest box office gross at the time was *Julia*, with $2.6 million after eleven weeks ["50 Top-Grossing Films," *Variety* (December 28, 1977): 9]. At the same moment, *Star Wars* and *Jaws* were in first and second place for all-time rentals to distributors ($127 million and $121 million, respectively), each 50% higher than the third-place *The Godfather* (1972) and fourth-place *The Exorcist* (1973). Only one film in the top five—*The Sound of Music* (1965) had been produced before 1972 [*Variety* (January 4, 1978): 25].

7. Tony Schwartz, "Stigwood's Midas Touch," *Newsweek* (January 23, 1978): 40; hereafter cited in text.

8. "A Man to Whom the Angels Flock," *Fortune* (June 1977): 44.

9. David Ansen, "Rock Tycoon," *Newsweek* (July 31, 1978): 41; hereafter cited in text.

10. For example, Stigwood purchased the rights to the song "Disco Duck" for $3,500 and earned a huge profit. With the help of Allan Carr, who would be his co-producer for *Grease*, Stigwood also purchased a low-budget Mexican exploitation film on cannibalism among the survivors of a plane crash in the Andes mountains. He dubbed it, renamed it *Survive*, and filled American screens in the summer with the result. See "Supermogul In the Land Of Opportunity," *Forbes* (July 10, 1978): 42.

11. *Doctor Doolittle* (Richard Fleischer, 1967), *Star!* (Robert Wise, 1968), *Hello, Dolly!* (Gene Kelly, 1969) all lost money for Twentieth Century Fox. The financial failure of *Goodbye, Mr. Chips* (Herbert Ross, 1969) resulted in a change of studio heads at MGM.

12. Molly Haskell, "J. C. Superstar Enterprises, Inc.," *Saturday Review* (October 30, 1971): 65–7, 82.

13. A few additional Who-composed songs were added to fill in the narrative gaps. Stigwood supplemented a cast headed by lead singer Roger Daltrey with a smattering of contemporary vocal talent (Elton John and Tina Turner) and film celebrities whose lack of musical abilities hardly interfered with their demonstrated cultural currency (Jack Nicholson, Ann-Margret, and Oliver Reed).

14. Travolta was a proven success through both the recently released *Saturday Night Fever* and the high-school slacker persona of Vinnie Barbarino that he had perfected in *Welcome Back, Kotter*.

15. Richard Hummler, "'Grease' Film Spurs B.O. for B-way Original," *Variety* (July 19, 1978): 107.

16. Robert Stigwood and Dee Anthony, *The Official Sgt. Pepper's Lonely Hearts Club Band Scrapbook* (New York: Pocket Books, 1978), 42.

17. Michel Foucault, "What Is an Author?," in *The Foucault Reader*, trans. Josué V. Havari, ed. Paul Rabinow (New York: Pantheon Books, 1984), 110.

18. Schultz had also recently directed *Cooley High* (1975), *Car Wash* (1976), and *Which Way Is Up?* (1977).

19. Stephen Harvey, "Eine Kleiser Rockmusik," *Film Comment* 14 (July–August 1978): 15.

20. Stigwood's elaborate promotional strategies for the film confirm the primacy of the dramatic and musical performers and performances. Five months before the film's release, Paramount negotiated a deal with National Screen to sell posters to both exhibitors and the public, featuring only the figure of the dance-floor-posed Travolta; see Addison Verrill, "Par, Nat'l Screen Riding U. S. Film Poster 'Boom,'" *Variety*, July 6, 1977, 4. Shortly before the film's release, RSO exhibited a three-minute trailer as a means of selling already-available soundtracks. The album cover appeared at the end of the trailer; see Todd Everett, "Trailers, Teasers vs. Screen Clutter," *Variety* (December 7, 1977): 67, 72.

21. Ed Zuckerman, "Sgt. Pepper Taught the Band to Play, and Stigwood's Gonna Make It Pay," *Rolling Stone* (April 20, 1978): 53; hereafter cited in text.

22. Henry Edwards, "Inventing a Plot for Sgt. Pepper," *New York Times* (July 16, 1978): sec. 2, p. 26.

23. Sales of singles and soundtrack albums made the returns significantly higher than $30 million, but even in considering grosses alone, *Saturday Night Fever* and *Grease* only shortly lagged behind *Close Encounters of the Third Kind*, the highest grossing American film of 1978.

24. David Ansen, "The Boogie Man," *Newsweek* (December 19, 1977): 65.

25. Frank Rich, "Discomania," *Time* (December 19, 1977): 69–70; Robert Asahina, "Slipped Disco," *The New Leader* (January 16, 1978): 24–5.

26. Frank Rich, "Black Hole," *Time* (June 19, 1978): 79. Stanley Kauffmann's review is similarly negative yet "forgiving" of Travolta's considerable attempts to rise above the quality of the production; see "Fin and Fantasy," *New Republic* (July 1, 1978): 18–19.

27. Rich suggests that "camera work is film school simple, and movement within shots does not even reach the levels we are accustomed to in TV, whence Kleiser sprang or, more properly, stumbled." In his scathing review of the film, John Simon observes that "Randal Kleiser's direction succeeds in making proliferation look lackluster, and frenzy, routine; see "Dog-Day Distemper," *National Review* (July 21, 1978): 908.

28. Roland Barthes, "The Death of the Author," *Image-Music-Text*, trans. Stephen Heath (New York: Hill and Wang, 1977), 147.

29. For a discussion of "noise," see Peter Wollen, *Signs and Meaning in the Cinema*, 2nd ed. (Bloomington: Indiana University Press, 1972), 104–5.

30. Alexander Doty, *Making Things Perfectly Queer: Interpreting Mass Culture* (Minneapolis: University of Minnesota Press, 1993), 26.

31. Simon Napier-Bell, *Black Vinyl, White Powder* (London: Ebury Press, 2001), 77.

32. John Lombardi, "Selling Gays to the Masses," *Village Voice* (June 30, 1975): 10.

33. On the roots and origins of disco, see Jamake Highwater, "Dancing in the Seventies," *Horizon* (May 1977): 30–3.

34. For an enlightening discussion of *Saturday Night Fever*'s central role in disco mass marketing, see Jesse Kornbluth, "Merchandising Disco for the Masses," *New York Times*, Sunday Magazine section (February 18, 1979): 18, 21–4, 44–5.

making films

asian american

fourteen

shopping for fangs

and the discursive

auteur

sarah projansky and kent a. ono

Few in contemporary film studies continue to write of the auteur, or filmmaker, as the originary and privileged location of a text's meaning. The advent of poststructuralism, the publication of key essays in film studies and in critical theory generally about the death of the author, and the emergence of spectatorship, reader-response, and audience studies have rendered it difficult (for some), if not impossible (for many), to emphasize (or even include) the author in any discussion of an author–text–reader triad. Despite the fact that film studies scholars, for the most part, now avoid modernist auteurship studies, in this chapter we study the author-function in relation to one film as a way of questioning the complete abandonment of the study of the author. Through analysis of media discourse about an independent film [*Shopping for Fangs* (1997)] and about the film's writers/directors (Quentin Lee and Justin Lin), and through analysis of our own unpublished interviews with Lee, we argue that the study of cinema profitably includes an understanding of the filmmaker's role as social subject. We also argue, however, that this critical focus makes sense only if it includes an examination of the author-function, or the production of the auteur in various public discourses about a particular filmmaker and her or his film, including discourses produced by the filmmaker herself or himself.

Although we (like many others, including Quentin Lee) would argue that textual meaning does not reside principally with the auteur, the filmmaker does exist, often produces discourse about her or his film, is often seen as the origin of textual meaning by members of the press and by the audience, is a subject positioned in particular ways in relation to the larger culture, and is a laborer within a global capitalist economy that continually masks the relationship between workers and products. In relation to Asian American cinema generally and Lee, Lin, and *Shopping for Fangs* specifically, historical and social processes, economic standing, immigrant status, racialization, gendered power, and sexuality all also frame and position the filmmaker.

If we focus not on languages and logics as artifacts of historical Western modern processes, but on what cultural studies scholars have termed "everyday life" or culture as "ordinary," we begin to recognize the positioning of the filmmaker as a particular subject within discourse. Indeed, we can see auteurs discursively as Michel Foucault encourages scholars to in his essay "What Is an Author?" that is "according to their modes of existence. The modes of circulation, valorization, attribution, and appropriation of discourses vary with each culture and are modified within each."[1] In this chapter we ask the following questions in relation to Lee, Lin, and *Shopping for Fangs*: What is the mode by which the auteur circulates as discourse? What is the mode by which the auteur is valorized in discourse? What is the mode by which attributions of origination are conferred onto the auteur? And what is the mode by which the auteur is appropriated within discourse?

We answer these questions by focusing on constructions of Asian Americanness—in critical scholarship (including our own), in the popular press, and in Lee's and Lin's own statements as writers/directors of *Shopping for Fangs*. After briefly discussing scholarship that helps us reclaim and reconstruct the concept of the author-function as having the potential to be analytically and politically useful, we discuss popular press discourse about Lee, Lin, and a particularly unproductive essentialized and racialized author-function, as well as Lee's negotiation with this author-function that we see taking place in his statements about himself as filmmaker. We develop this analysis by examining discourses about Lee and Lin as filmmakers, about the production and distribution of the film, and about the text of the film itself, in turn. Throughout, we argue that all these discourses construct *Shopping for Fangs* and the filmmakers as Asian American (albeit in multiple and sometimes contradictory ways); hence, our title: "Making Films Asian American." Arguably, Foucault's critique of the centrality of the author in a particular historical period can be understood to encourage this kind of analytic practice, one that regards large discursive processes as having systemic and particular effects within culture.

reconstructing the author-function

Contemporary Asian American film studies scholarship has begun to address the role of the author in ways that challenge both traditional modern humanist tenets and the absolute death of the author. For example, Peter X. Feng theorizes, complicates, and embraces a concept of identity in his essay "In Search of Asian American Cinema." Feng problematizes the term "Asian American," pointing to the diversity of cultures and nations contained within the term (e.g., Pakistani, Indian, Chinese, Japanese, Korean, Vietnamese, Laotian, Cambodian, Thai, Filipino), as well as the important historical differences that might affect identity formation. For example, Feng asks, "Have Korean Americans who have arrived since the Seventies found a place in American culture akin to that of the Korean immigrants who worked the sugar cane fields in the early part of [the twentieth] century?"[2]

Having problematized "Asian American" as a singular identity, Feng nevertheless goes on to discuss definitions of Asian American cinema that very much depend on a concept of identity. He suggests that although the definition needs to stay in flux, Asian American cinema can be defined as films made by Asian Americans or films about Asian Americans or, as filmworker Judi Nihei argues, films that tell "Asian American stories through the eyes of Asian American filmmakers" (quoted in Feng, 35). Importantly, Feng bases a great deal of his discussion of what Asian American cinema is on interviews with various Asian American filmmakers, writers, and actors, such as Nihei. Unlike for the popular press, which, as we argue presently, expresses a pervasive racialized scopophilic gaze at Asian American filmmakers and Asian American films, for Feng the identity of filmmakers as Asian American has political import, in part because it affects how those filmmakers are able to secure funding, distribution, and audiences. In a later essay, "The State of Asian American Cinema: In Search of Community," Feng expands on these issues of economics, representation, and identity when he notes that Asian and Asian American filmmakers tend to cross over to relatively big-budget Hollywood pictures only when they "have either submerged their Asian identities to make films about white Americans ([Ang] Lee's *The Ice Storm* [1997]) or have added Asian 'flavor' to Hollywood films ([John] Woo's *Face/Off* [1997])."[3]

As Catherine Grant (drawing on Timothy Corrigan) argues in her essay "www.auteur.com?" in the context of contemporary "globalization" and "deterritorialization," the auteur continues to exist as a "*commercial* strategy for organizing audience reception."[4] In other words, the auteur becomes a figure that exists across multiple texts, particularly in the digital/WWW/DVD age when the actual film text itself may no longer be necessary to the construction of the auteur. Furthermore, this version of the auteur (as well as other versions) can produce "identificatory pleasures." Grant draws on various scholars to point out that these pleasures might be, for example, (1) the pleasure of being interpellated as an "expert" spectator,[5] or (2) the pleasure of using "queer cultural competencies" to read "between the lines or against the grain" (106).[6] These two kinds of pleasures may reproduce problems associated with the bourgeois "free reader" of discourse because they privilege the individual reader/consumer as the site of textual address and meaning. Nevertheless, although we would like to remain skeptical and critical of privileging individual pleasure in discussions of the auteur, what is intriguing here is the way pleasure requires the resubjectification of the reader's identity. Thus, for example, one's pleasure may derive from being addressed as a queer subject in a world in which such hailing (at least within dominant popular culture) is rare. Additionally, the development of a queer vernacular of pleasure competencies is, in fact, a social, not individual, outcome of individual rereadings of the text. Moreover, such an approach to reading encourages resistance and thus potentially opens up space for future dissident readings. Drawing on Feng's work, to Grant's list we would add a politicized pleasure that we believe we share with Feng: (3) the Asian American or Asian American-identified critic's pleasure in finding and recognizing the role Asian American identities play in the independent films Asian American filmmakers can and do make. In other words, there is a political and personal pleasure in defining the representations we see as made by and about ourselves and/or people we care about—Asian Americans.

The flight from the auteur as sanctified origin of textual meaning parallels the postmodern cultural effect of liberating products from any and all sites of production and cultural contexts. When we no longer see an artisanal link between products and humans—between garments and sweatshop laborers, between produce and migrant field laborers, between domestic work and domestic laborers—labor is alienated from the existential moment of human production and products forever circulate as exchange value versus use value. Following this admittedly neomarxist sentiment, as academics, how do we work so as not to dispossess those who are already marginalized from their "rights" to intellectual property within a culture in which the ideograph "property" sits squarely at the center of corporate-driven juridical politics?

Working from this perspective, we turn now to an analysis of two sets of discourses—popular press discussions of Lee, Lin, and *Shopping for Fangs* and our own interviews with Lee—in order to argue that key political issues are at stake in the way that the auteur is, in fact, produced by discourse. In one sense, we are affirming Foucault's argument that saying that a particular work was created by a particular author "is a speech that must be received in a certain mode and that, in a given culture, must receive a certain status" (107). Attributions of authorship function to circumscribe the reception and reading of a text. The text is already to be received in a particular way once the author of that text is announced. However, whereas Foucault's primary concern is with the way the author-function works historically to communicate the importance of a work by drawing a connection between that work and an author whose status invests the work with significance (107), our concern is with how discourse constructs authors themselves in such a way as to contain certain textual possibilities, in this case possibilities that surround queer Asian American identities as they exist in discourse.[7]

the authors: quentin lee and justin lin

The popular press discussion of Lee and Lin as writers/directors of *Shopping for Fangs* is obsessed with their racial and national identities. Each article on the film that is long enough to provide background on the filmmakers tells (at least part of) virtually the same story:[8] Lee was born in Hong Kong but raised in Canada, and Lin was born in Taiwan and raised in Orange County, California. They met when they were both students at the University of California, Los Angeles's film school (e.g., Han, Iezzi, Brian D. Johnson, Voedisch). Additional details about Lee sometimes appear: the Montreal neighborhood in which he grew up was mostly Caucasian (Adilman), he has degrees in either English or literature from the University of California, Berkeley (undergraduate) and Yale [graduate, where he specialized in "post-structuralist theory and feminist criticism" (Iezzi)] (Hong, McCarthy), he is gay (Adilman, Hong), he grew up watching 1970s horror movies (Adilman), and, as a child, he made his own horror movies with a "Super 8 and fake blood" (Iezzi, see also Chao). The few additional details about Lin discussed in the discourse include working-class background (Chao), the fact that his family owned a fish-and-chips shop (Hong) where he worked (Chao), and that he was an Eagle Scout (Hong).

This loose narrative of migration and identity reveals anxiety about fluidity and a discomfort with what has now become a predominant mode for transnational subjects: inhabiting spaces of in-betweenness and criss-crossing social and geographic global spaces. Some articles try to assuage this anxiety by identifying fixed geographic, national, ideological, and political identities for Lee and Lin. One article, for example, links geographic location to ideological identity, saying Lin has lived in the United States since he was nine and achieved the all-American label of "Eagle Scout." This article also focuses on national identity, stating that Lee is a *Canadian* citizen (Hong). Another article focuses on political identity, defining Lee and Lin simply as "Asian American" (Moran).

Other articles, though, project the anxiety about identity onto Lee and Lin. For example, Sid Adilman of the *Toronto Star* quotes Lee as saying: "When you're born in a Crown colony you know is not going to exist any more, it's tough to have a national identity. . . . It's weird for my film to be in Perspective Canada and for me to be Canadian and to live in the U.S. where I'm not accepted as American. In Canada, people say I'm not really Canadian. And when I go back to Hong Kong, people say I'm really from the West." This quotation, along with Adilman's own observation that "Lee, who looks 18 but is 26, is gay," leads Adilman to comment: "No wonder Lee is fascinated by the question of identity." Although it is Adilman, himself, who expresses fascination with various aspects of Lee's identity (producing an infantilizing reading of the Asian American body as perpetually youthful in the process), he says that it is *Lee* who is "fascinated" by identity and that this identity is evidenced in his film. Nonetheless, in Adilman's quotation of Lee above, Lee's words can be interpreted to *reject* fixed identities ("It's tough to have a national identity"), to embrace transnational identity ("born in a Crown colony you know is not going to exist any more"), and to resist being positioned nationally ("It's weird for my film to be in Perspective Canada").

The attribution of concern about identity to Lee and sometimes Lin is commonplace in articles about the film. Peter Y. Hong begins his essay by quoting Lee saying "Boxes are the problem of our era. . . . You're lesbian, I'm white and heterosexual, and he's black . . . all these identities have become essential and stifling." Rather than embracing this antibox or antiessentialist position, rather than picking up on Lee's refusal to engage "real" identities (he uses a first-person pronoun to call "himself" "white and heterosexual," and he says "you're" a lesbian to the reviewer, *Peter* Y. Hong), Hong follows this quotation with the simple sentence: "Lee is 27, a filmmaker, and gay" (perhaps just in case his readers might think Lee "actually" *is* white and heterosexual). Hong then interprets Lee's comments to mean that he and Lin "decided to make a film pushing the limits of identity politics [and that to do so] all they had to do was point a camera at people like themselves."

Although we read Lee as offering an antiessentialist poststructuralist definition of identity implicitly in popular press quotations (such as those that appear in Hong's article) and explicitly in his interviews with us (which we discuss next), when popular press articles position this perspective under the rubric of "identity politics" they contain Lee's (and sometimes Lin's) larger conceptual comments about subjectivity within a more limited concept of identity. This logic posits Lee's and Lin's presumed interest in identity as an obvious effect of their bodies having crossed fixed cultural boundaries of nationality, age, race, and sexuality. This logic goes: because they are, in fact, not white and heterosexual, any film they might make must be, in fact, about themselves (whatever else they might be).[9] The issue for us is not so much that the popular press focuses on identity as that it draws on classic essentialist and metonymic fallacies to make assumptions about the filmmakers'

sarah projansky and kent a. ono

identities, often reading identity cues off of their bodies and then connecting (their readings of) those bodies to the subjects of the filmmakers' films.

Authorship and identity issues, then, are a dominant and powerful aspect of the discourse about *Shopping for Fangs*. Not surprisingly, Lee confronts these issues in various interviews. As he points out in an interview with the National Asian American Telecommunications Association (NAATA): "As a person of color making works with and about people of color (and being gay too), there's a strange compulsion for people to believe that those particular works are autobiographical. Remember how the publisher of Maxine Hong Kingston's first novel had published *Women Warrior* under autobiography for marketing? I'm always fighting this compulsion of ethnic authenticity over fictional imagination."[10] In our own interviews with him, Lee is even more resistant to taking up a particular identity, in this case our imposition of the category "queer Asian American filmmaker." When we asked him, for example, to discuss his "dedication to addressing Asian American and queer themes" he responded by saying, "I'm not dedicated. I just want to make whatever movies I want to make whether it is Asian American or queer or whatever. I'm dedicated to making films, because I feel passionate about making and watching films. I'm not dedicated to any genre or content." Concomitantly, in the same interview, Lee rejects the idea of "intentionality." When we asked him about tensions between his own "intentions" and comments he may have heard from audience members who had viewed *Shopping for Fangs*, he said, "I'm open to other people's interpretations. I don't really care as long as they pay to see it or rent it or buy it." Thus, although from our perspective as film critics/spectators nearly all (if not all) of Lee's films do address issues of Asian diaspora, Asian American experiences, and/or queer experiences, he refuses to take these issues up in the interview as if they derive from a particular identity position, insisting in this instance that he is just "making film." Here we read Lee as taking a poststructuralist position in order to avoid attempts to define his work as representing any particular political interest.

Taking this position of representing neither this political position nor that one allows Lee great flexibility in both potentially being interpreted through any and every lens and, simultaneously, being unable to be read at all. Concomitantly contemporary global capitalism assumes that products that can be purchased by any consumer but that cannot be said to have a particular meaning for all consumers have the greatest potential for garnering a broad-based consumer group. Lee's comments about wanting to reach bigger audiences suggest an awareness of the value of not being seen as filling a particular niche; in taking a not-this-identity-nor-that-one position, however, he fails to acknowledge, accept, and thank the broader Asian American audience that is, we would surmise, his primary one.[11] In other words, his unwillingness—

at least through his words—to take up (a version of) an Asian American identity, even if it is a strategic one, different from the ones that the press and various interviewers (including us) thrust upon him, has the side-effect of minimizing the social importance, and by extension discursive existence, of the complex, varied, and fluid Asian American audience that, in fact, watches Lee's films.

Despite denying loyalty to any particular identity group, Lee's disavowal of efforts to pigeonhole him do have other useful political effects. At another point in our interviews with him, he says, "it's a postmodern world; and the author is dead as much as we have the nostalgia for him/her." Here Lee's comments point to the danger in nostalgia for a fixed author figure, whether that nostalgia comes from the mainstream press, the independent media production community (e.g., NAATA), or scholars such as ourselves writing an academic article about his work.

In addressing Lee and Lin as film "authors," then, we note that many tensions exist between and among an emphasis on the determinative quality of identity in the popular press, the interest in Asian American cinema studies on the complex effects of identity (Feng, our own work), and Lee's insistence that his films are not for particular audiences and that the "author is dead," whether he directly states it as in his interviews with us or whether the quotations the popular media use allow a reading of his perspective as poststructuralist.

One of the ironies, of course, is that to make this argument we look to statements from Lee, thus taking as a given that, poststructuralist theory aside, a socially and historically situated body named Quentin Lee exists and that body has something important to say in relation to the film *Shopping for Fangs*. A further irony is that Lee, himself, is willing to fall back on the concept of the auteur, responding to our question about Hollywood influences by mentioning his favorite filmmakers: Brian de Palma, Dario Agento, Gus Van Sant, David Cronenberg, and Wes Craven. We mention this not to suggest that Lee is uncommitted to or does not understand the concept of "the death of the author" (quite the contrary), but to point out that the concept of the author, the authorfunction, continues to operate in powerful ways, whether as a way for Lee to resist how others position him or as a way for him to express his cinematic pleasures, or as a way for us to read questions of race and sexuality through Lee as a "queer Asian American filmmaker."

270

the production/distribution context: independent versus mainstream

The author-function emerges just as powerfully in discourse about the production and distribution of *Shopping for Fangs* as it does in discourse explicitly about authorship. Not only did Lee and Lin write and direct the film, but Lee raised funds (partly through a Canada Council grant and partly through contributions from friends and family) and managed distribution, including a limited theatrical release. As a very low-budget (usually reported as less than $100,000) independent film, Lee and Lin were necessarily heavily involved in most aspects of the production and distribution.

The press reveled in the independent nature of the film,[12] emphasizing the less than $100,000 price tag (e.g., Han, G. Allen Johnson, McCarthy), sometimes mentioning "'loans' from Lee's family friends in Hong Kong" (Adilman), "Canada and the U.S." (Iezzi), and using phrases such as "shoestring production" (*Daily News*) and "shoestring budget" (Chao). Some mention that the film was "shot in a rapid-fire 21 days" (McCarthy, also see Han). Adilman praises the film for its frugality: "Another thing *Shopping for Fangs* is not—and that is a $4 million or $5 million feature, though it looks like one. Lee reluctantly reveals that it cost $150,000 to make." Julie Chao calls Lee "enterprising and persuasive" for how he acquired and used his budget. Others use the budget to critique the film, writing that the film is "hindered by the raw edges of its low budget" (Birnie) and that it has "poor production values" (Guthmann). Chao praises the film's distribution: "the film [opened] in three cities, San Francisco, New York and Los Angeles. That rare feat, commercial release of an independent film with an Asian American cast, was accomplished by Lee harassing theater chains every week for more than six months." Often, the popular press articles quote the filmmakers stating that they were able to achieve much more than their budget suggests they should have been able to do. For example, Bob McCarthy quotes Lin talking about breaking "every rule of making low-budget film. . . . We had a lot of dolly shots and locations, including a supermarket, a movie theater, a dance club, and a million-dollar house, but pulled it off because a lot of our friends were willing to help us out." And Iezzi quotes Lee saying that the shoot was "totally guerrilla."[13]

Aspects of identity emerge in the popular press's discussion of and pleasure in the production process of the film within this independent context. For instance, many articles mention the location shooting, emphasizing that it was "shot mostly in the San Gabriel Valley (L.A.'s Asian American 'burb). *Shopping for Fangs* has an edgy sense of place. Forget sushi bars. At the Go-Go Cafe, you can nurse a tapioca milk tea or chow down on spaghetti."[14] Kevin Thomas of the *Los Angeles Times* calls the location the "burgeoning and prosperous suburban Asian community of the San Gabriel Valley."[15] Writing from a seemingly more knowledgeable position, Hong discusses the San Gabriel Valley as one of several places being "transformed" by "immigrants from Asia. . . . The San Gabriel Valley's cafes and nightclubs are a kind of cultural lode star. Much of *Shopping for Fangs* uses the Go Go Cafe, a flashy Hong Kong-style late-night San Gabriel joint that serves club sandwiches and dim sum, with lots of Cantonese torch singing in the background."

Teressa Iezzi uses the location shooting as an example to show how much Lee and Lin were able to achieve within the constraints of their budget: "Violating the rules of low-budget independent filmmaking, the shoot is a location extravaganza, with 'studio' work done out of Lee's apartment. All locations, including a supermarket, a theater and a restaurant called the Go-Go Cafe, which hosted the shoot for four days, are secured within the constraints of the film's budget, i.e., largely free of charge."

The press also quotes the filmmakers on issues of identity in relation to the production of the film. For example, when discussing the Go Go Cafe, Hong quotes Lee as saying that the message of the environment of the cafe is: "It's good for you to be Chinese! You should not look at it as something that causes [an identity] crisis." Hong also quotes Lin on the film's location shooting: "In old Chinatowns, every building looks like a temple to bring in the tourists. It's nice to see a place that doesn't have to do that to thrive. It's empowering."

Overall, this discussion of the production and distribution positions the film as marginal, in part through the construction of the filmmakers as Asian Americans and the link between that identity and the location shooting in the film, but does so through praise. Like the aspects of the popular press articles that assume that any film made by Asians or Asian Americans will be about Asians or Asian Americans, this discussion takes pleasure in the virtuosity of the filmmakers' ability to work within these constraints. Only one article we found actually begins to reflect on these constraints. Chao ends her article by quoting a conversation between Lee and Lin:

> These ambitious young filmmakers have an ongoing philosophical debate on money versus art: If you're offered to do *Mighty Ducks 4*, would you do it? "I would," Lin said without hesitation. "To me, selling out is if you do *Mighty Ducks 4* through 10. But if they pay me a million dollars to do it, I would do the best I can, then take that money and make little independent films that I like. It's all a balancing act." Lee looks on skeptically. "It would be the best Mighty Duck movie of the four," Lin said.

Here, Chao represents both Lee and Lin as suspicious of the "mainstream." Even Lin, who, Chao implies, would presumably make any movie asked of him if offered a million dollars, would only do so to further the cause of "little independent films."

In our interviews with him, however, Lee expresses an altogether different perspective on the tension between independent and mainstream production contexts. First, he points out that in distributing *Shopping for Fangs* he played it "more as a hip mainstream film, but it's really an art house product." Here he acknowledges an interest in the mainstream and then reinterprets his own film—not as an example of a film to celebrate because it did so much with so little (money), as the popular press does—but as what we would call a different kind of mainstream film, an art-house film. Elsewhere in the interviews he directly states: "I want to be mainstream, and I want to make bigger and big budget films. That doesn't mean I want to make the same films everyone else is making. I want as much budget [as possible] as long as it's economically prudent; and I want as wide an audience as possible."

We would argue that this perspective is not the same as making *Mighty Ducks 4* for a million dollars. Rather, here Lee articulates a theoretical perspective on the definition of "mainstream," acknowledging that it is linked to both economics and audience. Thus, while the press celebrates Lee and Lin as Asian American filmmakers whose film is to be praised because it achieves so much (particularly capturing the implicitly "authentic" locations of the Asian Californian San Gabriel Valley) within such a small budget, Lee does not link the definition of the "mainstream" versus "independent" versus "art-house" nature of his film either to his own identity or to the identities represented in the film. Rather, he addresses the complexity of what "mainstream" means in economic and political terms, and here claims the "mainstream" for himself while simultaneously redefining it so that it does not simply mean "schlock" (i.e., *Mighty Ducks 4*).

the film: *shopping for fangs*

The popular press's overwhelming focus on identity does not disappear when it addresses the film itself. As it does with the authors and the production/distribution of the film, the press focuses almost entirely on the representation of Asian American identity in the film.[16] Most articles define the film as definitively "Asian American" through the tag line "GenerAsian X" (*Daily News*, Sherman). Some ascribe the tag to Lee, as if he invented the term (e.g., *Daily News*), while others say that Lee dislikes the term and distances himself from it (e.g., Chao). At least one review recognizes the sexual politics of the film when it calls the film "gaysian" rather than "GenerAsian X" (Birnie). Additional definitions that emphasize Asian and/or Asian American themes include: "*Shopping for Fangs* . . . play[s] upon contrasting perceptions of Asians as submissive and repressed on the one hand, or as unleashed Kung-fu masters on the other hand" (Sherman). John Anderson ascribes his reading of the film as "Asian-centric" to the filmmakers when he says "What [Lee and Lin are] after is both the making of an Asian-centric movie, and the demolishing of stereotype, both inflicted and self-imposed." Thomas (1998) seems to be working more directly with statements from the filmmakers when he writes that the film "succeeds in its makers' stated goal of projecting a postmodern Asian American sensibility that's moved beyond the immigrant experience that is the traditional heart of the Asian American cinema." Edward Guthmann praises the film for "the effort it makes to open up Asian American cinema . . . and allow for stories that aren't bound up in immigrant conflicts and cross-generational cultural clash." Similarly, Sallie Han says, "Finally, someone has made a film about Asian-Americans that contains no intergenerational conflict over dating non-Asians, no pre-med or engineering students and no MSG." In a lukewarm review, G. Allen Johnson says that "underneath it all, there's a social statement about Asians in America, though it's all a bit murky. . . . What the movie is really about . . . is identity." In a decidedly negative review, Larry Worth says that the film's "one claim to fame is an all Asian-American cast and crew." And in one review, Lynn Voedisch (mis)identifies the main characters as "Filipino and Chinese, but other characters are from all over Asia." In yet another review, Anita Gates writes: "*Shopping for Fangs* . . . may become a hit among Asian-American moviegoers because it shows hip young Asian-Americans behaving pretty much as any other hip young Americans do." This article, in particular, denies the film's fictionality and draws a base correlation between the film's representationality and reality.

Some reviews link the film to Asian and Asian American themes through their discussion of the title. For example, the *Daily News* writes: the "lycanthropy of horror films [is] a metaphor for Asian identity crisis." Anderson writes: "fangs, apparently, [is] a symbol of finding one's nature." Adilman quotes Lee as saying that "the title refers to shopping for an identity." And Amy Taubin calls the film a "tender-hearted social satire about Asian and Asian American Gen X-ers in the throes of various identity crises."

As these examples suggest, the preponderance of the reviews of the film say the film is about Asian American identity and do so in primarily stereotypical ways. Nevertheless, at least one review claims that the film "choos[es] a familiar, universal theme [of] . . . struggling through the awkward period between college and commitments" and that, as a result, the film "assert[s] that being young, Asian American or gay influences one's vision, but does not have to define it."[17] This article distances the film from Asian Americanness, implying that race "makes no difference" when universal themes are addressed. Rather than relying on stereotypes, at least this section of this review relies on race blindness. This move is simply the flip side of the more dominant obsession with Asian American identity, however, in that it claims a "fixity" for Asian American identity; it simply then separates that fixed identity from other, more "universal" identities.

One article, though, does quote Lee arguing that the film is all about *unfixing* identities: "In our culture now we tend to think of people as having fixed identities. . . . We tried to use the myths in the film to make these identities fluid again and make us question what we're really about."[18] The article goes on to say that "Lee stays true to the film's treatment of identity, casting was not race-specific and represented a pan-Asian assembly of Chinese, Filipino, Korean and Vietnamese

274

actors." Here, by quoting Lee, Iezzi is able simultaneously to address the complexity of Asian American identity and to question the very idea of a singular or fixed identity.

Ironically, the fluidity of identity in the film is apparent in the various descriptions articles provide of the main characters.[19] For example, articles identify the character Trinh as either "Vietnamese" (Soe), "blond-wigged Asian," "Caucasian-looking" (Adilman), or even "Caucasian" (*Toronto Star*). The articles do everything from revealing that Trinh and Katherine are the same person (the same actor portrays the two characters, and these two characters are, in fact, both part of the same person/body within the diegesis) to missing the link between the two so badly that the author assumes Trinh is played by an "unbilled actress" (Guthmann). Thus, collectively, the articles represent the fluid identities that the relationship between Trinh and Katherine, as well as Trinh's use of a wig and sunglasses, suggest. Individually, however, the reviews seek to pin-down Trinh's identity by naming it. Katherine is similarly fluid in the collective reviews. Although many call her a housewife, some call her "meek" and "troubled" (Sherman), some call her "disillusioned" (Anderson) or "depressed" (*Daily News*), some call her "bored" (Birnie) or even "dangerously bored" (Thomas 1997), and one calls her "frigid" (Guthmann). Although on the one hand these articles each pick up on different aspects of her characterization, on the other hand the tension between representing her as passive and victimized (e.g., meek) and representing her as disturbed and dangerous (e.g., dangerously bored, frigid) highlights the complexity of her identity. Nevertheless, that complexity comes through only when reading the reviews collectively. Individually, the reviews use one particular adjective to explain her character.

Despite this definition of the film as unfailingly tied to a fixed Asian American identity, other aspects of the reviews reveal their hipness by pointing out all the Hollywood and Hollywoodesque references they see in the film. Quentin Tarantino is an obvious connection, as the following quotation makes clear: "One glance at the poster for *Shopping for Fangs* and you make the connection. A director with a first name of Quentin, a woman pointing one big, nickel-plated handgun in your face, a guy screaming bloody murder and a poker-faced couple fluent in body language. Only this isn't Tarantino" (McCarthy). Other reviews associate Trinh and her gun with Wong Kar-wai's *Chungking Express* (1996). Another common reference is John Woo. Individual reviews also associate *Shopping for Fangs* with *Broadway Danny Rose* (1984), Todd Haynes's *Safe* (1995), "schlocky horror films" (G. Allen Johnson), Hammer studios, nighttime soaps, Jack Nicholson in *Wolf* (1994), Marilyn from the television series *Northern Exposure*, and Julie Hagerty. Many reviews mention *The Joy Luck Club* (1993) in order to distance *Shopping for Fangs* from it. The reviews also associate the film with various genres, including "new age comedy-thriller" (Worth), film noir (McCarthy), dark comedy (Thomas), horror [citing Lee: "I grew up on horror movies made in the '70s; the title is a tribute to them" (Adilman)], and "satiric thriller" (Iezzi). We would add to this list myriad references to and reworkings of what we would call a "rape film genre," particularly rape-revenge films.[20]

Overall, even when the reviews focus on intertextuality rather than on the identities of characters in the film, they do so through constructions of identity, whether through the quintessential, contemporary auteur-figure of Tarantino or through the links between characters in *Shopping for Fangs* and characters in other more well-known films. When linking the film to Asian or Asian American texts, the reviews depend on a sense that readers will "of course" see the link. Here the press takes Asian Americanness to be transparent, while simultaneously obscuring it through the discursive practice of stating but not explaining a presumed citation. More commonly, though, the reviews link *Shopping for Fangs* to non-Asian and non-Asian American texts. This move reveals the stereotypic and simplistic ways in which the reviews elsewhere discuss Asian American identity in relation to the author-function. It is as if for a moment the reviewers try to think and write through an Asian American perspective, but they have no need to maintain that perspective themselves, as it is all neatly contained by their production of the author-function in relation to the film and the filmmakers. As a result, the reviewers can fall back on their own deracialized, but implicitly white, cultural competencies by congratulating themselves for finding lots of mainstream Hollywood citations within this "quirky" independent GenerAsian X film.

conclusion

In her essay "Bad Asians: New Film and Video by Queer Asian American Artists," Eve Oishi argues that queer Asian American cinema has moved away from a relatively early focus on ethnic and racial identity to more varied topics. Whereas ethnic and racial identity was foregrounded in earlier works, "a new movement in Asian American cinema, in queer Asian American cinema, and in experimental cinema in general, particularly in their awareness and treatment of racial identity and cultural representation" is afoot.[21] The new queer Asian American cinema has broken with "older humanist approaches and the films and tapes that accompanied identity politics. [The new] works are irreverent, energetic, alternately minimalist and excessive" (B. Ruby Rich, quoted in Oishi, 225). According to Oishi, these "new makers are producing work that understands racial and sexual identities as being formed out of and in conjunction with a larger set of cultural forces" (238).

Assuming that *Shopping for Fangs* falls into Oishi's category of new queer Asian American cinema, we want to challenge the way the press continues to read the film as definitive of a transparent fixed, essentialized, and often stereotyped Asian American identity that is nevertheless obscured by lack of explanation. We want to question the way the press keeps the film fixed in an "independent low-budget" category (despite its three-city theatrical release and current availability on video and DVD from Amazon.com and some video rental stores, among other corporate-capitalist locations). The key to challenging these moves is the critical act of calling attention to the discursive effect that mass media articles have in determining and sometimes limiting possibilities for a transformation in the mainstream cinematic aesthetic. Thus, we draw attention to the way, for example, the press expresses anxiety about fluidity with rhetorical moves such as using an explicitly post-structuralist statement from Lee as "evidence" of his supposed concern with identity and defining characters whose identities are profoundly fluid with one or two pithy adjectives. A second critical strategy, ironically, is to turn to Lee's and Lin's words themselves, to reread the quotations in the press through a poststructuralist and Asian Americanist lens, and to address our own interviews with Lee. From this perspective, we can read Lee, as author-function, to be resisting a nostalgia for the auteur and redefining the relationship between mainstream and independent.

By reading independent films such as *Shopping for Fangs* within a category they themselves marginalize, the popular press implicitly suggests that the mode of evaluation of the film, too, remains marginal. Roddy Bogawa addresses this issue in his essay, "An(other) Reflection on Race?" He suggests that "For artists of color, expectations of what their work should investigate simultaneously dictate what the work should not explore. In most contexts, for instance, I am introduced as an 'Asian-American filmmaker' or a variation of that description. These are not arbitrary or neutral labels. They construct Asian-American film-making as a uniform practice, ignoring the diverse complexities of each film and each filmmaker. Their function is to stereotype, control, and marginalize. To preface a work is to inherently reduce in many ways the discussions to one—is the film Asian-American or not?"[22] Independent filmmakers such as Lee and Lin (and Bogawa) are not only the auteurs of films, the principal subjects audiences associate with a text, in this case *Shopping for Fangs*. They are also resisting their own positioning within discourse (reviews, academic articles, etc.) that attempts to limit their identities, the genres of their films, their potential marketing and distribution, and the like.

We would argue that rather than seeing a dichotomy between mainstream and independent, deracialized (white) and Asian American, popular press constraints and filmmakers' resistances, it makes the most critical sense to see a negotiation taking place over the definitions of mainstream, identity, and race. From this perspective, both Lee (as author-function and as human being) and *Shopping for Fangs* (the film, but also the film in relation to its audiences) are constantly engaged in defining, transforming, and asserting what Asian Americanness is (despite Lee's explicit rejection of this identity as label). As many have argued, identity construction in discourse is a process, not a thing. Although articles in the popular press about the film overwhelmingly seek to pin down that definition, Lee and his film can be seen as constantly dodging that attempt at fixity, and therefore constantly reworking both Asian Americanness and identity. By focusing on the author-function in relation to this particular film, our goals are to draw attention to the "nostalgia" for the fixed Asian American filmmaker in the popular press, to challenge the racialized logic in that nostalgia, and, most importantly, to participate in Lee's, Lin's, and other scholars of contemporary queer Asian American cinema's efforts to embody, theorize, and produce a fluid Asian American identity, one that both acknowledges and attempts to transform the social, historical, and economic circumstances in which Asian Americans find ourselves/themselves.

notes

1. Michel Foucault, "What Is an Author?," in *Foucault Reader*, trans. Josué V. Havari, ed. Paul Rabinow (New York: Pantheon Books, 1984), 117.
2. Peter Feng, "In Search of Asian American Cinema," *Cineaste* 21, no. 1–2 (1995): 32–5.
3. Peter Feng, "The State of Asian American Cinema: In Search of Community," *Cineaste* 24, no. 4 (1999): 21.
4. Catherine Grant, www.auteur.com? *Screen* 41, no. 1 (2000): 103.
5. Rosanna Maule, "De-authorizing the Auteur: Postmodern Politics of Interpellation in Contemporary European Cinema," in *Postmodernism in the Cinema*, ed. Cristina Degli-Espositi (Oxford: Berghahn Books, 1998), 113–30; and William Routt, "L'Evidence," *Continuum: The Australian Journal of Media and Culture* 5, no. 2 (1990): http://wwwmcc.murdoch.edu/au/ReadingRoom/5.2/routt.html.
6. Richard Dyer, "Believing in Fairies: The Author and the Homosexual," in *Inside/Out: Lesbian Theories, Gay Theories*, ed. Diana Fuss (London: Routledge, 1991), 185–201; Andy Medhurst, "That Special Thrill: *Brief Encounter*, Homosexuality, and Authorship," *Screen* 32, no. 2 (1991): 197–208.
7. We thoroughly agree with Foucault's argument that there is no particular or necessary relationship between the author and the real writer. Nor is there a particular or necessary relationship between the writing and the writer (112). These are all relations constructed after the fact of the writing itself that work to establish status and power relations between the critic and the materials studied. Nevertheless, in the spirit of Foucault's conclusion to his essay, we are interested in the "point of insertion" of the author within the equation between author and text and the way that point functions in political ways to obviate against particular understandings of the text and of the author that emerge in popular discourses.
8. Sid Adilman, "Filmmaker Fascinated by Questions of Identity," *Toronto Star* (September 1, 1997): C4; Julie Chao,"Beyond Genre: Asian American Filmmakers Seek Wider Audience for 'Generasian X' Movie," *San Francisco Examiner* (May 5, 1998): C1; *Daily News* (May 10, 1998): 10; Sallie Han, "Asian-American *Fangs* Are Sharp," Peter Y. Hong, "New Voices Emerge to Tell the Story of Ordinary Americans," *Los Angeles Times* (May 23, 1998): B1; Teressa Iezzi, "Toronto International Film Festival: *Shopping for Fangs*," *Playback* (September 8, 1997): B11; Brian D. Johnson, "A Cinema of Extremes," *Maclean's* (September 15, 1997): 74; Bob McCarthy, "UCLA

Students Team Up for Noir," *Daily News of Los Angeles* (May 8, 1998), L.A. Life; Monica Moran, "Independents on Overdrive," *Variety* (July 21, 1997): 12; Lynn Voedisch, "Asian Artistry: Films with Bicultural Basis," *Chicago Sun-Times* (April 4, 1997): 38.

9. This insistence that U.S. filmmakers of color can make films only about themselves is neither new nor unique to Asian American/Asian Canadian filmmakers. For example, see Wahneema Lubiano, "But Compared to What?: Reading Realism, Representation, and Essentialism in *School Daze, Do the Right Thing*, and the Spike Lee Discourse," *Black American Literature Forum* 25, no. 2 (1991): 253–82.

10. National Asian American Telecommunication Association, "Filmmaker of the Month," http://naatanet.org/community/archives/arch_filmmaker/quentin_lee.html, June 2001.

11. NAATA's San Francisco International Asian American Film Festival was the site of the film's debut, after all. During an audience question and answer session at the festival the year the film debuted, one of us asked Lin and Lee publicly whether they felt any responsibility to the Asian American audiences of their films, as it was the Asian American audiences who were their primary supporters. They accepted this assertion but stated that they do not make films for particular audiences; rather, they try to bring to life a variety of ideas. In response to this same question, Lin also stated that he would want to make bigger budget films if he could get the financial backing.

12. Peter Birnie, "*Shopping for Fangs* Opens a Festival of Asian-American Films," *Vancouver Sun* (September 12, 1997): C2; Edward Guthmann, "Low-budget *Shopping* Buys Mix of Old, New," *Austin American-Statesman* (September 18, 1998): E5; G. Allen Johnson, "*Fangs* Is Fun, but Doesn't Have Teeth: Tale of Identity, Werewolves, and Suburbia Almost Gels," *San Francisco Examiner* (May 9, 1998): C1.

13. The following might be a good example of what Lee means by guerrilla filmmaking: At a public forum after the world premiere of *Shopping for Fangs*, Lee reported that they shot a pivotal scene including a standoff between two characters, Mr. Lee and Trinh, in which Trinh holds a gun on Mr. Lee, in the very early morning hours. Without a city permit to shoot, they depended on luck, hoping that no police officer would pass by and ask them what they were doing.

14. Amy Taubin, "The Sound and the Fury," *Village Voice* (May 12, 1998): 123.

15. Kevin Thomas, "Best for Last?" *Los Angeles Times* (August 21, 1997): F14. Also see Kevin Thomas, "*Shopping*: A Postmodern Take on Asian Americans," *Los Angeles Times* (May 8, 1998): F8.

16. John Anderson, "Stereotypes You Can Sink Your Fangs into," *Newsday* (May 18, 1998): B7; Anita Gates, "Is He a Werewolf, or Just a Little Hairy?" *New York Times* (May 15, 1998): E23; Betsy Sherman, "Feeling and Funk: The MFA's Asian-American Festival Ranges from the Touching to the Stylish," *Boston Globe* (March 14, 1999): N9; Larry Worth, "*Fangs* Neither Hair Nor There,"*New York Post* (May 15, 1998): 58.

17. Hong.

18. Qtd. in Iezzi.

19. Valerie Soe, "Pictures in Transition: 15th San Francisco International Asian American Film Festival," *Afterimage* 25, no. 1 (1997): 3; "Stylized Cultural Riff," *Toronto Star* (August 31, 1997): B8.

20. Sarah Projansky, *Watching Rape: Film and Television in Postfeminist Culture* (New York: New York University Press, 2001). In our interview with him, however, and in a distinctly postmodern fashion, Lee resists embracing these or other specific citations. "I don't want to see influences and inspiration as discreet and dichotomizing, as strategies and motifs which are academic and didactic. Influences and inspiration are passionate and intuitive."

21. Eve Oishi, "Bad Asians: New Film and Video by Queer Asian American Artists," in *Countervisions: Asian American Film Criticism*, ed. Darrell Y.

Hamamoto and Sandra Liu (Philadelphia: Temple University Press, 2000), 223.

22. Roddy Bogawa, "An(other) Reflection on Race?" in *Moving the Image: Independent Asian Pacific American Media Arts*, ed. Russell Leong (Los Angeles: UCLA Asian American Studies Center and Visual Communications, Southern California Asian American Studies Center, Inc., 1991), 208–9.

sarah projansky and kent a. ono

bibliography

Abbott, Spencer H. "Rough Cut Q & As: Sprungtime—and Love's in the Air." *Rough Cut* [electronic periodical] Turner Network Television. Updated May 16, 1997, cited May 2, 2000. http://roughcut.com/main/drive2_97may3.html.

Abrahams, Roger D. *Deep Down in the Jungle: Negro Narrative Folklore from the Streets of Philadelphia.* Hatboro, PA: Folklore Associates, 1964.

Abrams, M. H. *The Mirror and the Lamp: Romantic Theory and the Critical Tradition.* New York: Oxford University Press, 1953.

Adams, Rachel. *Sideshow U.S.A.: Freaks and the American Cultural Imagination.* Chicago: University of Chicago Press, 2001.

Adilman, Sid. "Filmmaker Fascinated by Questions of Identity." *Toronto Star,* September 1, 1997, C4.

Adorno, Theodor, and Max Horkheimer. *Dialectic of Enlightenment* [1947]. New York: Continuum, 1993.

Allen, Robert C., and Douglas Gomery. *Film History: Theory and Practice.* New York: McGraw-Hill, 1985.

Alpi, Deborah Lazaroff. *Robert Siodmak: A Biography, with Critical Analysis of His Film Noirs and a Filmography of All His Works.* Jefferson, NC and London: McFarland & Co. Inc., 1998.

Altman, Rick. *The American Film Musical.* Bloomington: Indiana University Press, 1989.

Alvarado, Manuel. "Authorship, Organization and Production." *Australian Journal of Screen Theory* no. 9/10 (1981): 11–35.

Anderson, Benedict. *Imagined Communities: Reflections on the Origin and Spread of Nationalism.* London: Verso, 1983.

Anderson, John. "Stereotypes You Can Sink Your Fangs into." *Newsday,* May 18, 1998, B7.

Andrew, Dudley. "The Unauthorized Auteur Today." In *Film Theory Goes to the Movies.* Edited by Jim Collins, Hilary Radner, and Ava Preacher Collins. New York: Routledge, 1993. Pp. 77–85.

Ansen, David. "The Boogie Man." *Newsweek,* December 19, 1977, 65.

———. "Rock Tycoon." *Newsweek,* July 31, 1978, 40–7.

Asahina, Robert. "Slipped Disco." *The New Leader,* January 16, 1978, 24–5.

Ashton, Dore. "Vision and Sound: Today's Art at Buffalo." *Studio International* 169 (May 1965): 211–12.

Astruc, Alexandre. "The Birth of a New Avant-Garde: La Caméra-Style [1948]." Translated by Peter Graham. Reprinted in *The New Wave.* Edited by Peter Graham. Garden City, NY: Doubleday & Company, 1968. Pp. 17–23.

Austin, J. L. *How To Do Things with Words,* 2nd ed. Cambridge, MA: Harvard University Press, 1975.

Bakhtin, M. M. "Forms of Time and of the Chronotope in the Novel [1937–1938]." Translated by Caryl Emerson and Michael Holquist. *The Dialogic Imagination: Four Essays.* Austin: University of Texas Press, 1981. Pp. 252–58.

Baraka, Amiri. "Spike Lee at the Movies." In *Black American Cinema.* Edited by Manthia Diawara. New York: Routledge, 1993. Pp. 145–53.

Barthes, Roland. "The Death of the Author [1968]." Translated by Stephen Heath. *Image, Music, Text*. New York: Hill and Wang, 1977. Pp. 142–48.

———. "From Work to Text" [1971]. Reprinted in *Art After Modernism: Rethinking Representation*. Edited by Brian Willis. New York: The New Museum of Contemporary Art, 1984. Pp. 169–74.

———. "La Mort de l'auteur," *Mantéia* 5 (1968): 12–16.

———. *The Pleasure of the Text* [1973]. Translated by Richard Miller. New York: Hill and Wang, 1975.

Bass, Ruth. "The Little Man." Reprinted in *Mother Wit from the Laughing Barrel: Readings in the Interpretation of Afro-American Folklore*. Edited by Alan Dundes. Jackson: University Press of Mississippi, 1990. Pp. 380–87.

———. "Mojo." Reprinted in *Mother Wit from the Laughing Barrel: Readings in the Interpretation of Afro-American Folklore*. Edited by Alan Dundes. Jackson: University Press of Mississippi, 1990. Pp. 388–96.

Baxandall, Michael. *Patterns of Intention: On the Historical Explanation of Pictures*. New Haven, CT: Yale University Press, 1985.

Bazin, André. "On the *Politique des auteurs* [1957]." Translated by Peter Graham. In *Cahiers du Cinéma: The 1950s: Neo-Realism, Hollywood, New Wave*. Edited by Jim Hillier. Cambridge, MA: Harvard University Press, 1985. Pp. 248–59.

Behlmer, Rudy, ed. *Memo From David O. Selznick*. New York: Viking Press, 1972.

———, ed. *The Sea Hawk*. Madison: University of Wisconsin Press, 1982.

Bell, Michael Davitt. *Culture, Genre, and Literary Vocation: Selected Essays on American Literature*. Chicago: University of Chicago Press, 2001.

Bellour, Raymond. *Le Cinéma Américain: Analyses de films*. Symboliques II. Paris: Flammariòn, 1980.

Belsey, Catherine. *Critical Practice*. London: Methuen, 1980.

Benjamin, Walter. "The Author as Producer [1934]." Translated by Edmund Jephcott. *Reflections: Essays, Aphorisms, Autobiographical Writing*. New York: Harcourt Brace Jovanovich, 1978. Pp. 220–38.

———. "Theses on the Philosophy of History [1939–40]." Translated by Harry Zohn. In *Illuminations*. Edited by Hannah Arendt. New York: Schocken Books, 1969. Pp. 253–64.

Benshoff, Harry M. "Blaxploitation Horror Films: Generic Reappropriation or Reinscription?" *Cinema Journal* 39, no. 2 (2000): 31–50.

Berch, Barbara. "A Hitchcock Alumna." *New York Times*, June 27, 1943, sec. II, 3.

Bergreen, Laurence. *As Thousands Cheer: The Life of Irving Berlin*. New York: Viking Press, 1990.

Biographer, The. "The Personal Side of the Pictures." *Reel Life*, July 25, 1914, 19.

Birnie, Peter. "*Shopping for Fangs* Opens a Festival of Asian-American Films." *Vancouver Sun*, September 12, 1997, C2.

Blakeston, Oswell. "Sketches by Len Lye." *Close Up* 6, no. 2 (February 1930): 155–56.

Bogawa, Roddy. "An(other) Reflection on Race?" In *Moving the Image: Independent Asian Pacific American Media Arts*. Edited by Russell Leong. Los Angeles: UCLA Asian American Studies Center and Visual Communications, Southern California Asian American Studies Center, Inc., 1991. Pp. 208–10.

Bogle, Donald. *Toms, Coons, Mulattoes, Mammies, and Bucks: An Interpretative History of Blacks in American Films*, 3rd ed. New York: Continuum, 1994.

Borde, Raymond, and Etienne Chaumeton. *Panorama du Film Noir Américain, 1941–1953* [1955]. Paris: Flammariòn, 1988.

Bordwell, David. "*Citizen Kane* [1971]." Reprinted in *Movies and Methods*, Vol. I. Edited by Bill Nichols. Berkeley: University of California Press, 1976. Pp. 273–90.

———. Lectures in Critical Film Analysis. University of Wisconsin-Madison. October 1977.

———. *The Films of Carl-Theodor Dreyer*. Berkeley: University of California Press, 1981.

————. *Ozu and the Poetics of Cinema*. Princeton, NJ: Princeton University Press, 1988.

————. *Making Meaning: Inference and Rhetoric in the Interpretation of Cinema*. Cambridge, MA: Harvard University Press, 1989.

————. *The Cinema of Eisenstein*. Cambridge, MA: Harvard University Press, 1993.

Bordwell, David, Janet Staiger, and Kristin Thompson. *The Classical Hollywood Cinema: Film Style and Mode of Production to 1960*. London: Routledge & Kegan Paul, 1985.

Bouhours, Jean-Michel, and Roger Horrocks, eds. *Len Lye*. Paris: Centre Pompidou, 2000.

Boultenhouse, Charles. "The Camera as God." *Film Culture* no. 29 (Summer 1963). Reprinted in *Film Culture Reader*. Edited by P. Adams Sitney. New York: Praeger Publishers, 1970. Pp. 136–40.

Bourdieu, Pierre. *The Field of Cultural Production: Essays on Art and Literature*. Edited by Randal Johnson. New York: Columbia University Press, 1993.

Bowser, Pearl, and Louise Spence. "Oscar Micheaux's *Body and Soul* and the Burden of Representation." *Cinema Journal* 39, no. 3 (Spring 2000): 3–29.

————. *Writing Himself into History: Oscar Micheaux, His Silent Films, and His Audiences*. New Brunswick, NJ: Rutgers University Press, 2000.

Bowser, Pearl, Jane Gaines, and Charles Musser, eds. *Oscar Micheaux and His Circle: African-American Filmmaking and Race Cinema of the Silent Era*. Bloomington: Indiana University Press, 2001.

Boyle, Deidre. *Subject to Change: Guerilla Television Revisited*. New York: Oxford University Press, 1987.

Braddock, Jeremy, and Stephen Hock, eds. *Directed by Allen Smithee*. Minneapolis: University of Minnesota Press, 2001.

Brakhage, Stan. "Len Lye." October 13, 1980. Rocky Mountain Film Center, Colorado.

Brion, Patrick. "Une vie dans le fantastique." *Cahiers du Cinéma* no. 550 (October 2000): 84–5.

Brooks, Cleanth. *The Well Wrought Urn: Studies in the Structure of Poetry*. New York: Harcourt, Brace & World, 1947.

Brown, Jeffrey A. "Comic Book Masculinity and the New Black Superhero." *African American Review* 33, no. 1 (1999): 25–42.

Browne, Nick. "The Spectator-in-the-Text: The Rhetoric of *Stagecoach* [1975]. Reprinted in *Movies and Methods*, Vol. 2. Edited by Bill Nichols. Berkeley: University of California Press, 1985. Pp. 458–75.

Brunvand, Jan Harold. *The Study of American Folklore: An Introduction*. New York: W. W. Norton, 1986.

Bürger, Peter. *Theory of the Avant-Garde* [1974, 1979]. Translated by Michael Shaw. Minneapolis: University of Minnesota Press, 1984.

Burnett, Kathleen. "Toward a Theory of Hypertextual Design." *Postmodern Culture* no. 2 (January 1993): http://jefferson.village.virginia.edu/pmc/issue.193/burnett.193. Accessed March 1, 2002.

Burnett, Ron, *Culture of Vision: Image Media and the Imaginary*. Bloomington: Indiana University Press, 1993.

Buscombe, Edward. "Ideas of Authorship." *Screen* 14, no. 3 (Autumn 1973): 75–85.

Butler, Judith. *Gender Trouble: Feminism and the Subversion of Identity*. New York: Routledge, 1990.

————. "Gender Trouble, Feminist Theory, and Psychoanalytic Discourse." In *Feminism/Postmodernism*. Edited by Linda J. Nicholson. New York: Routledge, 1990. Pp. 324–40.

————. *Bodies That Matter: On the Discursive Limits of "Sex."* New York: Routledge, 1993.

Cannon, Terry. "Willie Varela." Interview in *Spiral* no. 6 (January 1986): 51–3.

——. "Willie Varela: Deep in the Heart of Texas." *The Cinemanews* no. 81 (1982): 75–7.

Carnival Man, A. "Graft Death-Blow to Carnivals." *Show World* 2, no. 22 (May 23, 1908): 1.

Carringer, Robert L., ed. *The Jazz Singer*. Madison: University of Wisconsin Press, 1979.

——. "Collaboration and Concepts of Authorship." *PMLA* 116, no. 2 (March 2001): 370–79.

——. *The Making of "Citizen Kane."* Berkeley: University of California Press, 1985.

Caughie, John. "Preface" and "Introduction." In *Theories of Authorship*. Edited by John Caughie. London: Routledge & Kegan Paul, 1981. Pp. 1–6, *passim*.

Chao, Julie. "Beyond Genre: Asian American Filmmakers Seek Wider Audience for 'Generasian X' Movie." *San Francisco Examiner*, May 5, 1998, C1.

Clover, Carol. *Men, Women, and Chainsaws: Gender in the Modern Horror Film*. Princeton, NJ: Princeton University Press, 1992.

Cohen, Ralph. "Do Postmodern Genres Exist?" In *Postmodern Genres*. Edited by Marjorie Perloff. Norman: University of Oklahoma Press, 1988. Pp. 11–27.

Cook, Pam. "Duplicity in *Mildred Pierce*." In *Women and Film Noir*. Edited by E. Ann Kaplan. London: British Film Institute, 1978. Pp.68–82.

——. "The Point of Self-Expression in Avant-Garde Film [1977–1978]." Reprinted in *Theories of Authorship*. Edited by John Caughie. London: Routledge & Kegan Paul, 1981. Pp. 271–81.

——, ed. *Cinema Book*, 2nd ed. London: British Film Institute, 1999.

Cook, Pam, and Claire Johnston. "The Place of Woman in the Cinema of Raoul Walsh" [1974]. Reprinted in *Feminism and Film Theory*. Edited by Constance Penley. New York: Routledge, 1988.

Corrigan, Timothy. "The Commerce of Auteurism: Coppola, Kluge, Ruiz." In *A Cinema without Walls: Movies and Culture after Vietnam*. New Brunswick, NJ: Rutgers University Press, 1991. Pp. 101–36.

Couvares, Francis G., ed. *Movie Censorship and American Culture*. Washington, D.C.: Smithsonian Institution Press, 1996.

Crimp, Douglas. "Fassbinder, Franz, Fox, Elvira, Armin and All the Others." In *Queer Looks: Perspectives on Lesbian and Gay Film and Video*. Edited by Martha Gever, John Greyson, and Pratibha Parmar. New York: Routledge, 1993. Pp. 257–74.

Cripps, Thomas. *Slow Fade to Black: The Negro in American Film, 1900–1942*. New York: Oxford University Press, 1993.

Crofts, Stephen. "Authorship and Hollywood." *Wide Angle* 5, no. 3 (1983): 16–22.

——. "Authorship and Hollywood." In *American Cinema and Hollywood: Critical Approaches*. Edited by John Hill and Pamela Church Gibson. New York: Oxford University Press, 2000. Pp. 84–98.

Culler, Jonathan. *On Deconstruction: Theory and Criticism after Structuralism*. Ithaca, NY: Cornell University Press, 1982.

Curnow, Wystan. "Lye and Abstract Expressionism." In *Len Lye*. Edited by Jean-Michel Bourhours and Robert Horrocks. Paris: Centre Pompidou, 2000. Pp. 205–12.

Curtis, David. *Experimental Cinema*. London: Studio Vista, 1971.

Custen, George. *Bio/Pic: How Hollywood Constructed Public History*. New Brunswick, NJ: The Rutgers University Press, 1992.

——. *Twentieth Century's Fox: Darryl F. Zanuck and the Culture of Hollywood*. New York: Basic Books, 1997.

Daggett, Ann. "It's a Woman's World Too." *Modern Screen* (February 1945): 20, 22.

Davis, Angela. *Blues Legacies and Black Feminism: Gertrude "Ma" Rainey, Bessie Smith, and Billie Holiday*. New York: Pantheon Books, 1998.

Davis, Janet M. "'Instruct the Minds of All Classes': The Circus and American Culture at the Turn of the Century." Ph.D. dissertation, University of Wisconsin, Madison, 1998.

Davis, Mike. *City of Quartz: Excavating the Future of Los Angeles.* New York: Vintage Books, 1992.

Dayan, Daniel. "The Tutor-Code of Cinema" [1974]. Reprinted in *Movies and Methods*, Vol. 1. Edited by Bill Nichols. Berkeley: University of California Press, 1976. Pp. 438–51.

DeAngelis, Michael. *Gay Fandom and Crossover Stardom: James Dean, Mel Gibson, and Keanu Reeves.* Durham, NC: Duke University Press, 2001.

De Baecque, Antoine, and Serge Toubiana. *Truffaut.* Paris: Editions Gallimard, 1996.

De Certeau, Michel. *The Practice of Everyday Life.* Translated by Steven Rendall. Berkeley: University of California Press, 1984.

———. *Heterologies: Discourse on the Other* [1986]. Translated by Brain Massumi. Minneapolis: University of Minnesota Press, 1995.

Deleuze, Gilles. *Cinema 2: The Time-Image* [1985]. Translated by Hugh Tomlinson and Robert Galeta. Minneapolis: University of Minnesota Press, 1989.

———. *Cinema 1: The Image-Movement* [1983]. Translated by Hugh Tomlinson and Barbara Habberjam. Minneapolis: University of Minnesota Press, 1996.

Derrick, Scott S. *Monumental Anxieties: Homoerotic Desire and Feminine Influence in 19th-Century U.S. Literature.* New Brunswick, NJ: Rutgers University Press, 1997.

Derrida, Jacques. *Of Grammatology* [1974]. Translated by Gayatri Chakrovorty Spivak. Baltimore: Johns Hopkins University Press, 1974.

———. *Margins of Philosophy* [1982]. Translated by Alan Bass. Chicago: University of Chicago Press, 1986.

———. *Specters of Marx: The State of the Debt, the Work of Mourning, and the New International.* Translated by Peggy Kamuf. New York: Routledge, 1994.

Diawara, Manthia. "Black Spectatorship: Problems of Identification and Resistance." In *Black American Cinema.* Edited by Manthia Diawara. New York: Routledge, 1993. Pp. 211–20.

———. "Popular Culture and Oral Traditions in African Film." In *Film Quarterly: Forty Years—A Selection.* Edited by Brian Henderson and Ann Martin. Berkeley: University of California Press, 1999. Pp. 112–25.

Dickey, Joan. "A Maker of Mystery: Tod Browning is a Specialist in Building Thrills and Chills." *Motion Picture Classic* 27, no. 1 (March 1928): 33, 80.

Dickey, Sara. *Cinema and the Urban Poor in South India.* New York: Cambridge University Press, 1993.

DiMaggio, Paul, and Paul M. Hirsch. "Production Organizations in the Arts." *American Behavioral Scientist* 19, no. 6 (July/August 1976): 735–52.

Doane, Mary Ann. *The Desire to Desire: The Woman's Film of the 1940s.* Bloomington: Indiana University Press, 1987.

———. *Femmes Fatales: Feminism, Film Theory, Psychoanalysis.* New York: Routledge, 1991.

Doty, Alexander. *Making Things Perfectly Queer: Interpreting Mass Culture.* Minneapolis: University of Minnesota Press, 1993.

Douglas, Ann. *The Feminization of American Culture.* New York: Anchor Books, 1988.

Du Bois, W. E. B. "The Souls of Black Folk [1903]." In *The Norton Anthology of African-American Literature.* Edited by Henry Louis Gates, Jr., and Nellie Y. McKay. New York: W. W. Norton, 1997. Pp. 613–740.

Dundes, Alan. *Folklore Matters.* Knoxville: University of Tennessee Press, 1989.

———, ed. *Mother Wit from the Laughing Barrel: Readings in the Interpretation of Afro-American Folklore.* Jackson: University Press of Mississippi, 1990.

———, ed. *International Folkloristics.* New York: Rowman and Littlefield Publishers, 1999.

Durgnat, Raymond. *Films and Feelings*. Cambridge, MA: MIT Press, 1967.

Dyer, Richard. "Homosexuality and Film Noir." *Jump Cut* no. 16 (1977): 18–21.

———. "Believing in Fairies: The Author and the Homosexual." In *Inside/Out: Lesbian Theories, Gay Theories*. Edited by Diana Fuss. London: Routledge, 1991. Pp. 185–201.

Eagleton, Terry. *Literary Theory: An Introduction*. Minneapolis: University of Minnesota Press, 1983.

Eckert, Charles. "The English Cine-Structuralists"[1973]. Reprinted in *Theories of Authorship*. Edited by John Caughie. New York: Routledge & Kegan Paul, 1981. Pp. 152–65.

Edwards, Henry. "Inventing a Plot for Sgt. Pepper." *New York Times*, July 6, 1978, sec. 2.

Ehrenstein, David. "An Interview with Andy Warhol." *Film Culture* no. 40 (Spring 1966): 41.

Eisenstein, Sergei. "Dickens, Griffith, and the Film Today" [1944]. Reprinted in *Film Form: Essays in Film Theory* [1949]. Translated and edited by Jay Leyda. New York: Harcourt, Brace & Co., 1977. Pp. 195–255.

Eisner, Lotte. *The Haunted Screen* [1952/rev. 1965]. Translated by Roger Greaves. Reprinted Berkeley: University of California Press, 1969.

Elsaesser, Thomas. "Two Decades in Another Country: Hollywood and the Cinéphiles." In *Superculture: American Popular Culture and Europe*. Edited by C. W. E. Bigsby. Bowling Green, OH: Bowling Green University Press, 1975. Pp. 199–225.

———. "Vincente Minnelli [1969]." Reprinted in *Genre: The Musical: A Reader*. Edited by Rick Altman. London: Routledge & Kegan Paul, 1981. Pp. 8–27.

———. "Ethnicity, Authenticity, and Exile: A Counterfeit Trade? German Filmmakers and Hollywood." In *Home, Exile, Homeland: Film, Media, and the Politics of Place*. Edited by Hamid Naficy. New York: Routledge, 1999. Pp. 97–123.

———. "Tales of Sound and Fury: Observations on the Family Melodrama [1972]." Reprinted in *Home is Where the Heart Is: Studies in Melodrama and the Woman's Film*. Edited by Christine Gledhill. London: British Film Institute, 1992. Pp. 43–69.

Eng, David, and Shinhee Han. "A Dialogue on Racial Melancholia." *Psychoanalytic Dialogues* 10, no. 4 (2000): 667–700.

"Enjoin Sale of Negro Newspaper." *Chicago Broad-Ax*, May 13, 1920, 1.

Erickson, Hal. "Biography: John Waters." http://video.barnesandnoble.com/search/biography.asp?userid=1961I42I28&mscssid=6M09FW4X43CT9KS1Q232FB01M9SLES4C&CTR=748213.

Evans, Frank. "Picking the Best Films of the Year." *Evening Chronicle*, January 1, 1937. Ann Lye clipping file. New Plymouth: Len Lye Foundation Archive.

Everett, Todd. "Trailers, Teasers vs. Screen Clutter." *Variety*, December 7, 1977, 67, 72.

Ewen, Stuart. *Captains of Consciousness: Advertising and the Social Roots of the Consumer Culture*. New York: McGraw-Hill, 1988.

Feng, Peter X. "In Search of Asian American Cinema." *Cineaste* 21, nos. 1–2 (1995): 32–5.

———. "The State of Asian American Cinema: In Search of Community." *Cineaste* 24, no. 4 (1999): 20–4.

Feuer, Jane. *The Hollywood Film Musical*, 2nd ed. Bloomington: Indiana University Press, 1993.

"50 Top-Grossing Films." *Variety*, December 28, 1977, 9.

"Film Painter." *Time* 32, December 12, 1938, 50–1.

Foucault, Michel. *Discipline and Punish* [1975]. Translated by Alan Sheridan. New York: Vintage Books, 1977.

———. *History of Sexuality: An Introduction* [1976]. Vol. I. Translated by Robert Hurley. New York: Vintage Books, 1980.

————. *The Use of Pleasure: The History of Sexuality* [1984a], Vol. II. Translated by Robert Hurley. New York: Vintage Books, 1986.

————. "What Is an Author? [1975]." Translated by Josué V. Harari. Reprinted in *The Foucault Reader*. Edited by Paul Rabinow. New York: Pantheon, 1984. Pp. 101–20.

————. *The Care of the Self: The History of Sexuality* [1984b], Vol. III. Translated by Robert Hurley. New York: Vintage Books, 1988.

"Frances Calvert on Frank Hurley." *Metro* [Australia], no. 112 (1997): 14–16.

Freud, Sigmund. "Family Romances" [1909]. *The Standard Edition of the Complete Psychological Works*, Vol. IX. Translated by James Strachey. London: Hogarth Press, 1959. Pp. 237–41.

Fulmer, Jacqueline. "'Men Ain't All': A Reworking of Masculinity in *Tales from the Hood*, or, Grandma Meets the Zombie." *Journal of American Folklore* forthcoming (Fall 2002).

Furia, Philip. *Irving Berlin: A Life in Song*. New York: Schirmer Books, 1998.

Gaines, Jane. *Fire and Desire: Mixed-Race Movies in the Silent Era*. Chicago: University of Chicago Press, 2001.

Gates, Anita. "Is He a Werewolf, or Just a Little Hairy?" *New York Times*, May 15, 1998, E23.

Gates, Henry Louis. "Black Creativity: On the Cutting Edge." *Time* 144, no. 15 (October 10, 1994): 66.

Gaycken, Oliver. "Tod Browning and the Monstrosity of Hollywood Style." In *Screening Disability: Essays on Cinema and Disability*. Edited by Christopher R. Smit and Anthony Enns. Lanham, MD: University Press of America, 2001. Pp. 73–86.

Geertz, Clifford. "Blurred Genres: The Refiguration of Social Thought." *The American Scholar* 49 (Spring 1980): 165–76.

Geritz, Kathy. *Film Notes* 25, no. 4 (July–August 2001): 14.

Gerstner, David A. "Queer Angels of History Take It and Leave It from Behind." *Stanford Humanities Review: Inside the Film Archive: Practice, Theory, Canon* 7, no. 2 (Autumn 1999): 150–65.

————. "Queer Modernism: The Cinematic Aesthetic of Vincente Minnelli." *Modernity* 2, no. 1 (2000): *http://www.eiu.edu/~modernity/modernity.html*.

Goimard, Jacques. "Le jour où les maudits prirent la parole." *L'Avant-Scène du cinéma* no. 264 (March 15, 1981): 4–8.

Gorn, Elliott J. "Black Spirits: The Ghostlore of Afro-American Slaves." In *The Culture and Community of Slavery*. Edited by Paul Finkelman. New York: Garland Publishing, 1989.

Grant, Catherine. "www.auteur.com?" *Screen* 41, no. 1 (2000): 101–8.

————. "Secret Agents: Feminist Theories of Women's Film Authorship." *Feminist Theories* 2, no. 1 (2001): 113–30.

Green, J. Ronald. *Straight Lick: The Cinema of Oscar Micheaux*. Bloomington: Indiana University Press, 2000.

Guerrero, Ed. *Framing Blackness: The African American Image in Film*. Philadelphia: Temple University Press, 1993.

Gunning, Tom. *The Films of Fritz Lang: Allegories of Vision and Modernity*. London: British Film Institute, 2000.

Guthmann, Edward. "Low-budget *Shopping* Buys Mix of Old, New." *Austin American-Statesman*, September 18, 1998, E5.

Habermas, Jürgen. *The Structural Transformation of the Public Sphere*. Cambridge, MA: MIT Press, 1991.

Halleck, DeeDee. "Deep Dish TV: Community Video from Geostationary Orbit." *Leonardo* no. 5 (1993): 415–20.

Halliday, Jon. *Sirk on Sirk*. New York: Viking Press, 1972.

Han, Sallie. "Asian-American *Fangs* Are Sharp." *Daily News*, May 10, 1998, 10.

Haraway, Donna. "Situated Knowledges: The Science Question in Feminism and the Privilege of Partial Perspective." *Feminist Studies* 14, no. 3 (Fall 1988): 575–99.

Harmetz, Aljean. *Round Up The Usual Suspects: The Making of* Casablanca, *Bogart, Bergman, and World War Two*. New York: Hyperion Books, 1992.

Harris, Erich Leon. *African-American Screenwriters Now: Conversations with Hollywood's Black Pack*. Beverly Hills, CA: Silman-James Press, 1996.

Hartsock, Nancy. "Foucault on Power: A Theory for Women? [1987]." Reprinted in *Feminism/Postmodernism*. Edited by Linda J. Nicholson. New York: Routledge, 1990. Pp. 157–75.

Harvey, Stephen. "Eine Kleiser Rockmusik." *Film Comment* 14 (July–August 1978): 14–16.

Haskell, Molly. "J. C. Superstar Enterprises, Inc." *Saturday Review*, October 30, 1971, 65–67, 82.

Hazen, Don, and Julie Winokur, eds. *We the Media: A Citizens' Guide to Fighting for Media Democracy*. New York: The New Press, 1997.

Heath, Stephen. "Comment on 'The Idea of Authorship.'" *Screen* 14, no. 3 (Autumn 1973): 86–91.

———. "Film and System: Terms of Analysis." Part I, *Screen* 16, no. 1 (Spring 1975): 7–77. Part II, *Screen* 16, no. 2 (Summer 1975): 91–113.

Henderson, Brian. "Critique of Cine-Structuralism," Part I. *Film Quarterly* 27, no. 1 (Fall 1973): 25–34.

Herron, Leonora, and Alice M. Bacon. "Conjuring and Conjure-Doctors." Reprinted in *Mother Wit from the Laughing Barrel: Readings in the Interpretation of Afro-American Folklore*. Edited by Alan Dundes. Jackson: University Press of Mississippi, 1990. Pp. 359–68.

Hess, John. "*Auteurism* and After." *Film Quarterly* 27, no. 2 (Winter 1973–1974): 28–37.

———. "*La Politique des auteurs*." Part 1, *Jump Cut* 1 (May–June 1974): 19–22. Part 2, *Jump Cut* 2 (July–August 1974): 20–22.

Highwater, Jamake. "Dancing in the Seventies." *Horizon* 19, no. 3 (May 1977): 30–3.

Hillier, Jim. "Introduction." In *Cahiers du Cinéma: The 1950s: Neo-Realism, Hollywood, New Wave*. Edited by Jim Hillier. Cambridge, MA: Harvard University Press, 1985. Pp. 1–17.

Hirsch, Paul M. "Processing Fads and Fashions: An Organization-Set Analysis of Cultural Industry Systems." *American Journal of Sociology* 77, no. 4 (1972): 639–59.

———. "Occupational, Organizational, and Institutional Models in Mass Media Research: Toward an Integrated Framework." In *Strategies for Communication Research*. Beverly Hills, CA: Sage Publications, 1977. Pp. 13–42.

Hong, Peter Y. "New Voices Emerge to Tell the Story of Ordinary Americans." *Los Angeles Times*, May 23, 1998, B1.

Horkheimer, Max, and Theodor Adorno. *Dialectic of Enlightenment* [1944]. Translated by John Cumming. New York: Continuum, 1991.

Horrocks, Roger. *Len Lye: A Biography*. Auckland: Auckland University Press, 2001.

Hughes, Langston, and Arna Bontemps, eds. *The Book of Negro Folklore*. New York: Dodd, Mead and Co, 1966.

Hull, Bob. "Marry a Writer, Advises One Lady Producer: They're Quiet." *Hollywood Reporter* 30, April 5, 1968, 1, 9.

Hummler, Richard. "'Grease' Film Spurs B. O. for B-way Original." *Variety*, July 19, 1978, 1, 107.

Iezzi, Teressa. "Toronto International Film Festival: *Shopping for Fangs*." *Playback*, September 8, 1997, B11.

Ignatiev, Noel. *How the Irish Became White*. New York: Routledge, 1995.

Iris, no. 28 (1999). [Special issue on authorship.]

James, David E. *Allegories of the Cinema: American Film in the Sixties*. Princeton, NJ: Princeton University Press, 1989.

JanMohamed, Abdul R. "The Economy of Manichean Allegory: The Function of Racial Difference in Colonialist Literature." In *"Race," Writing, and Difference*.

Edited by Henry Louis Gates, Jr. Chicago: University of Chicago Press, 1985. Pp. 78–106.

Johnson, Brian D. "A Cinema of Extremes." *Maclean's*, September 15, 1997, 74.

Johnson, G. Allen. "*Fangs* Is Fun, but Doesn't Have Teeth: Tale of Identity, Werewolves, and Suburbia Almost Gels." *San Francisco Examiner*, May 9, 1998, C1.

Jones, Juli, Jr. "Motion Pictures and Inside Facts." *The Half-Century Magazine* 6, no. 7 (July 1919): 16–19.

Joyner, Charles. "The Trickster and the Fool: Folktales and Identity Among Southern Plantation Slaves." Reprinted in *The Culture and Community of Slavery*. Edited by Paul Finkelman. New York: Garland Publishing, 1989. Pp. 223–41.

Juhasz, Alexandra. *AIDS TV: Identity, Community, and Alternative Video*. Durham, NC: Duke University Press, 1995.

Kael, Pauline. "Circles and Squares." *Film Quarterly* 16, no. 3 (Spring 1963): 12–26.

———. *The Citizen Kane Book*. New York: Little Brown, 1971.

———. *I Lost It At The Movies*. New York: Holt Rinehart, 1982.

Kauffmann, Stanley. "Fin and Fantasy." *New Republic*, July 1, 1978, 18–19.

Kennedy, Joseph. "Len Lye—Composer of Motion." *Millimeter* 5 (February 1977): 18–22.

Kimball, Robert and Linda Emmet, eds. *The Complete Lyrics of Irving Berlin*. New York: Alfred A. Knopf, 2001.

Knowles, Dorothy. *The Censor, The Drama and the Film 1900–1934*. London: George Allen and Unwin, 1934.

Kornbluth, Jesse. "Merchandising Disco for the Masses." *New York Times*, Sunday Magazine section, February 8, 1979, 18, 21–24, 44–45.

Kracauer, Siegfried. *The Mass Ornament: Weimar Essays* [1963]. Translated by Thomas Y. Levin. Cambridge, MA: Harvard University Press, 1995.

"Labor Agents are Shunned in Chicago." *Chicago Defender*, May 17, 1919, 1.

Lapsley, Robert, and Michael Westlake. *Film Theory: An Introduction*. Manchester, England: Manchester University Press, 1988.

Lee, Quentin. Personal e-mail interview with Sarah Projanksy and Kent Ono. December 11, 2001.

———. Personal e-mail interview with Sarah Projanksy and Kent Ono. December 15, 2001.

Leggett, Paul. "The Noble Cynic: Michael Curtiz." *Focus on Film*, no. 23 (Winter 1975): 1–19.

LeGrice, Malcolm. *Abstract Film and Beyond*. London: Studio Vista, 1977.

Leja, Michael. *Reframing Abstract Expressionism: Subjectivity and Painting in the 1940s*. New Haven, CT: Yale University Press, 1993.

Levine, Lawrence W. *Highbrow/Lowbrow: The Emergence of Cultural Hierarchy in America*. Cambridge, MA: Harvard University Press, 1988.

Lewis, Jerry D. "'Murder,' She Says." *Colliers* 112 (August 10, 1943): 55, 70.

Linder, Laura R. *Public Access Television: America's Electronic Soapbox*. Westport, CT: Praeger Books, 1999.

Lindsey, Robert. "The New Tycoons of Hollywood." *New York Times Magazine*, August 7, 1977, 12–23.

Lombardi, John. "Selling Gays to the Masses." *Village Voice*, June 30, 1975, 10–11.

López, Ana. "The Melodrama in Latin America: Films, Telenovelas and the Currency of Popular Form." *Wide Angle* 7, no. 3 (1985): 5–13.

Low, Rachel. *A History of the British Film 1918–1929*. London: George Allen and Unwin, 1971.

Lubiano, Wahneema. "But Compared to What? Reading Realism, Representation, and Essentialism in *School Daze*, *Do the Right Thing*, and the Spike Lee Discourse." *Black American Literature Forum* 25, no. 2 (1991): 253–82.

Lye, Len. "Television: New Axes to Grind." *Sight and Sound* 8 (Summer 1939): 65–70.

————. "Sight Sound Consanguinity." New Plymouth: Len Lye Foundation Archive, 1966.

————. "Len Lye Speaks at the Film Makers' Cinematheque." *Film Culture* no. 44 (Spring 1967): 49–51.

————. "Somewhat Autobiographically." New Plymouth: Len Lye Foundation Archive, 1975.

————. "Is Film Art?" *Film Culture* no. 29 (Summer 1963), 38–9. Reprinted in *Figures of Motion: Len Lye Selected Writings*. Edited by Wystan Curnow and Roger Horrocks. Auckland: Auckland University Press, 1984. Pp. 52–4.

————. "A Kinetic Biography." New Plymouth: Len Lye Foundation Archive, n.d.

MacCabe, Colin. "Walsh an Author?" *Screen* 16, no. 1 (Spring 1975): 128–34.

"A Man to Whom the Angels Flock." *Fortune* 95, no. 6 (June 1977): 44.

Mancia, Adrienne, and Willard Van Dyke. "The Artist as Film-Maker: Len Lye." *Art in America* 54 (July–August 1966): 98–106.

Mankekar, Purnima. *Screening Culture, Viewing Politics An Ethnography of Television, Womanhood, and Nation in Postcolonial India.* Durham, NC: Duke University Press, 1999.

"Many Colored People Attending the Avenue Theatre Conduct Themselves in a Noisy or Boisterous Manner." *Chicago Broad-Ax*, May 13, 1920, 1.

Marks, Laura. "Here's Gazing at You: A New Spin on Old Porn Exposes Gender and Generation Gaps." *The Independent* (March 1993): 26–31.

Martin, Adrian. "Sign Your Name Across My Heart, or 'I Want to Write about Delbert Mann.'" *Screening the Past*, no. 13 (2001), www.latrobe.edu.au/www.screeningthepast.

Martinez, Wilton. "Who constructs anthropological knowledge? Toward a theory of ethnographic film spectatorship?" In *Film as Ethnography*. Edited by Peter Crawford and Ian Turton. Manchester: Manchester University Press, 1992. Pp. 131–64.

Marvin, Carolyn. *When Old Technologies Were New: Dealing with Electric Communication in the Late Nineteenth Century.* New York: Oxford University Press, 1989.

Marx, Karl. *Capital,* Vol. I [1867]. Translated by Ben Fowkes. London: Penguin Books, 1976.

Mast, Gerald. *Can't Help Singin': The American Musical on Stage and Screen.* Woodstock, NY: The Overlook Press, 1987.

Maule, Rosanna. "De-authorizing the Auteur: Postmodern Politics of Interpellation in Contemporary European Cinema." In *Postmodernism in the Cinema*. Edited by Cristina Degli-Espositi. Oxford: Berghahn Books, 1998. Pp. 113–30.

Mayer, Vicki. "Capturing Cultural Identity/Creating Community." *International Journal of Cultural Studies* 3 (2000): 57–78.

Mayne, Judith. *Directed by Dorothy Arzner.* Bloomington: Indiana University Press, 1994.

McCarthy, Bob. "UCLA Students Team Up for Noir." *Daily News of Los Angeles*, May 8, 1998, L.A. Life.

McChesney, Robert W. *Telecommunications, Mass Media, and Democracy: The Battle for the Control of U.S. Broadcasting, 1928–1935.* New York: Oxford University Press, 1995.

————. *Corporate Media and the Threat to Democracy.* New York: Seven Stories Press, 1997.

McDonogh, Gary, and Cindy Wong. "The Mediated Metropolis: Reflections on Anthropology and Communication." *American Anthropologist* 103, no. 1 (2001): 96–111.

————. "Orientalism Abroad: Hong Kong Readings of *The World of Suzie Wong*." In *Classic Hollywood, Classic Whiteness*. Edited by Daniel Bernadi. Minneapolis: University of Minnesota Press, 2001. Pp. 210–44.

McGilligan, Patrick. *Backstory: Interviews with Screenwriters from Hollywood's Golden Age.* Los Angeles and Berkeley: University of California Press, 1986.

McLuhan, Marshall. *Understanding Media: The Extensions of Man*. 1964. Reprint, Cambridge, MA: MIT Press, 1994.

Medhurst, Andy. "That Special Thrill: *Brief Encounter*, Homosexuality, and Authorship." *Screen* 32, no. 2 (1991): 197–208.

Mekas, Jonas. "Movie Journal." *Soho Weekly News*, December 6, 1976, n.p.

Michaels, Eric. *Bad Aboriginal Art: Traditions, Media and Technological Horizons*. Minneapolis: University of Minnesota Press, 1994.

Micheaux, Oscar. *The Forged Note*. Lincoln, NE: Western Book Supply, 1915.

———. "The Negro and the Photo-Play." *Half-Century Magazine* 6, no. 5 (May 1919): 5.

———. *The Conquest* [1913]. Lincoln: University of Nebraska Press, 1994.

Millstein, Gilbert. "Harrison Horror Story." *New York Times*, July 21, 1957, sec. 6, 44.

Mitchell-Kernan, Claudia. "Signifying." Reprinted in *Mother Wit from the Laughing Barrel: Readings in the Interpretation of Afro-American Folklore*. Edited by Alan Dundes. Jackson: University Press of Mississippi, 1990. Pp. 310–28.

Modleski, Tania. *The Women Who Knew Too Much: Hitchcock and Feminist Theory*. New York and London: Routledge, 1988.

Montagu, Ivor. *Film World*. Harmondsworth: Penguin, 1964.

Moon, Michael. *Disseminating Whitman: Revision and Corporeality in Leaves of Grass*. Cambridge, MA: Harvard University Press, 1991.

Moran, Monica. "Independents on Overdrive." *Variety*, July 21, 1997, 12.

Moritz, William. "Len Lye's Films in the Context of International Abstract Cinema." In *Len Lye*. Edited Jean-Michel Bouhours and Roger Horrocks. Paris: Centre Pompidou, 2000. Pp. 193–98.

Morson, Gary Saul, and Caryl Emerson. *Mikhail Bakhtin: Creation of a Prosaics*. Stanford, CA: Stanford University Press, 1990.

"The Movies Detrimental to the Negro Child." *Chicago Broad-Ax*, January 24, 1920, 1.

Muir, Florabel. "Joan Harrison Worrying about Butter." *Hollywood Citizen News*, January 16, 1946, n.p. Margaret Herrick Library, special collections, Joan Harrison clippings files.

Murdock, Graham. "Authorship and Organization." *Screen Education* no. 35 (Summer 1980): 19–34.

"Mystery Film Director." *New York Times*, November 24, 1929, sec. 10, p. 8.

Napier-Bell, Simon. *Black Vinyl, White Powder*. London: Ebury Press, 2001.

Naremore, James. "Authorship and the Cultural Politics of Film Criticism." *Film Quarterly* 44, no. 1 (Fall 1990): 14–22.

National Asian American Telecommunication Association. "Filmmaker of the Month." http://naatanet.org/community/archives/arch_filmmaker/quentin_lee.html. June 2001.

"New Movie Digest." *Daily News*, May 15, 1998, 58.

Nichols, Bill. "Introduction." In *Movies and Methods*. Vol. 1. Edited by Bill Nichols. Berkeley: University of California Press, 1976.

——— ed. *Movies and Methods*. Vol. 1. Berkeley: University of California Press, 1976.

———. *Representing Reality*. Bloomington: Indiana University Press, 1991.

"No Longer Chattels." *Chicago Defender*, May 24, 1919, 1.

Noriega, Chon A. "'Our Own Institutions': The Geopolitics of Chicano Professionalism." In *Film and Authorship*. Edited by Virginia Wexman. New Brunswick, NJ: Rutgers University Press, forthcoming, December 2002.

Nowell-Smith, Geoffrey. *[Luchino] Visconti* [1967]. Garden City, NY: Doubleday & Company, 1968.

———. "Six Authors in Pursuit of *The Searchers*." *Screen* 17, no. 1 (Spring 1976): 26–33.

———. "Minnelli and Melodrama [1969]." Reprinted in *Home is Where the Heart Is: Studies in Melodrama and the Woman's Film*. Edited by Christine Gledhill. London: British Film Institute, 1992. Pp. 70–4.

Oishi, Eve. "Bad Asians: New Film and Video by Queer Asian American Artists." In *Countervisions: Asian American Film Criticism.* Edited by Darrell Y. Hamamoto and Sandra Liu. Philadelphia: Temple University Press, 2000. Pp. 221–41.

O'Neill, Sean. "'Sprung' Fever: Triple-Threat Rusty Cundieff Directs, Scripts and Stars in His Third Film, Trimark's 'Sprung.'" *Boxoffice Online.* [electronic periodical] Updated April 1997; accessed March 3, 2000. Http.//www.boxoff.com/apr97sneak3.html.

Ossman, Susan, *Picturing Casablanca.* Berkeley: University of California Press, 1994.

Park, Robert E., Ernest Burgess, and Roderick Mackenzie, eds. *The City.* Chicago: University of Chicago Press, 1925.

Penley, Constance. "Introduction—The Lady Doesn't Vanish: Feminism and Film Theory." In *Feminism and Film Theory.* Edited by Constance Penley. New York: Routledge, 1988. Pp. 1–24.

Perkins, V. F. *Film as Film: Understanding and Judging Movies.* Middlesex, UK: Penguin Books, 1972.

Perloff, Marjorie, ed. *Postmodern Genres.* Norman: University of Oklahoma Press, 1988.

Petrie, Graham. "Alternatives to Auteurs," *Film Quarterly* 26, no. 3 (Spring 1973): 27–35.

———. *Hollywood Destinies: European Directors in America, 1922–1931.* London: Routledge & Kegan Paul, 1985.

Petro, Patrice. "Rematerializing the Vanishing 'Lady': Feminism, Hitchcock, and Interpretation." In *A Hitchcock Reader.* Edited by Marshall Deutelbaum and Leland Poague. Ames: Iowa State University Press, 1986. Pp. 122–33.

Polan, Dana. "Auteur Desire." *Screening the Past,* no. 12 (2001): www.latrobe.edu.au/www/screeningthepast. Accessed March 9, 2001.

Powell, Dilys. "The New Disney." *Sunday Times,* April 27, 1941. Ann Lye clipping file. New Plymouth: Len Lye Foundation Archives.

Projansky, Sarah. *Watching Rape: Film and Television in Postfeminist Culture.* New York: New York University Press, 2001.

Putnam, Robert, *Bowling Alone: The Collapse and Revival of American Community.* New York: Simon & Schuster, 2000.

Rabinovitz, Lauren. *Points of Resistance: Women, Power and Politics in the New York Avant-garde Cinema, 1943–71.* Urbana: University of Illinois Press, 1991.

"Rainbow Chasing." *Chicago Defender,* April 10, 1920, 1.

Ray, Robert. *A Certain Tendency of the Hollywood Cinema.* Princeton, NJ: Princeton University Press, 1985.

"Ray Thorburn Interviews Len Lye." *Art International* 19 (April 1975): 64.

Regester, Charlene. "Black Films, White Censors: Oscar Micheaux Confronts Censorship in New York, Virginia, and Chicago." In *Movie Censorship and American Culture.* Edited by Francis G. Couvares. Washington, D.C.: Smithsonian Institution Press, 1996. Pp. 159–86.

Renan, Sheldon. *An Introduction to American Underground Film.* New York: E. P. Dutton, 1967.

Rich, Frank. "Discomania." *Time,* December 19, 1977, 69–70.

———. "Black Hole." *Time,* June 19, 1978, 78–79.

Riding, Laura. *Len Lye and the Problem of Popular Film.* London: Seizin Press, 1938.

Roberts, John W. *From Trickster to Badman: The Black Folk Hero in Slavery and Freedom.* Philadelphia: University of Pennsylvania Press, 1989.

Robertson, James C. *The Casablanca Man.* London: Routledge, 1993.

Robinson, John. W. "Can the Negro Solve His Own Problem." *Half-Century Magazine* 6, no. 6 (June 1919): 16.

Roddick, Nick. *A New Deal In Entertainment.* London: British Film Institute, 1983.

Rosenau, Pauline Marie. *Post-modernism and the Social Sciences*. Princeton, NJ: Princeton University Press, 1992.

Routt, William. "L'Evidence." *Continuum: The Australian Journal of Media and Culture* 5, no. 2 (1990). http:wwwmcc.murdoch.edu.au/ReadingRoom/5.2/Routt.html.

Rubins, Josh. "Genius Without Tears." *The New York Review of Books*, June 16, 1988, 30–3.

Ryall, Thomas. *Alfred Hitchcock and the British Cinema*. Urbana and Chicago: University of Illinois Press, 1986.

Said, Edward. *Orientalism*. New York: Vintage Books, 1979.

Sarris, Andrew. "The American Cinema." *Film Culture* no. 28 (Spring 1963): 1–51.

———. *The American Cinema*. New York: E. P. Dutton, 1968.

———. *Confessions of a Cultist: On the Cinema, 1955–1969*. New York: Simon & Schuster, 1970.

———. "Notes on the Auteur Theory in 1962." *Film Culture* no. 27 (Winter 1962–1963). Reprinted in *Film Culture Reader*. Edited by P. Adams Sitney. New York: Praeger Publishers, 1970. Pp. 121–35.

———. "The World of Howard Hawks [1962]." Reprinted in *Focus on Howard Hawks*. Edited by Joseph McBride. Englewood Cliffs, NJ: Prentice-Hall, 1972. Pp. 35–63.

Scharrer, Gary. "Christians Rally to Squelch Pornography." *El Paso Times*, May 18, 1980, 1–B.

Schatz, Thomas. *The Genius of the System: Hollywood Filmmaking in the Studio Era*. New York: Pantheon, 1988.

———. *Boom and Bust: American Cinema in the 1940s*. Los Angeles and Berkeley: University of California Press, 1997.

Scheuer, Philip K. "Producer's Spurs Won by Woman." *Los Angeles Times*, February 23, 1944, n.p. Margaret Herrick Library, special collections, Joan Harrison clippings files.

Schwartz, Tony. "Stigwood's Midas Touch." *Newsweek*, January 23, 1978, 40, 50.

Sedgwick, Eve Kosofsky. *Epistemology of the Closet*. Berkeley: University of California Press, 1990.

Sgt. Pepper's Lonely Hearts Club Bank Pressbook. New York: Val Ventures, Inc., 1978.

Sherman, Betsy. "Feeling and Funk: The MFA's Asian-American Festival Ranges from the Touching to the Stylish." *Boston Globe*, March 14, 1999, N9.

Silver, Brenda R. "Mis-fits: The Monstrous Union of Virginia Woolf and Marilyn Monroe." *Discourse* 16, no. 1 (Fall 1993): 71–108.

Silverman, Kaja. *The Acoustic Mirror: The Female Voice in Psychoanalysis and Cinema*. Bloomington: Indiana University Press, 1988.

———. "The Author as Receiver." *October*, no. 96 (Spring 2001): 17–34.

Simon, John. "Dog-Day Distemper." *National Review*, July 21, 1978, 908.

Skal, David J., and Elias Savada. *Dark Carnival: The Secret World of Tod Browning, Hollywood's Master of the Macabre*. New York: Anchor Books, 1995.

Smith, Jack. "The Perfect Filmic Appositeness of Maria Montez." *Film Culture*, no. 27 (Winter 1962–1963): 28–32.

Smith, Jean Voltaire. "Our Need For More Films." *The Half-Century Magazine* 9, no. 4 (April 1922): 8.

Smitherman, Geneva. *Talkin' and Testifyin': The Language of Black America*. Detroit, MI: Wayne State University Press, 1977.

———. *Black Talk: Words and Phrases from the Hood to the Amen Corner*. Boston: Houghton Mifflin Company, 1994.

Snyder, Robert. *The Voice of the City: Vaudeville and Popular Culture*. New York: Oxford University Press, 1989.

Sobchack, Vivian. "Tod Browning: Raising the Dead, or the Film Historian as Archeologist." Unpublished paper, 1974.

Soe, Valerie. "Pictures in Transition: 15th San Francisco International Asian American Film Festival." *Afterimage* 25, no. 1 (1997): 3.

Solanas, Fernando, and Octavio Getino. "Toward a Third Cinema." *Cineaste* 4, no. 3 (Winter 1970–71): 1–10.

Solomon, Matthew. "Stage Magic and the Silent Cinema: Méliès, Houdini, Browning." Ph.D. dissertation, University of California, Los Angeles, 2001.

Spiegel, Alan. *Fiction and the Camera Eye: Visual Consciousness in Film and the Modern Novel.* Charlottesville: University Press of Virginia, 1976.

Spoto, Donald. *Dark Side of Genius: The Life of Alfred Hitchcock.* New York: Ballantine Books, 1983.

Sreberny-Mohammadi, Annabelle. *Small Media, Big Revolution: Communication, Culture, and the Iranian Revolution.* Minneapolis: University of Minnesota Press, 1994.

Stabiner, Karen. "Tapping the Homosexual Market." *New York Times*, May 2, 1982, sec. 6, 34.

Staiger, Janet. "*Theorist*, yes, but what *of*? Bazin and History." *Iris* 2, no. 2 (1984): 99–109.

———. "The Politics of Film Canons." *Cinema Journal* 24, no. 3 (Spring 1985): 4–23.

———. *Interpreting Films: Studies in the Historical Reception of American Cinema.* Princeton, NJ: Princeton University Press, 1992.

———. "Introduction." In *The Studio System.* Edited by Janet Staiger. New Brunswick, NJ: Rutgers University Press, 1995. Pp. 1–9.

———. *Perverse Spectators: The Practices of Film Reception.* New York: New York University Press, 2000.

———. "Authorship Approaches." In *Authorship and Film.* Edited by David A. Gerstner and Janet Staiger. New York: Routledge, 2002. Pp. 27–57.

Staples, Donald E. "The Auteur Theory Reexamined." *Cinema Journal* 6 (1966–1967): 1–7.

Stigwood, Robert, and Dee Anthony. *The Official Sgt. Pepper's Lonely Hearts Club Band Scrapbook.* New York: Pocket Books, 1978.

Stillinger, Jack. *Multiple Authorship and The Myth Of The Solitary Genius.* Oxford: Oxford University Press, 1991.

"Stylized Cultural Riff." *Toronto Star*, August 31, 1997, B8.

Sullivan, Monica. "Joan Harrison." *Movie Magazine International* (7 September 1994): World Wide Web Document. http://www.shoestring.org.mmi_revs/joan-harr.html. Accessed November 25, 2001.

"Supermogul in the Land of Opportunity." *Forbes*, July 10, 1978, 42.

Sypher, Wylie. *Rococo to Cubism in Art and Literature: Transformations in Style, in Art and Literature from the Eighteenth to the Twentieth Century.* New York: Vintage Books, 1960.

Taubin, Amy. "The Sound and the Fury." *Village Voice*, May 12, 1998, 123.

Taylor, Charles B. "Film Controversy Percolates." Letter to the editor in *The Prospector*, December 7, 1976, 9.

Taylor, Greg. *Artists in the Audience: Cults, Camp and American Film Criticism.* Princeton, NJ: Princeton University Press, 1999.

Taylor, John Russell. *Hitch: The Life and Work of Alfred Hitchcock.* London: Faber and Faber, 1978.

Tesson, Charles. "Le monstreux sentiment de l'espèce humaine." *Trafic*, no. 8 (Autumn 1993): 39–63.

Thomas, Kevin. "Best for Last?" *Los Angeles Times*, August 21, 1997, F14.

———. "*Shopping*: A Postmodern Take on Asian Americans." *Los Angeles Times*, May 8, 1998, F8.

"Tod Browning." *Motion Picture News* 23, no. 1 (December 25, 1920): 212.

Trachtenberg, Alan. *The Incorporation of America.* New York: Hill and Wang, 1982.

"Travolta's 'Fever' Infects 'Grease' Bookings in May." *Variety*, January 25, 1978, 1, 93.

Treviño, Jesús Salvador. "Chicano Cinema Overview." *Areito* no. 37 (1984): 40.

Truffaut, François. "A Certain Tendency of the French Cinema [1954]." Reprinted in *Movies and Methods.* Vol. 1. Edited by Bill Nichols. Berkeley: University of California Press, 1976. Pp. 224–37.

Turow, Joseph. "Unconventional Programs on Commercial Television: An Organizational Perspective." In *Mass Communication in Context*. Edited by D. Charles Whitney and James Ettema. Beverly Hills, CA: Sage Publications, 1982. Pp. 107–29.

———. *Media Industries: The Production of News and Entertainment*. New York: Longman, 1984.

Ulmer, Edgar G. "Entretein avec Edgar G. Ulmer." Interviewed by Bernard Eisenschitz and Jean-Claude Romer. *Midi-minuit fantastique* no. 13 (November 1965): 1–14.

Varela, Willie. "Art in Spite of El Paso." *MAIN: Media Arts Information Network* (June 1993): 4, 13.

———. "Chicano Personal Cinema." *Jump Cut* no. 39 (1994): 96–9.

Verrill, Addison. "Par, Nat'l Screen Riding U. S. Film Poster 'Boom.'" *Variety*, July 6, 1977, 4.

Vesselo, Anthony. "*The Colour Box.*" *Sight and Sound* 4, no. 15 (Autumn 1935): 117.

Voedisch, Lynn. "Asian Artistry: Films with Bicultural Basis." *Chicago Sun-Times*, April 4, 1997, 38.

Wallis, H.B. and Charles Higham. *Star-Maker: The Autobiography of Hal Wallis*. New York: Macmillan Publishing Co., 1980.

Warhol, Andy, and Pat Hackett. *Popism: The Warhol Sixties*. San Diego, CA: Harcourt, Brace, 1980.

Waters, John. *Crackpot: The Obsessions of John Waters*. New York: Vintage Press, 1986.

———. *Shock Value: A Tasteful Book About Bad Taste*, 2nd ed. New York: Thunder's Mouth Press, 1995.

Watts, Richard, Jr. "A Glance at Tod Browning, An Original of the Cinema." *New York Herald-Tribune*, March 20, 1927, sec. 6, p. 3.

———. "Mr. Tod Browning Continues His Grand Guignol Exploits." *New York Herald-Tribune*, June 19, 1927, n.p., clipping, Billy Rose Theatre Collection, New York Public Library for the Performing Arts.

———. "The Directorial Stylist—Has He Passed from the Picture?" *Motion Picture Classic* 102, no. 13 (March 28, 1931): 95.

Weber, Samuel. *Mass Mediauras: Form Technics Media*. Stanford, CA: Stanford University Press, 1996.

Weinberg, Gretchen. "Interview with Len Lye." *Film Culture* no. 29 (Summer 1963): 40–5.

"Welcome Stranger." *Chicago Defender*, April 17, 1920, 1.

"Where Children May Hiss." *World Film News* 1 (May 1936): n.p.

Wilde, Oscar. *The Complete Works of Oscar Wilde: Stories, Plays, Poems, and Essay*. New York: Harper & Row, 1989.

Willemann, Paul. "The Fugitive Subject." In *Raoul Walsh*. Edited by Phil Hardy. Colchester, England: Vinegard Press, 1974. Pp. 63–89.

Williams, Linda. "Feminism Film Theory: *Mildred Pierce* and the Second World War." In *Female Spectators: Looking at Film and Television*. Edited by E. Deidre Pribram. London: Verso, 1988. Pp. 12–30.

Wimsatt, W. K. "Genesis: A Fallacy Revisited." In *The Disciplines of Criticism*. Edited by Peter Demetz, Thomas Greene, and Lowry Nelson, Jr. New Haven, CT: Yale University Press, 1968. Pp. 193–225.

Wimsatt, W. K., Jr., and M. C. Beardsley, "The Intentional Fallacy," *Sewanee Review* 54 (1946): 468–88.

———. "The Affective Fallacy." *Sewanee Review* 57, no. 1 (January–March 1949): 31–55.

Wollen, Peter. *Signs and Meaning in the Cinema*. Bloomington: Indiana University Press, 1969.

———. *Signs and Meaning in the Cinema*, rev. ed. Bloomington: Indiana University Press, 1972. Pp. 74–115.

Wood, Robin. "Bernado Bertolucci" In *Cinema: A Critical Dictionary*. Edited by Richard Roud. New York: Viking Press, 1980. Pp. 125–32.

295

Wong, Cindy. "Community Through the Lens: An Ethnographic Study of Grassroots Video." Unpublished Ph.D Dissertation, Annenberg School for Communication, University of Pennsylvania, 1997.

———. "Understanding Grassroots Audiences: Imagination, Reception, and Use in Community Videography." *The Velvet Light Trap* no. 42 (1999): 91–102.

Worth, Larry. "*Fangs* Neither Hair Nor There." *New York Post*, May 15, 1998, 58.

Ya Salaam, Kalamu. "Black Macho: The Myth of the Positive Message." *Black Film Review* 7, no. 1 (1995): 6–9.

Zimmermann, Patricia. *States of Emergency: Documentaries, Wars, Democracy.* Berkeley: University of California Press, 2000.

Zuckerman, Ed. "Sgt. Pepper Taught the Band to Play, and Stigwood's Gonna Make It Pay." *Rolling Stone*, April 20, 1978, 50–54.

biographies

Hugh Bartling is Assistant Professor of Political Science at the University of Central Florida where he teaches courses in political science, political theory, and urbanism.

George F. Custen is Professor of Communications and Cinema Studies and Chairperson of the Department of Media Culture at City University of New York, College of Staten Island. He is the author of *Bio/Pics: How Hollywood Constructed Public History* and *Twentieth Century's Fox: Darryl F. Zanuck and the Culture of Hollywood* as well as Series Editor of the Rutgers Series in Communications, Media and Culture. He is a frequent contributor to both *The New York Times* and *The Los Angeles Times* and is currently working on a critical biography of George Stevens.

Michael deAngelis is Assistant Professor at DePaul University's School for New Learning, where he teaches film, television, and cultural studies. He is the author of *Gay Fandom and Crossover Stardom: James Dean, Mel Gibson, and Keanu Reeves* as well as articles in anthologies and the journals *Spectator* and *Cultural Critique*. His current project is a history of art cinema distribution and exhibition practices in the 1960s and 1970s.

Jacqueline Fulmer holds a Ph.D. in Rhetoric from the University of California, Berkeley. Her dissertation, "Strategies of Indirection in African American and Irish Contemporary Fiction, Zora Neale Hurston to Toni Morrison and Mary Lavin to Éilís Ní Dhuibhne," compares the line of descent from Lavin to Ní Dhuibhne to that from Hurston and Morrison by examining three strategies of indirect argument: "sly civility," folklore, and humor. She has published in the *Journal of American Folklore* and *Christianity and Literature*, teaches comparative literature and American cultures studies at the University of California, Berkeley, and is writing a book on indirection in Morrison's *Paradise*.

David A. Gerstner is Assistant Professor and Program Coordinator of Cinema Studies at City University of New York, College of Staten Island. He has published on issues of masculinity and queer cinema in journals such as *The Velvet Light Trap*, *Cultural Critique*, *The Stanford Humanities Review*, and *Film Quarterly*. He has also written on New Zealand cinema in *CineAction* and in the forthcoming collection, *New Zealand Filmmakers*, edited by Stuart Murray and Ian Conrich. His current book project explores issues of masculinity and aesthetics in early American cinema.

Roger Horrocks is head of the Department of Film, Television and Media Studies at the University of Auckland in New Zealand. He has been involved in documentary filmmaking and in media policy, serving as the Deputy Chair of the New Zealand Broadcasting Commission (NZ On Air). His most recent book is a biography of the artist and filmmaker Len Lye. In New York he worked as an assistant to Lye during the last year of the artist's life.

Christina Lane is Assistant Professor in the Motion Picture Program at the University of Miami. She is the author of *Feminist Hollywood: From Born in Flames to Point Break* and has published articles in *Cinema Journal* and the *Journal of Popular Film and Television*. She is working on a book-length manuscript of Joan Harrison and the women behind Alfred Hitchcock.

Walter Metz is writing a textbook on film and theatre tentatively entitled *Dramatic Intertexts: Encountering Theatre via Mass Media*. He is an Assistant Professor in the Department of Media and Theatre Arts at Montana State University–Bozeman, where he teaches the history, theory, and criticism of film, theatre, and television. His previous publications involve genre and intertextuality in cinema, for journals such as *The Journal of Contemporary Thought*, *Film Quarterly*, *The Journal of Film and Video*, *Film Criticism*, and *Literature/Film Quarterly*. He wrote the chapter on the 1960s American avant-garde for Paul Monaco's *The Sixties*.

Chon A. Noriega is a Professor in the UCLA Department of Film, Television, and Digital Media and Associate Director of the UCLA Chicano Studies Research Center. He is author of *Shot in America: Television, the State, and the Rise of Chicano Cinema* and editor of eight books on Latino media, performance, and visual art. Since 1996, he has been editor of *Aztlan: A Journal of Chicano Studies*. In 1999, he co-founded the 400-member National Association of Latino Independent Producers. He is currently working on book projects on Chicano feature films and on a Latino art exhibition.

Kent A. Ono is an Associate Professor in the American Studies and Asian American Studies programs at the University of California, Davis. His research emphasis is on critical and theoretical analysis of print, film, and television media, specifically focusing on representations of race, gender, sexuality, class, and nation. He has contributed articles to numerous journals and anthologies, in addition to co-authoring *Shifting Borders: Rhetoric, Immigration, and California's Proposition 187* and co-editing *Enterprise Zones: Critical Positions on Star Trek*.

Sarah Projansky is Associate Professor of Women and Gender Studies at the University of California, Davis, where she also teaches film studies and cultural studies. She is author of *Watching Rape: Film and Television in Postfeminist Culture* and co-editor of *Enterprise Zones: Critical Positions on Star Trek*. She has published essays on film history, the representation of girls in popular culture, the representation of whiteness in cinema, and gender and sports in *Cinema Journal, Signs*, and various anthologies.

Matthew Solomon is a Lecturer in the Department of Communication and Culture at Indiana University where he teaches European and American film history. He received his Ph.D. from the Department of Film and Television at the University of California, Los Angeles in 2001. His essays have appeared in the *Quarterly Review of Film and Video* and *Meta-Morphing*.

Janet Staiger teaches cultural, gender, and media studies at The University of Texas at Austin. Her recent books are *Perverse Spectators: The Practices of Film Reception* and *Blockbuster TV: Must-See Sitcoms in the Network Era*. She directs the University's Center for Women's Studies and is the William P. Hobby Centennial Professor in Communication.

Peter Wollen is Professor and Chair in the Department of Film, Television and New Media at the University of California, Los Angeles. His books include *Signs and Meaning in the Cinema, Raiding The Icebox: Reflections on Twentieth Century Culture, Howard Hawks: American Artist* (edited, with Jim Hillier), *Visual Display* (edited, with Lynne Cooke), and *Singin' In The Rain*. He was co-writer of Michelangelo Antonioni's film *The Passenger* and subsequently made a series of films in Britain, including *Penthesilea, Riddles of the Sphinx, Crystal Gazing*, and *The Bad Sister*, all co-directed with Laura Mulvey, as well as *Friendship's Death*, directed solo.

Cindy Hing-Yuk Wong is Assistant Professor of Communications in the Department of Media Culture at the City University of New York, College of Staten Island. Her areas of research include grassroots media, Hong Kong cinema culture, and film festivals. A co-editor of the *Encyclopedia of Contemporary American Culture,* she also has published articles in *American Anthropologist, Postscript, The Velvet Light Trap,* and *Amerasia* and contributed chapters to *Classic Whiteness* and *Consuming Hong Kong.*

indexes

index of films and videos

Adventures of Robin Hood, The (1938), 62, 64, 66, 74

Alexander's Ragtime Band (1938), 77–94

All That Heaven Allows (1956), 161

American Graffiti (1973), 251

Angels With Dirty Faces (1938), 64, 66, 74

April 1977 (1977), 196

Baby Doll (1956), 169

Bad Girl, The (1994), 209

Ballad of Gregorio Cortez, The (1982) 201

Ballet Mécanique (1924), 179

Bamboozled (2000), 122, 134

Battleship Potemkin, The. See Potemkin

Becky's Eye (1975), 196

Before the Revolution (1965), 88

Beggars on Horseback (1926), 242

Big City, The (1920), 245

Big Sleep, The (1946), 72

Bingo Long Traveling All Stars, The (1976), 253–254

Black Fury (1935), 74

Blue Angel, The (1930), 242

Body and Soul (1925), 134

Bombing of Osage Avenue (1986), 215

Booty Call (1997), 134

Border Crossing (1988), 198

Boy in the Plastic Bubble, The (1976), 254

Brewster McCloud (1970), 252

Broadway Danny Rose (1984), 275

Buffalo Bill and the Indians (1975), 252

Cabin in the Cotton (1932), 74

California Split (1973), 252

Captain Blood (1936), 63, 66, 74

Casablanca (1942), 61–75

Cecil B. Demented (2000), 157–159, 162, 164, 166, 169, 171

Charge of the Light Brigade, The (1936), 63, 66, 67

Christmas Evil (1980), 165

Chronicle of Anna Magdalena Bach, The (1968), 3

Chung King Express (1996), 275

Circle of Danger (1950), 98

Circus, The (1928), 243

Citizen Kane (1941), 31, 32, 65, 69

Colour Box, A (1935), 183–184

Colour Flight (1938), 184

Count of Monte Cristo, The (1934), 63

Cry-Baby (1990), 157, 162, 167, 169, 170–171

Dark Waters (1944), 97

Desperate Living (1977), 158, 161, 166–168, 171

Detritus (1989), 198

Devil's Circus, the (1926), 243

Disraeli (1929), 79

Divine Trash (1998), 159

Dodge City (1939), 69

Dracula (1931), 236, 242

Earthquake (1974), 255

Easy Rider (1969), 252

Erogeny (1976), 196

Exquisite Thief (1919), 244

Face/Off (1997), 265

Face to Face: It's Not What You Think (1996), 214, 218, 221–222, 224

Fantasia (1940), 184

Fearless Leader (1985), 197

Fear of a Black Hat (1993), 137, 139–144, 147, 149–150, 152

Female Trouble (1975), 162, 164–165, 168, 170–171

Fetish Footage (1981), 197

5th & Market (1983), 197

Fighting for Our Schools (2001), 222

Flaming Creatures (1963), 168

Forest Gump (1994), 169–170

Forest Lawn (1982), 197

Forged Note, The (1915), 127–129

Four Devils (1929), 243

Four's a Crowd (1930), 73

Four Weddings and a Funeral (1994), 150

Freaks (1932), 235–236, 239–245

Free Radicals (1958), 176–177, 186, 188

Fuses (1967), 196

General Line, The (1929), 185

Gerald McBoing Boing (1951), 187

Ghost (1990), 151

Gold is Where You Find It (1937), 64, 73

Gone With the Wind (1939), 73

Grease (1978), 248, 251–252, 254–258
Greed (1924), 241
Green Light (1974), 196

Hairspray (1988), 157, 162, 169
Harry Potter and the Sorcerer's Stone (2001), 160
He Who Gets Slapped (1924), 243
Hold Me While I'm Naked (1966), 196
House Beautiful (1988), 197
Housekeeper (1992), 208
House of Cards, A (1988), 197
House of Rothschild, The (1934), 79

I Am a Fugitive From a Chain Gang (1932), 79
I Am Joaquin (1969), 193
Ice Storm, The (1997), 265
Images (1972), 252
In Old Chicago (1938), 87
In Progress (1985), 197
In the Flesh (1982), 197, 199

Jamaica Inn (1939), 100–101
Jane Eyre (1944), 101
Jaws (1975), 249
Jazz Singer, The (1927), 78, 83, 85
Jesus Christ Superstar (1973), 248, 251
JLG/JLG: Self Portrait in December (1995), 20
Joy Luck Club, The (1993), 275

Lady Vanishes, The (1938), 99–101, 104
Last Laugh, The (1925), 237
Laugh, Clown, Laugh (1928), 243
Leaves of Grass (1979), 196
London After Midnight (1927), 236
Lost Horizon (1973), 251
Lost Man, A (1992), 198, 200–209

Making Is Choosing (1989), 198, 200
Man Who Knew Too Much, The (1934), 100
March of Time, The (1944–1951), 185
Mark of the Vampire (1935), 240
M*A*S*H (1970), 252
Merry Widow, The ((1925), 242
Meshes of the Afternoon (1943), 203
Mildred Pierce (1945), 65, 67, 70, 72–74, 203
Miracles for Sale (1939), 240
Mission to Moscow (1942), 74
Moana (1925), 180
Mondo Trasho (1969), 158, 161, 168, 171
Moondance I & II (1974), 196
Motor Kings (1976), 254
Mr. Arkadin (1955), 65, 72
Multiple Maniacs (1970), 158, 160, 168, 170–171
Murder in Harlem (1935), 129
Musketeers of Pig Alley (1912), 240
My Darling Clementine (1946), 65–66
Mystery of the Wax Museum (1939), 74

Nashville (1975), 252
Neon Crescent, A (1975), 196
Nightmare Alley (1947), 87, 236
Night Porter, The (1971), 163
Nocturne (1946), 98, 108, 112–113
Nosferatu (1922), 242
Now Voyager (1942), 72

Once More, My Darling (1949), 98, 102, 113
On the Avenue (1937), 82
Outside the Law (1920), 238

Particles in Space (1979), 176
Passage to Marseille (1944), 74
Pearls and Savages (1921), 180
Pecker (1998), 157–159, 162, 164, 169, 172
Pépé Le Moko (1937), 66
Phantom Lady (1944), 97, 99, 102–107, 113
Piano, The (1993), 179
Pink Flamingos (1972), 157–159, 161, 165, 168–169, 171–172
Polyester (1981), 157, 160–161, 168–169
Potemkin (1925), 159–160, 162, 185
Power to Change, The (2001), 221
Private Life of Henry VIII, The (1933), 63
Private Lives of Elizabeth and Essex, The (1939), 66, 73
Puppets (1916), 245
Pursued (1947), 48

Queen Christina (1933), 63

Reaching for the Moon (1931), 82
Reaffirmation (1990), 198
Rebecca (1940), 100–102, 105
Rebel Without a Cause (1955), 170
Recuerdos de flores muertas (1982), 197
Red River (1948), 72
Ride the Pink Horse (1947), 98, 102, 112–113
River, The (1948), 72
Rocky (1976), 253
Rules of the Game (1939), 72

Saboteur (1942), 104
Safe (1995), 275
Sally of the Sawdust (1925), 243
Santa Fe Trail (1940), 66, 73
Saturday Night Fever (1977), 248, 252–255, 258
Scorpio Rising (1963), 161
Sea Hawk, The (1940), 66, 74–76
Sea-Shell and the Clergyman (1928), 181
Secret Agent (1936), 184–185
Searchers, The (1956), 63, 72
Sergeant York (1941), 63
Serial Mom (1994), 157, 160, 162, 179, 171
Sgt. Pepper's Lonely Hearts Club Band (1978), 247–248, 251–256
Shadow of A Doubt (1943), 100–102
Shane (1953), 65
Sherman's March (1986), 219

Shopping for Fangs (1997), 263–278
Show, The (1927), 235, 239–243
Silly Symphonies (1929–1939), 184
Sixteen Candles (1984), 223
Sons of Liberty (1939), 74
So This is Paris (1926), 242
Sound of Music, The (1965), 252
Sprung (1997), 137, 139–140, 150–152
Stagecoach (1939), 64
Stan and Jane Brakhage (1980), 197
Strange Affair of Uncle Harry, The (1944), 98, 102, 107–108
Strangers on a Train (1951), 41
Star Wars (1977), 249
Strictly Business (1991), 140
Struggle in Futility (1983), 197
Suspicion (1941), 100–102

Tales From the Hood (1995), 137–152
Thelma and Louise (1991), 167
They Won't Believe Me (1947), 98–99, 107–113
Third Degree, The (1926), 243
Thirteenth Chair, The (1929), 240, 245
Thirty Nine Steps, The (1935), 98, 104
This is Spinal Tap (1984), 141
Thoughts of a Dry Brain (1988), 199
Thriller (1979), 160
Tin Pan Alley (1940), 91
Titanic (1998), 159
Tommy (1975), 248, 251, 253, 258
To School or Not to School (1993), 225, 229
Touch of Evil (1958), 48
Treasure Island (1934), 63
Tusalava (1929), 176, 180–182
TV Playland (1974), 199

Unholy Three, The (1925), 235–236, 239, 241, 243
Unknown, The (1927), 235–236, 241–243

Variety (1926), 237
Version One (1988), 198
Vertigo (1958), 63
Viaggio in Italia (1953), 72
Virginia City (1940), 66
Virgin of Stamboul, The (1920), 238

W. E. B. Du Bois: A Biography in Four Voices ((1995), 215
West of Zanzibar (1928), 240, 245
Wicked Darling, The (1919), 244
Within Our Gates (1920), 119, 127, 134
Wizard of Oz, The (1939), 72, 168
Wolf (1994), 275
Woman in the Moon (1929), 242
World of Suzie Wong, The (1960), 223

Yankee Doodle Dandy (1942), 65, 67–69, 74
You Better Watch Out (1980), 165
Young Man With a Horn (1950), 74

Young Mr. Lincoln (1939), 10, 47–48
Your Witness (1950), 102

general index

Abrams, M. H., 33
abstract expressionism, 188
Adams, Rachel, 235
Adilman, Sid, 267, 271, 274
Adorno, Theodor, 4, 123, 132
African American folklore, 138–153
African Americans, 79–85, 93–94, 119–134, 137–153
Agee, James, 8
agency, 43, 46, 49, 51, 99, 113, 120
Agento, Dario, 270
Alfred Hitchcock Hour (TV series), 113
Alfred Hitchcock Presents (TV series), 97, 113
Allen, Robert, 237
Alpi, Deborah Lazaroff, 103
Alvarado, Manuel, 29, 42, 45
Althusser, Louis, 10, 41–42
Altman, Robert, 252
Ameche, Don, 87
Anderson, John, 273–274
Anger, Kenneth, 6, 158–161, 196
animation, 182–185
Ansen, David, 252–253
Archer, Eugene, 72
Aristotle, 201
Arnheim, Rudolf, 5
Arzner, Dorothy, 6, 19–20, 52
Ashton, Dore, 189
Astruc, Alexandre, 6, 16, 34–35
Asian-American cinema, 263–278
Aurenche, Jean, 36
Austin, J. L., 50
auteur debate, 9–11, 37–40, 61
auteur theory, 5–7, 8–11, 35–40, 61–76, 263–278
author/artist, 4
author-creator, 12, 20
author-function, 28, 42, 50, 69, 122, 264, 267, 270, 276, 278
author intention, 12, 16
author as producer, 4, 13, 124, 129
authorial suicide, 20
author of text, 4, 28, 159
authorship
    approaches, 27–57
    biographical factors, 235–245
    as collaboration, 41–42
    collective, 213–229
    as discourse, 10–17, 46–49, 263–278
    as origin, 30–33
    as personality, 33–40
    practices, 3–25
    as reading strategy, 45–46
    as signature, 43–45

indexes

303

as sociology of production, 40–43
as technique of the self, 49–50
avant-garde cinema, 151, 162, 175–183, 193–195, 198–200
Avildsen, John, 253

B., Beth and Scott, 196
Badham, John, 253
Baille, Bruce, 196
Baker, Belle, 78
Bakhtin, Mikhail, 12–15, 20
Ballin, Hugo, 237
Bambara, Toni Cade, 215
Baraka, Amiri, 134
Barnes, Paul, 182, 187
Barr, Charles, 40
Barthes, Roland, 14–15, 20, 29, 45–47, 69, 158, 172, 256
Bazin, André, 7, 34–37, 40, 64–66, 72
Beardsley, Monroe, 11, 31
Beatles, The (musical group), 247, 251
Bee Gees, The (musical group), 247–248, 254
Beiderbecke, Bix, 74
Bellour, Raymond, 74
Belsey, Catherine, 33
Benjamin, Walter, 4, 12–15, 124, 129, 133
Bennett, Charles, 101–102
Benshoff, Harry, 147, 149
Bergman, Ingrid, 66
Berlin, Irving, 77–94
Bertolucci, Bernardo, 88
Bhabha, Homi, 18
biopics, 78–79, 82–83, 89–91
Blakeston, Oswell, 180
body, 17, 20, 175–182, 258
Boetticher, Budd, 64
Bogart, Humphrey, 62, 66–68
Bogawa, Roddy, 277
Bogdanovich, Peter, 69
Booth, Elmer, 240
Borde, Raymond, 68
Borden, Lizzie, 28
Bordwell, David, 3, 30–33, 38, 52, 237, 242
Bost, Pierre, 36
Boulanger, Nadia, 83
Boultenhouse, Charles, 39
Bourdieu, Pierre, 15
Bowie, David, 248
Bowser, Pearl, 19
Brakhage, Stan, 176, 179, 194–197, 200, 206–207
Brecht, Bertolt, 13
Breen, Joseph, 98, 107, 109–112
Breer, Robert, 176
Brenon, Herbert, 243
Bresson, Robert, 7
Brooks, Cleanth, 31–32
Broughton, James, 196
Brown, Jeffrey, 149, 152
Brown, Kay, 101
Browne, Nick, 10

Browning, Tod, 235–245
Brunius, Jacques, 242
Burns, George, 247
Buscombe, Ed, 10–11, 40–41
Butler, Judith, 19–20, 50–51, 152

Cagney, James, 64, 66, 68, 182
Cahiers du Cinéma (journal), 6–8, 10, 35, 38, 47–48, 63, 65, 72, 161
caméra-stylo, 6, 16, 34
Campion, Jane, 179
Cannon, Robert D., 187
carnivals, 235–245
Carr, Allan, 254, 256
Carringer, Robert L., 41–42, 69
Carroll, Madeleine, 98
Castle, William, 158, 160, 209
Caughie, John, 7–8, 47
cavalcade format, 84, 94
Cavani, Liliana, 163
Chabrol, Claude, 7
Chao, Julie, 271–272
Chaplin, Charlie, 72, 179, 243
Christensen, Benjamin, 236, 243
circuses, 235–245
Clarke, Shirley, 19
class, 5, 80–89, 107, 128
Cocteau, Jean, 7
Coffee, Lenore, 71
Cohl, Emile, 187
collaboration, 97–99, 213–229, 254
Columbus, Chris, 160
Community Visions, 215–221, 224–225, 227–228
Comolli, Jean-Louis, 42
Conrad, Tony, 16
Cook, Pam, 6, 9, 19, 49, 52
Cooper, Gary, 182
Coppola, Francis Ford, 8, 177, 252
Corman Roger, 8
Corrigan, Timothy, 265
Crawford, Joan, 67
Crimp, Douglas, 20
Cream (musical group), 248
Cronenberg, David, 270
Cruze, James, 241–242
Cukor, George, 35
Culler, Jonathan, 16
Cundieff, Rusty, 137–153
Curtis, David, 184
Curtiz, Michael, 40, 61–76, 243

Dalio, Marcel, 73
Daltrey, Roger, 258
Dash, Julie, 6
Davis, Bette, 73–74
Davis, Janet, 239
David, Mike, 206
Dayan, Daniel, 10
Dean, James, 182
death of the author, 14, 21, 45, 270

de Certeau, Michel, 15
De Havilland, Olivia, 63, 65, 67, 73
Deleuze, Gilles, 16, 35
de Palma, Brian, 270
Deren, Maya, 6, 19, 194, 203
Derrida, Jacques, 14, 16–17
de Saussure, Ferdinand, 43
de Tocqueville, Alexis, 120
Devereaux, Oscar, 127
Dieterle, William, 243
Di Maggio, Paul, 41
direct film, 176
Disney, Walt, 182–184, 187
Divine, 157, 160–170, 172
Doane, Mary Ann, 203
Domarchi, Jean, 7
Donne, John, 32
Dorff, Steven, 158
Doty, Alexander, 257
Dreyer, Carl-Theodor, 16, 32, 237
Du Bois, W. E. B., 125–126, 129, 133
du Maurier, Daphne, 101
Dundes, Alan, 139, 145
Dupont, E. A., 237
Durkheim, Emile, 41

Eagle, Arnold, 186
Eagleton, Terry, 41
Eckert, Charles, 45
écriture, 5, 16
Edison, Thomas Alva, 166
Edwards, Henry, 254–255
Ehrenstein, David, 39
Eisenstein, Sergei, 32–33, 72, 159–160,
     184–185
Eisner, Lotte, 35–36
Ellis, John, 40
Ellison, Ralph, 141
Ellitt, Jack, 183
Elsaesser, Thomas, 29, 35, 40, 243–244
Eng, David, 29
Epstein, Brian, 248
Epstein, Julius, 71
Evans, Frank, 184
Ewen, Stuart, 126

Fassbinder, Rainer Werner, 6, 20
Faulkner, William, 70
Fawcett-Majors, Farrah, 258
Faye, Alice, 87
Fellini, Federico, 35
feminism, 19, 98–99, 102–113, 200
Feng, Peter X., 265–266
Film Culture (journal), 38–39, 75–76
Fischinger, Oskar, 181
Flaherty, Robert, 180
Fleming, Victor, 63
Flynn, Errol, 62–63, 65, 67–68, 73
Ford, John, 8, 10, 44, 63–64, 66, 70
Foster, Stephen, 79
Foucault, Michel, 12, 14–15, 17–18, 28–29,

37, 42, 46, 49–50, 69, 125, 158, 172,
     253, 266–267
Fox, Maxine, 251
Frampton, Peter, 247
Frankfurt School, 134
French cinema, 6–7
Freud, Sigmund, 15, 163–167, 170
Friedrich, Su, 196
Fry, Roger, 181
Fuller, Buckminster, 188
Fuller, Sam, 44–45
Furlong, Edward, 158
Furthman, Jules, 70

Gabin, Jean, 66
Gaines, Jane, 19
Gallagher, Tag, 29
Gance, Abel, 7
Garbo, Greta, 40, 63
Gates, Anita, 274
Gates, Henry Louis, Jr., 137–138, 144
Gaumont-British, 185
gay culture, 249, 256–259, 274
gay filmmakers, 159–160, 270
Geertz, Clifford, 201
gender, 6, 19–20, 52, 98–106, 137–150,
     200–209, 264
gender role stereotyping, 140, 143–144, 151
genre, 64–66, 74, 82, 87, 97–98, 140–141,
     157, 178, 200–209
Geritz, Kathy, 176
German cinema, 237, 242–243
Gershwin, George, 81, 83–85, 91, 93
Gidal, Peter, 196
Gilliatt, Sydney, 100–101
Godard, Jean-Luc, 16, 20–21
Gomery, Douglas, 237
Goodman, Benny, 92
Gordon, William, 109–111
Gould, Elliott, 182
Goulding, Edmund, 236
Granger, Farley, 41
Grant, Catherine, 51, 265–266
Green, J. Ronald, 18, 129, 133
Grierson, John, 183, 186
Griffith, D. W., 8, 72, 187, 189, 240–241,
     243
Gross, Jack, 109–110
Grand Guignol, 241
Gunning, Tom, 48
Guthmann, Edward, 273

Habermas, Jurgen, 126
Hagerty, Julie, 275
Halliday, Jon, 39
Hammer Studios, 275
Hammid, Alexander, 203
Han, Shinhee, 29, 267, 271
Harrison, Joan, 97–113
Hart, Lorenz, 78
Hart, Mrs. William S., Sr., 243

Happy Days (TV series), 251
Hartmann, Sadakichi, 5
Hartstock, Nancy, 49
Harvey, Stephen, 254
Hawks, Howard, 8, 10, 35, 44, 62–64, 68,
  70, 72
Hawn, Goldie, 208
Haynes, Todd, 275
Hayter, Stanley, 186
HBO, 162
Hearst, Patty, 166
Heath, Stephen, 10–11, 43, 45, 48
Henderson, Brian, 45
Henreid, Paul, 68
Herrera, Raul Lopez, 196
Herrmann, Leon, 240
Hess, John, 36
Hillier, Jim, 7, 36
Hindle, Ann, 186
Hirsch, Paul M., 41
Hitchcock, Alfred, 16, 41, 44, 63, 68, 70, 72,
  97–106, 113, 184–185, 228, 243
Hollywood, historical context, 3–5
Home Box Office. *See* HBO
Hong, Peter Y., 268
Horkheimer, Max, 123, 132
Houseman, John, 99
Hugo, Ian, 186
Hunter, Tab, 161
Hurley, Frank, 180
Huston, John, 35, 64
Huston, Penelope, 37

identity politics, 268–270
ideology, 3–4, 6, 10–11, 13, 17, 33, 99
Iezzi, Teressa, 271–272
Ignatiev, Noel, 81
independent cinema, 266, 270–273, 277
Ingram, Rex, 237
Irish, William, 103, 105

James, David, 194, 206, 208
JanMohamed, Abdul R., 18
Jarman, Derek, 6
Jews, 80–82, 94
Johnson, Brian D., 267
Johnson, Nunnally, 82
Johnston, Claire, 19, 52
Jolson, Al, 78, 83
Jost, Jon, 196
Julien, Isaac, 6
Jung, C. G., 189

Kael, Pauline, 9, 31–32, 38–39, 61, 69
Kaler, James, 238
Kar-wai, Wong, 275
Kazan, Elia, 169
Keighley, William, 64
Kelly, Gene, 186
Kern, Jerome, 82
Kingston, Maxine Hong, 269

Kitses, Jim, 43
Kleiser, Randal, 254–255
Korda, Alexander, 63
Koch, Howard, 71
Kracauer, Siegfried, 119–121
Kren, Kurt, 196
Kuchar Brothers 159, 196
Kun, Bela, 75
Kurosawa, Akira, 228

Landry, Sylvia, 127
Lang, Fritz, 35–36, 48–49, 242
Latimer, Jonathan, 109, 111–112
Latin-American cinema, 193–195
Laughton, Charles, 101
Launder, Frank, 100
Lee, Ang, 265
Lee, Bruce, 258
Lee, Francis, 196
Lee, Quentin, 263–278
Lee, Spike, 122, 134
Léger, Fernand, 179
Leggett, Paul, 70
Le Grice, Malcolm, 183
Lennon, John, 195
Leone, Sergio, 64
Lévi-Strauss, Claude, 43, 68
Lewis, Hershell Gordon, 158
Lewis, Jerry, 35
Lewton, Val, 40
Lin, Justin, 263–278
Little Richard, 161–162
Lloyd, Norman, 113
Lochary, David, 165
Lockwood, Margaret, 100
Lovell, Alan, 43
Lubitsch, Ernst, 241–244
Lye, Jane, 185
Lye, Len, 175–190
Lynch, David, 177
Lyndsay, Vachel, 5
Lyon, Danny, 196

MacCabe, Colin, 40, 46
McCormick, Kevin, 252
Macherey, Pierre, 40, 42, 47
McLaren, Norman, 176
Mamoulian, Rouben, 63
Man From Uncle, The (TV series), 187
Mankiewicz, Herman, 31–32
Mann, Anthony, 64
Mansfield, Jayne, 168
Manson, Charles, 165
Marshall, Brenda, 73
Martin, Adrian, 29
Martin, Steve, 208
Martin-Márquez, Susan, 51
Marvin, Carolyn, 80
Marxism, 9, 13, 29, 41–42
Marx, Karl, 15, 122, 123
masculinity, 137–153

mass culture, 122–126, 132–134, 252
Massiah, Louis, 215
Mast, Gerald, 86
Mayne, Judith, 20, 52
Medhurst, Andy, 52
Mekas, Jonas, 38–39, 194, 196
Meredyth, Bess, 70–71
Merritt, James, 186
Metro-Goldwyn-Mayer. *See* MGM
metteurs-en-scène, 18, 36, 240–241
MGM, 63, 236, 239, 241, 243–244
Micheaux, Oscar, 6, 18–19, 119–134
Miller, Nancy K., 19, 49
Milstead, Glenn Harris. *See* Divine
Minnelli, Vincente, 8, 40
mise-en-scène, 7, 73, 239
Montagu, Ivon, 185
Montez, Maria, 39
Montgomery, Robert, 102
Moon, Michael, 20
Moritz, William, 176, 184
Movie (journal), 9, 37
Murnau, F. W., 35–36, 237, 242–243
Murphy, Dudley, 179
Murphy, J. J., 196

Naipaul, V. S., 18
New Criticism, 11, 16, 31–33, 44
New Deal, The (historical period), 74–75
Newman, Alfred, 84
Newton-John, Olivia, 251, 255
Nichols, Bill, 35, 226
Nicholson, Jack, 275
Nihei, Judi, 265
Northern Exposure (TV series), 275
nouvelle vague, 7
Nowell-Smith, Geoffrey, 43–47

O'Hara, Maureen, 101
Oishi, Eve, 276
Olson, Charles, 188
O'Neill, Sean, 140
Ophuls, Max, 7
Ozu, Yasujiro, 32–33

Pacino, Al, 258
Pal, George, 184
Paley, William, 85
Palomino, Ernie, 194
Panofsky, Erwin, 5
pantheon directors, 8
Park, Robert, 125
Paramount Pictures, 248, 254
parody, 137, 142, 157, 162
Penley, Constance, 19
Perez, Severo, 194
Perkins, V. F., 40
Perloff, Marjorie, 201
Petrie, Graham, 40, 243
Pichel, Irving, 109, 112
Polan, Dana, 5

popular culture, 79, 83–90, 247, 257
Positif (journal), 35
poststructuralism, 5, 17, 21, 27, 29, 42–43,
    163–164, 172–173, 263, 268
primitivism, 179–180, 188–190
Production Code, 88, 98, 109–112
Powdermaker, Hortense, 8
Power, Tyrone, 87, 90
Preminger, Otto, 35
psychoanalysis, 48, 68, 158
psychology, 11, 31, 158, 163, 253

queer theory, 20

Rabelais, François, 12–13
Rabinowitz, Lauren, 19, 203
race, 5, 18–19, 79–85, 93–94, 120
Ranown, 64
Ray, Nicholas, 8, 35
Ray, Robert, 65
Razaf, Andy, 80
reader, the, 12–13, 45–46
Reagan, Ronald, 197
Reid, Alastair, 175
Reliance, 63
Renan, Sheldon, 194–195
Renoir, Jean, 7, 72–73
Reville, Alma, 99
Rich, Frank, 255
Richter, Hans, 181
Riding, Laura, 183
Riggs, Marlon, 6
RKO, 110–111
Robbins, Tod, 242
Robertson, James, 63, 70
Robinson, Casey, 71
Robinson, William Ellsworth. *See* Soo, Chung
    Ling
Roddick, Nick, 62
Rodgers, Richard, 78, 84
Rohmer, Eric, 7, 65
romanticism, 33–34, 42
Roosevelt, Franklin Delano, 75
Rossellini, Roberto, 72
Rowling, J. K., 160
Ruskin, John, 33
Russell, Ken, 253
Russell, Lee, 71
Ryall, Tom, 99

Sabatini, Rafael, 63
Said, Edward, 18
Sarris, Andrew, 8–10, 34–40, 61, 63, 70–76
Sartre, Jean Paul, 68, 205, 208
Savada, Elias, 239
Savoy Films, 162
Scandinavian cinema, 237, 243
Schneemann, Carolee, 196
Schoenfeld, Bernard C., 103
Schultz, Michael, 254–255
Schwartz, Tony, 257

Scola, Kathryn, 84
Scorsese, Martin, 176–177, 252
Scott, Darin, 137, 145
Scribe Video Center, 215–229
Sedgwick, Eve Kosofsky, 19
Selznick, David O., 99, 101
Sequence (journal), 9
Sharits, Paul, 196
Sherwood, Robert, 101
Shiozaki, Erik, 188
sideshows, 235–245
Siegel, Don, 8
Sight and Sound (journal), 9, 37
Silverman, Kaja, 20–21, 158–159, 163, 173
Siodmak, Robert, 102
Sirk, Douglas, 39–40, 72, 157, 161–162, 166
Sjöström, Victor, 236, 242
Skal, David J., 239
Smith, Jack, 39, 158, 168
Smith, Jean Voltaire, 130–131
Smith, Kate, 160
Smitherman, Geneva, 138–141
Socrates, 17
Soo, Chung Ling, 240
Spence, Louise, 19
Spielberg, Steven, 28
Spivak, Gaytatri Chakravorty, 16
Spoto, Donald, 98
stage musical, 248, 250–259
Staiger, Janet, 138
Stanlaws, Penrhyn, 237
Stanwyck, Barbara, 87
Sternberg, Josef von. *See* von Sternberg, Josef
Stigwood, Robert, 247–259
Stillinger, Jack, 69–70
Stole, Mink, 165, 170, 172
Strand, Chick, 196
Stroheim, Erich von. *See* von Stroheim, Erich
structuralism, 43
Sullivan, Monica, 104

Tarantino, Quentin, 275–276
Tati, Jacques, 7
Taubin, Amy, 274
Tesson, Charles, 240
text, 4–5, 14, 20, 28, 43, 68–69, 159, 256, 265–267
Thomas, Kevin, 271, 273
Thompson, Jane, 182
Tin Pan Alley, 77, 83, 91–92
Toland, Gregg, 40
Tomashevsky, Boris, 32
Trachtenberg, Alan, 126
Travolta, John, 251–258
Tretiakov, Sergei, 124
Trevelyan, Julian, 181
Trotti, Lamar, 82, 84
Truffaut, François, 6–7, 36, 62, 69
Turner, Kathleen, 162

Turow, Joseph, 41
Twentieth Century-Fox, 78, 82, 251
Tyler, Parker, 8, 39

Ulmer, Edgar, 242
underground cinema. *See* avant-garde cinema
United Artists, 82
Universal Studios, 238

Valdez, Luis, 193
Van Peebles, Melvin, 134
Van Sant, Gus, 270
Varela, Willie, 193–209
Vasulka, Steina and Woody, 196
vaudeville, 83, 90–93
Vesselo, Anthony, 184
video, 213–229
Visconti, Luchino, 43–44
von Sternberg, Josef, 241–242
von Stroheim, Erich, 241–242

Waissman, Ken, 251
Walker, Robert, 41
Waller, Fats, 80
Wallis, Hal, 61, 63, 67, 70–71
Walsh, Raoul, 38, 40, 48
Warhol, Andy, 6, 17, 38, 157–159, 166, 194
Warner Bros., 40, 61–64, 67, 71–75, 78
Warner, Jack, 63–64
Washington, Booker T., 133
Waters, John, 157–173
Watts, Richard, Jr., 241–242
Weber, Lois, 6
Weber, Max, 41
Weber, Samuel, 17
Welles, Orson, 4, 8, 31–32, 65, 69, 72
Whiteman, Paul, 81, 91, 93
Whitman, Walt, 20, 34
Who, The (musical group), 251
Wilde, Oscar, 17
Wilder, Billy, 62
Willeman, Paul, 48
Williams, Raymond, 42
Williams, William Carlos, 196
Willkie, Wendell, 186
Wimsatt, W. K., 11, 31
Wollen, Peter, 10, 44, 48, 163, 240–241
Woo, John, 265, 275
Woolcott, Alexander, 83
Woolf, Virginia, 205
Wyeth, Sidney, 127–128
Wyler, William, 72

ya Salaam, Kalamu, 147
Yeager, Steve, 159
Young, Joseph, 129

Zanuck, Darryl F., 77–93
Ziegfeld, Florenz, 78